DIMENSIONS OF CHARACTER

By Ernest M. Ligon

THE PSYCHOLOGY OF CHRISTIAN PERSONALITY

THEIR FUTURE IS NOW

A GREATER GENERATION

DIMENSIONS OF CHARACTER

Dimensions of

Character

ERNEST M. LIGON

NEW YORK

THE MACMILLAN COMPANY

1956

© THE MACMILLAN COMPANY 1956

PUBLISHED SIMULTANEOUSLY IN CANADA

PRINTED IN THE UNITED STATES OF AMERICA

FIRST PRINTING

LIBRARY OF CONGRESS CATALOG CARD NUMBER: 56-9363

ACKNOWLEDGMENTS

Grateful acknowledgment is made to the following publishers for permission to quote from the publications indicated:

To Abingdon Press, Nashville, Tenn., for permission to quote from *Orientation in Religious Education,* edited by Philip Henry Lotz, copyright 1950 by Pierce and Smith. The quotations are from "The Home and Parent Education," by Wesner Fallaw; "The Total Church As An Agency in Religious Education," by Donald M. Maynard; "Trends in Educational Philosophy," by Frank M. Mc-Kibben; "The Christian Education of Adults," by Harry C. Munro; "Experimentation and Research," by Ross Snyder; "The Aim and Scope of Religious Education," by Luther A. Weigle; and "Newer Techniques in Teaching," by Mildred Moody Eakin. Also for permission to quote from *The Interpreter's Bible,* by George A. Buttrick, Vol. 7, copyright 1951 by Pierce and Smith.

To American Association of School Administrators, Washington, D.C., for permission to quote from the Department of Superintendence *Tenth Yearbook: Character Education,* published 1932 by the Department of Superintendence of the National Education Association of the United States.

To American Psychological Association, Washington, D.C., for permission to quote from *The American Psychologist,* Vol. 3, No. 9, September, 1948; Vol. 3, No. 10, October, 1948; and Vol. 5, No. 9, September, 1950.

To Appleton-Century-Crofts, Inc., New York, N.Y., for permission to quote from *Experimental Child Study,* by Florence L. Goodenough and John E. Anderson, copyright 1931 by The Century Company.

To Erik Erikson, Stockbridge, Mass., and Josiah Macy, Jr. Foundation Conference Program, New York, N.Y., for permission to quote from "Growth and Crisis of the 'Healthy Personality,'" in *Problems of Infancy and Childhood,* Supplement II, Josiah Macy, Jr. Foundation, New York. 1950.

To Harper and Brothers, New York, N.Y., for permission to quote from *Personality in the Making,* edited by Helen L. Witmer and Ruth Kotinsky, copyright 1952 by Harper and Brothers.

To Henry Holt and Company, Inc., New York, N.Y., for permission to quote from *Personality,* by Gordon W. Allport, copyright 1937 by Henry Holt and Company, Inc.

To The Journal Press, Provincetown, Mass., for permission to quote from the *Journal of General Psychology,* Vol. 24, October, 1941, copyright 1941 by The Journal Press.

To William A. Koppe, Schenectady, N.Y., for permission to quote from Studies in Psychological Ecology: A Behavior Setting Survey of the Town of Midwest. Unpublished thesis, 1954.

To The Macmillan Company, New York, N.Y., for permission to quote from *The "Why" of Man's Experience*, by Hadley Cantril, copyright 1950 by The Macmillan Company.
To McGraw-Hill Book Company, Inc., New York, N.Y., for permission to quote from *Fundamental Statistics in Psychology and Education*, by J. P. Guilford, Second Edition, copyright 1942, 1950, by McGraw-Hill Book Company, Inc.
To National Council of Churches, Division of Christian Education, Chicago, Ill., for permission to quote from the *Revised Standard Version of the Bible*, copyright 1946 and 1952 by the Division of Christian Education of the National Council of Churches.
To Religious Education Association, Oberlin, Ohio, for permission to quote from *Religious Education*, Vol. XLVII, No. 5, September–October 1952.

TO

LOIS

WHOSE DIMENSIONS OF CHARACTER

HAVE, FOR MORE THAN THIRTY YEARS,

DEMONSTRATED TO ME THE INFINITY PRINCIPLE IN

INSPIRATION, CHALLENGE, AND LOVE

PREFACE

WE HAVE long realized that man's growth in the moral and spiritual values has lagged dangerously behind his advances in technology. We have thought that the powerful tools of the scientific method were limited to the natural and biological sciences, and required the skills of the highly trained professional scientist for their use. This is very far from being true.

Almost every phase of the moral and spiritual growth of personality can now be attacked effectively by scientific research. Furthermore, many of the new developments in experimental design are not only powerful but can be used by any intelligent layman. The major purpose of this book is to bring some of these tools within the reach of all who are concerned with this phase of education—whether professional scientists, educators, leaders in the character-building agencies, religious educators, teachers, parents, or even some of our more able youth.

Religious educators and the character-building agencies could double their effectiveness every decade for the foreseeable future. If their leaders will master these great tools, I am sure that this will come about.

This presentation of scientific methods is being set in the framework of the history of the Union College Character Research Project. Many of our findings are important in themselves. They will bring about drastic changes in current methods of religious and character education. However, their major purpose in this book is to illustrate how science can be applied to such problems by lay leaders, and with what kinds of results.

Our story represents a period of twenty years, during which we have had, for our task, the best energies of more than a hundred people who, at one time or another, have worked on our Union

College Character Research Project staff. They have been assisted by many thousands of parents, youth leaders, and children all over the country who have participated in our Project. More than a million dollars have been spent in this effort. I hope that the account of this adventure will inspire the parents and youth in our homes, teachers, youth leaders, and ministers, students in our seminaries and teachers' colleges, many of my colleagues in the American Psychological Association, educational leaders over the country, and religious educators generally to believe that the tools of science which are now available to them are indispensable for finding solutions to even their most critical problems. The mastery and use of such skills can vastly increase their effectiveness.

Secular educators and professional scientists may feel some misgivings about setting such a discussion in a religious frame of reference. I hope they will examine with some care the conviction running throughout this book that the maximum potential of human personality can be achieved only on the basis of a religious faith.

We are at a historical moment in the history of religious and character education. Some leaders are turning away from the scientific method as having no value for them. This can only be compared to the legendary story of the member of the Patent Office who is said to have resigned many years ago because "almost everything has been invented which can be invented." Such leaders do not realize that scientific methods of great power for this field have been and are being developed at the present time.

Other leaders in this area are turning to the scientific method with high hopes. It would be tragic indeed, however, if, in their enthusiasm, they should set up badly designed research, get the inevitable useless results, and then discard the method which has so transformed our modern civilization. To make sure that this does not happen, they must not delegate their efforts entirely to the professional scientist: they must learn some of the skills of science themselves.

Perhaps the central principle of this book is the co-scientist concept. It is based on the hypothesis that the phenomena of personality and social relationships cannot possibly be explored scientifically to their maximum fruitfulness unless lay people cease to be guinea pigs—even willing guinea pigs—for such research, and instead become active co-scientists.

Many techniques which are now available for such co-scientists will be described in this book. These techniques make it possible for them to observe phenomena and discover forces which are far too complex to be seen without them.

There are four other concepts so basic to this book that you ought to be aware of them before you start reading the book.

The first we refer to as the *infinity principle*. This principle states that since truth is infinite, we shall never find final answers. Each new insight becomes not only a step in progress, but, even more important, a guidepost to the next step. Furthermore, truth is always in the direction of a better world. Even when new evidence seems to upset our cherished beliefs, we need have no fear. Finer and better concepts will inevitably emerge. Religionists will recognize that these concepts are based on the faith that God is infinite and that God is good.

Another of these basic concepts is that the individual influences his environment far more than his environment influences him. Our educational procedures are a part of youth's environment. It follows, therefore, that the effectiveness of such procedures is determined in large part by youth himself. The effect of this concept on our educational procedures is obvious.

This leads naturally to the third concept. It has to do with the fact that individuals differ widely among themselves. Any educational procedure which does not take into account the enormous variety of these individual differences is doomed to failure before it starts. We use a process to which we refer as the *adaptation procedure*. It consists of adapting all educational materials to each individual exposed to them.

Finally, there is the *positive potential concept*. It is based on the assumption that man has not even begun to approach his maximum potential. Furthermore, an educational philosophy based simply on the satisfaction of needs will never reach that potential. I would hazard the guess that every need that man can have could be satisfied without leading him to more than one-third of his potential.

The learning process has probably been subjected to more research than any other area of psychology. The findings which have come from that research have as yet made only a modest dent in our educational procedures, especially in the field of religious and character education. And yet, the implications of these findings are far-reaching. For example, I have already referred to the adaptation procedure and individual differences. There is growing evidence, too, that little, if any, learning occurs without application of that learning to daily life experience. This is true even of content learning. Even more significant is the fact that most forgetting is due to what the psychologist calls retroactive inhibition. This comes about when the learning of one body of material retroactively inhibits retention of what has been learned before. It is highly probable that the amount of content included in many of our religious education curricula is so great that retroactive inhibition alone almost guarantees that none of it can be retained.

Even in the field of theology, this learning process is relevant. This book is not concerned with theology as such. There are probably not more than fifty theological concepts in the whole book. Those whose task it is to deal more specifically with theology, and to give its inspiration to the next generation, must come to realize that these same principles about the learning process are inexorable and must be taken into consideration no matter what it is that is to be learned.

Research is done by people. Today, most of it must be done by research teams. The techniques by which research teams, or any other kind of teams, can work effectively together are relatively unknown. The fact is, most group efforts fall far short of their maximum potential. We have found some effective procedures which can make significant contributions in this area.

When I seek to acknowledge the assistance given me in the growth of this volume, the task seems impossible. Literally hundreds of people have contributed directly or indirectly to it. The injustice of this section, therefore, is going to be in its omissions. My only hope is that all concerned will accept my thanks.

This assistance has been of at least three kinds, in varying degrees of directness.

In the first place, during the years of writing I made three series of lectures. None of them is here in full. All of them are here in part. The Mead-Swing Lectures made at the Oberlin Graduate School of Theology in 1947 became the basis for much of the first four chapters of the book. The Earl Lectures made at the Pacific School of Religion in 1950 were the basis for Chapters V through VIII. The Robert F. Jones Lectures made at the Austin Presbyterian

Theological Seminary in Austin, Texas, in 1951 were based on the concept of individual differences which permeates almost the whole book. To those who made these lectures possible, and to the many hearers who offered helpful criticisms, I am genuinely indebted.

Then, too, we have a policy in the Character Research Project Laboratory of inviting distinguished scholars to spend periods of time with us in the capacity of consultants. As is said on radio, the principles set forth here do not necessarily reflect their opinions. Nevertheless I am deeply grateful to them for the many ways they have influenced our theory and research. Among them are the following psychologists: John E. Anderson, Walter Van Dyke Bingham, Gardner Murphy, Carney Landis, Jack W. Dunlap, Roger G. Barker, Vernon Jones, Harold E. Jones, Howard Y. McClusky, Fred McKinney, Louis G. Schmidt, Alfred L. Baldwin, and Robert J. Havighurst. Among the religious and character education leaders are Leonard A. Stidley, Raymond A. Vogeley, Harry T. Stock, Herman E. Wornom, Paul E. Johnson, Donald M. Maynard, Walter L. Holcomb, Gerald E. Knopf, Denton Coker, Ronald Bridges, Reynold E. Carlson, George Corwin, John A. Ledlie, and James F. Bunting.

The continuing faith of the Lilly Endowment in their support of the Project has, of course, made this book possible. I want to mention in particular the inspiring counsel of Mr. Eli Lilly and the invaluable advice and encouragement of Mr. G. Harold Duling.

Dr. Carter Davidson, President of Union College, through his constant support and encouragement is also an important factor in the work of the Project and therefore in the development of this book. The members of the Department of Psychology contributed much to my thinking. This is particularly true of Professor Franklin C. Chillrud and Professor Clifford H. Pearce.

Finally, there are the many members of my staff who have contributed substantially. In fact, all of them have. Those who have been most closely involved in the preparation of the manuscript are Leonard A. Sibley, Jr., Mervyn M. Morse, Richard S. Doty, William A. Koppe, Kearney Kirkby, Elizabeth H. Hovey, Mary A. O'Brien, Leona J. Smith, and Celia A. Larned. And as always, my wife, Lois, has contributed in countless ways, only one of which was the final reading of the manuscript.

ERNEST M. LIGON

January 1956

CONTENTS

CONTENTS — xxiii

CHAPTER I

THE POWER OF RESEARCH AND
THE PEOPLE WHO DO IT

RESEARCH IS neither impersonal nor dull. It has all the personal interest of a political campaign, all the thrills of a championship football game, and can be engaged in at some level by everyone from a Junior High to an Einstein.

Picking up the usual volume in experimental design makes the average person shudder. It looks as unintelligible as quantum theory is to most of us, and as uninteresting as the compound interest problems of the Junior High were. Research is neither of those.

Science has transformed our physical ways of living and dying in the last fifty years. That, all will agree. We have made as little progress in our social order over the centuries, however, as we had in our physical ways of living up to 1900. We now have the tools by which to make as great progress in our social problems between now and the year 2000 as we did in the physical sciences between 1900 and now.

Furthermore, every one of you can and indeed must play an active role in the process. The term *co-scientist* may not seem very exciting to you now. I think before you have finished reading this book, it will.

The Challenge   In this first chapter I want to introduce you to the road to infinite truth that we call research. I'll show you its major characteristics and especially the possibilities in it with which this book is primarily concerned. Of course, you will need to get a gen-

1

eral picture of the theory of scientific research. But research is done by people, and you won't have a realistic picture of it until you see something of how human nature handles that theory in practice. Then finally I want to give you a preview of how we very human people can take research theory and perform the kinds of miracles which may yet save our civilization.

RESEARCH—A ROAD TO INFINITE TRUTH

A boy was telling his friend that, when he grew up, he planned to buy an airplane and fly up to heaven to see his father. His friend informed him that this was impossible. When asked why, he replied, "If you buy the biggest airplane there ever was and fly forever you can't get there, because heaven doesn't have any end."

The theology or astronomy involved in this statement may be a little doubtful, but the boy had discovered one truth that many people have never realized; that is, that heaven hasn't any end. People often seem to think of the universe as consisting only of that which is inside the circle of their awareness. "Out of sight is out of mind" is altogether too often an equally accurate description of the content of our minds. And yet, most of our greatest advances have come about when someone explored beyond the horizon not only of what we know, but of what we didn't know that we didn't know.

But, you say, how is it possible to find out what is outside this circle of knowledge, with any hope of being even partially right? The scientific method is surely the most fruitful guide thus far conceived for doing so. The whole purpose of this book is to show the abundant rewards that can come to everyone if they seek to learn the secrets of the universe, by using this form of prayer—for all genuine scientific endeavor is a form of prayer. All of us are dissatisfied with the present-day "circle" in which we find ourselves. The pessimist looks only within that circle and says, "You can't change human nature." We say, let's take a look outside the circle.

Everyone Can Do Research and Help to Discover New Truth "I'm just not scientifically minded," say many people. In a vast majority of cases that is not true, although it doesn't come naturally; it has to be learned. Anyone with a mental age above nine years can acquire some facility with some of the basic tools of the scientific method and gain greatly increased power through their use. There are some scientific tools as simple as third-grade arithmetic, as well as others which require advanced study to master. Everyone can and should learn some of them. Every minister, every teacher, social leader, businessman, politician, parent, and even youth will find himself far better able to cope with the world in which he lives and to make his contribution to it if he acquires skill with some of these tools.

In this book I am going to describe several levels of scientific procedures, ranging from those available to almost everyone to some requiring specialized training in science to use. Of course, there are still others beyond these, but there are many fine texts from which they can be learned. Here I want to talk especially to those of you who are not professional scientists, and make available to you techniques which you can and should use. I also want you to gain some appreciation of the more advanced methods. I shall be particularly concerned with religious leaders—for they have pretty largely left the scientific method out of their training and, as a result, religion has suffered in attaining its potential power as a dominating force in society.

Our Major Basic Assumption—The Infinity Principle Scientists have not always believed in an infinite God; neither have theologians. The concepts of determinism and mechanism which dominated the scientific philosophy for a time assumed that there are definite and final laws governing the universe—and that is all there is to it. The theologian of that day talked about God being infinite, but usually constructed a finite theology which he then felt impelled to defend at whatever cost. He was even prepared to go to war if necessary to defend his concept of the message of the Prince of Peace.

It is this faith in an infinite God which gives direction to and vision for the scientific method. Since science has come to be inspired by this new guiding principle, it has in it the potential to lead us into a new and finer social order. Probably not even all scientists themselves have seen the full significance of this new scientific revolution. Many of them have. It underlies our whole research philosophy in the Union College Character Research Project.[1] It is a basic principle in science. Let us refer to it as the *infinity principle*.

[1] We use the initials CRP to refer to the Union College Character Research Project. These initials will be used hereafter throughout the book.

Put in scientific terms, it means that *however significant our progress in gaining new insights and formulating new theories, there are always still greater ones to be found.* Put in theological language, it can be stated as the belief that *if God is infinite, we can never exhaust any important aspect of his truth.* This, in turn, means that *however great our present conceptions of truth, there are always greater ones to be found.* Let us see how this concept shows itself in modern scientific thinking.

When I first studied science, even as a graduate student, we talked much about *scientific laws.* Most scientists at that time believed that there were such laws in the very nature of things, waiting for us to discover them. Once discovered, they were the final answers. Then, too, in research, we were seeking "cause and effect" relationships. The terms *laws* and *cause and effect* have about disappeared from our scientific vocabulary. This is one major result of the infinity principle.

The transition to our present frames of reference was so gradual that until very recently most of us were hardly aware of the transformation. If you read my book *A Greater Generation* (82),* published in 1948, you will still find some use of the term *scientific laws.* If you read carefully, however, you will see that even then the infinity principle was emerging, in that I believed we would never discover final laws, which could be thought of as constituting a sort of ultimate will of God.

The Term *Hypothesis* Has More Significance for You Than You Might Imagine   The term that has replaced the concept of *law* is *hypothesis.* You will find that it is indicative of a whole new way of thinking. It has taken on many new connotations which make it far more significant today than it ever was before. *A hypothesis is the best interpretation a scientist can give to a body of data, not only as a guide to action but also as the basis for further research and further explorations beyond the present frontiers of knowledge.* If it is more fruitful than previous concepts, it represents a genuine *insight,* but is never to be regarded as the final one. The term *insight,*

---

* Figures in parentheses refer to works cited in the Bibliography. Thus the citation (112, 113) refers to bibliographical entries 112 and 113; (65: Ch. IV) refers to entry 65, chapter IV; and (127:408) refers to entry 127, page 408, and so on.

then, comes to mean, not "This is the answer" but "Here is a better answer." It is a hypothesis.

Scientists have insights which create methods of destruction as well as discoveries in the search for good. But I believe that the scientist can be as spiritually inspired as the preacher, and the preacher as scientifically minded as the scientist. I also believe that the Church commits sacrilege whenever it refuses to use to the fullest possible extent any method by which to learn more about the will of God, and science is certainly one of the most effective.

But now let's get back to that concept of *hypothesis* and see how you formulate useful hypotheses. Try a little experiment. Make a set of systematic observations of some common type of human behavior. For example, record the behavior of a group of children fifteen minutes a day for a week. Then see what characteristics you are able to identify in this evidence. You can usually proceed this far without much feeling of achievement. But now you try to create some hypotheses to explain why these characteristics were present. Let us take a specific example. We have frequently brought to the Laboratory of Psychology at Union College groups of high school young people coming from various sections of the United States. They are exposed to a week's program of testing and lecture-discussions. Almost without exception, these young people come to the end of this experience with high visions of future achievement. Some follow-up studies of these groups indicate that they do not quickly lose these visions. Thus far, I have simply described a body of data, and made two broad generalizations, which seem to be descriptive of that data. But now comes the question that keeps the scientist awake nights. *Why?* Why do these phenomena take place? There could be many possible answers. The scientist examines the data with all the intelligence he can muster, and forms some hypotheses. He then constructs research designs to test them and does appropriate experiments for that purpose.

And now comes an important point. You might expect that the result of such experiments would be simply to confirm or reject these hypotheses. This is a very common misconception of the purpose of science. Such a conclusion is seldom ever justified. Oh, you can set down some scores, compute some reliability coefficients, and then conclude your investigation by accepting some, rejecting others of your hypotheses. But to the scientist, that would be like stopping just as the real fun begins. All data has meaning. So, no matter what the outcome of the experiment, he expects it to be the basis for formulating better hypotheses. This shift from the first hypothesis to the new hypothesis is usually what is implied in the scientific use of the word *insight*. From the time Archimedes jumped out of the bathtub and ran down the street shouting "Eureka!" this kind of insight has regularly given man some of his greatest thrills. And if the infinity principle is true, this will go on forever. He does not find the final answer, but he does find a new and better answer. To the layman the word *insight* may sound like a final answer. The word *hypothesis* is another guess. Perhaps the term *insight-hypothesis* is the way to show how the infinity principle operates. Our new insight is a real advance in knowledge, one with which we can do things. But it is also a hypothesis which will one day lead to a better insight-hypothesis.

But does research and its resultant insight-hypotheses always lead to better answers? We sometimes find new data which seem to upset our most cherished beliefs. One can certainly formulate hypotheses which represent regress instead of progress. If, however, we believe sincerely that God is good as well as infinite, we never need to be afraid of truth. When we are finished with the matter, even if we get temporarily off the track, we shall always come out with finer and nobler concepts than those we lost in the process. Later on I am going to describe some methods for avoiding shortsighted and shallow hypotheses which are often dismaying and which sometimes produce tragic results when put into practice.

Behavior, Even in Children, Is Never the Result of a Single Cause The term *cause and effect* has given way in science to the term *correlation*. That statement, too, may not seem very exciting to those of you who are not scientists until you come to appreciate its full implication. You see, when we talk about cause and effect between two variables, we are making a serious error. The forces in the universe are interactive. It probably never happens that any two of them get off in a corner and play only with each other. "Why did you do that?" the mother asks the child. You've got a genius if he really knows. Actually, it may happen that two factors do seem to vary together, in that when you find one you find the other, and so forth. The child may get angry most often at his brother. But there is seldom any simple explanation as to why there is this correlation between them. As a matter of fact, this never is the whole story. Such relationships, then, are simply observed characteristics of the data. They then become part of the basis for this most exciting of all scientific achievement, formulating a new hypothesis, getting a new insight; not that one causes the other, but what the factors are which result in their tending to be associated with each other.

THE BASIC NATURE OF RESEARCH IN THEORY

Research Makes It Possible to Predict and Utilize the Forces of Nature A new hypothesis is usually stated in the form of a *prediction*. In a sense, this is the chief goal of science: to predict! We watch the astronomer predict with split-second accuracy the position and time of the appearance of a new star. The physicist predicts in advance the enormous power to be derived from splitting an atom. Scientific progress consists, then, in predicting the unknown from our knowledge of the known. The further away we get from the known, the more difficult accurate prediction becomes. Usually conservative progress is the best progress, and can be made by attempting to predict only as far as we can do so with relative confidence, although this often takes courageous daring. This is why science sometimes seems to the experimenter to be the slowest method in the world. A look at the history of scientific progress proves that the scientific method reveals new truth many times faster than any other method ever suggested.

The Gateway to Science—Unbiased Evidence If we are to predict, we must, of course, get *evidence*. Furthermore, we must obtain significant evidence. It is easy to get false, useless, and misleading evidence. It is almost as easy to obtain accurate and fruitful evidence. Here is the gateway to science. Before you enter it you are not a scientist. As soon as you enter it you are a scientist, although you may explore only a small portion of its mysteries. Let's put it this way. *If habitually you make a judgment and then look for evidence to support it, you are not a scientist. If, however, you make a judgment and then collect a body of unbiased evidence by which to evaluate it, you are a scientist.* Perhaps you have decided that modern young people are going to the dogs. If you then watch for

all the evidence you can find to support this hypothesis, you are
not a scientist. If, on the other hand, you keep a record of all the
behavior of the young people you meet or observe, for a week or a
month, and then see how this evidence fits your hypothesis, you are
a scientist. Getting unbiased evidence is the key to the scientific
method. Almost all the rest is commentary—refinements for doing
this better.

**The Measure of Scientific Ability—Finding the Best Possible
Insight-Hypothesis** Having got the evidence, our next task is to
interpret it. To be sure, the evidence itself usually makes it possible
to eliminate many tentative hypotheses at once. But as a rule there
will still be a number of possible ways to interpret almost any set
of data. To be sure, every one of them constitutes a new hypothesis,
a new prediction, which needs to be explored with further evidence.
The more wisdom we use, however, in selecting the right hypothesis
to begin with, the faster progress we make.

**Research Design Is Our Plan of Attack—to Get Significant Evi-
dence and to Find Its Meaning** Most scientific evidence is the result of some sort of measurement. This means that we must find
fruitful dimensions of our data, so that we can carry out such measurements. I must admit that saying that we ought to measure and doing it are two different things. The fact is, it has taken us in the
Character Research Project many years to get our research design to
its present point, and we certainly have not completed the job, for
we ought always to be revising our plan of attack. But I'll show
you how we have progressed up to now.

Frames of Reference and Dimensions to Explore One of the
first practical problems in the construction of such research designs as this one is the selection of useful *frames of reference*. Let
me show those of you to whom this term is unfamiliar what we
mean by frames of reference. A frame of reference is a useful set
of categories into which to organize our data, and usually indicates
the dimension in terms of which to carry out our measurements.
Perhaps you can understand this idea better by performing a simple
experiment. Take a group of behavior items, each written on a
separate card, which have been observed in a class of school children. Ask each of several people independently to take these items
and, with no instructions as to how many or what, put them into
a number of categories. You will probably discover that no two

people will organize them in exactly the same way. Each of them can be said to be using a different frame of reference, his own system of categories. Which frame of reference you eventually adopt will depend on what purpose you have in mind and will determine how significant your research is going to be. We have often used precisely this method in some stages of many of our CRP research problems. It is particularly valuable if we are looking for some fresh new leads in attacking a problem.

The history of psychology—and for that matter of all science—can be looked at in one way as the search for more and more useful frames of reference. In general the best frame of reference is the one which, when it becomes a dimension, makes possible the best prediction. Personality is a highly complex, integrated whole. It is, however, much too complex to be treated as if it were just one thing. Of course, there are over-all characteristics of the behavior of a person as a whole which can be investigated as such, and these are useful dimensions. But most of the problems of personality require much more detailed analysis. In research, therefore, the data of personality have to be organized into fruitful categories, or frames of reference, in order to be attacked effectively. How this has operated in our research in CRP and what results have come from it will be described in Chapters V–X.

Finding the True Prophets Among Many Theories Is Achieved by a Process Which We Call Pragmatic Eclecticism We are sometimes asked, "What conception of the nature of personality do you hold?" Our research is not built on the formulation of any single existing conception of the nature of personality. Each of the major theories of personality is used when problems are attacked which can be dealt with best in the light of it.

A great many theoretical frames of reference have been formulated which are relevant to character education. They range from revolutionary to reactionary, from fantastic to common sense, from challenging and inspiring to pessimistic and hopeless. Out of all of them, how shall we select those which hold the highest promise of being both scientifically sound and productive of a greater generation? The position which we take can be called *pragmatic eclecticism*.

By eclecticism we refer to the practice of integrating into our hypotheses and methods the well established findings, concepts, and procedures of all approaches to the investigation of personality, whether from the investigation of other scientists, or growing out of our own research. This principle of eclecticism constitutes the most effective way to make sure that we revise our hypotheses and that when we do so there is a good chance that we are bringing about progress and not regress. At the same time, it also makes more certain the retention of such progress as has already been made. It is highly unlikely that those basic conceptions of universal values which have been held by a number of intelligent men over a period of time will ever be found to be totally without significance. It is even more certain that such conceptions never constitute final answers. The goal of eclecticism, then, is to hold on to the values that have been gained and to add them to more fruitful hypotheses, designed to replace those whose usefulness no longer justifies their retention.

The term *pragmatic* has to do with our criteria for determining those concepts from current scientific thought or from our own thinking which shall be integrated into our hypotheses. This cannot be just a matter of personal opinion. Needless to say, then, the value of eclecticism depends on the wisdom used in accepting and rejecting various points of view.

Fruitful Eclecticism Must Avoid the Dangers of Faddism   Fruitful eclecticism does not consist in wholesale discarding of existing hypotheses and sudden enthusiasms for new fads. In fact at one time we referred to our position in this matter as conservative eclecticism. The centuries of trial-and-error search for principles on which to bring up our children have led to countless widely accepted beliefs. Consider, for example, how many have been related to the problem of discipline alone, ranging from "spare the rod and spoil the child" to our more recent philosophy of extreme "permissiveness." The fact is, man is not by nature very scientific. As a result, we too often make cults out of these concepts, and so keep them from being the milestones in progress toward greater and greater understanding of personality that they ought to be.

Our present moral code is a pertinent example of a splendid ideal which obviously falls far short of being perfect, and needs much development if it is to achieve its maximum value in terms of strong, healthy personality. It is highly unlikely, however, that the longstanding cultural patterns, however inadequate, will be found to be entirely worthless. They almost certainly have in them values which must not be lost. Indeed, the burden of proof lies on those who would change them, not so much in *whether* to change them, as *how* to change them.

We Can't Progress, However, If We Close Our Eyes and Shut Our Ears Our second criterion can be described as a principle of *progressive hypotheses.* This means that we accept or formulate hypotheses which by their very nature lead on to other hypotheses, when the evidence concerning them is examined. They ought to represent progress over existing hypotheses and at the same time point the way to still better ones. Another sort of theory has to do with what is known as reasoning in a circle. When theories are so stated that there is no conceivable evidence to disprove or even modify them, they constitute sterile hypotheses. Unfortunately, there are many such theories, both in science and religion. For example, some of the more extreme Freudian concepts have sometimes been so conceived that no matter what the individual does, his behavior can be fitted into them. For example, I once knew a psychiatrist whose concept of the Oedipus complex could be used to explain an individual's behavior regardless of whether he demonstrated love, hate, or indifference toward his mother. If the infinity principle is valid, there can never be final answers; therefore, a useful scientific hypothesis must always be so stated that when experiments are constructed to test it the resulting evidence will in part support but also in part refute the hypotheses being tested. For example, in CRP we recently set forth some hypotheses concerning the "development of creative imagination in the youth's growth of high vision for his life work" (112, 113). We are reasonably sure that these hypotheses will be very fruitful in character education. We are equally sure that the evidence gathered about them will reveal their weaknesses and make it possible for us to formulate better ones.

Immature Theories Can Lead to the Kinds of Disasters Which Are Characteristic of Immaturity Our third principle for pragmatic eclecticism is that *new or different concepts are included in our curricular procedures only when they have been well established and when they can be effectively integrated into our total design.* It is not uncommon for us to see a new and promising concept come into a field like that of child development, and almost immediately begin to hear popular lecturers urging parents and teachers to use it at once. A few preach it with all the fervor of the old-time evangelist, promising psychological heaven if it is accepted and even more enthusiastically warning against the dire tragedies of psychological hell if it is not accepted. The scientists who conceived and developed these concepts are almost never the cultists who preach them as panaceas. Furthermore, eventually these hypotheses result in important and fruitful contributions to our educational procedures. However, to abandon completely and at once the concepts whose weaknesses have given rise to these new concepts and to accept them as complete substitutes is a form of emotional instability the scientist ought to avoid. Most new hypotheses are developed, in the first place, to correct weaknesses in older concepts. They represent ways of organizing some existing data for purposes of prediction. Experiments must be set up to test the extent and nature of their validity. The resulting evidence regularly shows that they have both values and inadequacies, areas of useful application and areas in which they are not applicable. In other words, it is important that the new hypotheses add to the older ones, but at the same time do not lose any of their values. The best ways to guarantee that this takes place as far as possible are to distinguish between those new concepts which have been extensively explored experimentally, thus making it probable that their findings will be more mature, and those new concepts which are still in early formulative stages; and to take great care to integrate them thoroughly into our own theoretical framework, so that they are not mere appendages of little or no basic significance to our over-all design, but become important elements in our basic procedures.

As an example of this principle, here are some theoretical developments for which a sufficient body of evidence has been found to demonstrate their value to us. We are at present in the process of integrating them into our CRP basic concepts. Among the many important Gestalt concepts, one—growing especially out of the work of Kurt Lewin—has especial significance for us. It is the concept of restructuring the field (65: Ch. IV). A good way to conceive of "the field" is to think of behavior as the interaction between an individual and all of the elements of his environment; that is, his field. The emphasis is on the interaction, not on either the individual or the environment as such. Restructuring the field comes about when some new element enters into the environment which changes the whole picture of the field for the individual. A simple example is the effect of falling in love on the total outlook of a youth. He restructures his field. Because of the occasional apparent completeness of such changes which comes about as a result of "restructuring the field," as the leading Gestalters themselves have pointed out, extremists have sometimes tended to minimize the value of character education. "What is the use of it if he is going to change his whole philosophy of life in the twinkling of an eye?" But we need to put over against this concept the Freudian emphasis on the fact that early childhood experiences have permanent effects on our personalities. This, too, can be carried to extremes, thus blaming everything on early childhood. Gesell and his associates have shown beyond all reasonable doubt that, in general, development proceeds in an orderly and predictable fashion. Extremists for this concept sometimes insist, then, that character is very little more susceptible to training than is growth in height. They suggest that about all we adults need to do is to get out of the way and let nature take its course. In fact, they place great emphasis on the many ways in which we get in the way and warn us against them. Such a concept is of considerable value in developing effective programs of character education, but it, too, needs to be balanced by such a hypothesis as the behavioristic concept of conditioning. This, in its extreme form, eliminates any dynamic influence of the individual as such almost completely from the picture, and puts the emphasis in education on creating the kinds of environmental influences which determine thereafter how the individual will react to them. Carried to its extreme, this could be interpreted so as to leave almost no room for maturation at all, and almost no place for the dynamic role played by the individual in the process of his own growth. But the individual does play an important role in his own development. *Self psychology,* with its emphasis on the factors of autonomy in the individual, is now coming again into its own, and may prove to be the most significant trend in developmental psychology in the last decade. The concept of the self (109: Chs. 21–23) rests on such facts as that the way an individual sees himself and how he thinks others see him are powerful determiners of his behavior.

Now put all these partial truths together, and we begin to have a picture of personality and character which has power and far-reaching implications for educational methods.

Our Children Are Not Guinea Pigs and Should Not Be Treated As Such Finally, another principle which influences our eclecticism is imperative in a practical educational program such as ours. Let me, first, state it negatively. In CRP we are opposed to any aspects of what is sometimes called "guinea-pigism." In the practical application of experimental designs, especially those involving the use of control groups, it has often been the procedure to subject one group to a given type of training and to withhold that training from another. In such cases the procedure followed in the experiment is anticipated to be desirable for one group and undesirable for the other. In medical research and in biology such experiments have been done most commonly with animals. This has been true to some extent in psychology, too. It is, however, quite impossible to test theories of character education on white rats. How shall we deal with this problem in this kind of research? Our own position can be described by two principles of procedure.

Our curricular methods and procedures will aways expect parents and teachers to use the best methods and exert their maximum effort to practice the wisest possible guidance of the children for whom they are in part responsible. In other words, we never— even for scientific purposes—carry out procedures which our best judgment and evidence indicate are likely to be wrong or even less than the best.

Recent Developments in Factorial Design Make Guinea-Pigism Obsolete But, you say, does this not almost rule out the control-group method of experiment? To a certain extent it does. To be sure, many "after-the-fact" control-group studies can be made. One curriculum contains a procedure which another does not. Groups using the second one can serve as control groups to those using the one which includes the procedure. How this is done will be described fully in Chapters XI and XII. But this is not guinea-pigism. How, then, can we proceed? The answer is that methods which presuppose guinea-pigism are not the only ones available. Methods have been or can be created which render guinea-pigism obsolete. One of the most promising is that known as *factorial design*. A great deal will be said about factorial design when we talk about statistical tools, especially in Chapter XII. It is based on the assumption that in practical application, most of the forces involved in the process of character education will differ among themselves from situation to situation. Size and constitution of classes, nature of leadership, socioeconomic and educational status of parents, morale factors in the home, individual differences in the native endowments of children, acquired skills and attitudes are among these. I think you can realize also that even when parents and teachers do the very best they can in this matter of character education, they will differ a great deal from one another in the emphases and skills. If, then, we can measure all of these factors as they appear in different combinations, it will be possible to estimate their relative importance by observing their presence or absence in different situations and combinations. This is basically what is meant by factorial design. The technical statistical procedures used in such designs simply make it possible for us to carry out this process with more factors and with greater precision.

What, Then, Can Scientific Theory Contribute Toward a Greater Generation?   All of us are interested in a greater generation. The infinity principle, which is at the core of scientific philosophy, tells us that greater and greater achievements are possible toward producing it. It is obvious that our biases and prejudices, our ego-involvements and personal limitations, set up serious obstacles toward achieving that end. It is through the method of experiment, involving fruitful dimensions, unbiased evidence, and systematic analysis that we are able to achieve fruitful insight-hypotheses in spite of personal bias. By means of the techniques of pragmatic eclecticism, we can integrate these hypotheses into educational progress. New scientific techniques have made obsolete the method involving guinea-pigism in doing research with our children. The concepts underlying factorial design permit us to explore with them the dynamic forces within them, their use of which determines the level of their achievements.

RESEARCH IS DONE BY PEOPLE—AND THAT PRODUCES PROBLEMS

Many years ago an astronomer found that he and his assistant arrived at different solutions to a problem but that their differences were consistent. As a result he discovered that we must consider the personal element in any research procedure. All of it that was involved in that first experience was simple reaction time. When, however, groups of people try to constitute themselves into research teams which can achieve results impossible in individual research, then the personal equation, as the astronomer named it, becomes far more complex and difficult to solve. The plain fact is that research is done by people and social research with people. No discussion of research methods, therefore, is complete without consideration of this factor.

An individual personality includes an intricate set of dynamic energies. It is almost impossible for a person to integrate those energies even within himself. Small wonder that when groups of such individuals come together, it is exceedingly difficult for them to make themselves into the powerful team which their individual energies make possible. Peace on earth and good will among men is a wonderful idea. The dynamic principles by which it is to be achieved are, for the most part, still to be found.

We Can Be Scientists, Co-Scientists, Guinea Pigs, or Obstructionists Research theory in and of itself is as hollow as a mirage. It is the scientist who does the research and gives life to the design. Research methods without the scientist would be like surgical instruments without a surgeon. The analogy holds in the other direction, too. The scientist without research tools is as handicapped as the surgeon would be without instruments.

When you add human nature to any situation, however, you immediately add problems. When you expect a number of people to work together in teams, these problems are multiplied many times. In CRP we go still further, and expect teamwork among literally thousands of people scattered all over the nation.

When such teamwork can be brought about, the results are incredible. They are many times greater than the thousands of individuals working individually could produce. Can such teamwork be achieved? That is the problem in this next section.

The physical sciences developed first, because their subject matter was inorganic. The biological sciences have considerable control over their animal subjects. In medical research we are pretty much at the guinea-pig level. In the social sciences, however, it is the concept of the co-scientist that will open up to us levels of insight comparable to those of the physical and biological sciences. A major purpose of this book is to challenge people to accept their roles as co-scientists and to describe some of the skills necessary for carrying out that role.

When people talk to each other, their words usually carry different meanings to the speaker and the listener. They have strong convictions, concerning which they are often so ego-involved that conflicts are inevitable. And yet the world needs men of strong convictions. How to have strong convictions without intolerance is a problem as yet unsolved.

Does this mean we must choose between being guinea pigs or obstructionists? At present it almost seems that way. Yet who can doubt that if all sincere men of good will could throw all of their combined energies—yes, and their convictions—into one united high purpose, that it would be a force of incalculable magnitude and irresistible strength. We believe that this can be done through the techniques of the co-scientist concept.

The More Complex the Problem, the More We Need Research Teamwork In a research project such as ours, in which the ultimate purpose demands highly complex program design, progress can be made effectively only when its research program is carried out by teams rather than by individuals. In his presidential address to the American Psychological Association in 1948, Donald Marquis said:

The first requisite of program design is that projects must be planned on a bigger scale than that to which we are accustomed. They must extend over a number of years and must involve a number of investigators if they are to meet the requirements. . . . I am convinced that planning by a group of scientists is superior to individual planning (93).

The number of variables involved in research problems which concern personality are so numerous and the dynamics of their interrelationships so complex that it is quite impossible for any investigator to deal with all of them at one time. Yet, their interdependency is so great that this is precisely what has to be done. Just to give you some idea of what this means, try this little experiment. Take four variables found in any group of children; for example, physical maturity, intelligence, aggressiveness, and social skills. We will assume that these children are all fifth graders. You want to place them into groups that constitute good working teams.

If you divide them on the basis of any one of these variables, they will not be equal in any of the other three. You must divide them so that the children in each group are so chosen in terms of all these characteristics that they constitute a harmonious, effective team. You'll find that just trying to keep all four of these variables in mind is a difficult task. In our Dynamics Diagram, with which you will become acquainted in Chapter VI, there are more than sixty such factors described. No one person could possibly be brilliant enough to deal with such complex problems, even with the statistical tools and computing machines now available. This means that most of our research thinking must be done by research teams if it is to be done at all. The most important thing is that these people shall be able to do collectively what they could not do individually; namely, observe the interactions among all the factors of these complex data simultaneously. If the members of such a team have varied training and interests, they will probably tend to look at the data from different points of view somewhat naturally. It is good practice, however, in such group conferences, to list the important factors involved and actually to assign them to the members of the team, to make sure that none is lost sight of.

Gaining maximum achievement on the part of such teams is not nearly as simple in practice as it sounds in theory. Let us look at three important areas in which difficulties arise. One, of course, has to do with the personnel of the team. Then when a team is as decentralized as ours, there is disagreement as to which problems should be attacked first. Finally, and probably most important, is the question of how decisions are made.

Teams with Varied Interests and Skills Can Produce Integrated Power or Interconflict Weakness   Members of research teams theoretically ought to have varied interests, but they can be ineffective if these interests tend to pull them apart and make cooperative action impossible. It is obvious that if each member of the team insists on going in his own particular direction, teamwork is impossible. In CRP we are always attempting to improve the creativeness of our teams, both of our Union College staff and among the institutions working with us. Each member of such teams should be constructively critical of all our hypotheses—that is one mark of being a scientist—but at the same time he must integrate his thinking with that of the team.

The solution to this problem of group design rests heavily on the assembling of the teams in the first place. If you need an expert in statistics, for example, you will, of course, seek a person so trained. But make sure also that he can function in the team. Genuine scientific humility which can make for maximum individual contribution and also for maximum teamwork is a difficult skill to master, but an invaluable one in program design.

The Five Faiths of Good Research Team Members   Research teams of either kind can fail to achieve their group potential even when every member of the team is intensely sincere and completely dedicated to his cause. The number of people who have worked on our CRP staff at Union College is well over a hundred. The stresses and frustrations we have experienced have centered almost entirely around those who have been completely earnest in their desire to help achieve this high vision of ours. How can teams made up of dedicated people work together effectively? Let me set forth a hypothesis based on twenty years of dealing with just such people. I believe that if the members of such a research team have personality structures characterized by five basic tenets of faith, most of our group-process difficulties will never arise. Of course, no person or team has them entirely, and, on the other hand, none is completely without such faith. The extent to which they can become the working philosophy of the members of a team will in the long run go far to determine how much the team will accomplish. I would guess that these factors are even more important than skills, training, and aptitudes.

These five tenets of faith are: faith in the ultimate importance of the research; faith in the importance of every task that has to be done in it, however routine; basic faith in the leadership of the project; faith in the good will and basic integrity of one's fellow workers; and faith in oneself.

But now comes a most interesting fact. Even assuming the complete validity of this set of categories, it is highly improbable that knowledge of this fact will appreciably help any research team. Why not? It is because of the method by which this descriptive classification was achieved in the first place. A list was made of many of the morale difficulties which we have experienced. Then these were sorted into convenient logical categories. The five faiths are those categories. They fit nicely, and probably almost everyone on the staff would agree to them. But what next? This is little better than listing the difficulties in the first place and saying, "Stop having them." We do not recognize some of these attitudes in ourselves; others we may feel to be just statements of the facts in the case; still others seem to us to be impossible to do anything about.

Let's contrast this state of affairs with a finding in another of our studies, the Home Dynamics Study.[2] This particular finding was the identification of three dimensions of mother's effectiveness in the character education of her children. None of these three dimensions grew out of such a superficial classification of her difficulties and successes but out of an experimental analysis of the dynamics in the case. In these dimensions the mothers can see challenges for new achievements, and they set out with zest to achieve them.

What is the difference between the two? The first are purely descriptive categories. The latter are dynamics derived from experimental analysis. They are fundamental and can be dealt with effectively by the person possessing them. I suspect that a large proportion of our failures in group work has been due to our method of attack on the problem. If, by making use of some of the powerful tools of science, we can discover the dynamic forces which underlie our group failures and successes, we can reach levels of group performance compared to which our present efforts will seem like the efforts of Indian medicine men for curing our ills.

The same concept of the integrated research team applies to our co-scientist ideal also. A considerable number of churches, YMCA's, schools, and other groups—extending all over the country—are working with us. Our maximum achievement depends on the ability of all of these people, as well as of our Union College staff, to work as a team. Representing as they do widely different theological opinions, and with their pressing local problems, the level of their cooperation thus far has been remarkable. If we can continue to integrate all of their skills into our total design, we shall have a team of probably unprecedented potential in the area of the moral and spiritual values. Again it is true that the more varied these churches and other institutions are in all the ways in which such groups can differ, the richer our findings are, to the extent that

---

[2] The Home Dynamics Study is one of our most extensive CRP pieces of research. Many references to it will be made throughout the book.

these differences are enriching through teamwork and do not result in conflict.

In addition to the Union College CRP staff itself, and this wider co-scientist staff, more and more we are coming to use consultants who are experts in the various phases of our total problem. Thus, we have brought in for consultation not only other scientists but also educators and leaders of youth to help us with our problems. Even this aspect of group design is difficult to utilize to its maximum efficiency. On the one hand, it is dependent on the ability of the consultant to grasp our problems and to present his own contribution in terms of them, making his suggestions in the form of challenge, not destructive criticism. It is perhaps even more dependent on our ability to understand what he says and to integrate it effectively into our procedures.

Isolated Experiments to Solve Localized Problems Represent Profligate Waste The potential of integrated research is so great that isolated research, whether in a central research laboratory or to solve some local problem in the field, is criminal waste. This does not mean that the local problems should not be solved, but it does mean they should be a part of a total design.

These two types of problems appear on the surface to be completely independent of each other. The fact is, this is just the difficulty. Too often they are independent of each other, or even conflict with each other. If the total efforts of our research resources in religious education could be integrated, we could have in religion one of the most powerful research programs in the world.

On the one hand, there is central research planning, with designs which reach out into local research centers. Such planning is a constant problem in any program design which is so complex that team procedures are necessary. It takes a great deal of skill to make progress as rapidly and as economically as possible. Some groups, for example, exhaust most of their energies and resources either in the process of planning itself or in the solution of minor problems which contribute only remotely to the total program of research. To be sure, at the other extreme, they can plan so carelessly that too many things are done which serve no useful purpose. If, after adequate planning, we can carry out extensive research with the cooperation of local research committees, we can do a great deal of significant research with a modest investment of time and energy.

On the other hand, many local problems arise in the use of our methods and materials in our CRP churches and participating groups. Understandably they request or do research in connection with these problems. Such research is unrelated to the whole, and involves the expenditure of valuable time and energy. It requires wise judgment to decide which problems should have priority and to keep the whole integrated. With the pressures of existing emergencies, a great deal of vision on their part is necessary to be willing to cooperate fully with the seemingly slow working of the scientific method.

Consider what can be done if all these local designs are brought together with the help of our entire research team into a general program design. Every one of these local experiments could constitute a significant contribution to the total ongoing body of research, and could be so planned as to be an integral part of the total program.

It Is Decision Making That Makes or Breaks Research Teams The critical point in any group design is when and how decisions are reached. At first glance you may not see the full significance of this. The fact of the matter is that it finds mankind at his weakest point. If group research is to be highly productive, then men of strong but varied conviction must produce creative results growing out of the fertility of their varied points of view rather than out of compromise. In general, however, our convictions make us dogmatic, intolerant, and divide us. What a tragedy! I have seen churches and even denominations torn asunder by internal dissension, when they could have been all the more powerful because of the very richness of the diverse thinking within their memberships, if they had learned this secret of creative group experience.

Morale Is a Symptom of Group Creativity, Not a Cause of It Creative groups probably always have high interpersonal morale. If a group or team is made up of people sincerely dedicated to its purpose, their morale has little to do with salaries, working conditions, prestige, or lines of authority. The crux of the matter comes at this point of decision making. This matter of significant group decisions sounds simple enough when you read a statement like that of Dr. Marquis, mentioned before: [3] "I am convinced that planning

[3] See Marquis quotation, p. 17.

by a group of scientists is superior to individual planning." But I wonder if the verb in that quotation ought not to have been "can be" instead of "is." The way Marquis stated it, you might think that if you put a group of scientists in a room they will inevitably demonstrate this prediction. If you do believe that, you are probably in for some disillusioning moments. Anyone who has had much experience in working with groups of any considerable size knows that as long as they are made up of human beings, the personal equation is going to play a very persistent role—for even scientists are human. For example, our central CRP staff averages around twenty-five people. Suppose each one of them had a personal altercation with each of the others just once a year. The total number would be three hundred, almost one a day.

Let me describe some common types of group effort. I think you will recognize them at once.

Some groups unfortunately are characterized primarily by conflict, jealousy, suspicion, and self-seeking. Each member or subgroup seeks the advantage in prestige, power, and income. Such groups are numerous, but the returns on investments in them are usually small. I am convinced that our management-labor disputes could make inspiring contributions to our concepts of democracy if they were not so frequently of this type.

A second type of research group has found one way in which conflict can be minimized. In it, each individual just goes his separate way—or they may divide into small cliques—with the result that there is little or no real group work at all. Oh, they may ask one another for advice once in a while, but their contacts are for the most part confined to lunchtime and staff meetings. Usually each one is sure that he has the final answer, or is interested only in his individual research. Not infrequently, his attitude toward his colleagues is marked by indifference or even suspicion and jealousy. To be sure, such a group achieves more than the first group, for an armed truce is still better than war. But in so doing, they lower the ceiling of their potential achievement, to whatever extent they curtail the number of their members who can achieve team decisions.

What Do You Do with Your Disagreements? The core of the problem lies at the point of what the group does with its disagreements. Everyone, in theory, would agree that disagreement is potentially good because of "the value of different points of view." Unfortunately, the theory so often does not work out that way. It depends a lot on the disagreers. Let me describe the philosophy that has often been proposed in an effort to deal with such conflict. It might be stated like this: "If each member of the group defends his point of view to the highest level of his ability, in the end the group will be able to decide which is the best." This is the theory of the majority vote. Note, however, that if this is carried out completely no decision can possibly be reached above the level of the best idea submitted. Often such irrelevant factors as ego-involved prejudices, the prestige of the people involved, and the skills with which each one presents his point of view, may result in a decision being reached which is far from being the best submitted. In any case, new concepts which are more fruitful than those held by any members of the group must grow out of conflicting opinions, and it is impossible for this process to take place when the method of ego-involved defense is used.

A third type of group, which has considerable vogue nowadays, is one which makes practically a cult of the group process. Group decisions are considered better, not necessarily because of any intrinsic value they have, but just because they are group decisions. I imagine that it could be shown that such extremist group-process zealots sometimes create as much conflict as they do group action. In the minds of such extremists, decisions made without the "consent of the group" are depicted practically as being un-American, simply because they are not "group decisions." Individual decisions are, by implication, condemned as "autocratic."

Principles of great value have and will come from this type of group-work research. Most groups, however, do not exist for themselves, but for some purpose which brought them together. The value of group decisions in research is to be measured in terms of their greater effectiveness in the search for truth, not as a sort of religious rite which is good just for its own sake. Probably many such groups waste countless hours in reaching minor decisions which could just as effectively be made by an individual trained for that particular job.

Possibly the most common variety of research group is one which grows up around the dreams of a single individual. Often he has found some promising leads into important problems and has received enough backing in terms of financial resources to invite others to help him explore his vision. His challenge to those who join him in this work may vary widely. He may simply assign them various tasks to perform, in the conducting of his work, and ask them to assume few of the responsible decisions characteristic of any important research. In doing so, of course, he makes it impossible to gain the value of creative group achievement, or even to find answers greater than he himself can make.

On the other hand, it usually happens that because he has committed himself to a particular area of research, and set forth some general guiding principles, the group attracted will consist of those who feel as deeply as he does the challenge of this program of research. As a matter of fact, individual "visions" are never really created by individuals at all, but arise because the time is ripe for such research in the development of science. The individual, you might say, is in the right place at the right time to lead in this development. It usually places a great sense of responsibility on him. Those who are attracted to his team, therefore, are those who see the same vision.

How productive such a group is will depend, first and foremost, on the significance of the research vision itself; second, on the leader's ability to create a climate in which every member of the team can make the maximum contribution of which he is capable to its development; and, third, on the quality of cooperation given by every other member of the team. Each one of them by his actions decides what his contribution shall be: a form of continual destructive conflict, a neutral carrying out of assigned tasks, perhaps his own individual best, or a contribution to creative group achievement.

Maximum Creativity, As Well As Destructiveness, Comes Out of Conflict Here is the central method for effective decision making —*creative conflict*. At one time I believed that conflict was in its very nature evil. One of the eight major goals in our Christian Hypothesis was stated as "a determination to resolve conflict." Now, however, I think that the world would be poor indeed without conflict. Indeed, progress would almost stop. To be sure, the tragedies in man's history have been almost entirely the result of conflict. But the power of that conflict can be made creative as well as destructive. In the past, conflict has produced serious declines in the growth of civilization. Used creatively, it can result in equally great progress.

This principle of group design consists of three basic research attitudes. I believe that they would be found to be quite as valid in the major councils of religious—and political—groups as in research groups. Let me show you how they apply in attacking a particular research problem. I shall use one which will be described more fully later on but which required us to arrive at some important decisions. In this case our responsibility was all the greater because the decisions we made had implications in the lives of thousands of children.

We were studying the problem of how to help our growing youth learn to make creative use of their imaginations. It turned out to be one of the most satisfying experiences of my research career because it revealed promising insights into this baffling problem of making it possible for groups to achieve their maximum potential.

I suppose no one, who is at all informed, would question the fact that among all of our personality resources, our "imagination potential" is often used least effectively. It can easily be demonstrated that very few people even approach their full potential in this area.

We proceeded to study the problem in this way. The entire staff spent some weeks in searching the literature as well as our own evidence for leads. Some of us, who were professionally trained psychologists, then took this accumulated evidence and tentatively decided upon some goal and method hypotheses for the various age levels. Then, completely independently, the members of our curricular staff who at the time were working at these various age levels did the same thing. Then we compared notes. In not one instance did we find ourselves in very close agreement—and note that we had eight two-year age levels, ranging from Nursery (two- and three-year-olds) to Senior II (grades eleven and twelve). In some instances our disagreements were marked, and sometimes we defended our points of view with considerable enthusiasm. Who won, the psychologists or the educators? Here is the miracle. In not one instance among the eight did we end with either of the initial points of view. We invariably came out with a concept which was superior to either of the ones with which we went into the conference! Why? I think the answer is highly promising for the future of group work, for here is the key to what we have come to call the concept of *creative conflict*.

This concept involves three basic convictions or assumptions on the part of the members of the group. The first one is the infinity principle. "If God is infinite, there must always be better answers than any thus far conceived. It follows, then, that however thrilled I may be at my achieved concepts, I can be certain that there are still better ones." The second assumption is this: "Differing concepts held with enthusiasm by other members of the group almost certainly have some values in them which mine do not have, and mine have values which theirs do not have. I must make sure that we do not lose their values any more than my own. In fact, it is these differing values which usually provide the key to the new and greater concepts!" We must find new concepts which include them all.

This is the way in which conflict can become the key to progress, not an obstacle to it!

There is one more step in this procedure. We are not likely, nor is it even desirable for us, to reach complete agreement. There will probably still be areas of disagreement even when we have gone as far as we can with this process. This is where our third assumption comes into the picture. It is this. "If we sharply define our areas of disagreement, consider the kinds of evidence needed to explore our different hypotheses, and set up experimental designs by which to test them, we can be confident that when we have done so the infinity principle will certainly operate again, and we shall again come out with concepts superior to any of those represented in our disagreement."

One needs to be highly suspicious of panaceas. But are we being unrealistic in seeing in this concept possibilities of such proportions as to give high hope for new levels of insight into the great problems which bewilder our present social order? We are being frustrated at every turn by seemingly irreconcilable conflicts among religious and educational leaders—even though the level of sincerity and depth of conviction among these people is of a very high order. Some of us can find flaws in almost any proposed religious efforts, and we are tempted to try to keep these efforts from being made—generally with success. Sometimes it looks as though we have become more skilled in religious work in preventing something than we are in doing something. Even for the local minister, note what proportion of his energy is commonly used in dealing with destructive conflict within his own congregation, as compared to the amount he can employ in fighting the forces of evil in his community. Suppose all of this conflict could be made creative!

A note of caution needs to be pointed out. Creative-conflict decisions are costly in research. Research economy requires that the investment be proportioned to the importance of the decision. Unimportant decisions ought to be made arbitrarily by one or two persons. Highly significant decisions on the level of heroic hypotheses can use large measures of creative conflict. To be sure, you don't always know how important a decision is going to be. The fact remains that the smallest number of people who can do a job as well as its importance justifies is the best number. When groups increase beyond five active participants, the cost rises sharply and is justified only in the case of very important decisions.

How Can Our Human Conflict-Producing Qualities Be Guided by Science into Insights?   Research is done by people, all of whom are human. But social problems, of which educational procedures are among the most important, demand that research be done by effective teams, sometimes involving thousands of people. Effective research teams must include members with varied interests and skills. If, however, their basic attitudes toward the purposes and procedures of the team, and their roles in them, make them sources of destructive conflict, fruitful research is impossible. It is the principles of the co-scientist and creative conflict by which these sources of conflict can be made creative instead of destructive. The critical point of team research comes at the point of decision making. Morale is a function of the team's perception of the creativeness of these decisions. Isolated and independent study of "local" problems is profligate waste, as compared to the potential of carefully integrated program design. The principles described here offer methods by which these sources of conflict can be used creatively instead of destructively.

PEOPLE, RESEARCH, CURRICULA, AND CHARACTER

"People in the field of religious education need to come together and to map out the most strategic points of attack for experimentation and research, the most strategic ideas and methods to be tested, and where such experimentation could be done" (127:408). This is a statement to which everyone would give verbal agreement.

The trouble is that the word "need" in the minds of most of us is not one which represents an emergency. It has about the same strength as saying, "I need to find a good hobby to fall back on when I retire." If somehow people could see the tremendous potential of religious education which could be released by the use of scientific methods, this need would quickly reach the level of action. Financing such research would not be difficult. In the first place, religious and character-building agencies would place research high in priority on their budgets, probably involving at least a quarter of their total budget. Furthermore, there are numerous foundations seeking eagerly for promising research projects in which to invest.

Financial resources are granted for the purpose of conducting a carefully planned program of research toward definite and important objectives. In our case, it is the exploration of the Christian Hypothesis for the development of character. A proper stewardship of funds implies that they must show a "substantial return on the investment" for that purpose. Of course, a foundation such as the one which gives the major support to our work [4] will urge revisions of hypotheses as rapidly as the evidence indicates. That is the surest evidence of progress when this revision has been based on pragmatic eclecticism. I know that our stewardship responsibilities in CRP are heavy indeed. Not only the finances placed at our disposal but the children whose lives we influence and the areas of truth still unexplored give us no alternative except using all of the skill and wisdom at our disposal for discharging these responsibilities, whether as members of the Union College CRP staff or as members of the nation-wide co-scientist staff.

Research Is the Most Fruitful Single Form of Service Now Available in Education   One of the oldest delusions existing in regard to educational research is the mythical conflict between research and service. Research still seems to many to be theoretical, whereas service is practical and shows immediate values. To be sure, some research has to do with pure methodology and still other parts of it with prerequisite problems. The fact remains that in the long run research is far and away the best kind of service. In fact, it is doubtful if any very far-reaching educational service can be done

[4] The Lilly Endowment, Inc., of Indianapolis, has for some years been the chief source of our financial support.

without it. A form of service which is useful today may be as obsolete as the village blacksmith shop tomorrow. All too often in religious education we find ourselves trying to make covered-wagon religious education meet the needs of our jet atomic age. Without basic research the only improvements we can make are like an increase of speed from five miles an hour to six miles an hour. If we are to lay hold on the power of Jesus' philosophy for our youth, we shall need to make progress much faster than that, and that means research, program research, and a great deal of it, not only in such projects as CRP but throughout the field of character and religious education.

A good friend of mine, a former director of religious education in one of our Project churches, used to say to me, after one of my discussions on CRP theory with a group of teachers, "That is all well and good, but what we want to know is what do we do when we meet our church school classes next Sunday?" The spirit of that question is what makes many people think of research as being not very practical. "Tested by research" sounds as if all research could do would be to put its stamp of approval or disapproval on your methods. No misconception could be more wrong than that. Modern research is creative—indeed, it is by far the most creative educational method in the world.

I had better try to prove so emphatic an assertion as that. So far we have looked at scientific theory with all its precision, its unerring accuracy, its ability to trace myriad forces in their behavior and interactions. We have also considered human nature with its living dynamic, its biases and prejudices, its dreams and visions, its enormous potential. Scientific theory without the human factor is as empty as a deserted barn. Human nature without science, even with the best of intentions, goes on in its bungling, interpersonal conflicts from strife to strife. What happens when human nature and science get together?

I should like to use the curriculum as the very practical focus for answering that question. The curriculum is the crucial point at which one generation tries to give all that it can to the next. What it gives, how it gives it, and what it inspires the next generation to do is one of the critical problems of our time.

In CRP, for example, we have constructed a research curriculum for the purpose of Christian character education. We are preparing soon to revise our curricular materials for the third time. We have in the past and certainly will in the future attempt to bring to bear on the revision process all that the scientific method can give us, plus all that several thousands of human beings, both the central staff and our many co-scientists, can add. I want to demonstrate what this can be like by showing you how a curricular writer can go about making full use of the method of science in approaching his critical task. In Chapter XVI I shall also show you the scientific tools that are going to be available to our CRP curricular staff for that purpose.

What Happens When Science Guides the Curriculum? It is clear to anyone who looks at the situation that religious education is entering the period of the greatest opportunity in its history. Educational buildings are being constructed by our churches at an incredible rate. They are symptoms, not causes, of effective education. Directors of religious education are at a premium. Their actual value is a small fraction of their potential value, with this tool of science placed at their disposal. Almost every denominational board either has recently made or is presently making major revisions of its curricula. What will come of it?

The answer to that question depends on the curricula we produce. These embody our best hypotheses as to what our objectives in religious education ought to be and the best ways to achieve them. Our educational leaders in religion are taking greater care nowadays in describing their objectives. They are bringing to bear upon the preparation of their curricula all the brains and skills they have available. But if they leave out the step of scientific evaluation, their end results will be negligible.

Most of us have quite definite notions as to how the next generation ought to be educated. In fact, we get ego-involved about them. Most of us are unconsciously afraid of evaluation for fear it will prove us wrong. That is like being lost in a forest and throwing away our compass for fear it will tell us that the direction in which we are going is wrong. The compass is not valuable so much because it tells us that we are wrong, as because it tells us the right direction. That is the way it is with the scientific method. If we make full use of it, we shall find our true course many times faster. You have undoubtedly played the old parlor game of "warm and cold" in which the audience helps you find a predetermined object by telling you, as you search, whether you are getting warmer or not. Try that game without audience help. You'll find that it takes much longer, and even then the searcher will usually be wrong in his decision. That is the difference between educational progress with and without the scientific method constantly telling us whether we are getting warmer or colder.

Our curricular writers can make or break our efforts to produce a better generation. And here the human factors can come tragically into the picture again. If we let prejudice, subjective opinions, and dogmatism enter in, however careful the planning which characterizes our work, then our objectives will almost certainly not be achieved. How can the scientific method meet this problem? Here is a curricular writer who says, "All right, just what do I do in my job, to carry out these principles of science?" I will put the answer in a series of steps in the process of revising a single lesson. These steps are adaptations of the major steps in scientific thinking described earlier.

Here we are then, instructing a curricular writer as to how to proceed. This is the sort of procedure we may suggest to him.

Take as a starting point a time in your work when you have in front of you a lesson to be revised which has been used. Scientifically speaking, this is a set of existing hypotheses. Bring together also all of the available evidence concerning it—reports from parents and teachers who have used the lesson, comments and criticisms from informed people in the field, and whatever else is available. Make sure that this is as unbiased as possible.

Make a careful analysis of the objective(s) the lesson was designed to achieve, the methods suggested for doing so, and the criteria which will indicate success or failure. Then examine the evidence obtained for these criteria to find out how well the objectives were achieved by this lesson.

Next, in light of these findings, define carefully the task you have before you, which is, of course, revision. This, put in scientific terms, means that you must end up with some new curricular hypotheses in terms of methods and/or objectives. If the infinity principle is true, each successive revision will be increasingly more far-reaching than the last.

Your next step is to formulate as many tentative hypotheses as you can find or create. There should always be more than one. Don't just jump at the first one that comes to mind. There are many sources to which you can turn for such hypotheses. (*a*) There are some hypotheses which grow out of the old hypotheses, in terms of what the evidence says about strengths and weaknesses. (*b*) Then there is the "heritage of the ages," the traditional answers to the problem; these must not be discarded without strong evidence, for they have been achieved at great cost. It would be as foolish for the scientist to ignore this heritage as it would be to hold on to it without making it grow through the method of science.

The experimental method is fruitful, not when it is used without pre-suppositions or content, but when it is applied to new material in the full light of what we already know and believe. Genuine creative teaching takes place [and the same holds for research], not in the absence of trans-mission of a heritage, but where transmission is so adequate that it serves as a base for further action and inquiry (143:89–90).

(*c*) There are the "modern" educational and psychological theories —and don't be too gullible; none of them is universally "accepted." (*d*) You will want to consider the creations of your own imagina-tion as you study the evidence; but don't get ego-involved about them, no matter how thrilling they look. (*e*) Then, there will be the implications for revision which have grown out of research findings in our own and other laboratories. (*f*) Finally, there are the hypotheses suggested by other members of your own research team. Take them seriously but cautiously.

Your next step is one of *integration*. There are usually certain definite directions toward which a project as a whole is committed— for example, in CRP, exploring the potential of the Christian Hypothesis. Make sure that your new hypotheses are clear-cut steps in this over-all purpose, and that they become integral parts of it, not mere appendages. Formulate your experimental designs so that they integrate with and implement those of other related researches going on in the project. You may need the help of the research "experts" in doing this.

Your next step has to do with creative conflict. The many vari-ables in any problem in character education are so numerous that no one person can keep them all in mind. You must seek the assistance of the group. In the last analysis, however, you must usually accept responsibility for the final decisions, however much you would like to avoid that responsibility. And if, at any time, you feel perfectly confident of the validity of your answer, you had better beware, for this is certainly one type of "pride" which really does "go before destruction"—and in this case often the destruction of important values for thousands of growing children. Look more carefully at how you can use this group assistance. You must first give the whole group a comprehensive vision for your goal. If their varied interests result in frustration conflicts, or if you have to resort to majority votes, or if they do not have a creative morale for the task—one that makes your ultimate goals help them to transcend their selfish interests—you are not likely to gain much from the group process. Instead of frustration conflicts, then, seek to bring about creative conflict. Furthermore, as they suggest hypotheses which do not agree with your own, explore these disagreements together, never giving up until you have found hypotheses better than any of the divergent ones with which the conference began. Finally, as you consider the disagreements that remain, begin to think of new experimental designs to get new evidence on the basis of which still more confident and effective judgments can be made.

You are now finally ready to bring to completion the formulation of your new curricular hypotheses. These will usually be in the form of some new curricular goals and methods, to be used in participating institutions and groups. Here is the climax of your work! It must represent several significant characteristics. Remember that the infinity principle still holds. You must so create your hypotheses and curricula that they will, in the very process of being used, bring forth the kinds of evidence that will make possible further progress into new areas of truth. This means that the methods for getting this evidence must be an integral part of the curricular procedures themselves. Make sure that the evidence to be secured will reveal the weaknesses of your hypotheses as well as their strengths.

There they are, then, some major steps in scientific thinking, as they might be used in the process of curricular revision. This may seem like a long and tedious method for creating curricula. It has been demonstrated many times in the history of science that progress made in this fashion, slow and laborious though it seems, in the long run far outstrips nonscientific methods, however thorough they may be. McKibben says:

There is every evidence of the increasing reliance of public education upon research of all kinds for the determination of its procedures in the classroom. The practitioner is leaning more heavily upon the research expert than upon the normal-school theorizer or armchair philosopher for guidance in the direction and improvement of practice (99:56).

Well indeed may he say that!

SOME IMPORTANT CONCEPTS DESCRIBED IN THIS CHAPTER

Some level of scientific research is possible for everyone and will vastly increase the validity and accuracy of his judgments. Even more important, the tools of science—even the simplest ones —open doors to new truth, which cannot be discovered without them.

A major concept in research philosophy is *the infinity principle*. This is the concept that the universe is infinite and that we shall never exhaust any important aspect of truth. In the history of science, this concept is reflected in the gradual disappearance of mechanism and determinism in scientific philosophy, in the transition from concepts of scientific laws to scientific insight-hypotheses. Terms like "cause and effect" have given place to "correlation" and "total personality interaction dynamics." The leaven of the infinity principle is especially stimulating in areas of research in human relations.

The gateway to science consists in collecting unbiased evidence. That is, it must not be evidence sought to confirm or reject a hypothesis, but a body of evidence representative of the whole situation. It must be collected with no bias for or against any hypothesis.

And now comes the next of the major concepts of this chapter, the concept of *creative conflict*. Conflict can be creative as well as destructive. Its basic principles are there. If the infinity principle is true, then no matter how significant an insight I have, there is a better one. If others disagree with me, each of our insights probably has values the others do not. If we share our ideas long enough, a new concept must therefore emerge, of greater value than any of the individual concepts held at the beginning.

In the construction of curricula, which embody our best contributions to the next generation, scientific research is by far the most creative procedure now available.

We are publishing some "Learning Projects" which people wishing to use this book as a text may secure by writing to the Union College Character Research Project, Laboratory of Psychology, Union College, Schenectady, New York.

CHAPTER II

——◆◆——

BIOGRAPHY OF A RESEARCH PROJECT
A. FROM ENDS TO BEGINNINGS

A VISITOR in our laboratory recently asked, "What have you found out about character so far?" That is a good question. The fact is, we expend our efforts so completely, wrestling with the problems at hand, that we don't often take time to look back to see how far we have come. Let's take a look, because actually we have come a long way and had a thrilling time doing it. How significant have our findings been? Let me show you a few of the high points of our journey so far; then you can judge for yourself.

More important than this, however, is what our experiences have to say about the question, "Can the scientific method produce answers to some of the age-old problems which have thus far seemed insoluble?" A national leader says in a speech, "If everybody would start practicing the Golden Rule and the Sermon on the Mount, our world's troubles would be over." Almost everyone would agree to that, but very few even dream that we are going to start doing it. Centuries of great preaching have long since convinced us that this is not a matter to be achieved by admonition. Many believe that human nature is just the way it is and that nothing can be done about it. Wanting to control my temper and doing it are two different things. Believing that I ought to love my enemies is a far cry from even knowing who they are, much less how to go about loving them. We in CRP set out to discover whether such ideals are possible for human nature. Here is the story of our experiences in the process.

Science Is Seeing Something in the Future, Not Proving Something to Be True Scientific progress proceeds from one insight-hypothesis to another. Our visitor's question revealed a common misconception about science. Scientific progress is not a set of conclusions which can be drawn from a letter-perfect experiment. These are at best just the raw materials from which insights can be drawn. Rather, science is looking at whatever evidence you have and formulating hypotheses concerning the problems with which you are concerned. You don't then so much set out to prove or disprove these hypotheses as you do to find better ones.

The basic key to scientific progress is the scientific attitude. This involves the humility of the infinity principle, that makes you always regard your insights, not as findings on which to rest your case, but as beginnings on which to base your future investigations. The attitude of seeking unbiased evidence is half the battle. That overcomes your greatest handicap, the powerful urge to become ego-involved about a point of view.

To be sure, the range of evidence you get will set limits to the outreach of your possible hypotheses. Some evidence is easily obtained and can be observed by anyone. Some is deep in the nature of people and society, and can be obtained only with highly technical methods. The sample of people from whom your evidence is obtained makes a difference, too. The wider the range of people to whom we can give the co-scientist vision, the more rapid our progress becomes. The more skills they can learn about objective evidence, the more significant the insights we can derive from their evidence. Then there are the research methods that are constantly being developed by scientists, and the flow of new statistical tools for analyzing the data. Scores of them exist today which did not exist twenty years ago, and which multiply our progress over and over again. All this influences the speed of insight. The fact remains that significant progress can be made even with serious lacks in all these areas. Read this story of our early experiences and judge for yourself how true this is. It is a long way, in terms of scientific know-how, from our original attitude questionnaires to those developed for our recent Home Dynamics Study. Nevertheless the age-level calibrations based on those early, comparatively crude instruments are standing the test of validating evidence astonishingly well. When we began the curriculum in 1944 we had available for its construction only a fraction of the resources in terms of personnel, techniques of construction, and guiding evidence available for the 1957 revision. Yet, its use brought in the first of the hundreds of thousands of parent and teacher reports, on which our present exciting Positive Potential Study is being made.

Our story represents a period of twenty years, during which we have had for the task the best energies of the more than a hundred people who have, at one time or another, worked on our Union College staff. They have been assisted by many thousands of parents, youth leaders, and children who have participated in our Project. More than a million dollars have been spent in this effort.

Can There Be Any Real Progress Without Research?   Our modern concept of progress has grown almost entirely from the spectacular successes of the scientific method. It was not characteristic of men's thinking until the last few centuries. One may well wonder if we shall make any greater progress in character and religious education without science than we did in the physical world without it.

Nowadays we are seeing a flurry of research studies done or proposed in religious education, along with a veritable flood of new curricula. It is my conviction that new curricula ought to be beginnings, not ends, and that these, like those before them, will make hardly a dent in our civilization unless denominations and character-building agencies invest at least a third of their income in research—scientific research!

Furthermore, this research must not be a succession of isolated studies, but a full-orbed program integrated into the very core of our educational procedures themselves. In our own research again and again we have found ourselves spreading our energies too thin, in the multiplicity of the problems we were doing. We could not help that, because the whole picture is an integrated one. Every part of it depends on every other part of it.

Hypothesis curricula—here is the door to progress in our field. Curricula are beginnings, not ends. In the future only those who fail to sense the significance of the infinity of God will create curricula which are not set in extensive research frames of reference.

Our Task As It Looked Twenty Years Ago   The history of science is the story of men who became obsessed with a driving desire to find meaning and power in a seemingly hopeless chaos of baffling facts. Through the intricate mazes of apparently meaningless data, they have seen glimpses of light and visions of new adventure. That is the way it has been for us in the Character Research Project.

If the scientific method consists of techniques by which to discover consistencies in what seems like meaningless data, the value of a research program depends on the degree to which it makes possible for the scientist to find meaning and predictive order in that chaos. It may be that when you have finished these chapters, you will realize that it is possible to make significant progress even with fairly simple techniques. No matter how limited your resources or training, you can still make some effective use of the scientific method.

A Third of a Century in Retrospect As I look back over the years, I am tempted to recall for you scores of the thrilling experiences we have had. It is the aim of this chapter, rather, to have you sense the adventures in ideas as they come to the person who makes use of the tools of science. I shall first give you only the very briefest outline of the chronology of the Project, so that later you will be able to orient the many insights—which are the important things—into their historical context.

A convenient way to outline the development of the Project is to divide it into four periods.

Fourteen Years of Groundwork The first is largely personal to the author, and pre-experimental. It can be dated as covering the years 1920 through 1934. It was during these years that the vision grew and finally reached sufficient maturity to become the basis for research. To be sure, valuable research has been done when the only purpose was to measure something accurately. In such research as this, however, it makes little sense to start out without a vision of where you want to go. We need to state this vision in terms of a clear-cut problem which we hope to solve. The first formulation of the vision now implemented in CRP culminated in *The Psychology of Christian Personality* (67). This book reported the results of some years of study, designed to translate the basic philosophy of Jesus into modern psychological concepts and into modern life conditions. When you do scientific research you must start with hypotheses. You do everything you can to make them the best hypotheses you can create; but at the same time you realize that they represent only a starting point. You know that your future experiences will become increasingly meaningful because God is infinite and because the scientific method will make it possible for you to find ever increasing insights into truth.

Science is done by scientists, and scientists are people who live with other people. As I look back over these periods in the history of CRP, I am tempted to add chapters of biography about the many people without whose help and encouragement even the vision would never have been formulated. I am thinking of the inspiration of my parents, the influence of a number of fine teachers, scores of great books, the encouragement of close friends, and the high visions of institutions. Not long ago I spoke to a youth group about the factors leading to my own vision. When I had finished listing only the most important ones, it was obviously on the mind of every young person there to ask, "What did you contribute to all this?" Indeed, it is a question I frequently ask myself. When I think of the many people and events without which none of this would have taken place, I realize that I purposely sought out these people and shaped these events only a very small percentage of the times. There are those who look with askance on a concept of guidance by a power outside of and greater than ourselves. It would be difficult indeed for me not to believe in one.

Ten Years of Basic Foundations The second phase covered the years 1935 through 1944. We call it the *Individual Phase of the Project*. During this period almost all of our research was with individuals, seldom with groups. The Personality Profile, to be described in Chapter VII, and *Their Future Is Now* (73) are the landmarks of that period. In 1935 the Westminster Presbyterian Church of Albany urged us to begin our research with the children in their church school. It was four years later when a second church joined us, and still two years later a third. Our first significant financial support came in 1941. Our failures during this period far outnumbered our successes, and yet they were exciting years.

Again, I am tempted to tell you of the personalities who played major and often heroic roles during this period. There was a minister, the late Kenneth B. Welles, who gave up his greatest ministerial opportunities to stand by the Project in its beginnings; a director who had to modify practically a life of training in other methods;

a wife who performed miracles in two of the early churches in times of emergency; a secretary who did the impossible at great personal sacrifice; a church board with sufficient vision to keep faith in the possibilities of this research in spite of repeated failures and mistakes; scores of parents who filled out endless questionnaires and rating scales; a philanthropist who began to give financial undergirding, when none of the larger foundations would have taken a second look at our vision. I remember vividly the first experimental proof of the effectiveness of some of our methods, which came at the Nursery level; the first quantitative evidence that we had successfully modified an attitude in an age-level group; the early thrills with the testing program, especially the demonstration of the fact that high achievement is quite as possible for those of modest endowment as for those of high endowment. And these are only a few of many such experiences.

Seven Years Building Curricular Hypotheses The third period, during the years 1944 through 1951, was characterized by the *development of a curriculum*. If genuine character research is to be done, its central hypotheses must be embodied in some form of a curriculum. Only when this has been accomplished is it possible to do over-all research to test your hypotheses. This is an undertaking of some size. Our first efforts at so extensive an undertaking—six units, more than six hundred lessons, with many different sorts of forms and techniques for gathering evidence—were bound to be inadequate at many points. We revised these lessons three full rounds, largely on the basis of parent and teacher reports, before we let any of them be used a second time unrevised. As you will see in Chapter XVI, most of our research at present is pointing to a still more extensive revision. Attitude scales, forms for obtaining information from parents, teachers, and youth, and many other instruments had to be created and revised over and over again. It was indeed a busy period. Churches all over the country decided to join us, until the number reached approximately fifty. YMCA boys' clubs, a boys' school, and a summer camp also joined in the effort. Our financial resources increased many times in volume. Our staff jumped from one person to about thirty. It was during this period that we were able to complete a full-orbed research design.

Perhaps you may overlook the significance of this last statement, unless you examine it carefully. I become increasingly convinced that program research in a field like character education, which deals with an individual's reactions to his whole environment, can be carried out effectively only when that research studies him in the normal operation of that total environment. The traditional definition of an experiment was, "Hold all factors constant except one; vary that one systematically, and measure the results." The modern definition, especially in research like this, might read, "Measure all the factors you can; vary the educational-method variables systematically, and measure the total results in terms of the interaction among all these variables." This can be done only when adequate planning and groundwork have been laid. This had been reasonably well accomplished for us by the end of this third period. It is my firm conviction that research problems oriented in such a total setting are likely to yield results of far greater significance than those carried out under conditions where only a few factors can be studied. Such limited research necessarily leaves out the countless important dynamic patterns involved in the interrelationships of the factors studied with the ones not studied. Program research designed to study the whole process at once must of necessity be very complex. As the vision for research grows among educators I hear of hundreds of specific studies being proposed. Even assuming their value, I do not believe we can ever get at the heart of the matter that way. What we need is a nationally conceived program of research into which all these isolated studies can be integrated.

Again, the human element comes crowding into the picture. I am thinking of a University of Michigan professor who almost singlehandedly brought about the rapid expansion of the Project; of a young associate minister who with his pastor took it to the West Coast; of an Episcopal rector who led that denomination into close denominational cooperation; of the gradually increasing group of young leaders who began to invest the best years of their lives in this unproved dream—a number of them are or have been on my staff; of a staff, many of whom have come to us at considerable financial and sometimes professional sacrifice; of others who have contributed additional financial support, especially Mr. Eli Lilly, and the Lilly Endowment; of hundreds of parents and teachers who have sent an ever increasing volume of evidence to Schenectady as a basis for our further progress. It was during this period that *A Greater Generation* (82) was published.

It was during this period, too, that we faced our greatest temptation. It would probably have been very easy about 1950 to have let the Project become a "national movement," involving hundreds, perhaps thousands, of churches and other institutions. Such a movement would probably have flourished, gained some renown, incurred much bitter opposition, and died with little or nothing accomplished. Once a person has tasted the thrill of scientific insight in his search for truth, however, he is not likely to be moved from working steadily toward this central goal.

The Present Harvest and Future Prospect   The fourth period, beginning in 1951 and still under way, is *the period of endless harvest*. The foundations are well laid. Expansion has slowed down. Any further growth will be through denominational boards or other character-building organizations. All this makes possible more intensive work with more experienced people over the country. You will see, as you read the rest of this chapter, that this period, characterized by intensive and technical research, produces increasingly more and better results. We are having a dozen insights now to one in any of the first three periods. Some of the concepts which are maturing in our research now will certainly influence religious and character education more significantly than has ever been possible before.

It would be impossible to list even a small fraction of the people who are contributing now to the growth of the Project. Their number increases daily. Parents, teachers, directors, youth leaders, youth —as they gain a vision for the Project they give their best to it, sometimes in spite of great handicaps. I am thinking of the high-school youth who have made our Youth Workshops so significant; of the hundreds of parents who have done the tedious and, as it seemed to some, futile labor of the dynamics studies; of the groups who have carried on when their churches have withdrawn from active cooperation; of the staff whose spirit is beyond any I have ever known before; of the increasing number of leaders in the denominations and character-building agencies who are using our results and seeking insight into our methods. The technical series *Union*

College Studies in Character Research is read by religious, psychological, and educational leaders everywhere.

The Ingredients of a Vision Now let us return to the problem of vision. It is not difficult to find a felt need. The world is full of them. The question is, Where do you take hold? That usually means spelling out the vision of your felt need—in our case, Christian character development—in terms of tangible facts which offer promise that the vision can be achieved. It isn't much help to decry the continued existence of war, for instance, if all we do is to exhort men and nations to stop it. If, however, there are significant bodies of evidence that point to the possibility of peace, then we have the ingredients of a hopeful vision.

Let me show you in outline the kinds of bodies of data which made it possible for us to clarify our vision and build a program of research.

In educational research the major independent variable (the portion of the child's environment which is varied systematically to bring about desirable results) is the curriculum. But curricula exist in great numbers and varieties. Despite man's incurable optimism that makes him sure the next one will be wonderful, the fact of the matter is that we aren't even in sight of one which will achieve the major objectives of which we dream in the area of Christian character.

Fallaw expresses the greatest pessimism, as follows: "Parents as well as church-school teachers know quite well that most Christian education programs are puny affairs—if they do not know it, they need but ask the children" (38:241).

Our task, then, is to create a curriculum which will challenge youth to attempt the full level of Christian living and help him to develop the necessary skills to do so. That is a task on which, up to now, we have been unable to make even a good beginning.

Some Striking Facts That Give Us Hope and Determination In our efforts to envision an effective curriculum, then, we looked for significant bodies of known facts. We wanted facts which would give us a clear picture of what our objectives should be and would also provide promising leads as to the nature of the kind of curriculum which would lead to those objectives. We found four such significant bodies of data. Two of them showed us the enormity of our task. The other two showed us what sources of hope we had to start with.

A Generation of Youth Who Need Our Insights As the Basis for Far Greater Ones The first, which we have in common with all curriculum builders, is the fact that a curriculum is actually to be used with children. Put yourself in the shoes of those of us who set out to formulate our original curriculum. It took us ten years to do it. When it was used for the first time, there were almost two thousand children in the Project. The figure now is many times that number. That meant that we realized that what we put into that curriculum could influence—or, more important, fail to influence—that many lives for better or worse. That is a heavy responsibility as well as a great opportunity. Many of my psychological colleagues would not dream of assuming so great a responsibility. This in itself is surely enough to make us want to use the scientific method. How could anyone dare to deal with so many children's lives without making every possible effort to test the validity of their methods and to be continually seeking better ones?

The Astounding Contrasts Between Caesar and Christ Where can we look for clues as to how we can hope to discharge that responsibility? This question led us to our second body of facts. Consider the contrast between the influence on civilization of Caesar and of Christ. Caesar had access to all of the recognized sources of power by which men and nations have tried to build strength and wealth. Jesus had none of them. Yet Jesus' influence on the course of history has been many times greater than that of Caesar. Does it not follow that Jesus revealed in his life sources of power as much greater than Caesar's as atomic energy compares with a child's firecracker? Who can doubt, then, that if we can just find the secrets of this power for future generations, a social order can surely arise in which, for example, so primitive a phenomenon as war actually will become obsolete. It has not been common enough for professional psychologists to make studies based on the teachings of Jesus. Studying Freud has been far more fashionable. I have no quarrel with those who wish to explore the brilliant hypotheses of Freud. But it has surely been a tragic oversight to have neglected the obvious forces in human personality which have grown out of the teachings of Jesus. To be sure, men have stood in almost universal awe before that great personality.

But the forces involved have too often been regarded as incomprehensible, despite Jesus' repeated insistence that they are not. The scientific method could certainly open the doors to many of them which are as yet almost untried and too often regarded as unrealistic, if not impossible.

The Sword of Damocles of Our Generation The third body of facts are those set forth in the morning newspaper, with its ever present foreboding of the imminent destruction of our modern civilization. Leaders are almost unanimously agreed that the only thing that can prevent such disaster is a generation with strength and quality of character far exceeding what any generations have thus far produced. The scientific method has given us incredible insights into the physical universe. Is it not probable that one reason why our progress in moral and spiritual values has been so small is that we have not made use of this form of prayer which we call science in our attempts to utilize these values?

The Body of Research in Child Development Is of Formidable Size, and Increasing Rapidly Our fourth and final body of data has come from the more than half-century of research in hundreds of psychological laboratories, as well as research in education, sociology, psychiatry, and mental hygiene. These studies have gradually been building an increasing volume of well established facts about the nature and dynamics of human personality. In our research we no longer need to start from scratch. This body of exciting knowledge gives us much that will help in our search for new truth in this area of human endeavor.

Here, then, is the basis for a more meaningful vision. We set ourselves to the task of trying to utilize the body of knowledge thus far accumulated by scientists; seeking at the same time to gain insights into the sources of power obviously inherent in the teachings of Jesus, in an effort to create a curriculum which would place that quality of character within the reach of the growing generation. This was surely an ambitious undertaking. Certainly it was reason enough to make us eager to get criticism, even if emotionally worded, so that we can become aware, at the earliest possible moment, of major errors we are making and of new leads with greater promise than those we have found. There are many psychologists who would never dare to present such a program of value education, for fear of its errors. Medicine, however, would never have come into being with that attitude. I believe that we must, therefore, walk with fear and trembling, but with firmness toward this goal.

AS OUR RESEARCH DESIGN GREW, MANY DECISIONS HAD TO BE MADE

When you engage in program research—the study of some general area such as character education—you will discover that not only can you not make all of your decisions on the basis of adequate scientific evidence; you won't be able to set up scientific research designs until some important decisions are made. Making the wrong ones will lead you into some costly blind alleys, and you are certain to make some of them. Jesus himself suggested that the best way to distinguish between true and false prophets is by their fruits. Let me illustrate this by some of the decisions we have made through the years in CRP.

In Exploratory Research, Some of These Decisions Grow Out of Practical Necessity The most persistent type of problems requiring such decisions comes about when what you would like to do in a sort of ideal scientific heaven comes up abruptly against reality. This is particularly true when you are doing exploratory research. The frontiers of ignorance are no different in this regard from the frontiers of civilization. When tools and methods with all the refinements of modern scientific technology are not available, you have to devise the best tools you can for the purpose. Only experience will teach you skills in making this kind of decisions.

I suppose that in CRP our two most common types of situations of this sort are these. The first has to do with scientific tools. There are many ideal methods and instruments available, which can be used with great power by highly trained technicians. Most of our procedures, however, must be used by lay parents and teachers, sometimes even by youth. The second has to do with deadlines. Time limits force us to make many judgments long before we have done all that we would like to do. Our answers to these two problems must not consist in a form of frustration surrender, or, as it is more commonly called, compromise. We must be continually searching for techniques which make possible good scientific work under realistic conditions.

For example, building as we have on the co-scientist principle, there is the ever present problem of orientation and training of teachers, parents, interviewers, observers, and others. They can't all take Ph.D. training in preparation for their roles in character education. On the other hand, superficial training may leave them pretty well baffled as to what to do. Our task was to create procedures which required a minimum of technical training to use, yet which were scientifically valid.

In our search for answers based on this hypothesis we have developed a concept which we call *motivated capacity*. Its philosophy is that effective methods of character education can be found which are within the "capacity" of parents and teachers, and which will challenge their best "motivations" to carry out. To say that we have solved all our problems in this regard would be a masterpiece of overstatement. Nevertheless, this philosophy has certainly kept us from surrendering either to the necessity of frustrating procedures or of diluted compromise. We always assume that there must be third alternatives.

This concept of motivated capacity should not be interpreted to mean that the way to get things done by laymen is to make them easy. Nothing could be further from the facts. I am sure that part of the reason for the attactiveness of CRP has been its very difficultness. People like to do difficult things, whether in athletics, exploration, games, or even character education, as long as they do not exceed people's capacities. Hundreds of our reports from parents and teachers show abundant evidence of heroic effort and correspondingly great enthusiasm. A vast majority of parents want the best for their children and will pay whatever price is necessary to get it, once they are really convinced that it is the best. They do, however, want these things to be possible. We must bring them within the range of their capacities. They want the sense of achievement, which is probably man's strongest motivation. Motivated capacity, then, is just another way of saying that we believe they will do with enthusiasm those things which are possible for them, and from which they get a sense of achievement.

Some Decisions Had to Be Made About Human Nature Itself
Do not confuse the terms *basic assumptions* and *theoretical decisions*. Basic assumptions are those aspects of your educational philosophy which you start with, although they ought always to be

as subject to change as anything else. Theoretical decisions, on the other hand, are hypotheses which you make in order to plan your actual research program. They are made because you must start in some direction. As is true of your basic assumptions, part of the purpose of your research will be to test the validity of these decisions.

To be sure, you try to make the wisest decisions you can. You choose from all the possibilities with a great deal of humility. In the paragraphs which follow are some of our theoretical decisions, as they stand at the present time. Many of them represent distinct changes from our position in 1935 when we began research. We gain more confidence in them when they grow out of research and of course when they stand the test of repeated research attack.

Positive Goodness As Opposed to Negative Ethics Our first decision came about at the very beginning of the Project. It is based on the fact that we describe behavior as "good" only when it is a positive act, never when it consists merely of the absence of behavior, even undesirable behavior. A "good boy," then, is one who does that which is good, not one who simply does not do that which is bad. Sins of omission in light of such a concept become more serious than sins of commission. If you will examine our educational goals in CRP, you will discover that every one of them is positive, what children are challenged *to do*, not what they are urged *not to do*. "Dominating purpose in the service of mankind," "Sensitiveness to the needs of others," "Being determined to see that every man gets his full chance at happiness and success," three of our major Character Research Project objectives—these can hardly be thought of as "Thou shalt not" goals.

This point of view is easy to accept in theory but not so simple in practice. I think you will agree, for example, that it is much easier to see those things which we do not like, or with which we disagree, than those things which we do like in individuals or movements or institutions. It is common practice to judge most things in terms of their flaws. Most of us take the boy next door pretty much for granted until he annoys us. The same too often holds with regard to one's judgment about his husband or wife. With one unpopular decision a boss can wipe out the positive effects of scores of good ones. I have noted that criticisms of CRP are far more frequently in terms of what we do not do than of what we do do. Scholars judge one another's books in terms of their blind spots instead of their visions.

Despite these serious difficulties, which seem to be basic in human nature, we have chosen a positive concept of goodness, on the grounds that it has more challenge to youth's highest potential. This in turn rests on our "potential" concept of character education, which will be described shortly. In a very real sense, then, what we are saying here is that "human nature can be changed," not biologically, of course, but in the quality of its common performances in daily life.

Children Are Not Plastic Clay   Here is another theoretical decision. This has to do especially with the respective roles of the teacher and the youth in the job of character education. In the more traditional "plastic clay" theory, it is the teacher who plays the leading role. The child is pretty much a pawn in the situation, a bit of molding clay at the mercy of his elders. We believe on the contrary—and we have some very revealing evidence to support it—that the major role in learning is played by the child. The best way to describe the ideal role of the teacher and parent in the process is that of creating a "favorable climate" in which the child can learn. A favorable climate may involve making the child's way easy or making it difficult. It may mean direct challenge or indirect motivation. It may involve being very permissive in some things and using strict discipline in others. But the fact remains that the main job—namely, learning —is done by the growing child, not by the teacher. We want teachers and parents to be good ones, but we are far more concerned with calling out in the child a determination to learn, even from a bad teacher, and to grow in strong personality even with the worst of parents. Our reasons for believing that this can be done are based on obvious evidence that the child's behavior resembles boundless energy far more than molding clay. The implications of this decision will appear repeatedly throughout this book.

Strong Personality Is Positive, Not Just the Absence of Maladjustment   A third decision which we have made is at variance with the concepts of many of my psychological colleagues. It has to do with the commonly used clinical frame of reference. While not all clinical psychologists and psychiatrists hold the same point of view, a concept common to many of them is that the betterment of human nature consists in finding and getting rid of maladjustive patterns of response. Most texts on "pastoral psychology" are actually texts on clinical psychology.

Our own point of view in this regard is that eliminating the weaknesses in personalities brings us up only to the zero point, and that the most important elements in character education are over and above this point, sometimes actually in spite of these weaknesses. Even more uncommon is our practice of dealing with undesirable behavior patterns by attempting to form positive ones instead of emphasizing the undesirable ones at all. For example, if a child has a fear, we attempt first to teach a corresponding courage, assuming that if he learns it the fear just will not be there. Only if this fails do we consider dealing with the fear as such. I think our experience indicates that this method is successful a vast majority of the times.

We find ourselves at some disadvantage in this effort, because of the preponderance of psychological work done with the negative emotions and the dearth of that relating to the positive ones (137: 330). It is significant that the emotion which is the opposite of anger, magnanimity, is an almost forgotten word in the language. Or again, you can find many studies describing the fears which are common at the various age levels. Where in the literature will you find studies describing the forms of courage common to these same age levels? In CRP we are at present engaged in studies for this very purpose.

Clinical psychologists often tend, for example, to make parents and teachers anxious lest they develop anxieties in their children. Since anxiety begets anxiety, no surer way could be conceived to develop anxieties in children than to make their parents and teachers anxious. Granted that many clinical psychologists use highly positive methods, these negative trends are more common among them. We have chosen to set our course on the hypothesis that human nature in general is mentally sound and responds to challenge more powerfully than to negative therapy. We believe that even if we eliminated all of the pathological in men, we still would have left untouched the most powerful elements in their personalities.

Man Has Positive Potential Far Beyond His Basic Needs A fourth decision of a similar nature which we have made is closely related to this third one. It has to do with a current emphasis in modern psychology on "needs" as the major drives in human motivation. The core of this concept of motivation is that the reasons behind most of the things we do are rooted in needs which we want to satisfy. Usually the physiological needs are set forth as the most basic of these. To be sure, such concepts as the need for security and the need for achievement are included in most such lists. Even the more unselfish and sacrificial aspects of the parental drive are depicted as coming about because they satisfy needs which the mother or father feel as a result of their basic nature as parents. In other words, parents satisfy the needs of their children not because of the needs of the children, but because of their own needs.

No one could question the presence of needs, nor of their role in motivation. However, to rest the whole of human motivation on needs is to imply that man is entirely egocentric; that even his apparently unselfish behavior is done for what is essentially a selfish purpose. In CRP we have used as a basic principle another explanation. Let us conceive a dimension which from zero to its negative end is need, but from zero to its positive end is potential.

$$- \quad\quad\quad 0 \quad\quad\quad\quad\quad\quad\quad\quad +$$

$$\text{need} \quad\quad\quad\quad\quad\quad \text{potential}$$

This implies that when there are felt needs, to be sure, we want to satisfy them. When they are not satisfied we feel discontented. When I am hungry, I am dissatisfied until I eat. The same holds for thirst, pain, fatigue, sex, need of security, need of belonging, need for achievement.

But that, it seems to us, is not the whole of the matter. For example, one ambition I have for this book is that it will give educators, especially religious educators, a vision for the potential of the scientific method, even for statistics. Yet, it is obvious that thousands of people go through life and feel that it has been entirely satisfactory without either. They have no felt needs for learning scientific methods. Personally, I dislike the use of the term *religious needs,* for the same reason. Granted that religion can satisfy some needs. Most of them, however, could be satisfied without religion. On the other hand, as will be pointed out in a comparison of one "needs philosophy" of personality development and our own in Chapters VIII and IX, the thrilling thing about religion is how tremendously it adds to man's potential, challenging him to levels of nobility not possible without it.

For the parents, especially, who read this book, it ought to be pointed out that these four principles underlie our present CRP curriculum. You ought to make sure that you want a curriculum based on such hypotheses for your children before they are exposed to a curriculum teaching them.

ADVENTURES IN INSIGHT-HYPOTHESES

The Most Exciting Experience in Research Is Insight Certainly the most exciting experience in science is *insight*. An insight is reaching another milestone in the search for infinite truth. No insight is final. That is why we use the term *insight-hypothesis*. Each insight becomes a new hypothesis, which in turn starts us out on another search. It comes about when a new piece is put in the puzzle, giving us a new and more meaningful idea of the whole picture. It may be that within a very short time another piece added to the puzzle may make possible a still greater insight-hypothesis. No scientist is disturbed when a thrilling insight gives way to another one. That is what he lives for. Indeed, one mark of a great insight is that it does point the way toward a greater one.

One who sees in the scientific method only its measurement techniques misses its greatest thrill. A child looking at a picture puzzle is told that he will find a face in it if he looks long enough. The thrill of finding the face is known to everyone. So it is in science. Just working out a mathematics problem, for its own sake, is not very exciting for most of us, although we may get a satisfaction of achievement from it. In science, the tables and graphs which are based on simple measurement do not often look particularly interesting. They are, however, the necessary foundations for insight. The great adventures in science are the insights which come not from deduction, but from induction; not simply a process of stating one's measurement findings in words, but concepts of possible meanings, based on these experimental findings. Almost always they are in essence the scientist's prediction as to what we will find at the next turn in the road.

Few, if any, of the great principles of science have been the result of straight deduction. They have much more frequently come about when the scientist has looked at a mass of data to which he has been unable to ascribe meaning, organized it in this way and that until he discovers a meaningful interpretation of it. This has often been as sudden as the child finding the face in the picture puzzle.

This may sound as if insight and sheer flights of imagination are about the same thing. Gossip is, in a sense, insight based on evidence. No one, however, would classify gossip as science. It is based on a minimum of evidence, usually selected by wishful thinking to "prove" a prejudgment, and completely unbridled. How, then, shall we make sure that our insights are significant and lead to new areas of truth? Let me point out at least some important characteristics of such insights, or insight-hypotheses.

Fruitful Insights Come Only from Unbiased Evidence Perhaps I have seemed to imply that the great insights have come without experimentation and collection of data. Nothing could be further from the facts. Here is the way it is. Usually the scientist has brought together a body of data, which not only does not confirm his original hypothesis but for which he can find no adequate interpretation. It may be a problem on which thousands of pages have been written, based on opinion, none of which adequately accounts for the data. He has, therefore, done some systematic experimenting to discover previously unknown facts, and sets about determining relationships among them. Gradually these increase his ability to see characteristics of this data until finally the insights come about.

Let's take an example from one of our CRP areas of study. Possibly no social problem concerns religious leaders today more than our so-called "youth problem." Here are our youth, facing a world in which they will surely have more difficult moral and spiritual problems to solve than any generation before in history. And yet, far too few of them seem to be much concerned about getting any basic training in the matter of dealing with such problems. What, if anything, can we do about it? One thing is certain. The newspaper is no place to go for unbiased evidence. A teen-ager can make the headlines by murder or vandalism. He cannot make the headlines by getting an A in chemistry, although the latter event may be a thousand times as important in the history of the world.

So let us do some research, gather a body of unbiased data, and reach for previously unknown relationships among them. Suppose we discover that an important difference between those teen-agers who do have real interest in moral and spiritual values and those who do not is that the former have far-reaching goals, and also a sense of confidence that they are accepted by their associates. As a matter of fact, we have some evidence that suggests just this. Then supposing we see further evidence that this social self-confidence depends more on the quality of their relationships with their parents than on those with their associates as such. Would these trends in our data give you a basis for some new insight-hypotheses on the youth problem? Note that we have not done any experiments which tell us the answer directly. We have done experiments which were not prejudiced toward any given answer and which threw new light on the problem, giving us the basis for developing new insight-hypotheses. Here, then, is the core of the matter! Once we have exhausted the possibilities of opinion, however wise, then we shall probably make little, if any, further progress until we have got some new data through research and discover new interrelationships among them on which to base our new insights.

The Most Important Value of an Insight Is the Problem It Opens Up, Not the One It Solves   Another principle in this matter of getting good insights has to do with the infinity principle. Every insight constitutes a hypothesis which we can neither prove nor disprove without new facts. Do you see why research, looked at this way, cannot be a succession of isolated studies? It is an ongoing, ever developing process, by which our educational procedures "increase in wisdom and strength and in favor with God and man." Having insights, especially when we have worked long and hard on a problem, is likely to be a thrilling experience. Being human, we are also certain to find much ego satisfaction in them. This in turn tempts us to regard our insights as final answers, and to spend more time in selling them to a great many people than in dreaming of greater insights. If, however, one believes in the infinity principle, each new insight thrill will simply whet his appetite for the next one, and he will always formulate his insight-hypothesis to bring that about.

Consider, as an example of this insight-hypothesis growth process, our progress, thus far, in CRP with our psychometrics program, as it is related to character education. When we began actual research in 1935, previous evidence had strongly indicated that awareness of individual differences is a prerequisite to effective character education. "A character trait has no meaning apart from the individual of whom it is characteristic." This was one of our first basic principles. We set up a testing program and applied it to all of the children in our first two experimental schools. The results in terms of effectiveness were spectacular. Our insight in this regard certainly seemed to receive abundant verification. But was that the end of the matter?

It wasn't long until an equally spectacular failure made us start looking for additional insights. It happened when a church introduced a testing program which was not really integrated into the educational philosophy of that church. We collected and studied all the facts we could find about this failure. This led to a second insight, which was that a measurement program must be oriented into the educational philosophy of the whole program of which it is a part. Because in our case this was Christian-character education, we began to integrate and interpret our study of individual differences into the Christian philosophy. You see, tests can also be used in other ways, for example, in the clinical frame of reference. Using them this way in our program proved disastrous. This study eventually resulted in two of our most effective curricular units, the Vocational Guidance Unit and the Vision Unit. Out of it also grew our "Workshops for Youth," which have constituted our most important contribution to youth work so far. But was this the end of our task? Far from it.

The next step, again based on the careful observation of objective evidence, turned out to be our *vision concept of vocational guidance*. It is based on the hypothesis, which was also an insight, that one should choose a vocation on the basis of what one would like to accomplish in the world, instead of first choosing a vocation purely on the basis of aptitudes and interests, and then trying to find what one can do with it. This is where we are now, but is this the best we can ever hope to do? Let's look at some facts for which we have tentative hypotheses, but far from adequate ones.

What of the obvious determination of so many youth, seemingly due to their immaturity at the Junior High, High School, and College levels, systematically to lower the ceiling of their achievement potential; that is, to waste their best potentialities. This they do, not because of bad intentions, but simply because of their inability to see the implications for what they are doing. My faith in a good God makes me certain that this tragedy is not inevitable. What about the divorce of parents from their teen-age children, with youth thereby losing the values which could come from building on the broader experience of their parents? What about our inability to

challenge so many of our modern teen-agers to anything except a
"fun" philosophy of life? The fact is, we have hardly scratched the
surface in finding solutions to these problems. Not only have we not
reached the end of our new insights; we have only really begun. The
thrills that await us in the future will, by comparison, pale to insignificance those which thus far we have had. Here again is an
illustration of insights becoming hypothesis milestones to future
insights. Note that each succeeding level becomes more far-reaching
than its predecessor.

An Interesting Insight Which Is a Challenging Hypothesis By
way of demonstrating how these characteristics of good insight-
hypotheses operate, let me relate them to another of our current
CRP problems. Let's take a problem on which we have begun to
make a systematic attack. What religious leader has not been discouraged by internal conflicts within his organization? We have
faced this problem in CRP. We needed some new evidence, so we
set out to get it. We did an interview study of a representative sample of a church population. As I write this, I have no idea what the
data will tell us. I certainly will have, long before the book is published. Let me describe this effort in this diary form.

[April 25, 1953] One of our best interviewers has, during the past week,
interviewed a representative group of parents in one of our churches. She
conducted interviews in 36 homes. These homes were selected from
several times that number by careful sampling techniques involving both
stratification and randomization. They ranged from homes enthusiastic
about the Character Research Project to homes strongly skeptical of the
Character Research Project. A number of varied questions were asked
and the answers noted in great detail.

The church in point is being studied at the request of its leaders. The
CRP curriculum has been used in it for several years. People's attitudes
toward this curriculum range from very enthusiastic protagonism to determined antagonism. The principles we discover, if any, will probably
apply in some degree to all so-called "church fights," all the more tragic
because both sides are equally sincere. People's strong convictions ought
to give a church strength. They often do almost destroy it. Up to now no
one has been able to come up with very productive answers. Yet, everyone
in religion knows that when we find such answers, the power of religion
as demonstrated in a church will be increased many times over.

Here were our next steps. It was fairly easy to arrange the thirty-
six families along a scale from most enthusiastic to most antagonistic.

This we did. The answers to the interview questions were recorded, question by question. We then proceeded to make up pairs of sets of answers to each question. For example, the answers of the most enthusiastic parents to question one were recorded in a set. The answers of the most antagonistic of the parents to the same question were recorded in a corresponding set. This was done for each of the questions.

These paired sets of answers were then given to judges—who did not know which were which—with the instructions that they try to discover some characteristic differences between the two sets. We continued this procedure with a number of judges until we had found most of the clearly discernible differences. This we call our *method of characteristic differences* (88). Note that up to this point we had just collected facts and were trying to find interrelationships among them. No effort had thus far been made to explain them.

The next step was to examine the suggested characteristic differences with the purpose of finding promising hypotheses—significant insights. Let me refer to an entry in the diary of the study, written a few weeks later.

[May 25, 1953] The insights gained from this initial exploratory study have far exceeded our fondest expectations. These results are being used as the basis for a theory of adaptation procedure for the orientation of new parents and teachers to the Project. We have been able to identify fourteen fairly definite variables describing different ways in which parents look at things. Their standing with respect to each of these variables has proved to be significant in determining their attitude toward CRP. We are now able to define nine types of orientation which can be used with parents. We have already done some preliminary thinking as to the types of orientation needed for each type of parent. Further studies will be needed to refine and enlarge this significant beginning. It may well be that in this study we have laid the foundations for discovering the nature of religious conflicts of all kinds, and transforming them into creative instead of destructive conflict.

THE CHARACTER RESEARCH PROJECT AS A PROTOTYPE OF INSIGHT-HYPOTHESIS RESEARCH

The ultimate value of a research program is not measured in terms of the multiplicity of experiments which have been done in it, but in terms of its creative promise, which is determined by the patterns and fruitfulness of its insight-hypotheses. I should like to describe briefly our experiences in CRP in terms of such insight-hypotheses. It is not nearly so important, however, that you learn these particular insights nor even how valid they are or are not. It is important that you come to understand how this process of insight, as hypothesis for further insight, takes place in scientific research. Careful experimentation, with complete analysis of its results, is usually the process of deduction in scientific method. Such experimentation is the foundation without which no strong superstructure could be erected. But the building itself, on which scientific progress depends, is insight, induction. Without it the adventure and outreach of science would be lacking.

Insights Which Are Not Made Research Hypotheses Are Extremely Dangerous When I see some new concept in the field of child development seized upon as a panacea, I am depressed, even though it be alive with possibilities as an insight-hypothesis. Consider, for example, a present conviction among some educators which makes them go overboard for an almost "no discipline" concept of child training. A large portion of our coming generation is being used as the "proof" of its validity. The great danger lies in the fact that for the most part it is being used with so little effort at research design that we may never be able fully to evaluate its validity, nor to discover from it the next possible insight, which could utilize its strengths and eliminate its weaknesses. If this widespread concept of discipline proves to be widely in error, one of the great tragedies of history may well be in the making. The point is: Don't forget the infinity principle. Look for the limitations as well as the values of your insights, and look forward to the next step. There are no final answers, no panaceas.

Despite our conservatism in this regard, I am amazed at the number of the insights we have gained during these many years of research, and stand in humility when I consider their implications for the next generation. But of one thing you can be sure: we will test them. I should like to describe some of these insights, and thus demonstrate how objective facts can lead to insights which have fruitful results, and which at the same time constitute hypotheses on which to find better ones. Note that in every case the insight came only after some new relationships among some new objective data had been observed. And when new insights are used in our curricula.

evaluational procedures always accompany them to get more such data. When discussion of any problem in education comes to the point of insoluble argument, you are in a blind alley from which you can escape only by getting more unbiased evidence and finding some previously unknown relationships among them.

The Key to Fruitful Research Is Finding the Right Dimensions to Measure Progress in science depends on our choice of dimensions by which to measure our data, more than on any other one thing. One could describe personality in terms of a hundred dimensions, none of which would contribute appreciably to our progress. On the other hand, consider the ultimate results of Newton's laws of motion. How much real progress a research program makes may depend more on what kinds of dimension insights it produces than on any other thing in it. Chapters VI–X in this book will be devoted entirely to this topic, but at this point I will cite a few of our CRP adventures in our search for dimensions.

Fourteen years may seem to be a long time to take to construct eight dimensional concepts with which to start, but that is how long it did take to arrive at the initial formulation of our Christian Hypothesis. The task was obviously one on which a great deal depended. The proposed eight dimensions of Christian character were the chief result of a study which was done during the years 1920 to 1934. We knew that our progress in character education would be rapid or slow, depending on how wisely we chose these dimensions and how effectively we could describe our aims and measure our results in terms of them. A good example of what I mean is the concept that parental love rather than brotherly love is the basic characteristic of Jesus' teaching (67: Ch. III). The concept of brotherly love did not seem to conform to many of the realities of daily life. For example, brothers in general don't return good for evil, nor turn the other cheek. Indeed, trying to teach brothers to do so might almost smack of making them queer, to say the least. Parents, however, do these things normally, so that this kind of behavior can be anticipated from them. Furthermore, children show parental behavior, as for example, toward dolls, pets, and younger children. When these two groups of facts were brought together into this concept, we found that we had a basis for teaching one whole area of Christian ethics in a way which looked more psychologically sound and educationally possible. The brotherly love concept had previously seemed overidealistic and impractical. Many people still doubt the practical possibility of a "turn the other cheek" philosophy. Our work since that time has done much to confirm this concept but also to refine the original insight.

Our psychological interpretation of the Beatitude concerning the "peacemakers" is a good example of the way in which new concepts can enlarge and enrich old ones. When we first used the Beatitude, its educational interpretation was stated, "Being determined to resolve the conflicts within and between and among men." This obviously was based on the hypothesis that conflict is essentially undesirable, and that an ideal world would be one in which no conflict was present.

As time went by, however, data began to come into the laboratory describing people's experiences with this concept. It soon became obvious that some types of conflict seemed actually to bring about highly desirable results. There were, then, two conflicting sets of data in the same field. They ought to give rise to a new insight, better than the old one. Experience has proved this to be true in our own laboratory over and over again. In this instance, the concept of creative conflict, described in the first chapter, emerged. Once having gotten this new insight, it was not far to the concept that "peace" is something positive, not just the absence of conflict. This led to a reinterpretation of the Beatitude which might be stated in this way, "Being determined to make conflict creative instead of destructive." A whole curricular unit was rewritten. A new insight, which will be described fully in Chapter IX, had come into being. This insight will, of course, just as surely give way one day to a still better one.

Our Search for Specific Educational Goals Led to Many New Insights Much of the first ten years of the Project research was spent in finding specific goals for the various age levels. This was achieved on the basis of a large body of facts. Organizing and interpreting all of these facts for our purposes was a big task. One insight after another, however, made possible more and more meaning and resulted in the gradual emergence of an integrated program of character-education goal hypotheses. This program had to be one with which we could proceed with the conviction that through it we were giving to children the best possible guidance within our wisdom to determine. It also had to produce evidence from which to gain still better insights. Let me show you how all this was worked out.

Having established our eight general goals or dimensions, we then began to search for relevant data on which to base our choice of specific goals. First we needed facts. This involved bringing together the results of all of the attitude research which had been done in the various fields of personality study. By a process of classification made possible by pooling the independent judgments of a number of scholars, these findings were distributed among the eight general objectives which constitute our Christian Hypothesis.

The list was many times too long. Which ones should be eliminated and which retained? We had to get some objective facts before we could answer this question with confidence. In this case we conducted a questionnaire study, asking parents of children of all ages to rate their children with respect to all of these hundreds of attitudes. When the results were analyzed, we found a number of significant characteristics of the various attitudes, which helped us to choose among them. We discovered that some of them were learned by almost all youth by the time they had reached maturity. These we eliminated from our list on the theory that children would learn them in the process of growing up in our culture.

This same set of data revealed the age levels at which the various attitudes began to be present in any considerable number of the children. This gave rise to our next concept, that of *age-level calibration*. We tried to verify our findings by experimenting with individual children, and this one study gave us an astonishingly accurate age-level calibration for our various objectives. We are at present conducting research, however, which ought to broaden our concepts of age-level potentials enormously.

Another insight needs to be mentioned along with this one. It is the *concept of optimum age level*. It is good common sense—even though very often violated—not to try to teach things before they can be learned. But there also comes a time later on when things can be learned less well because the individual has passed the best age at which to learn them. This concept of optimum age level grew out of a succession of reported experiences among teachers and parents, who, on the one hand, described highly effective experiences with a particular attitude with one age level and, on the other, unsatisfactory ones with it at a later age level. We have not fully explored the possibilities of this concept. As we watch Junior High and High School youth lose interest in religious education, we are still certain that there are ways of challenging them to the moral and spiritual values. It may well be that one of the important approaches to the solution of this problem is finding attitude goals which are geared to these age levels as the optimum.

The next insight is one to which I have referred before, especially in the description of some of our basic decisions. It has to do with the concept of *positive goodness*. In the development of the initial attitude list, we had to translate many of the attitudes which were retained from "what not to do" to "what to do." This was more easily said than done. We soon discovered that having stated an attitude positively in a lesson does not mean that it will be used that way in practice. Parents and teachers—and for that matter the children and youth themselves—still interpreted some of them negatively. We then studied our attitude statements, our lesson materials, and Parents' Reports, to see if we could find out why they had been interpreted negatively. We then tried to change them until they were seen regularly as positive.

This experience gave rise to another insight which has proved of value in a great many aspects of our work. Indeed, it has significance in all kinds of social relationships. It is that *the test of a procedure lies in the way it is used by the people who use it, not in the intentions of those who create it.* With regard to this particular problem; namely, stating our objectives, it relates to the interest, the challenge, and the difficulty which parents and teachers ascribe to our goals and procedures as well as the meaning. For example, people sometimes say of our curriculum, "There is not enough Bible in it." This cannot be true in any objective educational sense, because there is more Bible in the curriculum than can be learned in the time given by any of our youth to religious education. But if people think this is the case, as far as their use of the curriculum is concerned, it is. The same can be said about criticisms that the material is too technical, and so on. A very important practical impact of this insight on our methods for revision of curriculum is that the curriculum must be changed until it gives the desired meaning to those who use it. This is not accomplished by an editorial process alone, but by actual experimentation with it. Here is another instance in which an hour of pre-test is worth four hours of armchair theory.

Having learned this principle, you may very well jump from the frying pan into the fire. For example, if you are dealing with a curriculum, every time anyone says there is not enough Bible in it, just put in some more and see what happens. Or if they say the language is too technical, just go through and change all three-syllable words to one-syllable words wherever you can. Then see what happens. You will very quickly find yourself in far worse difficulties than you were before, as we certainly did. What, then, ought to be done?

The answer is a sort of double principle. (1) *Count noses* and (2) *find out the real reasons*. The two are related. If most people cite a particular objection, it has a greater chance of being valid on face value. If a very few do so, then the reason is almost certainly not to be the one which is given. For example, consider the "not enough Bible" criticism. Probably this comes most often from a sense of insecurity in this matter of character education, and a desire to find something which tradition says will certainly work.

"My child already has this trait." "He can already distinguish between imagination and reality." Statements like these came back to us many times in Parents' Reports. In fact, all three of these have been used by parents to describe children as young as Kindergarten level. The fact is that certainly neither of the last two of these statements could be made completely about even the best of adults, much less about Kindergarteners. This led us to our *concept of infinite traits*. On the one hand, this concept implied that we must select attitude goals which have infinite possibilities. "Making friends with all kinds of people" would be such an attitude. "Learning to go to bed when asked" would not. But even more important, we must state them so that parents, teachers, and youth can see this quality of infinite capacity in them.

We are far from having reached the end of this problem. "That again! We've had that a million times before!" This we hear at almost all age levels, especially at the High School age. Actually, we do not have a single attitude repeated in the Project. What are the characteristics of our goals, then, which give this impression to the youth? The fact is, we don't know, but are at present doing some research from which we hope we can achieve effective insights.

Some more recent evidence gives us reason to believe more

strongly than ever in a very interesting insight which originally grew out of an impressionistic judgment based on reasonably objective data. This we call the *concept of positive acceleration*. It is that the more a child has learned in any particular area, the more rapidly he can learn further skills in it. It is common for parents to think that character traits are finite entities; if a child has half learned a trait, his remaining potential is only half as great as the child who has learned none of it. "We don't get at the children who really need this," is a common statement of those who think that the child who has the least can learn the most. Of course, looked at in terms of a sort of mythical ultimate capacity, this may be true. But in terms of how much progress the child can make this week, or in this unit, or during this year, the opposite is true.

These last two concepts led very quickly to results which brought about another insight which is needed to make them effective. Our ambitions, inspired by the concepts of infinite traits and positive acceleration, outran the capacities of our children to achieve them, and of parents and teachers to teach them. Then, there came from the Gestalt laboratories, especially the Lewinian research, the concept of *levels of aspiration*. This, in brief, stated that if goals are too small or too large, they fail to challenge the child, but that achievable aspirations are important determiners of one's performance. This means that we must study our goals to make sure that they are modest enough to be within the capacity of the child to achieve and at the same time large enough to challenge his best. Much of this has to be achieved in the choice of goals. Note, too, that our thousands of parents and teachers who do the daily task of challenging youth, and our youth who meet the challenge with their efforts, are piling up evidence, from which will certainly come new and un-dreamed-of insights about this process.

Pay especial attention now to this last insight. It has to do with attitudes in the abstract and attitudes in personality. Consider this experience of ours. We have been criticized repeatedly for trying to teach attitudes as separate and isolated things apart from the total personality. Yet, a basic principle of the Project is, "A character trait has no meaning apart from the individual of whom it is characteristic." Does this not look like a matter of simple failure on the part of our critics to study our materials? Yet, evidence continued to accumulate concerning this isolation idea. Not only outside critics but also reports from parents and teachers showed that they often in practice really taught attitudes in an unrealistic fashion. On analysis it often proved to be that, in practice, they were not considering the total personality of the learners. Even some of us on the staff talked about attitudes as if they had reality in themselves. The very neglect of parents and teachers to use the adaptation procedure in lesson preparation showed that they were thinking of the attitude as something which could almost be imposed on the child, or at least "sold" to him as an entity in itself.

Then came the new insight. It is that *we must make a clear distinction between the attitude in the abstract and an attitude in a personality.* In other words, the attitude statement at the beginning of the lesson plan does not have any real existence. Use the analogy of painting a portrait. In a sense this is what character education is. Consider your red paint as an attitude. How much of it you use and where you use it is far more a function of the portrait than it is of the paint itself. Just throw it on slapdash and you will hardly get a masterpiece. It must be blended into the total portrait. This is the way it is with an attitude. An attitude becomes real only when blended into the total personality, influencing it and being influenced by it. This is what is really behind the adaptation procedure.[1] In a very real sense the adaptation procedure can be defined as transforming an idealistic abstraction into flesh-and-blood reality, changing a mythical dream into a social force, through the dynamic of a personality.

Of one thing you can be sure: there is no end to the process. We shall always be finding out more significant things about these objectives in character education, and finding out more significant ways of finding them out.

SOME IMPORTANT CONCEPTS DESCRIBED IN THIS CHAPTER

Note that while this history of our CRP research has involved many people, special skills, and considerable financial backing, many of the techniques can be used by anyone, even parents deal-

[1] The adaptation procedure is one of our teaching techniques in which we ask teachers and parents to adapt the lesson materials to the personality of each individual child.

ing with their children. In other words, the scientific method has great value for everyone, especially the layman.

The chronological story of CRP certainly demonstrates the importance of making haste slowly and laying solid foundations. Fruitful research starts out from hypotheses, and the more carefully one formulates his initial hypotheses, the better. From these initial hypotheses one builds carefully, step by step, toward a fully developed research design. We started from a fourteen-year study of Jesus' philosophy of life, spent ten years in dealing directly with individual children to find workable procedures and to eliminate ineffective ones, another six years formulating an initial curriculum embodying the best hypotheses we could find for effective character education. Then for a period already lasting several years and projected for several more, we have been testing these hypotheses and exploring promising areas for new insights into our problems.

Even more important, a number of decision-hypotheses also had to be made. In our case we decided, for example, to put emphasis on a positive concept of goodness as over against negative ethics; on an energy concept of personality as over against a plastic-clay concept; on the hypothesis that wholesome personality development consists in the formation of positive patterns of adjustment, not in the elimination of maladjustive patterns; and on the concept that the major areas of human achievement are to be found in levels of potential which are far beyond the satisfaction of human needs, however broadly defined.

The most important concept in this chapter is *insight-hypothesis*. An insight is a new hypothesis which offers a fuller and more useful explanation of certain observed phenomena than any previous hypothesis. Such an insight-hypothesis is based on an unbiased sample of data, and is stated in terms of the infinity principle. Indeed, it includes as an integral part experimental-design elements which lead to its replacement by a still better insight.

No extensive progress is going to be made in the field of religious and character education until scientific research becomes a major part of its ongoing program. At least a third of our educational budgets must be spent this way, not in a series of isolated evaluative studies, but as an integral part of the educative process itself.

CHAPTER III

———— • • ————

BIOGRAPHY OF A RESEARCH PROJECT
B. LEARNING IS DONE BY THE
LEARNERS, AND THEY ARE
ALL DIFFERENT

CHARACTER EDUCATION. The word "education" implies that some learning and teaching must take place. We are now emerging from a period in this country in which all the emphasis in our educational philosophy was on teaching and very little on learning. For instance, there are many times as many books on teaching methods as there are on learning methods. We are now coming to realize that the learner plays the leading role. In one of our own current researches in CRP, we are finding that the two most important things for a teacher to know are: first, the age-level characteristics of the children being taught and, second, the personalities of the individual children in the class. Teaching methods as such seem to be relatively much less important.

Most of the recent change in educational psychology from emphasis on the teacher and the curriculum to emphasis on the learner has come about during the years of the history of CRP. The story of our own experiences in dealing with the problem of learning reflect this trend.

If the learner is the important factor, it follows that we must find systematic ways to describe him and his efforts to learn. In this chapter, then, I shall describe very briefly the growth and development of our two principal tools for depicting the personality and its functioning. Then the development of our curriculum will show the course of our explorations into the learning process.

TOOLS WITH WHICH TO DESCRIBE PERSONALITY AND ITS FUNCTIONING

There are a thousand dimensions by which personality could be described. A very common statement which one is tempted to accept as a truism is: "The more we know about a child, the better we can deal with him." Actually, there are countless things we could know about any child that would not be of the slightest use to us in education. Indeed, such a multiplicity of facts could be more confusing than helpful.

The problem is, then, what dimensions of his personality are useful and helpful to know? Many factors enter into the answer to this question. Because from the very beginning we have evaluated our procedures by finding out what the children learned, we become aware of our failures very quickly. As a result we have revised our learning theory rapidly over the years. This growth in learning theory can be seen clearly in the growth of two of our most important tools, the Personality Profile and the Dynamics Diagram. Both of them in their present form will be dealt with much more extensively in later chapters, but a brief history of their growth will show you how to go about learning how children learn.

What Dimensions of Personality Play Major Roles in the Learning Process?

Make a thorough study of the needs and interests of the people whom it [Christian education] is to serve. The list of needs that grows out of such a study should include, not only the needs more or less common to all, but those that are peculiar to the individual members of that church and community (95:222).

That sounds easy enough, but in our CRP research we have found it worth while to invest a great deal of time and effort in constructing useful tools for doing so. Examine some standard textbook in educational psychology. You will almost certainly find one pretty dull chapter on the learning curve. It will talk of plateaus, insight drops, physiological limits, and the like. It doesn't look very exciting. But behind every real learning curve is a personality. And the factors of that personality had a lot more to do with that curve than the textbook, school equipment, and teachers all put together. Gradually these two instruments of ours have made it possible for us to study these personality factors in learning systematically and fruitfully.

I do not know how many different instruments we have attempted to construct during our work in CRP. I imagine that they would number into the hundreds. A vast majority of them have been discarded. A few of them, however, have stood the test of experience and by gradual improvement have become relatively permanent tools for our work. To be sure, there are standardized tests and scales by the thousand in the literature of psychology and education (16). Some of them, of course, we have used. It would be foolish indeed for us to try to develop our own intelligence test or to try to improve on many of the best achievement tests. But there have been unique problems in our work for which we had to develop instruments of our own, among which are the Personality Profile and the Dynamics Diagram.

From 1935, when we first began actual experimentation, until 1944 we did hundreds of individual studies. These consisted essentially in trying to teach a specific attitude to a particular child, using various methods until we succeeded and then recording how we did it. All this was done, as you will remember, to make it possible to bring together a body of educational materials and methods which had actually proved to be effective, at least with someone. It was with this body of data that we finally hoped to be able to undertake the construction of an effective curriculum.

But doing individual studies is not as simple as it sounds. The human personality is very intricate and complex. We soon discovered that we needed to measure it in two fundamental ways. In the first place, people differ. We needed, therefore, an instrument by which we could describe these differences in terms of some useful dimensions. Then, secondly, although there are many characteristics of a personality, every individual is just one person. This means that we also needed an instrument by which to describe his intricate wholeness. Here is how we went about it.

When ethical ideals are presented to large groups, we can easily fall into the fallacy of thinking of these ideals as if they had some reality in themselves, and can be accepted by every individual in about the same way. In CRP we have been saying that when a new ideal becomes characteristic of a person, it must be an individual part of all of him. His own application of it will be as unique as he himself is. To be sure, it should color his personality, but his personality will color it even more. This concept—of learning "all over" as it were—was and still is the core of our personality theory, including learning. "Probably no finding in educational psychology has secured more universal support today than the principle that we learn as we live, and that information, knowledge, skills, habits, attitudes, appreciations, beliefs and ideals are acquired in one and the same process" (99:54).

This gave rise to one of our most commonly quoted principles: "You can no more solve the problems of the personal equation without knowing the factors in that equation than you can do the same for a mathematics equation." We began, therefore, in 1935 to develop a psychometric laboratory at Union College. Each year since then we have given psychological tests to numbers of people, ranging from two years of age to adulthood. Our emphasis on the personal equation, as we call it, has become more intense, rather than less so, through the years. This personal equation is the name we apply to a set of dimensions which experience has taught us are important ones to know in helping a growing youth to achieve his maximum potential.

What Are the Important Dimensions of Personality? The most important tool which grew out of this effort to discover useful dimensions by which to describe the personal equation is the *Personality Profile.*[1] Its purpose is to record in useful graphic form all of the significant facts we can gather from tests, rating scales, laboratory observations, and school records. In its first form in 1935 it included twenty-seven dimensions. After being revised a number of times, it at present lists sixty-one variables, including physical characteristics, mental abilities, special aptitudes, and traits of social and emotional maturity. More than four thousand of these individual profiles have been constructed concerning individuals tested. Not only has this enabled us to give useful guidance to hundreds of parents and youth, particularly with regard to the educational and

[1] *The Personality Profile* which is now being used is published by the Union College Laboratory of Psychology, and can be secured from it.

vocational problems, but it has also been a rich source of information about how children and youth learn.

The challenge to "Know thyself!" was surely not intended to be limited to problem cases. Our testing program attracts two fairly distinct groups of people. Much the larger group are not "problem cases" but CRP youth (and some others) who are being tested on our philosophy of positive potential. Our Youth Workshops, which are built around the testing program, attract the leaders of our young people in the churches all over the country. The rest of our testing program, and the smaller part of it, consists of children "referred" by the schools, because of educational difficulties; or of college students who come for the same reason; or people seeking vocational guidance because of dissatisfaction with their present jobs. This distinction between the positive potential role of mental measurements and the therapeutic role is, I believe, one of our most important contributions. It influences the tests we give, the procedures in interview concerning test results, and the people who come for testing.

An early notion about tests and vocational guidance was that an expert could look at the test results and immediately tell a youth what he ought to do in life. The fact is, no well trained guidance counselor uses tests that way. Furthermore, the notion that a person should go into one and only one vocation is a misconception. Psychologists refer to this as the "niche" fallacy. Most people can do a number of different things equally well.

General insights or principles have become a part of our procedures, as a result of this, all of which can be related to the idea of the dignity and autonomy of the individual youth.

The first one we have stated this way: Vocational guidance is the privilege of the counselor; but vocational choice is both the privilege and the responsibility of the youth. In our own work we have firmly refused to tell any youth what he should be, even if he urges us to do so. That is his task. We will, of course, give him every bit of evidence we can, on which to make the wisest decision he can. Note that this decision is a significant part of the youth's total education. In fact, we have built two of our curricular units around this decision which he must make.

The second insight is of a very different nature. You might expect that our modern-day worship of a high IQ would make interviews concerning children of modest endowment rather depressing and unhappy experiences. Once in a great while this is so, but this has been decidedly the exception. In general, the interviews concerning children of modest endowment have been among the most thrilling and satisfactory of them all. This happened so repeatedly that I knew that it would eventually lead to very important insights in our educational philosophy. It certainly did.

The idea growing out of such experiences was our *vision concept of vocational guidance.* From the very beginning we urged all the young people, having chosen vocations, to find high visions for them. This proved, however, to be superficial. Then we tried the idea of reversing the process. We ask the youth to consider the possibility that, being unique, as everyone is, he is destined for a unique task. He is told that he can change the world a little with his life. Discussion usually translates this abstract principle into practical and attainable form for each youth. This we call his vision. Then he is challenged to choose a vocation, by means of which to achieve the vision. The vocation becomes a means to an end, not an end in itself. This concept has proved to be one of the most effective we have ever developed.

What Is This Total Personality Like?   The Dynamics Diagram is our second major tool. Let me describe its development, for behind it is one of our most thrilling adventure stories. The secret of it is in the word *dynamic.* It has been a long time since psychologists have tried to describe personality in terms of structures. We don't talk any longer about "memory," but about "remembering," and so on. But the concept of dynamics goes even beyond that. For example, we frequently find two facts in personality whose influence in behavior is due, not to either or both of them, but to a force which results from the interrelationship between the two. Leverage is such a concept in physics. Self-confidence probably does not exist as such at all, but is probably a way of describing the quality of a personality which results from such interacting factors as ability, habits of success, competition, praise and criticism received, opportunity for expression, and degree of responsibility involved. The Dynamics Diagram grew out of an effort to find a tool by which to identify the most important interaction dynamics in personality; hence its name.

This concept of interaction dynamics did not exist in 1935. The first version of this diagram was called a Diagram of Behavior at that time. In fact, the concept of personality which we were using then was practically a modified form of behaviorism. To be sure, we never held such a mechanistic view as that involved in Watson's Stimulus-Response sequence. We never conceived of human personality as so complete a pawn in the drama of life. When the equation began to be written Stimulus-Organism-Response, so that the organism got in between the situation and the individual's reaction to it, the story began. In fact, I'd guess that this was a more significant event in the history of psychology than most of us have realized. As you will soon see, the environment has come to be less and less important and the organism more and more central in our thinking about the learning process.

We introduced another term, PS, perceived situation, between the S and R in our new diagram. The PS was defined as the way an individual interprets his environment. The O was one of its determiners as well as the S. It is interesting to note, in passing, that one of the modern developments in psychology is called phenomenological psychology. Its major tenet is that perception is the central data which psychology ought to study. In CRP we were insisting that the PS was the most important factor in behavior as early as 1935.

We also included a factor to which we referred as T, tensions, to indicate motivations inside the individual. We also divided the O into Oi (the innate organism, his constitutional traits), and Om (the modified organism, those characteristics which are a result of learning, using that term very broadly to include all changes due to experience). The Diagram then looked like this (73:5):

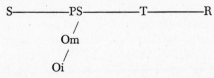

$$S\text{————}PS\text{————}T\text{————}R$$
$$/$$
$$Om$$
$$/$$
$$Oi$$

The most important term in this version of the Diagram was, however, the PS. Increasing force of evidence kept showing us that the way the individual interprets his environment, the meaning he attaches to it, is a far more important determiner of his behavior than the environment itself is.

Then came another important event in this adventure story. It was a piece of research using this Diagram which was reported before the American Psychological Association in 1941 (74). As the basis for that study we selected from our files the data on one hundred children with whom—using all the criteria available—we had been clearly successful in our efforts to stimulate changes in their personalities in the direction desired. We selected another hundred in whom we had been able to produce no such observable changes, so far as we could determine with the same criteria. In the meantime, another elaboration of the Diagram had taken place. It was the division of the Om (modified organism) into Attitudes and Skills. We prepared behavior diagrams on all of these two hundred cases to see if we could discover which factors had been most effective in our successes and failures. We found that we had changed the S (situation) about the same number of times in each of the two groups. These changes involved such things as "allowances," being assigned an "own room" at home, changing courses or teachers or grades at school, or, in a few instances, changing schools. It seemed apparent, therefore, to our surprise, that changing the S as such was followed by failure as often as by success. This was not interpreted as meaning that we can neglect the influence of the cultural determinants in human behavior, but that they won't do much good unless we also consider how the individual will regard them. In fact, we actually changed the S in a way that might on the surface have been expected to produce negative results in some cases. For example, we often suggested that a child remain in one school grade for a second year. In these cases, however, we were very careful to try to determine what meaning the child would give to such a change. He might see it as disgrace or as opportunity. It was necessary then to make sure that the child regarded the change as opportunity, not disgrace.

A second factor in the Diagram which we utilized frequently in our procedures was the Om_{sk} (modified organism, skills). We taught the children many skills: study skills, social skills, athletic skills, and so on. Again, only slightly more instances in which this was done were found in the group with whom we had been successful than in the unsuccessful group. The learning of skills, then, does not in and of itself apparently result in character growth. It is, of course, true that skills are often essential for effective character.

For example, if you wish to make character socially influential, it presupposes social skills. However, we discovered again that the meaning the child attached to the skill was the important thing.

Finally, we attempted also to change attitudes (Om_{Att}). When we were successful, the results were uniformly successful in terms of observable personality change. When we found negative results, we often discovered that attitudes had been changed there also, but they were not changed in the way we intended. This regular association of attitude change with personality change made it seem probable that the two were identical.

It was about this time that our Diagram was again enlarged significantly. It was in the area of the self. Many psychologists at the change of the century talked about the self. But the influence of behaviorism drove it temporarily out of the picture. It was inevitable, however, that the self should return. Our equations simply wouldn't balance without it. Freudianism may well have been the most important influence in this rebirth of the self concept. Whatever we may think of such concepts as the ego, the super-ego and the id, guilt elements are mighty hard to detect in muscle twitches.

This concept of the self assumes that there is something more basic in personality than native endowment or acquired skills. It is the person himself—that part of him to which he refers when he says "I." To be sure, this self is not obvious in infants. Because of this, many psychologists describe its development in such terms as "the interiorization of social experience." They think that it is a learned phenomenon. I should like to predict that we shall not find an adequate explanation of those personality phenomena which we call the self until we postulate the kind of personality structure religious thinkers through the ages have called a soul.

In any event, in our CRP Diagram we began to distinguish between self attitudes and other attitudes. As soon as we did so, other things became clear and new insights became possible.

Now we were ready for the final transition from a cause and effect concept like that of S—R, S—O—R, or even our early Diagrams, to a completely dynamic frame of reference. We took out the arrows on the Diagram leading from S and O to PS, and that to T and R. We kept finding these factors coming in different order and influencing one another in such intricate ways that we finally put

them all in a circle and described them as if they were a group of
ping-pong balls in a goldfish bowl, with their dynamic energies
causing them to move rapidly and to influence one another in many
ways. A study of their interactions becomes one of our most interesting areas for research. In fact, we become increasingly convinced that the forces resulting from the interaction among these
factors are more powerful than the factors themselves.

Let us note one striking fact. Traditionally we have thought of
the S as something to which the individual must adjust. He is almost a pawn in it. Now, we suddenly discover that in a far more real
sense the individual decides what S he will face. From the time in
early infancy when the child begins to decide that he will go to
this person and not that one, that he will eat this and not that, that
he will play with this here and not that there, he more and more
selects his own S, until in adult life he chooses most of it. The implication of this fact for our traditional notions of education, eco-
nomics, and personality are enormous.

The Diagram has now become in fact a Dynamics Diagram. The
interrelationships among its factors, the cluster patterns found in
their functioning set up some of the most interesting problems we
now face. This should lead to new achievements in the study of
personality, far beyond anything we have dreamed of up to now.

What Do We Mean by "Children of God"?   And now let me
describe the most recent and perhaps the most interesting and effective concept that has come into our thinking about all this. Let's
give it a religious name, for it presupposes an item of religious
faith. Many of my psychological colleagues will shy away from
this. Let me urge them to examine the facts before they do. I like to
call this the *Child of God concept*. It grows out of the fact of individual differences, and the corresponding fact that each person is
a unique individual. It also is related to this dynamics concept.

Note that in the Personality Profile we have described personality
in terms of a number of practical dimensions. In the minds of many
people these dimensions differ qualitatively as well as quantitatively. A high IQ is better than a low IQ. Good athletic aptitude is
better than modest athletic aptitude, and so on. I propose that this
notion that high endowment as the chief determiner of achievement is not true.

The concept behind our use of the Dynamics Diagram is based

on the hypothesis that the major forces of human nature are the interrelationships among these endowment factors and not the factors themselves. Let us suppose that the universe is so ordered that because each individual is unique in his make-up he has the capacity for a unique job; furthermore, that its importance is not a function of native endowment but of finding what one's unique job is. Here is some pertinent evidence.

In one part of the California study of genius, an analysis was made of the personality characteristics of some three hundred great men of history (24:223–710). Their IQ's were estimated by scientific methods, which can be demonstrated to have fair accuracy. Here are names of a group of men from that study: John Quincy Adams, Samuel T. Coleridge, Nicolaus Copernicus, Charles Darwin, George Fox, William Harvey, Thomas Jefferson, Blaise Pascal, and Friedrich Schleiermacher. I am listing them in alphabetical order. Rearrange them in the order you would rank them in terms of their greatness. At the bottom of the next page you will find them listed in the order of the estimate of their intelligence. How well does that agree with your order of greatness? When a number of our staff ranked them in order of greatness, and a pooling of these judgments was used as a final rank, the correlation between the pooled ranks and the estimated IQ's of the men was —.12.

Now do you see how we arrived at the term Child of God concept? Each individual, owing not to his particular native endowments, but owing to the maximum potential of his total personality, has the capacity for making an important contribution to the world. I have interviewed hundreds of parents and youth on the basis of their test results. As I pointed out before, seldom have I had a depressing interview where the endowment was modest. Such interviews have generally been very thrilling.

CHILDREN LEARN, BUT NOT ALWAYS WHAT WE WANT THEM TO

The scientific method is ruthless in its revelations of our failures. In no place has it been more so than in the field of learning. "Jesus increased in wisdom and in stature and in favor with God and man." That is what all of us want to have happen with our children, but except for the second, we have used some astonishingly ineffective procedures for bringing it about. Probably if the scientific method had not come along, we might have gone on forever, especially in religious education, depending on memory verses and verbalized theological formulae to do our work for us. If we had put our minds to it, we could not have produced a more ineffective method.

To us, at least, our own experiences in learning theory and methods thus far seem to be somewhat like conducting a scouting expedition into an almost uncharted wilderness. We had, when we started, few even moderately effective instruments to guide us, but a multitude of traditional myths to give us false leads, and a whole host of eager prophets holding out sure-cure panaceas. How indeed were we to distinguish between the more productive and sterile hypotheses among the hundreds offered in the field of education? It was not so much that no effective character education was being done as that we had little idea as to *how* it was being done. We couldn't be at all sure whether our educational procedures had anything to do with the child's character growth or not. He may have been growing in spite of rather than because of what we were doing. Or again, the individual carrying out these procedures and the way in which he did it may have been more important than what we did. In other words, curriculum builders just didn't know what was happening nor why.

You will remember that during the first years of the Project, we had dealt almost entirely with individuals. During this period we tried to record our successes and failures in order to build up a stockpile of effective procedures. It is my belief that our efforts at group curricula would never have been successful without this backlog of experience with individual children. The fact remained that if character education were to become a practical procedure, we had to develop general curricula, and this implied group methods. One thing, however, became very clear during the decade of individual studies. Character education, to be effective, must be individual in its nature. Group procedures which do not deal with each individual as an individual are probably doomed to failure

The order of the nine great men in terms of IQ is as follows: Pascal, Coleridge, Adams, Schleiermacher, Jefferson, Darwin, Harvey, Fox, Copernicus. Their IQ's ranged from between 180–190 for Pascal, to between 100–110 for Copernicus.

before they begin. The same is true of any sort of learning. To teach children verbalized formulae, even if they consist of theological concepts, will be meaningless unless they are individualized for each person learning them.

How Can Individual Differences Be Taken into Account in the Group Process? The first concept which helped us make this transition from the individual to the group phase in the development of our curricular procedures was what we called *drama-type education*. This can be described as the process of constructing group lessons or projects so that each member of a class plays a role which conforms to his own personality, somewhat as an actor in a drama plays a role which fits his personality. Note that this makes standardized curricula possible, even taking individual differences into account. A drama is a unified thing, even if each actor does play a different role. It does imply, however, that regimented procedures which set the same role for everyone are ineffective. Using this principle, each teacher or leader was asked to include materials in his plans for the class or project, some aspects of which would be applicable to each member of the class, and in each project to have a role especially suited to each member of the class. (The term *drama-type education* has gradually given way to the term *adaptation procedure*. The principle involved, however, is the same.)

Are There Different Types of Children? It is at this point that we face one of the most interesting problems in character education. Of one thing you can be reasonably certain: Curricula which treat all people as if they were alike, or which are aimed at "the average child," are certain to be ineffective.

But having said that, let's note two phenomena with which everyone is familiar. On the one hand, each individual is unique. No one just like him ever existed before. On the other hand, however, groups look astonishingly alike. Any teacher, no matter with what age group he deals, is impressed with the fact that from year to year each new class seems to be much like the one before it. The shy child, the aggressive child, the leader, the follower, the quick child and the slow child—they are all there in each successive class. This tempts us to classify children into types.

In the Morse Kindergarten study (104, 105) there was some evidence to indicate that when a lesson was adapted to a large portion of the twenty-four children in his experimental group, these adaptations proved to be effective for other members of the group as well. Now, suppose we repeat this research, adapting for different numbers of children, from one to whatever number results in these "spilled over" adaptations making the lesson effective for the whole group. We can note which children are affected by any one adaptation and study them to determine what characteristics in common among them bring about this result. Then, too, we can see how many such "adaptation groups" are necessary to affect the whole class. This should give us "types" which are based on the very nature of the personalities involved, and would show how many such types are needed for the learning involved.

THE CURRICULUM—INSIGHT-HYPOTHESES OR SEDATIVE

A host of new curricula are coming from our religious publishing houses these days. They represent the best that religious education has to offer. They have been achieved at great cost in time, money, and the best brains available. Yet, as I watch them, I am depressed, for their very values may lull us into as deep a sleep of false security as any sedatives could have done. Without research, and far-reaching research, they represent as grave a danger as the Church has to face, for they represent a temptation to stand still, believing that they are the best we can possibly achieve.

What chance has religious education in our culture? The movies, radio, TV, the comics, the myriad forms of pleasure have billions to match our pitiful millions. Trying to compete with them on a sheer glamour level is so pitiful as to be tragic. The thing that scares me about these new curricula is the zealous salesmanship that urges churches to buy them, with only the most superficial efforts to search for new insights in the nature of an infinite God.

We ought to be spending a large portion of our total religious budgets for research. We have not even got well started toward finding out how our youth can learn the religion of Jesus. Given real research, fifty years from now we shall have curricula which will be a thousand times as effective as the best we can produce now, and which can match and surpass the best that the secular world has to offer.

Our first general CRP curriculum was produced in 1945–1947.

Despite lack of time and personnel for an adequate job, this curriculum did serve as a foundation—a set of basic hypotheses—on which later revisions could be built.

The first step in the development of a curricular unit was the selection of a *typical class*. This was achieved by studying a number of Personality Profiles of actual children. An effort was made to select a group of these at each age level—usually Profiles of five boys and five girls—in such a way that they would represent as wide a variation from one another as possible. The assumption underlying this procedure was that if curricular writers kept each of these "typical" children in mind as they wrote, attempting to make sure that each lesson was adaptable to each one of them, the resultant materials would be more realistic and effective than if the task were primarily in terms of the content to be taught and secondarily geared somewhat vaguely to an "average" child of that age level.

You will note that this method automatically involved a practical form of age-level calibration. When this was coupled with the age-level calibration done in the construction of the attitude goal list, we could have considerable confidence in its validity. Of course, we made errors, and we still do. Nevertheless, each succeeding revision is more carefully geared to the age-level groups involved. This demonstrates the difference between doing age-level calibration by experiment and by armchair theory, even when based on existing studies.

The next step was the search for materials and methods from the existing literature of religious and character education, suited to the basic task of attitude formation. As you might expect, it was difficult to find such materials, geared to the particular purposes we had in mind. If, for example, we had chosen to use such traditional trait goals as honesty, loyalty, and so on, there was abundant existing material. We had, however, developed different objectives—our original attitude list (79). Few materials suitable for them could be found. This meant that we had to select from the endless available materials those which we could best adapt to our needs.

Interestingly enough, the construction of suitable projects was the most difficult part of the lesson, or program plan. We were able to find astonishingly few projects which met the needs of our drama-type approach. In most of those which were available, only one type of activity was employed. If one child drew pictures, they all did. We needed projects in which children of different abilities could contribute according to those abilities. In some of our recent research it is very interesting to discover that when church-school projects have allowed for individual differences, the effectiveness of the lesson during the following week in the home has been greater than when the church-school project had all children doing the same thing. The chief criteria for much project construction have apparently been "child interest" and "the appearance of religious value."

The use of activities in church schools at the present time can be described as mostly off-center. The value seen "in things to do" is mainly that they offer help to the teacher in his problems of holding pupil attention, keeping order, preventing situations from getting out of hand. Thanks to them he hopes to be able to salvage a few minutes of each session for having the lesson read and maybe talking about it to a passively listening group. (34:202).

THE LESSON PLAN—SUGAR-COATED PIETY OR CHALLENGE TO HIGH ACHIEVEMENT

Here is the focus of any educational venture. We must be more rigorously critical of the lesson or program plans than of anything else. And this brings us back again to that word *criterion*. By what criteria shall we judge our curricular materials?

On the one hand, we can use such criteria as readability, literary style, apparent interestingness, stated content objectives, ease of use, and even physical appearance. Such characteristics may have value in planning and writing curricula. They are quite secondary and futile in evaluating it. Although I do not have evidence to support this assertion, I would guess that the absence of these qualities would handicap a curriculum, but their presence would not add one iota to its effectiveness. The only way to test it is to use it with a group of children and then find out what they have learned.

We as curricular writers cannot wash our hands of responsibility if people don't use our materials and if children don't learn what we put in them. We must work on the premise that if our job is done well enough, both use and learning will follow. Our criteria of a good lesson then are clear. Is it used? Does it get the evidence by which we can measure its effectiveness? Does it reflect the infinity principle and lead to its own revision? What of value do the children learn who use it?

Because the lesson plan is actually the embodiment of our educational hypotheses, the format finally adopted for it needs to be described in terms of the experimental design of which it is a part. When a curriculum is being developed primarily to teach attitudes, as this one has been, the validity even of its outline construction is determined by different criteria than when the purpose is primarily to teach content materials. We regard our lesson plans in CRP as consisting essentially of instructions to parents, teachers, leaders, and youth on how to attack the problem of attitude formation. The underlying psychological principles of attitude formation (oriented to the particular attitude being learned, the age level to which it is taught, and the range of individual differences involved) have to be set forth in a form which makes it possible for the people who are to use them to be able to do so successfully in terms of our objectives. This would be more easily achieved if the people using the lesson plans were all technically trained in the relevant areas of scientific psychology. The fact that a vast majority of them are not makes the task one of immense difficulty.

Here is one of the central principles in our concept of curriculum construction. It involves the co-scientist ideal at its top point. The curriculum must not be regarded by parents, teachers, and youth as a finished product, in which they have no creative role. On the contrary, they must see themselves as scientists testing its values with their very lives and reporting back their experiences as evidence for creating new and vastly superior curricula. All of us who have faith in Christianity believe that in it lies the hope of the world. We also know that our comprehension of the will of God for our children is still pitifully small. Therefore we create the best curricula we can, and with the deepest of humility challenge our children and their teachers to lead us to greater insights by their co-scientist efforts. It is they, not we as its writers, who have the leading role.

The lesson plan is the keystone in the effectiveness of an educational program. To be sure, the teacher, the class, the classroom, the home, the school, the surrounding culture—these and many other factors play indispensable roles in the educative process—and the lesson plan must be a keystone that fits. The child himself plays the leading role. The fact remains that the lesson plan presents the vision to him. By it the child is bored or thrilled, challenged to petty goals or goals that inspire his best, learning that is static and dead, or learning that holds forth visions of infinite possibilities.

Perhaps those rather drastic assertions can be made clearer by suggesting an evaluation scale of types of lessons in ascending order of their potential.

1. The lowest point on the scale would be one in which the material to be learned is set forth with an accompanying admonition to the pupil, "Learn it!" With enough compulsion and drill, most of us learned the multiplication table, our Latin verbs, and the kings of England that way. In character education, it consisted of memorized mottoes and Bible verses. Research has thus far failed to find any measurable values in terms of strength of character in that. This is not to say there are none. The use of proverbs in all cultures has been much too widespread for them to be of no value. The chances are, however, that such values have come because of more fundamental factors, such as cultural approval, which underlie this simple procedure.

2. The second-level curriculum attempts to improve over the first by adding some applications to modern life. Cain and Abel are used as bad examples to admonish us against murder. Abraham and Lot teach us about selfishness. In such a curriculum, religious education becomes essentially an endless process of moralizing about passages of scripture. Such religious training has usually been repressive and in general unattractive to youth. Certainly few of them have found high adventure in it. Yet to many of them this is the only form of religious education they know. It is this kind of curriculum that has given rise to the term *goody-goody*, considered to be a major insult by most youth and their parents.

3. The next level involves a more serious effort at age-level calibration. It consists of an effort to teach at each age level what can be learned at that age level. This principle, it seems to me, underlies the first major effort at constructing curricula which have some chance of being met with interest and learning on the part of the child. Graded materials represented a great step forward in curriculum construction. Probably the reason for this improvement is not so much that they can be learned as that they tended to reach further into the child's learning potential.

4. The fourth level is the one now current among new curricula, and perhaps can be called *modern methods curricula*. All of the recent advances in education, Biblical scholarship, and child psychology are utilized to their fullest extent. All of the "established findings of science" are added. This again represents real progress. And yet, as I have said, their very values may create a spirit of false satisfaction with them. To stop now would be to stop at perhaps point IV in the diagram below.

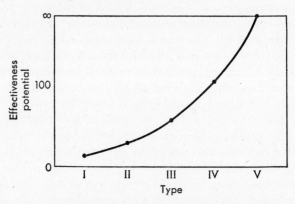

5. The fifth level can be called the *infinity principle curriculum*. I hope religious educators can come to see its potential. It is my firm belief that it can lead to achievement of many times greater Christian character than we have thus far produced. It involves the use of the powerful tools of science in the very center of the curriculum itself. This is a curriculum that embodies in its very nature the petition, "Thy will be done," with the faith that that will is infinite. I think our own experience with this kind of curriculum demonstrates its power beyond reasonable doubt.

Perhaps this simple graph will show its possibilities. As I describe our lesson plan, you will see how we have attempted to use it. I wonder if I can show you, then, how this infinity principle and the scientific method can result in a more powerful approach to curriculum construction than we have had before.

For example, one of our staff was recently teaching an adult class of women in church school. She asked them to cite instances of goodness, which were positive, rather than just the absence of sins that it is wrong to commit. She reports that they were almost helpless to do so. Contrast that to the situation our curricular writers will be in when we begin our next revision. From the reports of parents, teachers, and youth covering just one two-year period, we have collected 40,000 such positive items. This incredible achievement is just one example of the power of the co-scientist principle. Such an achievement is possible, however, only if the lesson is so constructed that our co-scientists can carry out their roles. This involves instructing them in what to do and how to do it.

Format of the Lesson Plan　The format of the lesson plan went through several exploratory phases before even its general outline could be determined. The lesson plan carries such heavy responsibilities that it was not easy to find a format designed to meet all of them. And here is a very important point I have made repeatedly before in various forms: Psychological organization is the criterion to be used—not logical organization. It would be easy to determine a logical order for the various elements of the lesson plan. This could easily result in decreasing its effectiveness drastically. For example, at one time we decided to put the Guide for the Parents at the beginning of the lesson, in order to emphasize the importance of home cooperation. We quickly discovered that this produced much confusion. The home teaching comes after the church-school lesson chronologically. We found we had to put it that way in the lesson plan. To assume that a logically systematic presentation of a body of materials is best may not be true at all. It may be far better to present that same material in some order determined by its relevance to the learner's daily life.

The Introduction (Where Are We Going? Why? And How Will We Know If and When We Get There?)　The *Introduction* is probably the most unique and ambitious section of a CRP lesson plan. It attempts to achieve four major purposes, all related to the infinity curriculum and the co-scientist principle.

In the first place it is the statement of a specific hypothesis and a corresponding criterion. That is to say, the goal of the lesson constitutes the hypothesis that here a potential area of growth which is open to a child or youth if he can be challenged to learn and master it. Alongside this is also stated the nature of the evidence—that is, the criteria—in the behavior and thinking of the child which would seem to constitute reasonable proof that the child has or has not learned it and also whether or not it actually does represent stronger character potential. If religious education is ever to gain for itself the power of the scientific method, its curricular elements will always have to contain this statement of hypothesis and criterion. Without it, we will inevitably continue our age-old procedure of wishful thinking and relative ineffectiveness.

Our principal attack on this problem has been to include in each Introduction the psychological and educational principles necessary to teach the particular attitude goal of the lesson to the particular age level. In this way we hope to make it possible for parents and teachers to use the general principles needed in specific situations with specific goals. They do not need to become educational psychologists to be able to take advantage of the skills of that field.

The other two major purposes of the Introduction are concerned with the integration of the specific lesson objective into the total ultimate goal of Christian personality.

In the first place, because personality is a whole, a specific attitude statement is only an abstraction until it becomes part of this total personality. For that matter, an attitude statement is simply a way of describing how a total personality will react under certain conditions. It is John who is kind and gentle. Kindness and gentleness are not separate entities which John can add to his repertoire like a new suit. The lesson Introduction must show how this integration is to be achieved.

In the second place, CRP is based on the Christian Hypothesis. A specific attitude goal can be described accurately only in terms of this total Christian picture. It has been a frequent experience for parents and teachers to deal with an attitude goal without this orientation. Whenever they do, they may interpret it in many different ways, some of them not Christian at all. The Introduction, then, should show the basic nature of this attitude in terms of the Christian Hypothesis.

The Church School Lesson—Helping Youth Find the Power of the Heritage of the Ages   The second section of the lesson plan is entitled *The Church School Lesson* and is designed to include the instructional materials necessary for showing youth the lesson goal and its meaning for them. Materials for direct instruction, story materials, biographical and historical materials, Biblical and other religious content, are used in this section. However, ours is not basically a content curriculum. The materials used are selected, not primarily for their own sake, but to set before the child a vision for the attitude objective of the lesson. They need to be evaluated and revised by this test: Do they or do they not produce understanding and challenge for the attitude goal? Research relative to this section will consist in measuring the effectiveness of the materials used in producing this result. It will be obvious that a crucial task in this research will be the construction of valid criteria for determining when this has been achieved. Note that this gives parents and teachers a purpose for teaching particular materials. Whether or not you agree with our purpose, no very effective teaching will take place unless you have such a purpose. I memorized certain rules in Latin to get a passing mark, and that is the only purpose they served.

The first concept we used in CRP was the common one of translating the attitude, with its religious implications, into modern life. More and more, however, the fact of individual differences has influenced this process. Illustrations of different kinds of children have been used. As our formulation of functional type concepts comes to maturity, these will certainly be the basis for more effective lesson illustrations.

The second concept grew naturally out of the first, and is an implementation of the adaptation procedure. Each element in the lesson should be so constructed that it can easily be adapted to the individual child. Indeed, we have even attempted to construct lesson elements so that they cannot be used without such adaptation. For example, stories are seldom written so fully that teachers can tell or read them as they appear. They must be adapted. This is a very important aspect of our concept of the curriculum.

The third phase of this process is setting up a criterion by which the effectiveness of this portion of the lesson can be evaluated in our search for ever better ones. It usually takes the form of questions which the teachers are asked to answer in their reports, and which will give us valid evidence for such an evaluation.

The Church School Project—In Which Youth Tries It Out in Practice   The third section of our lesson plan is *The Church School Project*. The major purpose of the project is to give each child in the group opportunity to practice the skills involved in the attitude, in terms of his own particular abilities and interests. It is a laboratory exercise in which each member of the class has an opportunity to practice applications of the attitude. The practical measure of its success is its demonstrated adaptability to the individual differences of the group and its challenge to the class as a whole and as individuals. I have already referred to the evidence recently found that the more varied the project is, the more effective it is, even as its results are observed in Parents' Reports. In general the project has proved to be the most difficult part of the lesson plan to develop. A few highly successful projects have been created; and in each succeeding revision it becomes easier to construct such projects, based on the evidence gained from previous uses of the material.

The significance of a church-school project in character education as implied in our CRP philosophy is threefold. All three purposes grow out of our increasing conviction that learning rather than teaching is the main element in education. The heaviest responsibility for character education rests on the child who must do the learning rather than on the teacher whose chief purpose is to make it easier and more challenging for the child to learn. The project, then, should make it possible first for the child to prove to his own satisfaction that the attitude is a valid one, and one by which he is willing to guide his behavior. Then, secondly, the project should make it possible for him to adapt the attitude to his own personality. To be sure, he will need much guidance and help from the teacher if he is to do this successfully. Nevertheless if it is really to be done, he must do it. Finally, the project gives him an opportunity for practice. It is becoming increasingly clear to educators that there is little, if any, learning without recitation. The project should make this possible. "I'll learn you" is bad English. "I'll teach you" is bad psychology if it carries a sort of plastic-clay concept with it. This whole principle is in line with our idea that the individual has far more to say about his environment than his environment does about him.

When all this has been done and the experiences have been described in reports from parents, teachers, and youth, we get invaluable co-scientist evidence on which to construct future projects many times more meaningful and challenging to those who use them.

Home Guide—Without Home Cooperation, the Church School and Character-Building Agencies Are Helpless Our emphasis in CRP on the home as the center of character education is not new in religious education. We have simply succeeded in bringing it about in large measure. To be sure, we have been as guilty as others of the creation of platitudes. "Character education must be a seven-day-a-week process." "Not only will we (the church school) not promise to do anything for your (parents') child without your cooperation; we'll promise not to." These are two of our best known platitudes. What success we have had, however, has not been in admonition, but in challenging parents to work at the job and, even more important, giving them some effective tools to work with.

Our central tool for this purpose has been the *Home Guide* in the lesson plan.

"Any curriculum would be as successful as yours [CRP] if parents worked at it as hard." This has been said repeatedly about our success in getting parental cooperation. Perhaps. Even if this is the case, it implies a measure of success in our work, for one major characteristic of a good curriculum is to get itself used. In this we have had considerable success, but only a fraction of the ultimate potential.

The important question then, is: Why do parents use it? Let's look at the major elements which through the years we have put into this section of the lesson plan and see if we can answer this question.

The purpose of the Home Guide is to provide instructions for the guidance of the parents in teaching the lesson at home. It must also allow for individual differences and must suggest practical situations in which the attitude can be applied.

The term *adaptation procedure,* as applied to the home, is the process of adapting the materials of the lesson to the individual child as a member of an integrated home. A major aspect of it in the home environment consists in discovering a project for the child —and often one for the parents, too—to carry out which, on the one hand, fits his particular needs and problems and, on the other, makes it possible to put the attitude into practice in his daily life, especially at home.

The use of the adaptation procedure in the home is proving to be one of the most important elements in success there. In one study it was found that observable character growth took place sixteen times as frequently in homes in which parents had used the adaptation procedure than it did in homes in which it was not used.

THE SEARCH FOR INSIGHTS INTO THE LEARNING PROCESS

The success of any exploration depends on the preparation made for it and the tools available for dealing with its problems. Exciting as have been our journeys into learning so far, we are completely aware of the fact that the future holds the possibility of new insights which will dwarf these by comparison. Let us look, for a few pages, at the methods we have available for our next attacks in the field of learning.

Learning is one of the oldest areas in which psychologists have done research. Ebbinghaus' memory experiments are still among the classics in the field. A bibliography of the research titles in the field of learning would fill a large volume. Theories of learning have so sprung up in recent years that now there are at least a dozen important ones, each explaining some kinds of learning, none explaining all kinds of learning. Needless to say, all this has had its influence on our thinking through the years. If you are doing educational research, you must of necessity keep up with trends in this field.

We in CRP have done little or no research in the problem of learning theory as such. Yet our policy of pragmatic eclecticism has resulted in continual growth in our basic assumptions about learning. I have already spoken of the drama-type approach of the early years, and the adaptation procedure, and of the steps in the concepts embodied in the lesson plan.

I suppose the concept which we have used which has caused the most comment is that embodied in our description of the "steps in the learning process." To many people the terms *exposure, repetition, understanding, conviction,* and *application,* have sounded pretty "old-fashioned." Yet when Hilgard (51) wrote his basic volume on theories of learning, he concluded the discussion of each theory by evaluating it in terms of how well it explains each of the major problems of learning. He listed six such problems: capacity, practice, understanding, motivation, remembering, and forgetting. Note how alike they are to steps set forth in our work, especially if our fifth step of application is replaced with his two problems of remembering and forgetting.

Each new theory of learning is established to explain some kind of learning. It follows that if this is the kind of learning you want to have take place, then this is probably the best theory by which to plan your procedures. Note some of the major factors which differ from one learning situation to another. There is, of course, the nature of the thing to be learned. A skill in athletics is not learned in the same way as is the multiplication table, nor that like a theory in philosophy, nor that like an evaluative attitude. Then there is the decision as to the criteria you will accept as evidence that the desired learning has been achieved. It may be that all you want is the ability to recognize what you are studying when you see it in the future. If so, then it is learned when that is the case. It may be, however, that you will want to be able to repeat it verbatim, or perhaps to understand its implications, or still more fully to put it into practice, or finally to have it become an integral part of your concept of your self. In other words, you must decide what level of learning you desire. Again, the learning situation differs, depending on who is doing the learning and upon his readiness for this particular kind of learning experience.

The teacher is usually a factor in the equation as he plays differing roles depending on his own personality and skills, and on his relations with his pupils. Even fellow learners may influence a learning situation very much, as every Sunday-school teacher of a group of twelve- and thirteen-year-old boys knows. This means that only when you have described your learning situation carefully in terms of all these variables can you decide what educational procedures to employ in the process.

How Can We Know When Growth in Character Has Taken Place? In the preceding discussion of eclecticism in learning, I touched upon the next insight that we are using in our concepts of learning. This has to do with the criteria of learning. I have repeatedly referred to this word *criterion*. It is with you always in the field of science. Our task is character education. When can you say that a person has grown in character? You cannot assume that if he has memorized or even come to understand your ethical principles, his character has improved. Our most confident learning criteria are embodied in the one of our trait-dimensional theories which we call the *Definition of Character*. It will be discussed fully in Chapter X. It contains six variables, which were first designed to serve as a cross-validation concept to test the validity of our Christian Hypothesis. However, they also constitute learning criteria. There are two social variables (social effectiveness and social breadth), and two personality variables (integration and maximum potential), and two ethical variables (ethical idealism and moral consistency). We say, then, that learning has taken place, in terms of character education, when the child has grown in one or more of these variables. I cannot overemphasize the importance of a criterion concept like this one, whatever your educational goals may be. The point is, make sure that you know what your educational objectives are and how you will know whether you have achieved them or not.

On Using Your Character When You Need It   You cannot stay very long in the field of learning without running into those troublesome twins known as *generalization* and *transfer*. Of what value is it to learn a specific skill or attitude if it never generalizes to any other situations than the one in which it was learned, or if you can never transfer your mastery of it to other types of situation? I would guess that one reason why so many people consider religion impractical is that they have practiced it in so few ways. They try returning good for evil once. Because the experience is not good, they conclude that Christianity will not work in our modern competitive cutthroat society.

Attitudes must be taught in such a way that they transfer, if we expect them to do so. We have used several methods to bring this about. The first of these can be called *application in roles*. In planning each week's work, parents, teachers, and children are urged to consider in what aspects of the child's daily life he can apply the attitude goal of the week. They help him work out a plan and challenge him to carry it through. This has been by far our most used and our most successful learning technique. The children themselves have participated in the planning of these objectives as much as they were able to do so. Because we believe that character and religious education is a seven-day-a-week process, these applications have been made in many aspects of the child's life as he participates in his various roles.

In regard to achieving transfer, two concepts have been especially effective. The first has been the basic conception of our Church School Projects, previously described. The major principle underlying our development of projects for the church school is that in them the individual child gets an opportunity to put the attitude goal into practice. When this is combined with the drama-type concept and the adaptation procedure, the project becomes both individual for each personality and socially integrated. It is hoped that such projects will frequently provide the child with skills for transferring this experience to his daily life.

The other transfer concept has had to do with parent participation. Parents have found that they must do some learning themselves, if their children are to learn. This led to the insight: "The best way to teach these attitudes to your child is to learn them with your child."

Then came the recognition of the fact that parent participation had values not at first realized. One of these is that as the parents learn, at their own level, what the child is learning at his level, they clearly demonstrate to the child that the attitude is of value to the adult as well as to the child. One of the problems of religious education has been the child's tendency to think that things learned at one childhood age level belong to that age level, and that they ought to be "put away with other childish things" when he is older. Someone has said that one of Jesus' greatest problems is "outgrowing his baby pictures." This problem of "dating," as we call it, is partly solved by parents learning the attitude with their children.

A less objectively demonstrable value is that the child sees, not only how the attitude is applicable to his present problems, but also how it will be applicable to the type of problems he will meet as an adult. This, of course, if true, is the very essence of the concept of transfer.

One more problem in this area of learning has been met repeatedly through the years of our work. This is the fact that we are always dealing with the total personality. How can we emphasize single attitudes from week to week and not be teaching piecemeal, isolated fragments of personality? A great deal of modern educational theory, especially in personality research, has emphasized the importance of the total personality. The situational approach to character education and the experience-centered approach have both been outgrowths of this emphasis.

We have certainly been fully aware of the importance of this principle of the total personality. On the other hand, the outstanding values of having specific and clear-cut objectives have made us strive diligently for ways in which these objectives could be emphasized in terms of the total personality. Here are a few of the methods we have used. Remember, of course, that an attitude is not an isolated aspect of personality anyway. It is the total personality looking at one aspect of life.

Our most extensively used method has been that of continual cross reference from one unit to another. This has had its disadvantages, especially in that it has given the child (notably in the later age levels) a feeling of repetition. "Oh, we've had that a thousand times before!" Actually, there is not a single repeated attitude in the whole Project attitude list. Nevertheless the fact that some of our youth think there is means that we must find out what the aspects of the lessons are that seem repetitious and how we can change them to be seen as new and challenging.

SOME IMPORTANT CONCEPTS DESCRIBED IN THIS CHAPTER

The learner, not the teacher, plays the central role in learning and carries the heavier responsibility.

Learning is a function of the total personality and can be brought about only with a knowledge of the relevant dimensions of the personality of the learner.

An interaction dynamic is a force which results from the interaction of two or more other things or forces. Achievement is a dynamic resulting from the interaction between one's abilities and the problems he attempts to solve.

The PS (situation as perceived) is one's environment as he sees it. It is usually far more important in his behavior than the objective situation itself.

From earliest childhood the individual plays an increasing role in choosing the environment to which he will adjust. Most adults choose a vast majority of the situations in which they live. The individual, then, is far from being a pawn to his environment. For the most part he decides what it will be.

Effective curricular material must take into consideration the full range of individual differences. Effective teaching of curricular materials presupposes their adaptation to the individual expected to do the learning.

Effective curricular materials must be calibrated to the age levels to which they are to be taught.

A systematic logical presentation of a body of material to be learned may not be the best psychological order in which to learn it. The best order is determined by experiment with children learning, not by logical analysis.

There are many different kinds of learning, of learning methods, and learning theories. In planning curricular materials, one does not adhere to this learning theory or that, but examines the nature of each learning experience to discover which theory or method is best suited to it.

Our elaborate new modern denominational curricula, produced at great expense and with the best brains available, can represent a major tragedy in our generation, if they lull us into a feeling of false security. Evaluational procedures should be so integrated into the very nature of the curriculum that it very soon brings about its own revision at a many times higher level.

A curriculum is not to be regarded by the parents, teachers, and youth who use it as a finished product to which they are exposed, but as a set of hypotheses which they are testing with their very lives. In so doing they play a creative, co-scientist role in producing the evidence on which a greater curriculum can be built.

The infinity concept of curriculum is demonstrated by the experience of one two-year cycle of reports in CRP producing more than 40,000 different examples of positive Christianity. An adult class could suggest almost none.

The problem of generalizing learned concepts is a very complex one. Learning something in one context is no guarantee that it will automatically become a generalized skill. In fact, usually it will not. One method of increasing the probability of generalization is to create learning situations in several roles in the learner's life experiences.

Related to this is the problem of transfer. When a thing has been learned in childhood, how can we have any assurance that in later years the individual will apply the same principle to his adult life? One method we have used is to encourage parents to learn the same thing at the same time, so that the child sees how it does apply to adult life. The effectiveness of this method has not been experimentally determined.

CHAPTER IV

—◆•◆—

BIOGRAPHY OF A RESEARCH PROJECT
C. YOUTH, HIS FAMILY AND THE COMMUNITY IN WHICH HE LIVES

IN A DAY when the newspapers are headlining a small minority of teen-agers who are involved in vandalism, crimes of various sorts, and even murder, it is good to take a look at another small minority who are going to be tomorrow's headliners as the world's leaders, and at the great majority of them—"fine, decent kids"—who could be the builders of a far greater social order, but won't unless we find out a great many secrets about personality we do not now know.

Headline Youth Who Don't Make the Headlines Here is a group of CRP teen-agers in our high schools and colleges all over the country who are undertaking the difficult, arduous, and sometimes even dangerous task of testing the social and personal concepts of Jesus in their daily lives. As we watch them, we are inspired by their seriousness and the remarkable insights that come from their experiences. Then we get a fleeting glimpse of what youth's potential actually is.

In this chapter I want to show you how far we have come in this regard in CRP during our twenty years of effort. First, I'll talk about youth himself; then about the family, which plays the leading role in his development; and finally about the few but interesting efforts we have made toward evaluating some of the community agencies designed to help youth meet this challenge.

ACRES OF DIAMONDS, BUT STILL IN THE ROUGH

The Church fails most completely in its work with young people between Junior High age and maturity, but they are its greatest opportunity. The curve of growth in Christian character levels off sharply in the beginning of the teens, when it ought to be turning up just as sharply. I doubt seriously if our present adult Christian generation is at one-quarter of its maximum spiritual and social potential.

When you hear the five-thousand-year-old wail that "Youth is going to the dogs," there appear to be only two alternatives, the Elder Brother or the Prodigal Son. The Elder Brother had respect for his elders, was dependable, and industrious; yet somehow he has commanded as little respect through the ages as he did in Jesus' day. The Prodigal Son wasted his birthright in riotous living and probably spent the rest of his life wishing the money had held out. The father, because of his parental love, was the only one of the three who contributed to a better world. Today there are still, generally speaking, those two alternatives between which youth must choose: dependability, respect for elders, and good marks in school—a youth who "never gives his parents a minute's worry"—and the one whose concept of life with a capital L is a wild orgy of waste in personality resources which spell a burnt-out adulthood, with only comfortable survival and respectability as a worthy goal.

Must our religious education curricula for these youth be either a "prescribed course to run," which they vigorously refuse to run, or letting them "take care of themselves," at which they rebel with even more violence? Usually they end up letting the motion-picture industry, the radio and TV producers, and other entertainment experts prescribe what course they are to run. Never in all history has there been a more dictatorial course set out, nor a generation of youth more docile in their submission to this dictatorship.

Our CRP findings in this area have been meager, because we have got the least co-scientist cooperation here. They have been enough, however, to convince us that here is our greatest opportunity. The dynamic capacity of youth for Christian adventure is almost unbelievable. We shall look at the achievements of our youth in this area twenty-five years from now with the same awe and wonder as we now do our achievements in the physical sciences. Let me see if I can show you the few glimpses that we have seen so far, that justify this assertion.

The youth problem presents two characteristics which make it especially dependent upon the scientific method. The first of these is that there is such an abundance of seemingly chaotic data. You could take a sound motion picture of the activities in one of our big high schools for a single day and have so many facts that it would take the rest of your natural life to give meaning to them. The fact is that the bewildering number of factors operating in teen-age personalities is so large that only our newest methods of multiple-factor statistics can hope to open up effective procedures for dealing with the problem with any significant success. The second characteristic of the problem is that there are more stereotyped panaceas about what to do with youth than about almost any other subject I know. Everyone has a definite notion about how to solve the youth problem. It is a pretty good bet that when we do begin to find far-reaching solutions, they will include almost none of these present-day stereotypes, except perhaps as partial steps toward real insights.

Autocracy Versus Laissez Faire? Or Is There a Third Alternative? The first and still the most persistent question we have faced in our approach to the youth problem has had to do with the selection of goals. Who should determine their goals? Shall we adults impose our goals on them? Surely our generation is not infallible enough to do that. Won't they learn more if they work out their own problems? Won't they be more interested in them? Won't the problems thus selected more nearly represent their real needs? These were questions which were being asked with great insistence by youth leaders when we began the Project. They still are being asked. Through the years we have examined whatever evidence we could find or observe. Here is the first thing we discovered. When we examined the literature about adolescents and itemized their "needs" on the basis of this information, we got one picture of the kinds of things we ought to do for youth. Then when we asked youth groups to list the needs of which they were conscious, the resultant goals were very far from being the same ones. As a result of this, we became convinced that the growing youth is not aware of nearly all his needs. Nor is his concept of their relative importance at all accurate.

We tried the following general procedure. Based on all that we could find out about the adolescent personality, we prepared lists of goals with curricular projects built around them. When these were presented to youth groups, they included many items which the young people themselves had never thought of, much less asked for, but which they accepted with great enthusiasm. For example, in our Youth Workshops we have sessions on study habits. Seldom do youth include study habits when they set their own goals. Yet these Youth Workshop groups have regularly evaluated these study-habit sessions as among the best they have. For several years a skills course on study habits was taught in the youth group in one of our churches. It was very popular every time it was taught. Yet to my knowledge it has not been taught now for several years, and no succeeding youth group has ever asked for it. In other words, it becomes clear that we must find additional ways of determining the best youth goals—both in terms of his needs and in terms of his own enthusiasm—than by simply asking him about the matter. And when all his needs have been adequately accounted for in our programs, we have barely tapped his maximum potential.

Having arrived at this insight, it was clear that we needed to find more effective methods for determining youth's goals than by simply asking the teen-agers themselves. In our efforts to do so, we examined the research results in all relevant fields to discover the kinds of attitudes which lead to integrated, well adjusted personality, as compared to those which lead to maladjustment. We tried them out with youth groups to see what the reaction to them would be. We compared their interest in them with their sustained interest in goals of their own choosing. One youth group, for instance, changed its program a half dozen times in a single year when its goals were of its own choosing. In that same group, the first year we set forth for it a full year's CRP program the group grew from 50 to 150, and continued its enthusiasm throughout the year.

Youth Sees Some of His Present Needs but Is Blind to His Future Potential   It must be admitted that conscious needs do set up immediate motivations which drive youth to doing something at once; potentials seldom do. For example, tests tell me that I have considerable musical ability. I have, however, had astonishingly little strong drive toward using this ability. Or again, the things that can be accomplished with the scientific method are breathtaking in their

magnitude. Yet I find that many of my associates in religious education are as yet not strongly motivated to master the basic skills of
this method. If we are to gear our concept of character education to
potential, we shall have to use educational methods and materials
which arouse challenge in our youth which they would seldom, if
ever, experience without them. I think this insight may have been
basically our most important up to now, as far as this youth problem
is concerned.

As we began searching for more and more effective ways of challenging our youth, experiencing many failures as well as a few
signal successes, we wanted to find some better evidence. The
thought came to us that we might get it by bringing small groups of
youth to Schenectady for vocational guidance testing, and then
setting up discussions and interviews to learn more about their inner
thinking in this area of potential. We were amazed at the success of
this new concept, which we call *Workshops for Youth*. We ask those
youth who come to discuss topics most of which they have never
heard of before. They not only do so; they are inspired by the experience, despite the fact that they have not chosen the topics themselves. With none of the common emotional paraphernalia of a youth
religious conference, they nevertheless become highly challenged.

It was also during a Youth Workshop that the concept of *a greater
generation* came to full development. This was another effort to
challenge youth. It is built around such questions as these: "Is the
idea of a greater generation realistic, or is it just a good book or
sermon title?" "How much could college students learn if they used
all that we now know about study skills, as compared to what they
usually do learn?" "How much of people's emotional energy that
now is wasted in destructive, disintegrating emotions could be
utilized in positive, integrating emotions?" "How much more socially
effective could people become, so that we could raise the present
low level of social skill—or lack of it—that results in so much social
strife and chaos as we find in our present culture?" "What about the
moral and spiritual insights of today's generation, as compared to
those which are possible for modern youth as they prepare to take
over the world's problems?" The inspiring nature of the answers to
these questions are obvious even to youth. They can see the unquestioned possibilities of a greater generation. This in turn strongly influences their plans for their own lives.

The youth problem, then, becomes: How can all this be accomplished? Here again the scientific method is the most promising approach with which to find answers. In CRP we have found the High School age much the most difficult about which to get good evidence. Parents turn in fewer reports. In fact, they seem to know the least about their children of this age. Youth in general have shown neither the maturity nor the long-time persistence to give us the best available evidence. We still do not have adequate answers. Our best source so far is the *Youth Report*. In this we ask the young people themselves to prepare reports comparable to the Parents' Reports at the lower age levels. We have succeeded in getting a number of such reports, but as yet far from the quantity or even the quality we need.

Youth has great creative potential, and it needs to be developed. The worst elements of autocracy may tend to suppress it. But youth also has immaturity, and left to his own devices he may be even more likely to destroy himself. Our task then is to construct an educational climate which stimulates his creative potential but safeguards him against his worst enemy, his own immaturity.

THERE IS NO "STAND IN" FOR THE FAMILY

Throughout the social history of mankind, many kinds and varieties of social theory have been attempted. One can find almost every conceivable attitude toward how our social institutions ought to be organized to bring about "heaven on earth." Contradictory theories are the rule rather than the exception. One principle, however, runs through most of them with astonishing consistency. It varies from time to time in its centrality, but never for long. One can almost offer as an axiom the principle that *the family is the fundamental social institution, on which all the others must depend!*

As Dr. Sherrill has pointed out, effective religious education was found among the Jews centuries before the Christian era. The family was the center of this education. The first teachers were the child's parents. The chief learning method was to arouse the child's curiosity by means of rituals, questions, and so on. The primary responsibility for answering these questions rested upon the parents themselves (125).

In fact, we are just emerging from an era in our American culture in which we have tried—with astounding lack of success—to delegate many of the guidance responsibilities of the home to a whole multitude of other agencies, ranging from the school and church, to campus and teen-age canteen. But when the results are examined, we come back to the basic fact that a successful social order must be based upon the home as its central institution.

Dr. Fallaw points out that the American family is today disintegrating as a social unit and spiritual matrix despite the fact that here people can discover that individual freedom is derived only at the price of subordination of self to the common good (37).

This is not to say that the character-building agencies have no value. But there is increasing evidence that they must have active home participation to succeed (87). The Y and the Scouts are asking for more and more parental cooperation in their boys' and girls' club programs. School people are coming to realize that they have gone too far in their laudable attempts to do some of the tasks the home was failing to do. They need now to rethink their programs to include more home participation.

Just admitting this, however, does not solve our problems in this area. Building successful homes has always been a difficult task. In our bewilderingly complex society, it becomes more difficult every day. There may have been a time when two young people could get married, build a house, have some children, and live with reasonable happiness ever after. That certainly is not the case today. Consider, for example, this matter of character education in the home. If parents don't try, of course they don't succeed. But the reverse of that is not always true. The success of home teaching is not just a matter of effort. Some of the most heartbreaking tragedies I have seen have taken place in homes in which the parents almost literally ate their hearts out for their children, and still failed tragically.

There is abundant evidence to show that the number of couples who achieve as great success in their marriages as they thought they would when they got married is very small indeed—probably not more than 1 per cent. On the other hand, the number that end up with homes characterized by continual conflict is well above the one-third mark. This is not because those couples didn't try. Most of them did try. It is because they didn't know how. Changing this condition is not a task for repentance but for research.

How Easy Is It to Build a Great Home? In order to make the extent and nature of the problem clearer, and to show you why only the scientific method gives us hope of finding solutions, let me introduce you to a family I know.

Frank J——— met Mary on a golf course. Each found the other attractive, and after considerable golf, a number of dances, dinners, theaters, and moons—none of which, by the way, had much to do with building a successful home—they were married. Let's enter their home seventeen years later, during which time two sons and a daughter have joined them. They have tried sincerely to build a happy and effective home. But note the principal ingredients they had to work with. I will describe each of the five members of the family in terms of general make-up, outstanding skills, characteristic attitudes, attitudes toward self, typical tensions or drives, and general outlook on life.

Frank J——— is a rather easygoing merchant. He shoots golf in the nineties; makes friends easily and is practical-minded; in general likes "peace and quiet," and is satisfied with the status quo. He recognizes that he is successful and well accepted among his fellows; has no very strong drives; in general sees his family as somewhat but not too much of a burden, and thinks his wife takes most things, especially the children, too seriously.

Mary, his wife, is beautiful, high tensioned, and socially energetic. She is skilled in music and participates in many community activities, including the church. She is socially ambitious, especially for her seventeen-year-old daughter. She regards herself as a person of outstanding endowment who could have gone far in a career if she hadn't given it up for marriage. All of her appetites and drives are strong ones; she thinks life has been unfair to her, but that she must bear her burden, if not cheerfully at least definitely.

Grace, seventeen, is energetic, socially active but not too successful socially. She is neither as beautiful nor as talented as her mother. She has been successful academically and would be terrified to make anything less than an A, but wishes she were far more skilled socially. Her concept of the most desirable things in life consists of food, clothes, use of the family car, dates, and freedom from parental discipline. She recognizes her need of social skills, and desperately fears social unpopularity. Her drives are of the all-or-none variety, with no happy mediums. She regards life as having been not too good to her, either in terms of her parents or her native endowment. Her mother is quite strict with her, and her father does not interfere.

Bill is thirteen. He is active, full of imagination, likes to run with the gang, is "allergic" to "church" or being "lectured to" by anyone. His skills are in avoiding work and keeping out of trouble despite his mischief. He is pretty sure his parents have it in for him, and never want him to have any fun. He sees himself as a successful "bad boy" and seldom thinks much about life beyond the next episode with the gang. His eating capacity is infinite and his energy boundless. School and church are necessary evils and his "god" is "fun."

Ben is eight. He is more introverted, quiet and sensitive. He is studious, already working with a chemistry set. His skills are academic and scientific, with much time spent in daydreaming. He prefers to be left alone and to stick to his many hobbies. He sees himself as a potential genius, who is superior to the rest of his family. He has no very strong physiological drives and sees his home life and school life as forms of nuisance to be patiently endured but not enjoyed.

You will not be surprised that this family has great difficulty avoiding a constant state of conflict. It takes great wisdom indeed to integrate such diverse personalities into a working team. I have estimated that there are some 450 obvious ways in which the various members of this one family can come into conflict with one another. It will take far more than good intentions to solve the bewildering problems involved in welding them into the powerful unit which their wide range of talents makes possible for them. At the same time I find a great many parents attempting with might and main to do just such a task. Indeed, I am sure that a part of the attractiveness of CRP to some parents lies in its contributions to the solutions of such overwhelming problems as involved in welding these five personalities into a great family team.

All this need not, therefore, make parents feel hopeless and fearsome. Challenge—yes! Frustration, guilt and fear—no! And this is the central theme of our CRP approach to this problem of character education in the home. Some parents are concerned only that they do nothing wrong with the child. They seldom dare to strike out in new directions for fear they may be doing something wrong. Fear is their major motivation. Child psychologists are responsible for much of this, for many of them have warned parents against error more than they have challenged them toward high achievement.

Let me list just a few of the problems in this area with which we have been concerned in CRP. Remember that we have looked at these in terms of only one function of the home: character education.

Will and Can Parents Perform the Role of Co-Scientists?   Of course, our first task was the basic one of securing parent cooperation. A whole generation of dumping the children on the Sunday-school doorstep at ten o'clock and picking them up at eleven was certainly not conducive to habits of extensive parental cooperation in this matter of religious education. To be sure, we have not succeeded 100 per cent, nor even 50 per cent. But if all of the parents who are members of Christian churches in America were writing proportionately as many Parents' Reports, or their equivalent, as our present CRP parents do, and these were bound in book form, each volume containing 500 reports, they would constitute 350,000 volumes each year. There are less than thirty public libraries in America with that many books on their shelves. Achieving this level of parent cooperation may well have been our outstanding achievement so far, both in terms of its quantity and of its implications for the future.

Is It Bad to Spank a Child?   Next, there is the ever present problem of discipline. We began pretty much on the Horace Bushnell philosophy of gradual emancipation. In recent years child psychologists have varied widely in their concepts, ranging from fairly strict discipline, to complete laissez faire. A full account of our CRP thinking in this regard would be a long one. In general, however, it might be summed up in this principle: Parents should create the kind of home climate which permits the child to develop to his maximum capacity. This, however, is far more easily said than done. Such a climate may and probably does include some strict discipline and close guidance, as well as permitting the child to learn some things for himself. We certainly do not want to impose our own culture on the child so rigidly that he can never transcend it; but we do want to give him the benefit of our experience on which to build a greater culture.

An important emphasis which we have made in CRP in regard to discipline is to point out that it is not synonymous with punishment. It is far more closely related to discipleship, from which the word itself was derived. One of our most quoted principles is: "You can punish any child you have the right and strength to punish. You can only discipline those children who make themselves your disciples." Winning the love and respect of the child is the main thing. What kind of punishment you use is quite secondary.

Because most families have more than one child, the problem of interchild conflicts is another one with which any program involving home participation must deal. The principle with which we have had the most success in this regard is that parental love is at the center of Jesus' philosophy of life. When we urge older children to use a parental attitude toward their younger siblings, we have been successful far more often than with any other motivation.

Then, there is the matter of giving the child increasing freedom. How much should he have and how rapidly should it be given to him? At one time in our CRP materials, we urged parents to include, among their children's Christmas presents, an "emancipation present." This was to be some new freedom. However, two guiding principles for choosing such "emancipations" were suggested. The first is to give the child freedom only as rapidly as he is mature enough and wise enough to use it well. The other is that the child needs to learn that freedom implies corresponding responsibilities. It has been far easier to find freedoms which the child wants than responsibilities to match them. Furthermore, a car without brakes is not one whit more dangerous than a youth with no controlling inhibitions, both within and without.

We began our research toward the end of the era in which the family was attempting to delegate its responsibilities to the Scouts, the school, the Y, and the many other "character-building" institutions. The first major insight that grew out of our evidence showed us that, in almost every instance in our early years of individual research, attitude formation took place only when there was home cooperation. It soon became clear that parents who deposited a child on the steps of the church for Sunday school were doomed to disappointment if they expected that institution to achieve much in the way of effective education, character, or anything else, as a result of his experience there. It became obvious that before Sunday dinner was over, the family could cancel out any influences felt there. The concept of home cooperation was, of course, not new with us, but it was certainly rare except in theory and admonition when we began our research. The whole body of our experience since has increased our conviction in its indispensable value. This conviction is shared now by almost all leaders in character and religious education. New curricular materials are including more and more home guidance.

Greater progress can be made by attacking specific problems than by trying to deal with indefinite generalities. Theories which talk about what "homes ought to do" are likely to fail because of their inability to come to grips with tangible aspects of the problem. Let me describe a few of the more specific problems with which we have dealt in this regard.

One of the first areas in which we were able to gain a new insight had to do with research concerning *fear of failure,* which we found to be a very common characteristic of children in at least some areas of their activity. Our study revealed that probably this was often true because parents and teachers depict failure to children as a disgrace. When we began, with the help of parents and teachers, to depict failure as the high road to success, as the inevitable beginnings of learning a new skill, we were able to produce a measurable change of attitude.

Next came our study on *sensitiveness to criticism.* Probably most of our present adult generation is sensitive to criticism, not because we do not think we could profit by it, but mostly because of wounded vanity. We set out, therefore, to discover its beginnings and probable causes. We found that it seemed to become prominent first at about the Primary level (school grades I and II). When we made a study of the kinds of criticisms children of that age receive, we found that scolding constituted the great majority. When parents in the Project tried the policy of matching every necessary scolding with a constructive criticism; that is, telling children how to do something better, the amount of sensitiveness seemed to become much less. We have never been able to make a good follow-up on the permanent effect of this procedure. But we have observed a few individual cases in which the children in this particular study, at upper High School age, have shown outstanding ability to take criticism, seeing it as coaching instead of as punishment, no matter how severely it is given.

Our concept of the *difference between chores and responsibilities* was another of those early insights. A chore is any routinely assigned task. A responsibility is a task one assumes because he believes it to be an important part of his contribution to the family. The same task can be a chore or a responsibility, depending on how the child sees it.

Then we began to develop the concept of *the family team*. This has been one of our central themes ever since. We found, however, that it was sometimes successful and sometimes unsuccessful. When we studied a number of cases to see if we could discover why, we came upon another important insight. If the term "family team" is used by the parents simply as a good excuse for urging the child not to do those things which "break up a good team," then in general the idea is unsuccessful. If, on the other hand, the family plans positive projects in which each member has an assignment of some importance, just as do the members of a football team, then the family-team principle is commonly much more successful.

The Power of Science in the Home   By far the greatest contribution we have made to this problem of family life has come about as a result of the creation of the *Parents' Report,* the *Attitude Scales,* the *Parent-Teacher Conference Worksheets,* and the like. Does that startle you? Probably many of the CRP parents who read this and remember the bother of "all the paper work" will have some skepticism concerning my evaluation of this aspect of our work. Too often they have thought of these things as having value—if at all—for our research in Schenectady but not for their home life. The essence of this role consists in observing and reporting accurately the interplay of the many personality factors that operate in a family. Such observation will guide the family itself toward building great family teams many times faster than without it. The evidence reported on the basis of this experience will be of inestimable value in our struggles toward a better world.

The fact is, the study of individual differences involved in families, the setting of positive goals, the evaluation of methods of procedure —these things have constituted significant contributions to the homes who have done them well. To be sure, there have been bad features, such as the reports becoming a burden in the minds of the parents and the guilt feelings often felt about them. These have been on the negative side, and we are always searching for ways to eliminate them, so that the process will regularly be one of satisfaction, thrill, and challenge.

Every Home Is Unique   Let me list one more concept which has recently come into our thinking about this problem of the home. It can be called *the concept of the unique home*. In our discussion of individual differences, the concept of the unique individual was pointed out. Each individual is unique and has a unique contribution to make. But homes are made up of individuals. If each individual is unique, then every home is also unique. If each individual has within his power a unique contribution, then each home, being unique, can also make a unique contribution of its own. We are now challenging our homes to think through for themselves what their unique contributions are; and to determine that they will each do something no other home could possibly do. Indeed, the Home Dynamics Study suggests that one of the four most important characteristics of a great home is the carrying out of family projects— each family doing something together for a cause outside itself.

Parents Sometimes Like Difficult Tasks Better Than Easy Ones
Why do parents work harder at CRP than they do with most curricular materials? If you had asked me that a year ago, I would have guessed that our definite goals, the practical suggestions in the lessons, their applicability to daily life, were the main reasons. But some new evidence has recently been uncovered which throws new light on that question. It will take about four steps to describe it and its apparent significance.

We recently interviewed two groups of CRP parents. Members of one group regularly turn in Parents' Reports from week to week. Members of the other group—all enthusiastic CRP parents—do not. One question we asked in the experiment was, "What difficulties do you experience with the various parts of the Parents' Reports?" We have always assumed that difficulty in preparing Parents' Reports is a major factor in why so many parents do not prepare them. Much to our astonishment the group who had turned in reports testified to having had far more difficulties with them than the other group! Does this mean that difficulty can be a positive as well as a negative factor in the matter?

This set us to looking for different kinds of difficulties, those which help and those which hinder. They were easily found. It quickly became obvious that the kinds of difficulty which are seen as challenge become a positive factor. In fact, people tend to lose interest without them. Who would want to play golf if everybody could make a hole-in-one every shot? Football squads do not like to "run signals" when there is no opposition, nor to play a team they can beat 100 to 0. On the other hand, however, some kinds of difficulty set up frustrations and are certainly negative factors. Not knowing how to write reports, or feeling that one's efforts are getting no results, for example, are not the kinds of things that motivate parents to write reports. This was the second insight in our search.

The third step is concerned with a motivation which probably few parents have recognized consciously, yet it seems probable that it is an important one. In recent years much has been said about scientists treating people like guinea pigs, to be used as subjects in an experiment. In CRP we have made every effort to transcend this condition of guinea-pigism—great as have been its contributions.

Finally, there is the ever important infinity principle. If the infinity principle is true, then there are new insights which go far beyond our present ones. The parents by their careful observation and reports can participate in gaining these new insights. Indeed, we are helpless without these reports. Carefully controlled experiments play their indispensable role in research. But careful observation in real-life situations plays a still more important role.

SCIENCE AND THE CHARACTER-BUILDING AGENCIES

The World Almanac lists well over a thousand clubs and societies in this country. A high percentage of them have philanthropic or character-building purposes. We support them with our Community Chest and other drives. For the most part we assume their values. Most of them are run by able and devoted people who have the noblest of purposes. Yet the return on our investment in them is only a small fraction of what it could be if they defined their objectives more clearly, made careful evaluations of their procedures, and continually revised them.

Unfortunately, most of them invest very little in evaluation of their achievements. They assume them. Once in a while someone does a study to discover whether or not one of them is achieving its goals. Almost all of them have merits as well as demerits. A careful research program would not threaten them, but continually strengthen them. What we need, then, is a change from the realm of good intentions to the policy of measurement and evaluation.

During the years of CRP we have been asked to consider doing research concerning the methods of a number of well known character-building agencies. For the most part we have not had the personnel or resources with which to do so.

Many such agencies have not realized the full possibilities of the scientific method for increasing their effectiveness. At one extreme, for example, was one whose leaders wanted us to do research "to prove that their methods were right." Needless to say, this is not research. Others with a misconception of the role of science wanted us to evaluate their procedures so that they could "correct the flaws in them." This narrow concept of the potential of science falls far short of the spirit of the infinity principle.

In CRP we have done some research with other groups in addition to our work with church schools. Let me describe briefly our explorations with other character-building institutions. We have made three such explorations: into YMCA summer camp work, YMCA boys' club work, and a private boys' school. I should like to report two of these.

Character Research in a YMCA Boys' Camp　Let's look first at our summer camp venture. This began in 1947, at Camp Chingachgook, the Schenectady YMCA boys' camp. At the time of this writing, we have completed our eighth season. The largest share of the work has been done by Richard S. Doty, who has, until this year, directed the camp and has been the chief YMCA member of our CRP staff. With his help, I am reporting here a few of the insights we have had during those seven years (32, 33).

Our first major insight concerning character education in the camping situation came about, curiously enough, as a result of the fact that we got negligible results during the first year's efforts. It was nevertheless a very significant insight. In brief, it is that you cannot impose a character-education program on a traditional camp program (42). You must start with your character-education objectives and build the camp program to achieve those objectives. This, of course, is in line with our experience in the church-school program. Any expectation that effective character education will be achieved as a secondary and indirect result of something else is doomed to failure unless some new methods are discovered of which we are at present unaware. It is very possible that character education is the most difficult of all kinds of education and must be approached with the greatest skill and planning. The common belief that "character is caught and not taught" may be regarded as among the most baseless of our folklore.

If this contention is true, it has far-reaching significance for our whole American program of character education. In recent years there has been a strong trend away from direct character education. Many believe that character growth comes best as a secondary result from other types of education. None of our research has seemed to justify this assumption.

Why? Of course, we don't know why. But here is a hypothesis which seems worth exploring. True character growth, perhaps more than any other kind of education, requires a modification of the total personality. If an attitude goal is to become part of a child's character, he must integrate it into his total personality. It is difficult to see how this can be done without some very definite cooperation on his part, including insight into the goals being sought.

This is not to say that a great many of his experiences do not modify his character; they probably do. But as a rule we cannot predict what these modifications will be. Certainly, facing injustice and persecution does not lead to character traits of magnanimity in all people. In fact, I think you will agree that it probably very rarely does so unless the child is given a vision for it. Will not "an eye for an eye" probably be the reaction far more frequently than "returning good for evil" unless some very wise guidance is present to give the child a vision and the skills for the latter?

It is not without interest that when we first began putting the emphasis on character education in our camp program, some had misgivings lest registrations fall off. "Boys come to camp for fun, don't they?" Not only did this not happen, but Chingachgook has grown steadily in popularity, until now the camp is filled almost as soon as registrations are accepted, with many applications which must be rejected. This is not true with all camps.

This leads to another interesting question. Does "fun" rank as high in the child's mind as we have come to believe that it does? Approach a group of prospective campers. Let one camp folder say this: "Come to our camp. We will have lots of fun." Then in small type add, "We will also do a little character education." Concerning the program of the other camp, say this: "The main business of this camp is to help you acquire the strengths and skills of character which will give you greater power to meet your future responsibilities in our society. We hope we will all have some fun in the process." Ask them to decide to which camp they wish to go. If your concept of the American youth is that his "god" is "fun," you may be in for a great surprise.

Another insight that has come from our camping experiences is that we must find an equivalent for the family group if we are to achieve results. This we did by making the tent or cabin group the family group and so adjusting the program that each such "family" had adequate opportunity to be together and do things together as a "family." This tended to pull the program away from an activity-centered type of program, and toward providing large blocks of time which were not structured by the staff, when these "family groups" could be encouraged to live, play, and work together in pursuits which demand creative imagination and expression for practicing the attitude objectives.

Everyone who has had anything to do with camping knows how often it comes about that a boy "learns," for example, a habit of neatness in camp, and then shows no sign of it when he gets back home. This is a typical example of the knotty problem of transfer. In our efforts to bring about more general transfer of such learning we have found it essential to get increasing amounts of parent co-operation. To whatever extent we have succeeded in this, there is evidence of greater permanent effectiveness.

Certainly the concept that having learned to apply an attitude in one situation guarantees its application in all others seems to be overwhelmingly disproved by the evidence. If you want transfer to take place you must bring about as many different kinds of application as possible. To achieve this, counselors often followed this kind of theme in evening discussions with their tent group: "You have found this principle [attitude] effective in your camp experience. How does it apply to situations which are likely to face you when you get back home? How can you go about applying it to them?" It was hoped that this would help the boys to generalize their learning more widely. Christmas letters are sometimes sent to the boys reminding them of their summer thinking, and challenging them to post-camp applications. We have still just scratched the surface in the problem of camp learning transfer, but these are illustrations of the kinds of insights by which we are making some progress toward that end.

Another problem which arises in all character education, and is sometimes exaggerated in the camp situation, is the effect of the boy's total adjustment on any particular learning experience. If he is very homesick, or unpopular, or seriously deficient in camping skills, can he be challenged to master our attitude goals? The point of view of many clinical psychologists is that all such maladjustments must be taken care of first. The psychologists who base their concepts of motivation on needs say that we can start on the positive traits of character only after all the basic needs are fully met.

There is no gainsaying that when these maladjustments are very serious and strong, we are not likely to make much headway toward other goals until they are taken care of. We have attempted to deal with this difficulty at Chingachgook by including among our attitude goals one which consists of an over-all adjustment to camp.

On the other hand, two important facts need to be taken into consideration. One is that perhaps the best way to make such adjustments consists, not in dealing with the maladjustments as such, but in learning corresponding positive attitudes, which by their very nature preclude the maladjustive attitudes.

The other fact is that there often seems to be a strong urge in human nature toward the heroic. All of us are challenged from time to time to deny ourselves the satisfaction of some of our basic needs because of challenge to some heroic achievement. If all appetitive needs, such as hunger, thirst, comfort, rest, and security, always had to be met before we could be expected to do anything positive, such thrilling human experiences as football, mountain climbing, lifesaving, the sacrificial vocations, heroism in war, the finer examples of parental behavior, giving one's life for friend or country—none of these would ever happen. So this "heroic" point of view toward maladjustment and needs has to be considered before we decide too fully on the optimum course of action in guiding the boy. The immediate satisfaction of needs may indeed deny him some of the finest values in human experience.

The next insight is more obvious. It has to do with leadership. We have been fortunate in the Chingachgook situation. Because of its widespread reputation we have been able to attract many gifted counselors from all over the country. Nevertheless the range from the best to the least skilled of them in any camping season is wide, and the effectiveness of their work correspondingly wide. Probably no camping program can fully transcend the prerequisite of good counselors.

A second element in this leadership picture, however, is the need of intensive training for these counselors. Certainly, one of the outstanding results of the Lewin, Lippitt, and White study (66) was the clear demonstration that leaders can be fairly quickly trained to use autocratic, democratic, or laissez-faire skills with remarkable thoroughness. In our work at Chingachgook, we have brought our counselors to Union College for a full week of intensive training in our objectives, procedures, and basic philosophy. This we have found to be an indispensable characteristic of a camping program which is designed to do more than provide a pleasant and safe summer vacation.

The scientific method is based strongly on the collection of representative evidence. That is, we should attempt to bring together a body of evidence which has the same characteristics that we would find if we had all of the evidence there is in the area being studied.

We have made several kinds of efforts to get evidence representative of the total stream of events, and therefore a more valid base for making judgments.

The most used form is the Leadership Observation Report, or, as we call them, LOR's. The counselors are asked to record every event they can observe which is relevant to the character-education objectives of the camp. Counselors vary widely in their ability to see these events and in the number of such LOR's recorded. They have nevertheless been comparable to the Parents' Reports in the church-school program and have thus far been our best source of data. It is still impossible to estimate how representative they are of all behavior. They probably do tend to be loaded with an undue proportion of the striking events. They have led us to some interesting insight-hypotheses in areas in which previously we had nothing but opinion.

During the last few years we have tried what we call the Teaching Technique Form, in which the counselor plans a teaching situation, carries it out, and then records its success or failure. This overcomes the error of after-the-fact thinking. It is always better scientific procedure to predict in advance what is going to happen and then observe what actually does happen.

How Can We Measure the Effectiveness of Our Camping Program? Finally, there is the difficult problem of measuring success or failure. How shall we know whether and to what extent attitudes have been changed? Different kinds of procedures have been used in our Chingachgook research which are typical of such methods in the field of psychology in general.

The first of these is a rating scale. We call the rating scale used in the camp the Leadership Progressive Appraisal, LPA. Each counselor rates the boys in his tent in regard to the attitude goals shortly after arrival, corrects it after closer acquaintance if necessary, and then makes a final rating at the end of the boys' camping season. It has been pretty difficult to evaluate the validity of such ratings. They seem to correlate highly with such factors as the boys' evaluation of the counselor, and supervisor's evaluation of the counselor. However, all of these may primarily be a function of how well the counselor gets along with his boys, with little evidence of actual success in character education.

Another technique, which we are using with increasing frequency and success, is that of sociometric procedures. We have constructed many sociograms (129) for all kinds of purposes. "If you were going on a canoe trip, which boy in this tent would you like to have as a companion?" "Which boy or boys do you think have this attitude [the character education goal] to the largest degree?" When the responses to such questions are plotted on a sociogram, many interpersonal relationships are observable.

Science Can Thrive Creatively in Camp As Well As in the Laboratory This description of our Chingachgook adventure is an excellent example of the value of the scientific method in a setting far removed from careful laboratory controls. It has often been assumed that unless research can be done under optimum conditions, there is no use doing it at all. Here is a striking demonstration of the fact that quite the contrary is true. In fact, if this sort of exploratory research were not done the highly controlled experiments would never be possible. The main point is that when we approach a problem with the scientific attitude, we already have made great progress. Let us note a few principles that apply.

As long as we leave our character-education problems in the area of vague felt needs, we shall make little progress toward solving them. Only as we identify tangible problems and try to construct research designs for solving them will we begin to get the results we want. Scientists will differ as to whether they prefer to work in highly controlled exact research or out on the frontiers of ignorance where they are forced to do the best they can. Both kinds of research are indispensable, and many of us prefer the adventure of pioneering.

We have made some other efforts in our relationship with the YMCA. The most extensive of these was with Gra-Y clubs. Judged by the usual criteria of widespread interest and positive findings, it was not successful. In terms of ultimate values, however, we learned much from it. The fact is, we often learn more from our failures than from our successes. I am not reporting it here, because we have not had time to study our evidence sufficiently thoroughly to suggest mature conclusions about it.

Our Secular Schools Are Interested in Character, Too Our other extensive exploration outside the churches has been in the Park School in Indianapolis, Indiana. Under the direct guidance of Dr. Norman Johnson, the headmaster during the first years of the Project there, and Mr. Gene Schwilck, Director of the Counseling Program, this phase of our program has produced a number of significant insights which constitute promising hypotheses. An exploration of these hypotheses by more technical methods is being undertaken by Mr. Schwilck. The whole problem of moral and spiritual values in the public-school curriculum is proving to be a very difficult one. This is especially true for a nation which is built on the Christian tradition but at the same time believes in the rigorous separation of Church and State. This experiment of ours is being carried out in a school in which there are Protestants, Catholics, and Jews.

The interest of school people in CRP dates back to its very beginning. Teachers and school leaders in Albany, New York, played a significant role in the early days of the Project there. At one stage when we were developing our first curriculum, a committee of about sixty from the Schenectady Public School staff gave a great many hours of work and much advice to help us in a very difficult part of this task. School people all over the United States have expressed serious interest in what we are doing. A second private day school in Jackson, Mississippi, the St. Andrew's Episcopal Day School, has joined in active participation.

To construct a curricular base for this secular school project, Dr. Johnson and, later, Mr. Schwilck edited the church-school lessons at the different age levels. They deleted all of the direct Biblical and theological references. On the other hand, such CRP techniques as parent-teacher interviews, parent classes and Parents' Reports are all utilized in somewhat the same pattern as in the church-school setup.

The program, as far as its actual day-to-day administration is concerned, however, is quite different from that in the church school. Each counselor or teacher has one class session each week with his CRP group. In addition to this group session, he holds an individual conference in which each boy is helped to plan his weekly project. The counselor has met with the parents before this personal conference and thus can give the boy not only his own help in planning the project but that of the parents. This makes the week's work a cooperative venture, including teacher, parents, and child. This is a level of cooperation we have seldom achieved in any of our other research groups.

A fairly extensive guidance program is also carried out with the boys in Park School. They have a testing laboratory which, using our Union College Personality Profile, serves not only the Park School body but many others who apply for its services.

I have attempted to set down the most significant insights which have come from this experience.

The first group of findings have to do with the counselors. In general, the only counselors who have proved effective are those who are sincerely convinced of the value of the aims and methods of CRP and are capable of a sympathetic understanding of the child. They must be ready to give generously of their time and energy in work with parents, in individual adaptations, and in making reports of their findings. This brings out an important aspect of effective leadership: sincerity and enthusiasm for one's objectives are powerful assets in any kind of leadership, especially educational leadership.

The second insight in this experiment also has to do with leadership. It confirms similar findings in every other phase of our work; namely, that effective leadership must and can be trained. Indeed, most of the Park School counselors have come at least once to the Union College Annual Workshop.

In all of our work, the training of parents has been a central problem. The major tool about which this training is organized is the parent class. Park School has been relatively freer to experiment in this regard than most of the churches. There were no traditions as to when, how often, how long, to hold sessions, nor what to do in them. To suggest that their experiences through the years were carefully controlled experiments would not, of course, be true. The fact remains that they have tried varying approaches and used them long enough to be able to make some objective evaluation of their effectiveness. While they have always asked parents to express their preferences, their decisions were made on what actually did happen rather than on what people thought might happen.

At Park School it was the practice at one time to have biweekly parents' meetings, with general introductory sessions followed by grade-level sessions. The latter made possible not only general orientation but personalized planning for individual children. It may well be that in this they have uncovered an important insight into the problem of parent participation. Parents must have an over-all understanding of the "why" of their objectives as well as specific help in their personal efforts to achieve those objectives.

Park School shared with the rest of CRP the problem of getting regular and meaningful Parents' Reports. From another study conducted in one of the local churches, there has come evidence that one important reason why parents are reluctant to submit Parents' Reports is that they do not know how to write them. In the Park School experiment the planning portion of the report is prepared in conference with the counselor during the parent class sessions. This means that after that the parents need only to record what happens as a result of carrying out these plans.

Another interesting insight which grew out of our experience in the Park School experiment had to do with age-level differences in the group aspects of planning. At first the assumption was made that the perfect setup is a general class session with individual conferences between the counselor and each boy. Experience, however, has shown that this seemingly common-sense concept is not always correct. At the lower age levels planning in fairly large groups proved to be more effective than individual planning. As the upper age levels are approached, the ideal number for such a planning group seems to decrease, so that at the top of the Senior High age level the optimum group contains two or three. It is significant, however, that completely individual planning has never been found superior at any age level. This insight undoubtedly has dynamic implications of which we are still largely in the dark.

Certainly the most interesting and surprising insight-hypothesis of all has to do with the religious content of the lessons. You will recall that we began on the assumption that the Biblical and theological materials must be deleted from the lessons to make them acceptable in a secular school situation where all faiths are represented. The interesting fact, however, is that so much power seemed to be lost from the lessons in this process that the Jewish and Catholic parents were quite as insistent that the religious factor be put back into the lessons as were the Protestants. Various public-school leaders who have since examined both the Park School versions of the lessons with religion deleted, and our church-school editions, have chosen the latter, even with a view to using them in the public-school situation.

The great significance of this is the overwhelming evidence it throws on the importance of religion in character education. A very common question which comes to us is: "Why character education in church school? Why not confine that element of education to the public schools and the institutions especially designed for character education? Character education and religious education are two different things." In Chapters VIII and IX on dimensions of personality, I am comparing our own dimensional concepts based on the Christian philosophy with those set forth in a secular report of a national scope. But here is another kind of evidence of the fact that a religious philosophy is essential to achieving man's maximum potential in terms of strength of character.

WHEN THE BIOGRAPHY OF CRP IS COMPLETED—WHAT THEN?

What is the major purpose of CRP? It is certainly not to compete with anything except ignorance. Nor is its chief goal the particular insights which have grown and will continue to grow out of it. Its major purpose is to bring into religious and character education the full power of the scientific method.

Recently I listened to two sales speeches. One speaker was talking about General Electric Company products. He spent most of his time telling a little girl about the GE products she probably would be able to buy when she had a home of her own. The things he described were fabulous and almost incredible. It made our most modern gadgets seem like products of the Dark Ages. Furthermore, both she and I believed him.

The other salesman was talking about a new religious education curriculum. He praised it in glowing terms, most of which it richly deserved. No one listening, however, would have suspected that it did not have all the final answers. There was not even a hint of the possible future achievements which could dwarf its present values into insignificance.

It would be a tragedy for CRP to cease its efforts until religious educators see visions of the future as thrilling and fabulous as our modern industrialists see for their future. This will come to pass only when as far-reaching a national research program has been established in religious and character education as now exists in industry.

Isolated studies, even hundreds of them, can contribute only a drop in the bucket. It will take the highly integrated efforts of all of us, inspired by the infinity principle, to achieve this goal. It ought to involve a multimillion dollar project.

Furthermore, now is the time! I doubt if money is the most difficult problem. It seems to me that foundations with funds to invest have more vision than the educators who apply for them. Let me show you three great resources now at our disposal which were not available even twenty years ago.

In the first place, experimental and statistical methods for this kind of research have been and are being developed at a rapid pace. I shall describe a number of them in Chapters XI and XII. Distinguished scientists are turning their best energies to just such exploratory and ecological studies.

Then, secondly, there is an increasing number of young and brilliant psychologists, sociologists, and religious leaders who have the courage, the vision, and the skills for doing this kind of research. There were very few of them twenty years ago.

Finally, there are the co-scientists. Not only the parents and teachers and leaders in our participating CRP research centers, but an ever increasing list of "individual subscribers" who are taking up the challenge of this difficult venture. They are not all people of high IQ and extensive education. Vision is more important than native endowment in this undertaking. Without them the first two resources would be seriously handicapped. With these co-scientists, our progress can be of great proportions.

SOME IMPORTANT CONCEPTS DESCRIBED IN THIS CHAPTER

The co-scientist principle has special meaning in the area of youth work. The youth has been regarded by some as the best final authority on his own problems. On the other hand, he has been used as a guinea pig for the theories of others. Our CRP philosophy is that while he is far from being an infallible authority about himself, the whole problem is solved more quickly and progress made more rapidly if he works with us in the role of co-scientist, investing his creativity but seeing the dangers of his immaturity, and believing that he plays an indispensable role in our task.

Youth has creative potential which ought not to be discouraged by adult control. But he also has immaturity which may lead him to personality failures unless his adult advisers can supply the ingredient of maturity for him.

A characteristic of youth's immaturity is that he is able to see his present conscious needs, but much less clearly his future potential. It is one of the roles of character education to give him vision for this potential, so that interest in his present needs does not destroy some of that potential.

Few families even approach their maximum potential. This is not a matter of guilt, for most of them try. It is a matter of understanding. We fail in family life just as we do in cancer therapy because we don't know enough. We need extensive research in discovering the basic dynamic influences in family life.

Discipline is more closely related to the concept of discipleship than to punishment. "You can punish any child you have the right and strength to punish. You can only discipline those children who make themselves your disciples."

In their co-scientist role of observing and reporting the interplay of the many personality factors that operate in a family, parents will discover that they are able to find the keys to family achievement many times faster than they can by haphazard observation. Their reports will be of inestimable value in the progress of the social sciences.

Camp programs are not necessarily character-building experiences. In fact, research shows that probably most of them are not. They can become so only if character education is a major factor in their program construction.

In general, only those teachers who have insight in and enthusiasm for the goals of a character-education program in secular education are effective in it.

The ultimate aim of CRP is not to compete with other curricula, nor even primarily to produce insights into the nature of character, although this latter is its main activity. Its chief goal is to bring into religious and character education the vision of the potential of research in the spirit of the infinity principle.

CHAPTER V

DIMENSIONS OF PERSONALITY
—WHICH DIMENSIONS
SHALL WE MEASURE?

As I looked, behold, a stormy wind came out of the north, and a great cloud, with brightness round about it, and fire flashing forth continually, and in the midst of the fire, as it were gleaming bronze. And from the midst of it came the likeness of four living creatures. And this was their appearance: they had the form of men, but each had four faces, and each of them had four wings. Their legs were straight, and the soles of their feet were like the sole of a calf's foot; and they sparkled like burnished bronze. Under their wings on their four sides they had human hands. . . . As for the likeness of their faces, each had the face of a man in front; . . . the face of a lion on the right side, the face of an ox on the left side, and the face of an eagle at the back. . . . And each went straight forward; wherever the spirit would go, they went, without turning as they went. In the midst of the living creatures there was something that looked like burning coals of fire, . . . And the living creatures darted to and fro, like a flash of lightning.

EZEKIEL 1:4–14

I CANNOT think of a better way to introduce the problem of trait theory than this quotation from the prophet Ezekiel. In fact, that was a trait theory. Ezekiel was trying to describe his vision in terms of traits and dimensions as he saw them. It was obviously a bewildering vision to him. But then, so is human personality to anyone who studies it. The bewildering complexities of personality, man's unrelenting inconsistencies, his kaleidoscopic qualities which almost defy description, his blinding energy, often "like a flash of lightning"—all these things confront anyone who attempts to find suitable dimensions for describing human personality. Surely few problems in science could be more baffling. Yet we must have dimensions if we are to apply the methods of science in the study of its problems. Don't be surprised if at times your efforts come to a conclusion as incomprehensible as did those of Ezekiel.

THE ROLE OF DIMENSIONAL-TRAIT THEORIES IN PERSONALITY RESEARCH

The word *trait* means any consistency in human nature. When you compare people with one another in terms of any constant characteristic, this is both a dimension and a trait. We call it a dimensional-trait. There are many other kinds of traits. But in our research we use almost entirely dimensional-traits. Hence I shall often use the two terms interchangeably.

You Can't Study Any Personality or Social Problem Without Relevant Dimensions Let's look at a few problems, which I believe can be tackled with the tools and methods we now have, or can construct. The first step in doing so, however, must be the selection of some appropriate dimensional-traits.

Love your enemies? A wonderful dream, that! But can it be done, man being what he is? We can't even love those who love us, yet! Go from house to house down your street. Ring the doorbell and find out how many of the families living there have achieved happiness on the level the father and mother dreamed about when they faced the minister and said, "I do!" Go to many a ministers' meeting. You may be deeply concerned at how much apparent jealousy and suspicion and interconflict you will sometimes find there. Sit in on a college faculty meeting, and all too frequently you will sense an undercurrent of bigotry, jealousy, and mutual distrust. Let the newspapers hint of war, and watch even the leaders of society begin to be swayed by emotional propaganda. Consider the emotional bitterness of a political campaign. And so on, ad infinitum. That is one side of the picture.

Yet, over against this, there is equally abundant reason to believe that a vast majority of mankind, including all these I have mentioned, are really good at heart. There are probably very few basically "mean" people. To be sure, that is an item of faith, but I think you will agree that almost every husband and wife want to build a great home. Ministers, for the most part, are sincerely devoted to their visions. Faculty members usually become teachers because they really are concerned to help produce good citizens. Most of us mean well; we just don't know how to do well! A world vote on war or peace would result in an almost unanimous vote for peace. Yet, here we are, unable to live peaceably together as nations or as neighbors or even as members of families.

But, you say, are you suggesting that all this could be changed with adequate trait concepts? That is a prerequisite part of it, all right. I believe much of our past confusion has been due to our inability to find useful and manageable ways of describing human personality, especially in its dynamic complexities. Now, however, the scientific tools are at hand by which we can do just that.

There are, however, thousands of possible dimensions. The fruitfulness of our research will depend on our ability to find the right ones for the problem at hand. Many a parent-child conflict has been solved when the parent stopped judging the child's behavior in terms of negative ethics and began to look for ways of using his potential. Many an adult has found life far happier when he no longer regarded his fears and angers as evils to suppress and began to search for ways to invest the emotional energies wasted in them into creative channels.

Dimensional-Trait Theory and Consistency in Human Personality

If we are to apply the powerful tools of experimental design to our study of personality, we must have dimensions in terms of which to measure it. These dimensions, of course, must be stable and consistent enough to be measured. And that is no small order. These dimensions must be observable ways in which people differ. People must be consistent enough in the way they exemplify them so that they measure about the same way from time to time. Furthermore, there are many different kinds of traits. I suppose the most commonly used classification among psychologists would be this fourfold one: (1) *constitutional traits,* which include anatomical features, such as height and weight, and other inborn physical characteristics of the individual; (2) *temperamental traits,* such as shyness or extroversion, which are probably also inborn or developed very early in life, but which are usually listed as a distinct group; (3) *ability traits,* which have to do with our consistent capacities for certain types of performance, such as mechanical aptitude or musical aptitude; and (4) *dynamic traits,* of which character traits constitute a good example.

It Takes a Detective to Discover Man's Consistencies   When we look closely at man and his social institutions, what we see dwarfs even Ezekiel's vision in terms of bewildering, conflicting currents and crosscurrents of powerful forces. Our first task is to find consistencies. To be sure, there are lots of them. But there are even more ways in which man is inconsistent too, very often in ways we wish he would be consistent. The frequent wail, "I just can't understand people," is our popular way of saying this.

The fact is, human nature is roughly consistent in a number of different ways. For example, read some of the literature on role psychology, of which Newcomb's (111) work is typical. We can see that, within their various roles, people tend to be fairly consistent— at home, at school, on the playground, at business, at Rotary, at church. We may find them much less consistent, however, when we try to predict their behavior from one role to another. Then, too, if we observe the behavior of any one individual over a period of time we discover that he is fairly consistent, especially if we study his behavior in all of his various roles. It may be that his consistencies are seldom found in other individuals. Then we begin to realize what Allport (2) was talking about in his concept of unique traits. This holds also for such individual behavior patterns as those to which Murray (60:3–34) refers as personality structure, and which are usually closely bound up with self concepts. Still again, we can find consistencies if we look at man in terms of his basic needs and drives (94), except that within each such "trait pattern" there are variations in terms of the other areas.

It will be obvious that these various systems of consistencies cannot be completely independent of one another. A person's intelligence strongly influences his reactions to and even participation in all of his various roles. His unique traits and personality structure are usually strongly influenced by his native endowment and the role subcultures in which he lives. As a result, we may begin to find some reasonably clear cultural consistencies, such as national behavior or traits connected with one's religious experience (60:161–

266). Finally, it is not impossible to identify some widely common varieties of human behavior, which McDougall (96) called instincts. If you will read McDougall's book, even today, you will be impressed by how convincing it is. We do not any longer identify these consistencies with the concept of instinct, as he did. Nevertheless, the consistencies are there when looked at from a relevant point of view.

Are all these various kinds of consistency so complex and mutually inconsistent that no rhyme or reason can come from any effort to describe over-all consistencies? Far from it. It does mean, however, that no simple approach is going to prove very effective. When we want to deal with human nature from any point of view, we must first study it in terms of the interaction among these major types of consistency. When we have studied our problems from each of the relevant consistency areas, then we can hope to study the interrelationships among them and to find meaningful dimensions by which to attack the problem with which we are concerned.

At one time, I was convinced that eventually we would discover "the final trait theory." I no longer believe that. I think that as our knowledge advances, we shall always be finding better frames of reference about which to formulate our problems in character education, and for that matter, in any other phase of personality.

Let me summarize this concept of frames of reference by quoting from J. P. Guilford's presidential address at the 1950 meetings of the American Psychological Association:

I have defined personality as a unique pattern of traits, and traits as a matter of individual differences. There are thousands of observable traits. The scientific urge for rational order and for economy in the description of persons directs us to look for a small number of descriptive categories. . . .

We do not need the thousands of descriptive terms because they are much interrelated, both positively and negatively. By intercorrelation procedures it is possible to determine the threads of consistency that run throughout the categories describing abilities, interests, and temperament variables. . . . If the idea of applying this type of description to a living, breathing individual is distasteful, remember that this geometric picture is merely a conceptual model designed to encompass the multitude of observable facts, and to do it in a rational, communicable, and economical manner (46).

Which Dimensions? That Depends on Your Purpose   Here is the
next major key to thinking clearly about traits and dimensions in
personality. Which traits you use is determined by your purpose,
although they must be consistencies in the personalities you are
describing. They have to fit personality—but hundreds of trait systems could be and have been devised which would do that. The
point is that dimensional-trait concepts are tools for the experimenter
and educator, not absolutes inherent in the personality. Let me
illustrate.

Suppose several people are asked to survey the houses in a city
and classify them into groups according to some convenient categories. Let us suppose that the first person represents a paint company and he classifies them by color—red, blue, white, gray, and
so on. Is that a valid "trait theory" for these houses? Well, for the
purposes of the paint company, it is. Then the next person is the
tax assessor. He classifies them according to value. Is that valid? For
his purpose it is. The next person may be an artist. He classifies them
in terms of beauty. I am sure you could add to this list. Notice that
each one establishes a "trait theory," and that in every case it is a
valid and useful trait theory. So it is with personality. What dimensions you use depends on your problem.

Consider a trait concept to which I have already referred—
courage. I suspect that we shall discover that every act of behavior
which we commonly call courage is motivated by something else
entirely in the individual. A mother saves her child from danger not
because she has courage but because she loves the child. A re-
former braves the taunts of his audience because of his convictions
for his cause. A fooball player risks injury because of his desire
to win, and so on. Psychologically speaking, there may be no such
entity as courage. Nevertheless, if a military leader is choosing some
men for a dangerous mission, he wants to know whether or not
their behavior during that mission will be courageous enough, regardless of what motives brought it about in the individual soldiers.
Therefore courage is still a useful dimension—from the point of
view of the military leader.

In any program of research, then, you may, and probably will,
need several trait systems, and you will probably be continually revising them as you approach new research to make them more
effective. For example, in CRP we are using five different major trait

systems at present. Each of them serves purposes the others cannot serve. Each of them has to be adapted for each specific purpose, as evidence indicates the desirability of doing so. Each of our five dimensional frames of reference or trait theories led to new areas of achievement in our quest of character.

A Few Adventures Made Possible by Our Dimensional-Trait Concepts As I look back over the years and recall some of our mountaintop experiences in CRP, the most exciting ones came about and were made possible only after one of these dimensional-trait systems had been formulated.

The first of these experiences I want to describe was one of our earliest. We had become pretty certain that character education is not a matter of teaching abstract ethical traits as such, however high sounding they may be. We began to test the hypothesis that character traits are integral characteristics of the total personality —having no more reality in themselves than the grin of the Cheshire cat after the cat had disappeared. This could only mean that individual differences must play a central role in our procedures, and it gave rise to our testing program and the adaptation procedure. The results of this concept have certainly had far-reaching effects. The lives of two churches were at once infused with a new youth dynamic, the like of which they had not seen before.

This experience followed, and had to follow, the development of that phase of our trait theory which we have set forth in our *Personality Profile*, to be described in Chapter VII. It has received many revisions as we have found better dimensions and tools by which to attack the problems of individual differences inherent in character education. It certainly committed us to a child-centered program in the most literal sense of that term.

The second experience grew naturally out of the first. It is a matter of common knowledge—not always utilized, however—that as the mind develops, new levels of ideas come within its grasp. Not nearly so well known is the corresponding fact that ideas can be presented to children too late as well as too early. We have found, for example, that moral and social learning can be a very exciting experience for the child if geared to his level of development. New challenges to Christian achievement which he could not comprehend last year and may find rather dull next year are sources of real adventure this year. I shall not soon forget the excitement of a group of third graders when confronted with the almost incredible idea—for them—that there are skills for learning to like and be liked by people you don't like. I remember vividly another group of fourth graders who changed from fear of failure to seeing many failures as challenge. They wrote a motto: "If at first you don't succeed, try, try again. If at first you do succeed, try something harder."

This potent insight became possible because we had formulated the third of our dimensional-trait frame of reference to which we refer as our *Attitude Goals.* As you might guess, it is revised more frequently and more extensively than any of the others.

Then there was the time when we instituted our Workshops for Youth, and found one of the most far-reaching principles we have thus far discovered—one which I have already mentioned. Groups of High School young people come to Schenectady in these workshops, primarily for vocational guidance. We test them and show them the picture of their native endowments. Then we challenge each of them to conceive in his mind a vision for his life—not just work he will like and which will pay him well, but a goal of how he, as a unique individual, can hope to make a significant difference in the world with his life. Having found this vision we urge him to choose a vocation in which, using his abilities, he can hope to achieve this goal.

Note, however, that this experience would never have come to us if we had not formulated that part of our trait theory to which we refer as the *Christian Hypothesis,* because the problems involved in this insight were attacked in terms of the dimensions to which we refer as *vision* and *dominating purpose in the service of mankind,* set forth in that hypothesis.

When it comes to our experiences with the *Dynamics Diagram,* it is hard to decide upon just one event. A long succession of insights has been made possible by it. The fact is that this dynamics concept, making possible the study of exceedingly intricate problems, results in our greatest thrills, whatever research is undertaken with it. It has taken many years to develop it, but its power as a research tool certainly justifies the cost a hundred times over.

Our very first achievement in CRP, of such magnitude as to be quantitatively measurable by significant differences, was the one I described earlier which had to do with "fear of failure." We framed our procedures in that study in terms of an early form of this diagram.

Then, there is some recent evidence in our dynamics research which looks as though it would give us the key to one of the most difficult problems we have faced. We have found, through the years, that many High School youth find in CRP a challenge to which they respond with vigor and enthusiasm. Others, however, will have none of it, and rebel with considerable emotion against it. Why? We had found no promising hypotheses until very recently. One of our researches with the Dynamics Diagram indicates that probably at the two extremes are youth who show the following characteristics. The enthusiastic ones have strong self goals; that is, they conceive themselves as going somewhere and achieving something in the world. Furthermore, they have strong, positive self other concepts; that is, they think of themselves as socially secure, well thought of and accepted by their fellows. At the other extreme, the antagonistic ones seem more frequently to be youth who have no strong self goals—having not much longer vision for their lives than next Friday night's date. Usually they also have pessimistic self other concepts; that is, they feel insecure among their fellows and fear to do anything which might endanger their popularity. If this hypothesis proves to have merit, the solution is not a matter merely of "challenging" youth to accept the sometimes apparently dangerous social goals of CRP. We must first give them purpose and social confidence. Then we can be more assured of their willingness to strive toward these goals, despite the possible heartaches and social struggles which may beset their paths in doing so. This insight would never have been possible without the Dynamics Diagram.

The last of these outstanding trait-theory experiences came about as a result of an effort to understand a significant group of events. From the beginning we had been asking ourselves: How can we be sure that these Christian goals we are holding before our children may not actually destroy rather than ensure their chances either at personal happiness or at social achievement? Religion has not always been healthy, much less creative, either in personality or in social relations.

It has been heartwarming, therefore, as we watch our CRP youth grow, to see homes revitalized, children and youth winning distinction among their fellows, moral and spiritual as well as social and intellectual achievements of a caliber our older generations seldom achieved. Our question was, did CRP have a significant role in those events? We couldn't answer that without some relevant dimensional concepts. This led to the formulation of our fifth dimensional frame of reference, our so-called *Definition of Character*. It makes possible a quantitative evaluation of our procedures. In studies based on this dimension we didn't expect to find the whole credit for these events to be due to CRP. Indeed, we would have been disappointed if we had. When you find the shortcomings of a procedure or concept, that very discovery, far from being a discouraging experience, is almost always accompanied by a new and more effective insight. This kind of insight—the very heart of the infinity principle—could never have come about for us if we had not been able to formulate that part of our trait theory to which we refer as our Definition of Character.

A Bird's-Eye View of the Problem of Traits and Dimensions
Finding dimensions of character and personality: that is the core of our problem! Our research successes and failures rest on what dimensions we use. Personality is so infinitely complex that finding ways it is consistent is not nearly as easy as finding ways in which it is inconsistent. There are, however, literally thousands of ways in which man is consistent. Our first task is to find out how to identify them. We watch man in his various roles, in regard to his individual make-up, as he faces his needs and self evaluation, in his adjustment to the culture about him. In all of these areas we can find consistencies. Using some of our modern research techniques, we can now study people and groups in terms of all of these consistencies simultaneously, and discover consistency patterns among their interactions. There is no final trait theory. New consistency patterns will always be found when we study different problems, and as man faces new situations. In CRP some of our most exciting adventures have come when we have developed some new dimensional-trait frame of reference with which to study his consistencies. I hope you will find these six chapters as fascinating as we have found the problem during the twenty years it has taken us to do the research on which they are based.

There is a hierarchy of facts: some have no reach; they teach us nothing but themselves. The scientist who has ascertained them has learned nothing but a fact, and has not become more capable of seeing new facts.

There are, on the other hand, facts of great yield; each of them teaches us a new law. And since a choice must be made, it is to these that the scientist should devote himself (119).

So it is with dimensional-trait theories. Their value depends on whether they "have reach" and make possible "great yield." Having found such trait-hypotheses, then the powerful tools of experimental design can be used to increase this yield a hundredfold.

MAJOR CRITERIA FOR EVALUATING DIMENSIONAL-TRAIT CONCEPTS

As you might imagine, a dozen trait concepts are suggested for every one that proves to be fruitful in terms of important new knowledge about personality. The test of a trait concept is the new insights to which it leads.

Is the construction of such concepts a matter of trial and error, a sort of shot-in-the-dark kind of thing? To be sure, the scientific method is not in itself creative. It is, however, a powerful tool by which the scientist can be creative. He will still have to conceive the new hypotheses in his search for good ones. The scientific method will do two things. It will help him to eliminate the sterile hypotheses quickly. It will also lead him to the kinds of evidence from which he can make more adequate formulations of good ones.

Complex and bewildering as human nature is, there are lots of methods available today for constructing valid dimensional-trait concepts. These have been achieved as a result of centuries of efforts to make some sort of hopeful sense out of personality.

In the accompanying table are some sixteen criteria which are important in developing dimensional concepts. Not all of them will be significant for any one trait concept or system. I have indicated in the same table the criteria which were used in the formulation of each of our five CRP trait theories. The next time you want to generalize about people, individually or in groups, look at page 138!

Let us examine each of these criteria in terms of its significance for different kinds of educational problems. You will sense the importance of this matter more clearly, as you go along, if you apply the criteria to some of your own problems.

Purpose and Validity Requirements of Dimensional-Trait Theories As Used in Five Major CRP Trait Theories

Validity Requirements	CRP Trait Theory A Dynamics Diagram	B Personality Profile	C Christian Hypothesis	D Definition of Character	E Attitude Goals
I. Psychological Validity					
1. Hereditary characteristics					
a. Human nature	#	#		#	#
b. Developmental			#		#
2. Social determinants					
a. Personal-social adjustment	#	#		#	#
b. Home-social determinants	#		#		#
II. Experimental Design					
1. People who use it					
a. Psychologists and educators	#	#	#	#	#
b. Parents, teachers, youth	#	#	#		#
2. Tools of experimental design					
a. Quantifiable	#	#	#	#	#
b. Indicators	#	#	#	#	#
III. Nature of Goals					
1. Moral and ethical					
a. Christian			#		#
b. Insight, conviction, skill			#		#
2. Internal consistency					
a. Trait consistency			#	#	#
b. Generalization and transfer			#		#
IV. Dynamics					
1. Dynamic concepts					
a. Plastic clay *vs* self-determination			#	#	#
b. Negative ethics *vs* positive goals			#	#	#
2. Goal requirements					
a. Challenge and the infinity principle			#	#	#
b. Levels of aspiration taught and learned			#	#	#

Choose at least two—preferably several—educational objectives from some curriculum or program with which you are concerned or at least familiar. Be sure they are different kinds of objectives. For example, one may consist in verbal learning and another in skill learning and still another in a basic attitude toward how to deal with some characteristic situation. Several of our CRP objectives, for instance, are based on returning good for evil, and discovering a Christian way to respond to some of the common forms of injustice.

PSYCHOLOGICAL VALIDITY

Are Your Traits Possible, Human Nature Being What It Is? In the first place, a good trait theory is psychologically valid. This means simply that it must take human nature into full account. In the past it has been a common practice to set up trait theories purely on the basis of "social desirability." In general, businessmen want "honest" employees. Children, therefore, are urged to be "honest." We sensed many difficulties with concepts like this, and finally the Character Education Inquiry (23: Vol. I) demonstrated that this method of selecting goals is not a sound one. At various times in its history, religion has tried to brand all sex behavior as sin. Human nature has always stepped in and proved that such a trait concept will not do. On the other hand, it is valid to build a trait concept on sympathy, for that is a natural expression in human nature. Parental behavior is also natural, and its drives can be used as motivation in trait theory.

Hereditary Characteristics: You Can't Change This Part of Human Nature You cannot expect human nature to do what it does not have the capacity to do, nor to leave unexpressed any of its natural drives.

"You can't change human nature!" When the word *nature* is used in its strictest sense—that which is inborn—this assertion is essentially true. Biologists once talked of the inheritance of acquired characteristics. They are pretty well convinced now that such an assumption is not justified. The inherited qualities of a man are largely determined at the moment of conception. After that, they achieve maturation in a fairly predictable fashion. Heredity, then, sets definite limits on what trait goals we can expect of our children, and produces energies which are going to express themselves one way or another.

Lest this seem to be a pessimistic point of view, it needs to be pointed out that these limits have, thus far, not even been remotely approximated, much less exhausted. I grant you that some students of human nature have built concepts of personality development limited entirely to the satisfaction of basic needs. But these have seemed to some of us to emphasize the animal and ignore the divine in us. The animal is all right, but why leave out the other? Take a look at some of the undeveloped resources in human nature. The creative potential in our inherited imagination has probably not been developed to even an approximation of its maximum in more than three or four out of every million of us. Our emotional drive is for the most part wasted in fears and angers rather than made a source of power in high achievement. Socially, we literally cannot live either with or without one another. The picture of a social order which utilized even a generous portion of man's social potential is challenging to say the least.

Many of our inherited characteristics appear in the process of our growing up. I suppose the term *developmental maturation* used in the chart is redundancy in a sense. I use it to emphasize the nature of maturation. We once thought that a child was just a small edition of an adult. We recognize, now, that this is about as inaccurate a picture of childhood as one could imagine. Incidentally, we also thought of maturity as taking place finally and completely at about eighteen to twenty-one years of age. Now we recognize that some of it goes on until at least fifty. Any college professor beyond the age of forty is impressed and even amused by the immaturities of his students, of which the students themselves are blissfully ignorant and to which they are emotionally blind.

In the growth of our Project, we have called this the problem of developmental calibration. It has been one of our most interesting problems. Our successes and failures have certainly been influenced by the accuracy of our developmental calibration. When we have aimed too high, nothing but confusion has resulted. When the goals have been on the immature side, the element of challenge has regularly been lacking. What Sunday-school teacher has not read the contempt in the eyes of a growing youth when the objective was one which he considered too infantile for him? It is even worse when he takes the concept indifferently, assuming that such is about all one can expect from religion anyway.

As a result of these two criteria, a very important principle has emerged, with important implications for curricula in religious education. We overestimate our children's learning ability quantitatively, and to an even greater degree we underestimate it qualitatively. Thus we expect them to learn many times more Biblical passages than their inherited intelligence makes it possible for them to learn in the time we devote to religious education. On the other hand, we assign to them very petty goals in Christian living, whereas their enormous personality energies make possible the heroic. What challenges, for example, do our religious-education curricula hold out to our High School youth that will utilize fully the potential reservoirs of their creative imaginations, call for positive investment of their endless emotional energies, or demand from them levels of social courage which have characterized the prophets of all the ages?

Social Determinants: We May Not Be Pawns of Our Social Environment, but We Have to Live in It How shall we satisfy our own personal needs and at the same time meet the demands of our society? We talk much about personality integration and maximum potential in personality. But does not such a self-centered concept of adjustment inevitably result in social conflict? Indeed, it may. That depends on the trait concepts about which we endeavor to build personality. The psychopath seeks only to satisfy his own wants, no matter what their social implications may be. At the other extreme is the person who is so afraid of the opinions of others that he has no mind of his own. But are these the only alternatives? Much of the material which we have put into our CRP concepts of leadership has been directed toward attitudes which demand the best from the individual and at the same time make him able to command the respect and affection of his fellows. Here again is an important limitation on the trait concepts which can be used. Consider our Junior High attitude mentioned in the growth of imagination: "Acquiring the courage and skills to exceed prevalent peer standards." This implies neither submission nor prudishness, but a concept which satisfies both personal and social demands.

It is important to look at these social determinants from the other side. We have talked about how personality integration can be achieved along with social adjustment. What about the rights of society? The individual has responsibilities toward it. He must find and play his responsibility role if he is to be an important part of his social institutions. I think you will see that an important factor in solving this problem is what trait goals are suggested. How can loyalty to the group and courage of one's convictions be held simultaneously when they conflict, as they very frequently do? How can the demands both of the home and of the gang be met without serious frustrations? It is the formulation of trait concepts which can provide the answer. They must lend themselves to adaptation both to individual and to social needs. Examine some of those we have endeavored to formulate in CRP. In them we have endeavored to make social responsibility lead to growth in personality. For example, we have several curricular objectives which have to do with acquiring attitudes which deal honestly and realistically with the intricate problems of prejudice, and others with being determined to see that every man gets his full chance at happiness and success. This relates to social contacts both inside and outside the family.

EXPERIMENTAL DESIGN CRITERIA

Scientific Research Has to Be Done Scientifically   As we prepare our experimental design, we must decide what statistical tools we are going to use. A statistical procedure always presupposes certain prerequisite conditions in the data. These then will set additional limitations on which dimensions we can use. Badly chosen dimensions usually result in large errors. Such errors make our observed differences obscure and our correlations approach zero. Anyone setting out to develop a research design of any considerable scope in a new area needs to expect many discouraging experiences before he finds dimensions which measure sharply and reveal the characteristics of the data clearly.

Your Scientific Techniques Are Useful Only If the People Who Use Them Find Them Useful   It will be obvious that if trait concepts are to be used accurately, they must make sense to the people who must use them. In our case, for example, our trait concepts must make it possible for psychologists and educators to make full use of their technical skills. The layman uses many trait names which are so vague in personality structure and difficult to agree upon that the psychologist stays away from them. Consider a term like *personal magnetism*. Experiments show that this is almost entirely a matter of individual opinion, so that it becomes impossible to measure.

I need not labor the point. I merely want to emphasize the fact that we will not have a very useful trait theory, unless it makes sense to psychologists and educators. This means that we must keep reasonably well abreast of psychological developments so that we know of the major advances in personality theory (14).

There are, on the other hand, many trait concepts which psychologists use which carry little or no meaning to laymen. Most of our CRP dimensional concepts must be used by parents and teachers; and sometimes youth must use them. It would be very difficult to develop an effective character-education program when those working on it did not know what its objectives were.

You Must Use Dimensional-Trait Concepts for Which Experimental Design Tools Are Available What good would it be to have an electric refrigerator in a place where there was no electricity? In later chapters a number of powerful tools for research are described. As I have already pointed out, each of them presupposes certain kinds of evidence. Unless that kind of evidence is available, the tools are of dubious value. I want here to point up two fairly basic requirements for trait hypotheses if we are to study them with our best tools of experimental design.

In theory almost any conceivable trait can be quantified. In psychology we have developed so many methods for determining units that anything which exists in variable amounts can be measured. This is in theory, however. In practice, the story is often different. For example, in our work in psychology errors of observation are a common barrier to accurate measurement.

Of course, this principle of quantifiability is a relative one. We can detect gross differences in almost any trait. At the other extreme, our precision of measurement for almost any trait is still below the level of the physical sciences. Nevertheless, one of the important elements to take into consideration in the choice of trait variables is the accuracy with which they can be measured.

Then, our dimensional-traits must be the kind which can be observed. It is much easier to measure a trait like activeness than one like introversion. The reason is that in the case of the former there are so many more indicators which can be easily observed and confidently evaluated.

A *trait indicator* is something which we can observe and measure objectively, and which we accept as valid evidence of the presence or absence of the trait itself. For example, suppose we are trying to challenge a boy "to return good for evil" and want to see what progress, if any, we have made. We observe the following items of behavior: (*a*) he assures us that he desires to return good for evil; (*b*) he gives a present to the bully who torments him; (*c*) he stanchly defends this same bully in his Scout troop. That looks pretty good. The trouble is, he may have said what he did because he thought his parents and teacher expected him to, and have given the present as a ransom to stop the bullying, and defended him in Scout troop because he didn't like the boys who objected to him. You can see at once, then, that this matter of finding infallible trait indicators is a difficult one.

The problem of consistency is also involved in our indicators. Many a parent has become discouraged because his child acts one way on Monday and the opposite on Tuesday; one way at home and another at school; one way with older people and another with his own age-level group. Thus it is no small task to find trait indicators which in the child's behavior indicate in the same direction all the time.

THE NATURE OF GOALS

There Are Many Ways to Choose Goals Which You Can't Reach or Which Don't Mean Anything If You Do Reach Them The nature of the goals we have in mind will be an important determiner of what trait frames of reference we use. Indeed, our choice of traits may largely determine whether or not we reach these goals. For example, let us suppose we are seeking ethical goals. A man might be described as being brilliant, clever, aggressive, extroverted, witty, athletic, artistic, and musical without ever mentioning a trait with definite moral and ethical significance. Furthermore, an equally long list of trait names could be used—such as those accompanying nominating speeches at a political convention—which would be useless in character or personality research because they were vague, not measurable, and did not reach into new levels of character achievement.

In Character Research These Goals Will Have Moral and Ethical

Significance First, then, let us look at a few of the determinants which are involved when our purposes have moral and ethical significance.

Here is a group of boys, ages approximately nine to twelve. The speaker has been describing a childhood experience of his in which he had tried to be scrupulously honest toward an older man, despite the latter's sullen disposition and obvious hatred of boys. This the speaker submitted as his concept of good behavior. When asked what was lacking in this story from a Christian point of view, most of these boys responded at once that the behavior of the boy had not gone far enough to be called Christian. We have not behaved in a Christian manner in such a case, they insisted, until we have actually made friends with the one whom we dislike.

When research goals have to do with ethical and moral values, then our dimensional-trait concepts must usually indicate in their very nature the requirements for achieving these goals, as well as constituting dimensions in terms of which to measure that achievement. Most negative-ethics goals require a minimum of understanding, depress rather than inspire us, and are lived by just not doing something. Using a concept of positive goodness raises a vastly different problem.

I want to emphasize especially the skill part of this last group. Our present adult generation has been a pretty good one, as measured by "good intentions." It is our lack of skills to carry out these intentions which has made us so ineffective. Here is a boy who has become convinced that he ought to control his temper—that is, redirect the wasted energy of destructive anger into useful channels —who says: "I'm convinced, all right. But how do you do it?" In CRP, we are putting more and more emphasis on the answers to this kind of question.

Your Dimensional Goals Must Have Consistency in Human Behavior Someone has said that the only consistent thing about human nature is its inconsistency. If that were true, then you can be sure that one trait included in many trait theories would be inconsistency; for one of the important criteria of a good trait concept is its consistency. When research began to throw strong doubts on the consistency of well known widely generalized traits, some scholars suggested that this might indicate that there are no consistent traits in human nature. Most psychologists were very reluctant to accept this verdict. They agreed that this research showed beyond all doubt that some trait concepts commonly used in the past are not consistent. At the same time they still believed that there is some consistency in human personality. This meant that instead of assuming that consistency is to be had for socially desirable traits just by admonition, we must examine human nature to find in what ways it is consistent, and then build dimensional-trait concepts in light of this evidence.

The two words *generalization* and *transfer* are among the most important in the language for the educator. In the last analysis, they are the embodiment of what he is trying to bring about in the new generation.

Transfer, as you know, is the concept we use in evaluating our educational procedures generally. Thus, we say that the purpose of education is to prepare us for life. Put more specifically, this means that we expect the things we teach children to carry over; that is, to transfer, to the problems they will meet later on. In our general education we are trying to develop ability traits. If I take a course in English usage, I am trying to develop an ability trait which can be described as "proficiency in English usage." The English course has achieved its transfer purpose if I actually am more proficient thereafter in English usage.

Now, this same principle can be applied to character traits. Most parents, for example, want their children to develop a trait of persistence. If a particular parent teaches a child to be persistent in some aspects of his daily life, and this results in the child being persistent in other aspects of his behavior, then we can say that the trait has *transferred* to other situations from the situation in which it was learned.

Generalization is the ultimate in transfer. If as a result of learning a trait in one situation, I find that it is shown in all others, then it has become a generalized trait. Men have aimed at such generalization throughout the whole history of character education. Unfortunately, when psychologists began to study those generalized traits scientifically, they found that few, if any, of them ever became completely generalized. Of course, this is not an all-or-none matter. We may generalize some traits in some of our daily life roles but not in all of them. Thus there are levels of generalization.

I think you can see that the degree to which a trait can be generalized or transferred is usually determined in part at least by whether or not it is an integral part of the personality. A trait like courtesy does not seem to transfer very well. For example, can you predict from observing a man's behavior at an afternoon tea how courteous he will be driving a car? Prejudice, on the other hand, seems to transfer altogether too easily and generally, at least within a particular social group. The point is, however, that psychologists would probably all agree that one way to distinguish between good and poor educational trait concepts is to determine the degree to which they can be generalized or transferred. This is just another way of saying that the individual's behavior becomes consistent in them.

Note, however, that this does not mean that such a trait as honesty, which has not been found to generalize too well, can never be a useful trait concept. A banker hiring an employee doesn't much care whether the employee has a generalized trait of honesty or whether he has just learned a large number of specific honest habits. As long as he behaves honestly in his banking associations, that is the thing that matters to the banker. A parent, however, trying to teach the child honesty may feel pretty frustrated if, when he has taught the child a great many specific honest habits, there is no apparent tendency for this trait to transfer to new situations. He will be very much interested in finding trait concepts which do transfer.

In passing, it is not without interest that the trait concept of honesty, which came to be so thoroughly discredited in the twenties, is described in a recent text in child psychology as "one of our most important moral-social values" (137:567f.). One needs to be cautious about speaking too caustically about "outmoded trait theories." They have a way of coming back into fashion, especially if they have behind them a long cultural history, which honesty certainly does.

Our Project began at a period in the history of child psychology which was being strongly influenced by the startling and disillusioning findings of the Character Education Inquiry (23). The most widely known concept suggested by this research is the Doctrine of Specificity. It suggested that perhaps there are no *generalized traits;* only a number of *"specific" habits.* Indeed, as a result of this research, it was being said that an approach to character education in terms of traits, virtues, and ideals is impossible for a number of reasons, best summarized in the *Tenth Yearbook* of the Department of Superintendence (26:43–59). The refining influence of all this body of research probably brought about more drastic changes in our thinking and methods than anything else which has happened in the history of character education. Like all new points of view, however, it was inevitable that the new hypotheses suggested would be carried too far by some.

This does not mean that we ought to reject the findings of this significant body of research (26:79–178). On the contrary, we must gain every advantage possible from them. The arguments given in the report of the Department of Superintendence (26:43–59), for example, for eliminating the use of "traits, virtues and ideals" in character education have certainly not resulted in such elimination. But they have clearly pointed out many limitations as to the sort of "traits, virtues and ideals" that can be used effectively. It does not follow, for example, that because some suggested virtues are of such nature that their value is destroyed if one seeks them consciously, that all virtues have the same drawback. It does follow perhaps that a wholesome character-education program must use objectives which can be sought with vigor and enthusiasm for motives other than priggish self-righteousness. Certainly generalization is far easier when we have insight into what it is we are expected to generalize. It would be discouraging indeed if the great moral concepts of Jesus had to be kept a secret from a generation which was being challenged to apply them to our chaotic social order.

DYNAMICS

If You Are Concerned with the Dynamics of Personality, Your Dimensions Will Have to Be Stated in Dynamic Frames of Reference Our last general group of criteria are relevant when we use dynamic frames of reference. It is becoming increasingly evident that dynamics play a more important role in personality than structures. A few illustrations will show why this is the case. For example, height is a structure, but if a girl who is tall develops a sense of conflict because of being too tall, then this conflict is a dynamic. Drives as such are also dynamics, but when they interact with the environment in the forms of motivations, then this interaction type of motivation is also a dynamic. An attitude is a dynamic concept because by definition it describes the interaction between an individual and his environment.

These interaction dynamics in personality are vastly important, too, in any form of education. Teaching, in such a frame of reference, is like turning on the light. Your pressing the light switch does not actually produce the light, but it does set in action a complex system of forces which do result in the light coming on. The teacher, then, is effective when he sets in action a number of forces in the child which result in the child's learning. What the child learns in character education is for the most part a set of dynamics patterns. This is another illustration of how one selects frames of reference in which to set his research procedures, by the nature of the problem he is attacking. If we are concerned with a problem such as the relationship between "body type" and "personality characteristics," some structural frame of reference would certainly be appropriate. Character, however, as we define it in CRP, has no meaning apart from action, feeling, or thinking. We speak, for example, of strength of character. When we look at a child, we do not judge his character by the color of his eyes or the length of his nose. We watch him as he meets his environment, and we observe the quality of that interaction.

Dynamics Dimensions Are Essential If Your Educational Aims Are to Challenge Youth, Instead of Just to Inform Him   The importance of dynamic frames of reference including dynamic dimensional-trait concepts increases as psychologists and educators abandon the plastic-clay theory of the learning process, in which the teacher plays the active role and the child the passive role. More and more we are assuming that the child's personality is an energy system and that learning is determined by him rather than by his teacher.

The older theory pretty much assumes that the child is a piece of molding clay which his elders shape in any way they desire. Such terms as "molding character" and even "character building" usually imply this theory. We are coming to see that the child is more like a speeding express train that needs to be guided into useful directions, or that his personality is like atomic energy which can be utilized by him either for his own and his fellow's happiness or for widespread destructiveness. Such technical terms as integration and achieving maximum potential are characteristic of the vocabulary of this approach to learning.

You can see how this point of view inevitably influences our choice of dimensional-trait concepts. For example, in our CRP trait concepts, dominating purpose is far more characteristic than negative ethics. Social vision plays a more positive role than social adjustment conceived of as primarily lack of social conflict. To be sure, both negative ethics and lack of social conflict could be studied dynamically, but the positive concepts are more likely to accompany dynamic concepts of personality. Striking evidence of the increasing use of dynamics is found in clinical psychology, where positive dynamic concepts are increasingly used to eliminate pathological adjustments from the personality.

In his presidential address before a section of the American Psychological Association, John E. Anderson said a number of things relevant to this dynamic conception of personality:

The personality of young children is frequently misrepresented. . . . Common types of misrepresentation are: (a) the child is passive and responds to all the stimulation to which he is exposed without action or selection on his part; (b) the child is so delicate and tender that he must be protected at all costs, and must have exceptional amounts of love, affection, and security. . . . In contrast to these, the following picture of the child as a personality system is presented: (a) the child is an active energy system that responds selectively to its environment and neglects as well as takes in many stimuli; (b) the child has substantial capacity to withstand stress and strain, and recovers quickly from deformation and has great capacity for self-repair and readjustment. . . . The child, then, is not a simple passive creature molded exclusively by external forces; he is very much a creature in his own right, moving through his own experience and creating his own world (7).

Traditionally, it has been common to think of good behavior as being the absence of bad behavior. A person's goodness is thus described as the amount of badness he does not exhibit. Working from a dynamic frame of reference, we tend to reverse the process. We think of goodness as the most desirable possible application of the ongoing energy of the child, and of badness as the inability to achieve goodness.

This at once sets some new limitations on what kind of dimensional-trait concepts we set up. It may be, as the theologians tell us, that awareness of sin is essential. Be that as it may, we must certainly describe goodness as more than just the absence of sin. And this is not so easy as it sounds. It is a lot simpler to interest people in eliminating the "sin of being angry" than it is to talk about "the strength of magnanimity." More books are written about how not to be unhappy in marriage than about positive ways to be happy.

Even with Dynamics Dimensions, There Are Limitations on What Goals You Can Use   A child can touch the electrodes of a dry-cell battery without feeling the current. Run the same current through an appropriate transformer, and you can knock down a horse. We are just beginning to realize that this is the way it is with the force of personality when we begin to understand these dynamic frames of reference. Differences in IQ are of little significance, compared to the power of the many dynamic forces which a personality can generate. That is why such dynamic realities as faith and love are so much more powerful than physical prowess or strong intellect.

It is inevitable, then, that these new insights will have far-reaching implications for our choice of educational goals. The full range of these implications is beyond the scope of this chapter. I would, however, like to discuss briefly two general ways in which these dynamic concepts are influencing our choice of educational goals, especially in character and religious education.

Human potential, as viewed from a dynamic point of view, is so great that for all practical purposes it can be described as infinite. That is, no man can ever achieve his maximum potential. And this is not humanism as I understand it; for the largest factor in that dynamic equation is the religious one. Let me show you what I mean.

Consider the formula all of us learned in physics; namely, that momentum is equal to mass times velocity. We see a light lineman in a football game completely outplay his much heavier opponent by simply moving faster than he. Outcharging the other lineman is the secret of success there, which is a practical application of this formula.

This same concept, with the velocity factor multiplied many times over, can be applied to personality. It is not uncommon to hear people brag about the "statics" they possess: IQ, race, size, natural abilities, handsomeness, nationality, even wealth, or ancestry. When we measure people in these qualities, there do seem to be large individual differences. But mass never achieves anything. Momentum only comes when mass is multiplied by velocity. And velocity in this case can be a many times larger factor than the mass. Just one more illustration from physics. Not long ago I watched a group of first graders learning about leverage. They were discovering how they could lift various heavy weights with different leverage ratios. One of the youngsters suddenly shouted, "If I had one long enough I could lift the whole world, couldn't I?" Not an original idea, but a discovery for him.

Now let us see how this relates to our trait concepts. To be sure, we need to take into consideration all that psychology and psychiatry have learned about personality, and personality integration and conflict. These principles are dynamics and belong in the velocity factors of our equation. But add to these the religious factor, and you may have squared or cubed the ultimate power of the personality on society. I shall attempt to prove this assertion in the two chapters on the Christian Hypothesis.

I think you can easily see, then, how this principle will influence our choice of trait goals. They must represent challenge and the infinity principle. "My child already has this trait," says a parent. If that is the case we have surely gone astray in the attitude goals, which should be such that no individual can "have" them completely. So we set out to change the attitude goal, until every parent and child sees in it challenge for greater achievement than he has thus far realized. Often this comment has resulted from misunderstanding of the attitudes. Some of our social-adjustment attitudes have been seen as lessons in etiquette, instead of in social vision. Attitudes about anger have been interpreted as saying that one ought not to be angry, instead of being a challenge to use in creative experience the driving emotional energies which waste themselves in anger. Attitudes about imagination have sometimes been seen as encouraging the child to freer use of phantasy, instead of urging him to gain the enormous potential of creativity which lies in native imagination. Such limited interpretations have ignored the infinite nature of the attitude goals.

Furthermore, it is important in educational research, and especially in religious and character educational research, that our trait-goal concepts inspire men toward their best and noblest. This is not to suggest that such concepts must not also conform to human nature; indeed they must. But they must have this characteristic, too. For example, I pointed out, on page 139, that religious concepts of "virtue" which attempt to make sex behavior, as such, a sin, have generally proved futile. The majority of mankind have rejected them. Those who haven't have all too often become neurotic and frustrated. But what is the alternative? Must we go along with one group of psychiatrists who insist that the alternative to an unrealistic and mentally unhealthy morality is no morality? I do not believe so. I believe we can develop a finer and nobler morality, which on the one hand utilizes—not represses—all of man's physical drive, and at the same time inspires him to his greatest idealism. Such a morality will need to be formulated in terms of dynamic concepts.

The very nature of the infinity principle implies that our maximum potential is not to be achieved as a single leap. We must take a step at a time. An achievable goal which we set for ourselves is called our level of aspiration. Loving one's enemies is an ideal, the power of which we sense. The child's first step in mastering it, however, may be learning to like the neighborhood bully. Dominating purpose is an ultimate ideal of great value. The Nursery child does well, however, if in his journey toward it he can discover that there is more thrill to building up blocks than kicking them down.

Education implies that someone is teaching something and someone is learning something. It wouldn't be of much use to construct a trait theory about Christian character if its suggested dimensions couldn't be taught and learned. In the "good old days" the problem seemed easy enough. You just told children what kind of behavior you expected of them; praised them if they behaved that way and punished them if they didn't. "Spare the rod and spoil the child" was pretty much an accepted theory of child training.

In CRP we are putting far more emphasis on learning than on teaching. In fact, we define teaching as creating an environment in which learning can take place. The spare-the-rod philosophy could produce a certain kind of learning. It does create a situation in which learning becomes desirable. In fact, probably some useful learning is brought about that way. Teaching a young child not to cross the street unattended or not to hit baby sister may often be accomplished more economically this way than in any other.

But when you are dealing with Christian attitudes, that is an entirely different matter. No one was ever punished into loving his enemies. Many a well meaning parent has tried to teach his child the "habit of giving" by forcing him to do so, only to discover that the resultant attitude was just the opposite of what he had been seeking to achieve. When we set our ultimate goals in terms of the Christian Hypothesis, we are talking about the quality of the total behavior of the personality. This means that creating a favorable teaching environment must take into consideration, not only information and reason, but also native endowment, skills, other attitudes, and tensions. Insight, conviction, vision, and application are difficult qualities to achieve.

This is not the place to discuss learning theory. The problem of learning does play a part, however, in the formulation of our trait concepts. For example, do you start with the attitude as a goal, and try to apply it to as many relevant situations as possible? Or do you start with life's experiences and try to discover what attitudes are relevant to dealing effectively with them? Of course, the answer is both. The second would be very difficult with the young child who had learned none of the major Christian concepts. But as new aspects of the Christian philosophy are mastered, they ought to be integrated into the total personality and then applied to all experience. Unless they are, the first process becomes fairly insignificant in its value.

Note, for example, how this dynamic concept of learning applies to the study of the Bible, in terms of its character-building purposes. Memorizing it or at least gaining familiarity with it is at best a skill. It does not exert much influence on the effectiveness of personality until it results in the formation of attitudes, which add to the integrative forces of the personality. Nor does it reach its maximum force until it becomes a part of the self—so much a part of the self that the individual is hardly aware of having such an attitude.

SOME IMPORTANT CONCEPTS DESCRIBED IN THIS CHAPTER

Human personality is a bewilderingly complex phenomenon involving literally thousands of dynamic interactions among its various forces. Any scientific study of it presupposes the formulation of useful dimensions by which it can be systematically described.

It is obvious that, in the whole field of religious and character education, we are as yet very far from having found the best possible dimensional-trait frames of reference, because so many major problems in our personal-social relations remain unsolved, even when everybody concerned sincerely wants to solve them. Bringing about good will on earth, even among men of good will, requires better understanding of the major dimensions of personality than we have thus far achieved.

The word "trait" has been used in many ways, some of them very inadequate for purposes of challenging a greater generation. A good definition of traits is that they are concepts formulated to identify the consistencies in human nature. Traits as isolated parts of personality have long since ceased to have general use in psychology. In modern psychology, trait concepts are any ways in which the total personality seems to have some measures of consistency.

Useful trait concepts in research also have to be dimensions, so that degrees of them can be observed and measured.

Most important of all, however: they are frames of reference by which the scientist describes personality, not something in the very nature of the personality, like anatomical features.

The value of a dimensional-trait theory depends on the purposes for which it is constructed and how fruitful it is in helping to achieve those purposes. In the history of CRP each of our five major trait theories has led to significant achievements which would have been impossible without it.

As a result of the work in the psychology of personality during the last half-century, we can now identify a number of criteria by which to formulate and evaluate dimensional-trait concepts. Not all of them are relevant to all problems, but as each research problem is approached, an appropriate frame of reference for it can be most quickly and effectively formulated by considering which criteria are relevant to it, and by using them as guides in the process.

Among the many possible criteria there are four major types. The first group has to do with psychological validity. For example, the organic nature of man must be considered. We cannot set up educational goals which are inconsistent with human nature. Then, too, as we examine our past efforts in religious and character education it becomes increasingly evident that we have overestimated children's ability to learn quantitatively and underestimated their ability to learn qualitatively.

If our purpose is research, our dimensions must constitute an appropriate frame of reference for our experimental design. For example, if these dimensions are to be used by lay people they must be understandable to them.

If the research is set in dynamic frames of reference, as is that of CRP, then the dimensions used must be such that dynamic patterns can be measured in terms of them. A plastic-clay concept of learning is not suitable for dynamic expressions of personality. Negative-ethics concepts do not lend themselves to ethical dynamic patterns as well as positive concepts of goodness.

Moreover, if these dimensions are to be used in the actual educational process with the child, then they must constitute challenge for him, but at the same time inspire levels of aspiration which he sees as attainable goals.

CHAPTER VI

———•———

DIMENSIONS OF PERSONALITY—
DYNAMIC FRAMES OF REFERENCE

SPEED PLAYS an increasingly important role in our civilization. Yet no one has ever studied it directly, because it does not exist as such. Speed consists of a dynamic interrelationship between other things, such as your car and the road. If we want to study speed, we have to deal with cars and roads, never with speed as such. That is the way it is with many dynamics. They are very real forces, among the most important in our lives. Yet they exist and can be studied only in terms of other things and forces.

Most character traits are dynamics. Faith, for example, does not exist as such, but is a result of the reactions of a person toward something outside himself which inspires faith in him. Probably one of the reasons why so much character education has been ineffective is that we have tried to produce a desirable dynamic—a character trait—in a child, as such, instead of by means of the interacting factors which produce it. For example, we speak of young people having "respect for their elders." I doubt if such a trait can be achieved, except perhaps in terms of very superficial behavior, unless their elders can merit that respect. The respect, then, is a dynamic which grows out of the interrelationships between adults and youth.

What is even more important is that probably a great many of the most important dynamics in personality have never been identified; dynamics, that is, which are important in the sense that they make possible higher levels of human achievement.

Definition of a Dynamic   If you have read very much in the literature of psychology, you may have got the impression that the term "dynamic" is used so broadly as to have no precise meaning. To a certain extent, that is true. However, there is a common core to all of its uses. Perhaps if I may point out a few systematic principles running through the wide variety of its uses, our explorations into dynamics will be clearer.

A simple, but fairly precise, definition of the term as we use it in psychology is that a dynamic is any force or energy in the personality which results in reactions or aspects of reactions which are not functions of the external situations in which they occur but of the personality involved.

Consider a series of illustrations on four arbitrary levels. These four levels have to do with the relative importance of the role played by the individual in what he does as compared to that played by the environment.

When a croquet ball is struck, for all practical purposes we can say that there are no dynamic elements in its behavior. Its behavior will be a result of the force with which it is struck, modified by such factors as the friction and slope of the path over which it travels. If you knew all of these things, you could predict its behavior completely. Some human behavior is like that of the croquet ball. If I fall on the ice and break my arm, the whole process is not too different from that involving the croquet ball. In this kind of behavior I am a pawn of my environment, and no important dynamics are involved.

When Herbart, the philosopher, described the mind as a *tabula rasa* (blank tablet) on which ideas impress themselves, he was setting forth a nondynamic psychology. The very term "association of ideas" originally meant that the ideas, as such, were the important forces in human behavior. The individual himself no more determined what happened than the blackboard determines what is written on it.

But now we can go a step further and begin to introduce a dynamic element. When John Watson, the behaviorist, with his S(timulus)—R(esponse) sequences insisted that if we could describe and control the S (Stimulus) completely, we could predict precisely what the individual would do, he still saw the role of the environment as dominant. However, he introduced another element into the picture. In an illustration I used before, I spoke of turning on the lights. Actually, I press a button which in turn releases a great deal of energy and which results in light. In a very real sense this is the way it is in behavioristic concepts of personality.

This brings us to the second step in the ladder. It depicts human personality as having energy (like the dynamo in the electric system) which influences the reactions of the personality. In general, however, as seen by the behaviorist, it has no initiative of its own. Watson believed that if we can measure accurately enough we shall eventually be able to control and predict behavior by controlling the situation, just as we do in the case of the electrical system.

Thus if I am hungry and food is placed in front of me, I shall eat. If a young man has matured far enough and a pretty girl appears, he will fall in love.

But now let's turn to a third level in this hierarchy. It is illustrated by Freudian concepts. We have certain urges—he referred to these as *libido*—which drive us all of the time. The environment can either facilitate or frustrate this ongoing energy but it cannot stop it. If, as is usually the case, frustrations appear, the personality must then find some way of using this displaced energy. Freud called these various forms of reaction *dynamisms*. Symonds (135) has described our present use of these dynamisms very clearly in his recent book on the subject. In Freudianism the individual is still somewhat at the mercy of his environment. But he does have energy which cannot be turned off and on, only channeled, modified, or distorted as a relentless environment sets obstacles in his path.

Perhaps the main core of Gestalt psychology can be placed at this level. We have certain purposes which make us strive toward desired goals. Those goals and purposes are far more determined by us than by the environment. If I am hungry, I do not just passively wait until by chance some food is found in my environment; I go out to seek a food-giving situation in the form, perhaps, of a restaurant.

The fourth level of dynamics begins here. When we reach the point where we no longer speak of the individual reacting to his environment, no matter how energetically, but of him as actually seeking out his environment, then we have reached another stage in dynamic psychology. It has been common for psychologists, talking of desirable child care, for example, to warn parents against countless dangers as if the child were a very delicate pawn in his environment.

I wonder if it is not actually closer to the facts to point out that almost as soon as the child is born he begins to say: "I will go to this person and not that one; I will play with this and not that; I will eat this and not that." This drive toward becoming the master of his destiny is certainly a force to be reckoned with for the rest of his life. William Koppe refers to this in his thesis.

One of the major findings in this thesis is that children select or are selected by behavior situations that are congruent with their interests and capacities, and that they are not often found in behavior situations that do not fit their capacities. In some way the environment to which the child must respond is at least in part a function of the child himself (61).

Are There Dynamic Patterns Previously Unknown? The most recent approach in the search for such dynamics is that made possible by the statistical tool of factor analysis. By means of this tool we are able to discover consistencies in behavior which would be completely beyond the capacity of even the most brilliant mind to observe directly. The best description of this approach is found in Cattell (21). A group of experimenters, using this tool, have attempted to describe and identify a number of traits in human nature never before discovered. Cattell's fourteen source traits are examples of the personality consistencies they have found. Our approach is based on the hypothesis that the key to a great many of our most difficult personal and social problems lies in the meaning which a person gives to his environment, and that the dynamics in our personalities play the leading roles in determining what this interpretation is to be. Not only that, I would also guess that the same dynamics are the forces in our personalities which bring it about that, for the most part, we select the environment to which we choose to adjust. Finally, I would guess that such dynamics change from time to time. In any case, here is the way we are going about it.

We try to observe how a number of people react in specific kinds of environments. This is a very important point. If you ask me,

"How do you get along with people?" I am very uncertain about my answer. If, however, you ask, "How did you get along with your family on that picnic last week?" that I can answer more confidently. The more specific the question, the more accurate the answers. In our CRP research we are trying to find the most general situations to which sufficiently accurate answers can be given.

THE CRP DYNAMICS DIAGRAM

Our CRP Dynamics Diagram, which I shall now describe, has reached its present status through twenty years of trial and error with various factor concepts. If observers could not describe these factor concepts sufficiently accurately, or if they did not appear in meaningful patterns, they were discarded and others tried. If by this procedure we can find dynamic patterns which are common and which are significant in terms of desirable and undesirable behavior, then we shall have formulated some new dynamics trait concepts.

Here we are, then, setting forth dynamic concepts which are based on the hypothesis that the individual is basically the determiner of his destiny far more than is his environment. In fact, it assumes that these dynamic energies which characterize his personality make it possible for him to decide pretty much what his environment is going to be, and to evaluate and interpret it himself. Such a theory of personality means that we must know these dynamics in people if we are to influence them one way or another. Even more important, perhaps, they must know them if they are to approach their maximum potential. Almost all psychologists nowadays would agree that personality problems can be studied effectively only if you have adequate frames of reference by which to identify personality dynamics; namely, the functioning of the personality as a whole. Character education certainly falls in this area, and in CRP we have constructed our Dynamics Diagram for this purpose. It is most nearly comparable to topological psychology (147: Ch. VII) and action theory (116).

Human personality has many characteristics. It is possible to measure a number of relatively stable aspects of personality; as, for example, intelligence, height, emotional control, or sense of values. The fact remains that in behavior we are dealing primarily with phenomena which are none of these external aspects, but a dynamic expression of all of them. We cannot study any of them very fruitfully except as its interrelationships with all the others are considered.

Our own dynamics frame of reference was first formulated in 1935, first published in 1939 (73:4–10), revised and expanded many times to its present form, which is shown in the accompanying figure.

An act of behavior is a very complex phenomenon. How can we construct a diagram by which to describe it? If you will examine a number of similar diagrams in the literature of psychology, you will see that they differ widely. Which one is right? The answer is that probably all of them are, for each of them is useful in the study of some particular problem. In research like ours, one important criterion to use in the choice of such dimensions is that they must be accurately identifiable by lay people. In our first efforts to construct such a diagram, the various factors were so complex that parents, for example, could not recognize them in their children with sufficient accuracy. We divided and redivided, defined and redefined them until now most of them show reasonably high reliability, even when they are used by parents and teachers who have no technical training in psychology.

The factors which we now have in our Dynamics Diagram can be described under eight broad areas of personality structure. These are: S, the general situation in which the behavior occurs; PS, the situation as perceived, the individual's interpretation of his environment; T, the tensions, the motivational tensions which are active in him at the time; R, the response, the reaction which the individual exhibits; Oi, the innate organism, or basic endowment of the individual; Sk, the skills which he has acquired; Att, the general system of his attitudes, for example, likes, dislikes, biases, and some of his value judgments; and the self, that part of him which he sees as himself and to which he refers as "I." The last three we include under the heading Om, modified organism, the individual as modified by his experience. This is, of course, an oversimplified picture of the dynamics of personality structure. The complete Diagram as we used it in the Home Dynamics Study contains more than sixty variables. The exact number varies from study to study. Each of these eight general headings is subdivided into a number of more

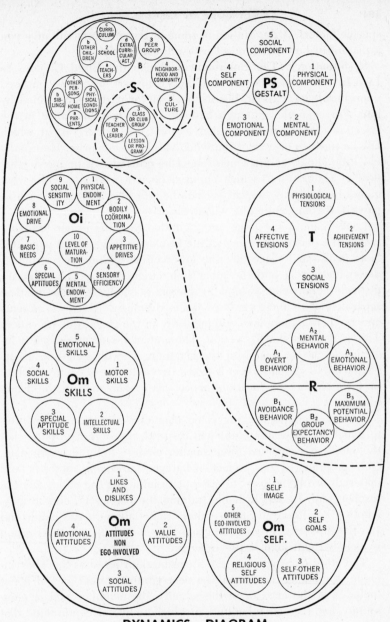

DYNAMICS DIAGRAM

163

specific factors. A description of some of these factors will give you a picture of how this kind of research can be done.

S (Situation): The Environment Which the Child Chooses to Live In The environment of a child is in part, of course, imposed upon him from without, but in much larger part is determined by him. For example, although biologically he has no choice in the selection of his parents, he has a great deal to say about which one he turns to or away from when various needs arise. He usually has little choice about which school he goes to, but he has a great deal of choice as to which children he will associate with, what games he will play, which teachers he will like, and usually which parts of the curriculum he will stress or neglect.

Look, then, at the large circle entitled S in the upper left-hand part of the personality circle of the Dynamics Diagram on page 163. Note in the first place that the lower circle within the S group is designated as S_A and the other four circles as S_B. This arbitrary distinction between S_A and S_B factors is made in order to deal separately with those parts of his environment which his parents and teachers manipulate systematically in the process of education. This is done in the S_A section. The rest of his environment is included in the S_B section of the Diagram. The ultimate aim of the Character Research Project is to discover effective ways in which to produce character education, hence this organization of the S factors.

S_A here includes our suggested character-education procedures, to which we hope the child will respond appropriately. Note that this circle, S_A, contains three smaller circles: (1) the lesson plan, club program, camp project—whatever curricular methods and materials are being used to attempt to influence the child; (2) the teacher, club leader, in home training the parent(s), and so on— whoever is attempting to use these materials with the child; and (3) the class, club group, tent group, family group—whatever group is included with him in this process.

The other five factors in the S can be designated as S_B. They include: the home, the school, the peer group (or that part of it not included in the class or in the school), the neighborhood or community, and the general culture in which he lives. Keep in mind that he must adjust in this entire situation, S_B as well as S_A, even when we may imagine that we have him entirely in our church-school class or club group. For example, his reactions to the teacher frequently may really represent reactions to his parents. Note, however, that each of these S_B factors in part he determines or at least gives meaning to, and in part they are the objective situation into which he has been born and lives. Let us look briefly at some of them.

S_{B1} is the home, and includes parents, siblings (brothers and sisters), other individuals living in the home, and the physical conditions of the home. One of the tendencies in religious and character-education curricula has been to describe the role of the home as if one home were pretty much like another. This is not true, of course. Then when you consider the fact that one child's home is not even like that of his brothers and sisters—owing to his own personal selecting and rejecting among its various possibilities—it is even more obvious that there must be wide differences among homes in their relationship to the problem of character education.

Second in importance to home usually is the school (if the child is old enough to go to school). We have tried to describe this phase of the child's environment in terms of four factors: the teacher(s), other children, the curriculum, and extracurricular activities within the school environment.

The part the child can play in the selection of his own environment is even more extensive here than in the case of the home. The child, in the pre-high school years, has little to say about the choice of his teacher. Among all the things his teacher says, however, the child has a great deal to do with which ones he pays attention to and likes, and which ones he neglects or is not interested in. Two children sitting in the same class could conceivably hear nothing in common, and thus be responding to entirely different environments as far as the teacher is concerned. As for the influence of other children in the school group, rarely, if ever, does the child respond to all of them. Even in the case of close paired-friendships, or in cliques, the effective environment will be very different for each child in any one class.

There are usually other children outside his school, class, or club, who may be regarded as his peers. The ones with whom he comes in contact will differ from situation to situation. For example, the group he meets at a movie may be almost entirely different from the neighborhood group with whom he plays each evening. Furthermore, which of these become important parts of the background S (S_B) during the process of character education (S_A) will differ widely. Clearly, here too, he has a great deal to say about which of his peers play a significant role in his total adjustment.

A great many studies, especially those of a sociological nature, dealing with such problems as juvenile delinquency, have taken into account the neighborhood and community influences as causal factors. Almost without exception, however, they have dealt with these factors measured objectively, and thus neglected the role each child in a given community plays in determining which parts of these factors he will react to. In other words, the S to which the child really adjusts in this matter of neighborhood and community influences is described accurately not only in terms of a sociological description of the neighborhood, but also in terms of which of those factors are effective after the child gets through his selecting and rejecting among them. Ninety per cent of the homes in his neighborhood could be criminal, but if he associates only with the other 10 per cent, he lives in a "good" environment. One can never evaluate the effect of a neighborhood on a child until he finds out just what part of that neighborhood the child has chosen as his S "neighborhood."

The most difficult of all the S factors to define accurately and even more difficult to measure is the culture. The general pattern of mores or culture in which the child lives is, of course, a very important part of his total S. In this case, however, not only does he select and reject among the many cultural possibilities open to him, but those who interpret the culture to him do the same thing. If we wish to describe the cultural influences in a community, we must discover which of these cultural influences his parents and teachers select and which they reject; and then which among these the child himself selects and rejects. This becomes a quite complex procedure and a very important one if our dreams of a better world are to be realized. As Munro puts it:

To be sure, we have been thrilled at "Christian Youth Building a New World." . . . If it were only that simple and easy! The world is controlled by adults. Christian youth can't build a new world as long as adults don't want one. And as rapidly as youth crosses the bridge into adult responsibilities, youth is assimilated, by those very responsibilities, to the existing adult ideals and patterns (107:304).

Dynamic Factors in Our Native Endowment Oi (Inherited Organism) Having got a general picture of the S (environment) in the study of this interdynamic relationship between the individual and his environment, we must now turn to those factors which have to do with the individual.

Oi, Inherited Organism: Every Individual Is Unique We don't make the best of even a good-sized fraction of the inherited nature we already have. We don't need any more. More than half of us are brighter than some of the greatest men and women in history. We could learn ten times as much in school as we do. We have enough emotional drive to make life and society heaven on earth. We have enough social endowment to make war as obsolete as a dodo. All of these achievements are possible without changing our native endowment one iota; simply by making the best possible use of the "human nature" we already have.

Let us look, then, at the circle in our Diagram which is designated as Oi (innate organism).

It is designed to indicate those aspects of the personality which are essentially a result of heredity. How many subdivisions are included in such an organization of hereditary traits is largely determined by the purpose for which the description is intended. On the Personality Profile, to be described in Chapter VII, we include more than forty such traits. For purposes of identifying dynamic patterns, however, ten are probably enough. These include physical endowment—height, weight, stamina, and so on; bodily coordination; the appetitive drives—hunger, thirst, sex, and so on; sensory efficiency—visual acuity, auditory acuity, pain sensitivity, and so on; the mental endowments; the special aptitudes—including imagination, art aptitude, musical aptitude, mechanical aptitude, and so on; the basic needs—including such things as the need for security and self-esteem; emotional drive; social sensitivity—referring to the degree to which an individual is able to sense the social and emotional reactions of others; and level of maturation.

We need to consider each of these in light of their dynamic and interdynamic significance. There are several ways in which the Oi exerts marked influences on the behavior of the individual. It has a great deal to do with which energies in the external world the individual will be aware of. Color-blind individuals fail to see many visual stimuli to which color-normal individuals are sensitive.

Young children are totally incapable of perceiving many things which the mature individual perceives. Factors in the Oi strongly influence the nature and strength of our motivations—the individual with a powerful hunger drive may be much more strongly motivated to "live to eat" than one who has less hunger drive. The Oi sets limits on the nature of one's capacity for adjustment—if a youth is modestly endowed athletically he cannot gain prestige through athletics, no matter how much he may wish to do so. The Oi also sets limits to achievement. Overambition—the desire to enter a vocation for which one does not have the necessary aptitudes—is quite as productive of unhappiness as underambition.

You Will Be Able to Think at Once of Many Ways in Which These Oi Factors Influence Character Education Many a father urges his young son to "fight back" when being bullied. This may have merits (of a doubtful nature) if the boy is well enough co-ordinated to be able to do so. He may even become a better bully. But if he is not, the results may be more disastrous than ever. The boy who "throws like a girl," or the girl who cannot learn to dance, can vouch for the enormous unhappiness that can arise from such "handicaps."

One of the great problems of democracy is that many people are asked to vote on issues which they cannot comprehend. Or again, consider two infants, one of whom explores every closet and drawer in the house while the other is content to play with a toy in the living room. They do not differ morally, nor necessarily because of parental training, but in terms of inherited characteristics which are expressed as curiosity.

Emotional Drive People differ enormously in how emotional they are. Emotion adds color to personality. It is essential in face-to-face leadership. It colors our interpretation of the world about us and surely is an important factor in our selection of our environment. It is not to be confused with emotional stability or instability, but is to be regarded rather as a potential source of power. Who has not wondered what would be possible in human achievement if children at Junior High and High School level were mature enough to use their educational opportunities to their fullest extent? For that matter, the same holds for College students. One of the problems in CRP is to explore the possibilities of achieving this very thing.

One can look at this organism and deal only with its needs. There surely are many of them, and they do constitute a major portion of our dynamics. I would urge you to go back over this description of the Oi and list all of the needs implied in it. For example, satisfaction of the appetites to a certain level is certainly a part of basic needs. Pick up the nearest popular magazine and look at the food advertising. How much of it has to do with real needs and how much to the sheer joy of living? I certainly need food to stay alive, but what need makes me seek the glories of the Thanksgiving table?

After you have listed all of the needs you can think of, then list the potential. Think of all the things that could be done with these endowments and various combinations of them. It is my guess that satisfaction of basic needs will never bring social harmony even in families, much less in world politics. That will have to come when men have explored far further than they have in the area of their social potential.

The Unique Individual in His Unique World Having used this organization of factors to describe the inherited nature of man, the bewildering complexity of behavior becomes more and more apparent. It is not the purpose of this chapter to add to the difficulty of psychological problems; but it is important to sense the full complexity of personality, especially in terms of the interdynamic relationships among its many facets. Note a few of the ways in which S factors and Oi factors influence each other.

On the side of Oi, it has already been pointed out that one's sensory efficiency plays a major role in determining which of the many energies of the external world are perceivable to the individual. The role of levels of maturation in determining the ultimate influence of the home and the school in the S complex will be obvious. The mental ability of the child will surely influence what aspects of his school situation will most influence his personality. His physical traits will have a great deal to do with which aspects of his peer environment will influence him and how. These are just a few of many possible illustrations.

The S does not influence the Oi directly, except in such extreme situations as starvation diets and rigorous climates. It does, however, have a great deal to do with how the Oi comes to be expressed. A child's education has much to do with the wisdom with which he uses his IQ. His home training will play a large part in how he uses his emotionality. His cultural and community influences will strongly direct the expression of his basic drives and appetites.

It is appropriate, here, to point out again the ultimate value of such frames of reference as those we are using. A quotation from Allport will serve our purposes:

> The desire of the present volume is to discover a type of element (trait) that will account without artificiality or undue multiplicity for the self-consistency of each individual personality. It is not so much a matter of being right or being wrong. It is rather a matter of selecting units that will best represent the structure of personality as personality (2:247).

Om (Modified Organism): Man's Nature As Modified by Learning and Experience   The next three groups of factors to be described have all been given the general designation of Om (modified organism). They have to do with those characteristics of personality which are a result of learning. Siberians and Californians do not speak the same language, nor eat the same food, nor engage in the same pleasures, nor believe in the same philosophy of values. In the development of trait-theory frames of reference, then, we must give a prominent place to learned characteristics. We find it useful, in terms of studying dynamics, to include these learned reactions in three groups: Om skills, Om non-ego-involved attitudes, and Om self (ego-involved attitudes).

Om Skills: It Takes As Much Skill to Use Your Emotions and Get Along with Your Friends As It Does to Throw a Ball or Study a Lesson   Man inherits aptitudes but not skills. These he must learn. In seeking for a useful way to classify skills, we have used five categories: motor skills, intellectual skills, special aptitude skills (including musical, artistic, and mechanical skills), social skills, emotional skills.

We learn new skills every day in our work with tools, our athletic achievements, and our ability to make war. We are making little, if any, progress on how to use our emotional, social, and spiritual potential. There is far greater possibility of developing new skills there than in the case of the former group.

There are many kinds of influence which the skills will have on character traits. The skills will certainly set definite limits on one's achievement. If character can be regarded in part as being measured by one's social influence, the skills will surely influence this aspect of it. The quality of character traits found in our greatest statesmen requires mental skills for the necessary depth of insight. Social skills are, of course, great determiners of one's social influence.

In passing, and with some relevance, it ought to be pointed out that achieving one's maximum skill in any area requires levels of insight possible only with expert coaching. This fact is generally recognized with regard to some kinds of skills but not with others. Coaching in athletics and such special-aptitude skills as art, music, and mechanical ability is a recognized necessity. Of course, the importance of teachers in acquiring intellectual proficiency is among the oldest principles of education. As for social skills, probably a vast majority of people, especially youth themselves, are sure that all they need is experience. We teach our young people social skills on somewhat the principle of throwing them into the water and letting them swim out or drown. A look at the capacity of our adult generation to make one another unhappy—and usually unintentionally—is ample evidence of the fallacy of this assumption. As for emotional skills, most people do not even know that there are such things. Yet, let each of us take stock of the amount of unhappiness, indigestion, and sleepless nights he suffers because of the gnawing tortures of fear, anger, suspicion, jealousy, and the like. Consider that for the most part these are due to faulty emotional training—and the value of emotional skills is evident.

Om Attitudes: Our Likes and Dislikes, Biases and Prejudices, and Self Evaluations—These Constitute Our Real Philosophy of Life
Now we come to the very core of personality. One's environment (S), one's native endowment (Oi), and one's skills (Om skills) are important determiners of action. But by far the most important determiners are the attitudes. Indeed, the chief significance of the first three in character is probably their role in the formation of attitudes. When we observe an individual react in a situation, if we wish to understand that reaction, understanding his relevant attitudes will help us far more than all of the other facts put together. The attitude seems to us by far the best to use in research of this nature.

Simple definitions of attitude are usually not very satisfactory. The individual tends to make value judgments and feeling-tone judgments about every situation. His consistent judgments are the attitudes which form his philosophy of living. They have been classified in literally scores of different ways. Thus far no one classification has received any wide acceptance among psychologists.

The classification we are using seems to be a convenient frame of reference in which to formulate our problems. In the first place, we distinguish between those attitudes which are ego-involved and those which are not. The former we call self attitudes; the latter, non-ego-involved attitudes.

Some attitudes seem to be a part of our selves. When anyone disagrees with them we take it as a personal matter. Other attitudes, however, do not seem to have much to do with us personally and we regard them as independent from our inner selves and change them freely. If I like apples and you do not, that rarely has much to do with our friendship. If, however, you cast aspersion on my family, my religion, my country, my profession, or my own personality I may become highly incensed. While attitudes probably do not fall into a sharp dichotomy, this distinction between self attitudes and non-ego-involved attitudes seems to be useful.

Om Non-Ego-Involved Attitudes—On Which We Invest Billions Every Year We think very highly of this part of our personality. For example, approximately 4,000 children were born in my home town last year. If they follow our example, they will earn about $400,000,000 before they die and spend $125,000,000 of it on "recreation," tobacco, and alcoholic beverages. They will spend less than $4,000,000 on religion and welfare. In fact, up to now, mankind in his search for happiness has assumed that satisfying his likes and dislikes, his interests and pleasures is the best road to that happiness. There seems to be little correlation between the amount of pleasure a man gets and his happiness, but we go on trying anyway.

A classification of the non-ego-involved attitudes which seems to be adequate in our search for the dynamic aspects of character describes them as: likes and dislikes, value attitudes, social attitudes, and emotional attitudes.

Our likes and dislikes for the most part have to do with our appetitive satisfactions. What foods, pleasures, and habits of living we like or dislike are the objects toward which these attitudes are directed. Some of them can become ego-involved, but this is the exception rather than the rule.

Because of their great influence in character research, the social group have been separately designated in our Diagram. The others may or may not become ego-involved. For example, in some cases religious attitudes are a very superficial part of a person's personality. In others they become strongly ego-involved. Research has shown that when they do, they are the most difficult of all attitudes to change.

The social attitudes have to do with our reaction toward people. They determine how we choose our friends and enemies, how we value them and what they do, and how we regard what they do to and with us. A slap on the back may be regarded either as an insult or a high degree of commendation, depending on our attitudes toward the person who does it.

Our emotional attitudes include our fears and angers, our habits of suspicion and jealousy, our enthusiasms and habits of courage, magnanimity and affection. These are almost always attached to specific things, and they frequently become highly ego-involved. This is especially true of anger, which almost always is regarded by the person expressing it as "righteous indignation."

Om Self: My Evaluation of My Self and of My Neighbors' Estimate of Me The attitudes which we designate as Om self are probably the most important ones for character research. If the non-ego-involved attitudes determine where we invest our money and time, the self attitudes decide very largely where we invest our emotions. We get angry nine times when our vanity is wounded to one time for everything else put together. We worry more about what the neighbors will think than about death, taxes, and war combined. By far the best way to a man's heart is flattery, not his stomach. Yes, we think highly of ourselves. If we have an inferiority complex, we get angry even more often and intensely if anyone reminds us of our supposed inferiority intentionally or unintentionally.

The concept of the self is not a new one in psychology. But for a time it was in some disrepute. However, psychologists discovered that unless we include such a concept, much human behavior cannot be accounted for. It was inevitable, therefore, that the concept of the self should come back into psychological theory.

The self is difficult to define. It is that part of me to which I refer when I say, "I." It is not my body, nor my special aptitudes, nor my intelligence. Even if my body is drastically changed, I still think of myself as the same "I" that I was before. It is what the Freudian calls an ego, and the Christian a soul. This is not to say that the terms "ego," "soul," and "self" are identical. They are not. But for our purpose they can all be grouped together. Trying to pin it down to something definite has given employment to philosophers for centuries. Since we are concerned only with its dynamics, we can describe it in terms of functions and operations.

For the purposes of our research design, the attitudes which it includes can be subsumed under the self image, self goals, self other attitudes, religious self attitudes, and other ego-involved attitudes.

The self image consists of those attitudes which represent how one sees his self. The development of these attitudes begins in infancy when the baby begins to distinguish that which is part of himself and that which is not-self. This process continues through the years, gradually developing a highly complex and varied self image.

Many influences contribute to its formation in the growing child. His native endowment, his Oi, and his acquired skills, are the evidences on which he arrives at some of his concepts of his self. What he hears others say about him, especially if they are people for whom he has great respect, will play a big role in this growing self image. As he associates and often competes with others, he also gets evidence on which to base self attitudes.

But by far the strongest influences in this process are inner pressures, which are a part of his very nature. These were included under the Oi, as the basic drives. These were set forth as: a need for security and a need for self-esteem. Each of us, then, has strong inner urges which have to do with this self image, two of the common expressions of which can be described as the need for security and the need for self-esteem. Conceit, on the one hand, and feelings of inferiority, on the other, are names which we apply to characteristic attitudes in the self-esteem category. Typical results in personality structure can be illustrated by Maslow's description of the four types of security—self-esteem combinations. One with high security and high self-esteem, has strength and affection for his fellow man, is kind and protective. If he has low security with high self-esteem, he has strength but feels hostility and fear of others, is ruthless and sadistic. When low security is associated with low self-esteem, one tends to be masochistic and something of a boot-licker. Finally, high security with low self-esteem results in a quiet, sweet, dependent person (94).

The self image one has may be very far from that which his associates have of him, and different from any which could be formed on the basis of objective measurements. One of the aims of good character education should be to achieve as objectively accurate a self image as possible. This requires objective insight of considerable magnitude on the part of a person.

This does not mean that people of modest endowment ought to have feelings of inferiority because of this fact. One of our most successful methods in CRP has consisted in making this accurate knowledge of oneself, plus faith in a Father God, the basis for an intelligent optimism. It has proved to be highly inspiring to youth of all levels of endowment.

Self goals are in part determined by the nature of one's self image. One may conceive of his self as worthless and act that way, or as bad and try to prove it, or as invincible and at least talk a good battle, or as having an immortal soul and live as if he did. In any event, he comes to have levels of aspiration which grow out of his self goals. They may in part be inspired by his contact with the group, by his perception of their expectancies, his ideal self, his experience in terms of success and failure, and his concept of what is possible for him.

The great study conducted by Terman and his associates (24, 136) seems to indicate that a determination to excel was the one characteristic most common to all of the distinguished men whose biographies they studied. This is an excellent illustration of the degree to which self attitudes can influence character. Many of the distinguished men described in Volume II of that series were not endowed much beyond the average of men in general. Yet they achieved distinction, partly because of this driving force in their nature. Through the vision concept of vocational guidance referred to above, we have been able to create in youth this determination, based on a challenging self image.

Self other concepts probably have more to do with our adjustments among our fellows than any other factor in our social behavior. What one thinks of his fellows; what he thinks they think of him; how this compares with what they do think of him and of what he thinks of them—these are the things on which our social structures are built and destroyed. I may admire another so much that I identify with him as completely as possible. Which of us has not identified with an athletic hero so completely that we experienced his successes and failures almost as though they were our own? Or we may project our own sins and shortcomings into others, hardly recognizing that they are our own. Paranoia is basically a system of intense self other attitudes.

Religious self attitudes have been shown to be among the most stable of all attitudes. By religious self attitudes, then, are meant those religious beliefs which have become so much a part of the self that to change them would require a change in one's inner self.

Some of these religious self attitudes can be undesirable. We may experience such strong prejudices in favor of our own sect and against others that we may be willing to believe the most incredible stories about the others and at the same time rationalize completely any sort of behavior on the part of those belonging to our group. Then there are those concepts of right and wrong associated with our own religion which become so deeply entrenched in our thinking that they can produce neuroses in their resultant conflicts. It is here that guilt and shame elements come most commonly into our personality structures.

By the same token, religious self attitudes can give us great strength of character. If religion is defined, psychologically, as "the sum total of our universal attitudes" (attitudes concerning the universe and its laws), then everyone is religious, whether he subscribes to one of the formal religious sects or not. The fact is, that although one may profess religious beliefs which are entirely at the verbal level and in no sense ego-involved, he may "believe" in loving his enemies, that it is more blessed to give than to receive, and in immortality; and yet live the exact opposite of them in his daily life. It is those attitudes toward universal concepts which are real dynamics in his behavior which we call religious self attitudes.

Other ego-involved attitudes include those from the group designated as Om attitudes which have become ego-involved. A woman may take a non-ego-involved attitude toward a hat in the store window but become highly ego-involved about it when she buys and wears it. Other attitudes may be non-ego-involved for a time, then ego-involved and then back again. For example, I may admire the YMCA, a non-ego-involved attitude. I become a member of the board of directors, and the same attitude becomes ego-involved. Then I retire from the board, and the process is reversed. One of the great psychological problems involved in our modern conceptions of social service is complicated by this very fact. The Community Chest idea has as one of its handicaps its inability to build ego-involved interests in people for the agencies themselves. In money-raising campaigns, then, we resort to teams, thermometers of goals, contests, "oughts," and the like, as substitutes for genuinely ego-involved motivations.

Most of our biases and prejudices come under this heading. Race-prejudice problems and other social prejudices, although sometimes religious in their nature, are more often of this sort.

Today most psychologists use some concept of the self. To be sure, many of them believe that it is developed by such processes as the "interiorization of social experience." Thus they still shy away from any concept involving a soul. Nevertheless, almost all of them acknowledge that something, to which the name "self" is usually given, must be hypothecated if we are to have much success in predicting behavior.

Note some of the common-sense evidences that the person does not act like plastic clay or a "soulless" machine. Rather, he tries very hard to be master of his destiny. The infant is hardly born before he begins to take initiative even in the selection of his own environment. He will go to this person and not that one. He will play with this and not that, he will eat this and not the other. To be sure, we, his teachers and parents, can stack the cards for or against him; but he still plays the major role in his biography. "Free will?" I don't know how free it is, but there is much will demonstrated in most of us.

Place a number of individuals in the same situation. Record the variations in their reactions. Then place one individual in a number of situations and do likewise. I'd guess that in such an experiment there would be more variations among the different individuals in the same situation than there would be with the same individual in different situations. This would indicate that the individual controls the environment more than the environment does the individual.

I want to be clear about the role I think this self plays. I do not believe that it is simply the sum of the other factors described in the Diagram—intelligence, the special aptitudes, the appetites, skills, tensions, and so on, or even the interiorization of social experience. I think it must be conceived of as the individual himself, a soul, if you wish. His performance is, of course, limited by intelligence and skills. His judgments are colored by his emotions. His evaluations are necessarily made in terms of his environmental opportunities as well as his capacities for learning evaluative criteria. And there certainly is some "interiorization of social experience." In fact, we regard the process of character education as having taken place when attitudes become "a part of the self." But I'd still guess that you could have two individuals exactly alike in environment, experience, and native endowment, who nevertheless would be as different as day and night because of their will to be so.

In other words, I do not believe the child starts with zero self and comes to have a self only as the product of his early experience. I believe that he begins with a self which actively interacts with his environment, making use of his native endowment and skills to produce his maturing personality.

The other three large circles in our Diagram have to do with dynamic factors operating in any single act of behavior. The four circles which we have described under the headings of Oi, Om skills, Om attitudes, and Om self have to do with relatively stable factors in personality. Part of the S circle can be regarded as having some permanency. The last three circles, PS, T, and R, however, have to do with the present psychological event only. They represent the personality in action.

T (The Tensions): What Happens When We Feel Hungry, Tired, Scared, Angry, or Full of Energy? The first of these is called T, and has to do with whatever tensions are operating at the moment. For example, one may have a big appetite as part of his Oi constitution. This becomes a tension, however, only when he is actually experiencing hunger.

Some psychologists and psychiatrists have said you can't expect anything else from a man so long as his tensions (felt needs) are unsatisfied. Parents of a new baby are assured that satisfying his needs 100 per cent is the best way to convince the child they love him. In fact, they are told that some very dire things will happen if they don't. I must admit that in my earlier writings I said that all behavior was to reduce tensions, although I did say that achievement tensions and social tensions are stronger than appetitive tensions for all normal people. I don't believe even that any more. Nevertheless the tensions still have to be taken into account in our behavior.

For some years, now, in the Character Research Project, we have found a fourfold classification of these tensions satisfactory in our frame of reference for formulating dynamic problems: physiological tensions, achievement tensions, social tensions, and affective tensions.

Our bodily needs set up physiological tensions in our organisms for their satisfaction, which we commonly refer to as appetites. They have been variously classified. Those most commonly listed are: hunger, thirst, sex, freedom from pain (comfort), freedom from fatigue (rest), elimination, and need for oxygen.

One characteristic of the appetites is that there are wide individual differences in their strength. For example, some people experience far greater feelings of hunger than others; some have greater sensitivity to pain than others; and in some the sex drive is stronger than in others. How major the role is that they play in human behavior depends in part on how strong they are, and in part on how strong the other tensions are.

A second characteristic of the appetites is that their psychological intensity does not always correspond closely to their biological value. Biologically, we eat to live. Psychologically, we eat to get the pleasure that comes from satisfying an appetite, or because the food tastes good. We often eat more than is biologically desirable and eat foods that are biologically unwholesome. In varying degrees this is true of all of the appetites.

A third characteristic of the appetites is that in general they are effective in motivation primarily only on the negative side. When we are in pain, we very much wish to be comfortable. When we are comfortable we don't think anything about it at all. A toothache makes us consider how much more pleasant life would be if that tooth did not ache. When we have no toothache, however, we do not give thanks to the Almighty for each and every tooth which does not ache. This, too, is true in varying degree of all of the appetites.

A biological concept which has attracted wide interest can be stated in this way. Living protoplasm tends to express itself. A simple example is that of a bee laying up honey. He gathers far more honey than he needs. In all probability he gathers all the honey he can, simply because he is made that way. He needs no other reward or punishment. His basic make-up carries its own motivation. This concept is a very important one in theories of human motivation. If it is true that living protoplasm tends to express itself, then the various aptitudes, including intelligence, will carry with them a strong motivation to use them. This certainly seems to be the case, and gives rise to our concept of achievement tensions. Musically inclined individuals tend to seek musical expression. Athletically endowed people go in for sports, and so on. To be sure, this becomes involved with the social tensions, the various attitudes, and even the situation itself, but in general this concept of achievement tension can be regarded as valid.

Our conscious experience of achievement tension is, of course, far more complex than just this biological nature of the organism. Our sense of "ambition" and our "levels of aspiration" rest on this biological basis, to be sure. There is also included, however, the effect of all of the relevant attitudes, especially the self attitudes included in the self image and the self goals. As a result, one can have strong tensions to do things which are far beyond the reach of his native endowment, and to avoid forms of activity which are directly in line with his native endowments. If a musically endowed boy thinks that playing the piano is "sissy," he may have stronger tensions against than toward musical performance.

All would agree that man is a social animal. To describe the nature of this social endowment in terms of specific factors, however, is far from having reached a point of common agreement. The nature and strength of the social tensions will certainly be in part a function of the Oi social aptitudes, the Om social skills, the Om social attitudes, and the Om self other attitudes. Of course, the environment—his social opportunities—will play a role. The fact remains that there are strong social tensions per se. Solitary confinement has been found to be one of the most severe forms of punishment, outweighing any sort of physical torture. The concept of gregariousness seems to be a useful frame of reference for this general tension, although some of the connotations that were attached to it in the early days of psychology would need to be avoided. Likewise, sympathy seems to be a natural reaction rooted in the Oi and expressed even in infancy. Possibly the parental drive is at least in part a function of the Oi, and productive of some of the strongest tensions in our nature. In our work in CRP, we have made wide use of this motivation.

It was pointed out in the discussion of the Oi that one of our inherited characteristics is emotionality. Obviously it, too, tends to express itself. The feelings and emotions are sometimes referred to as secondary tensions, because they are usually ways of expressing our evaluation of the satisfactions of the primary tensions. If in the satisfaction of a hunger tension we eat food that tastes good, we experience a feeling of pleasantness. If the food is disliked, the feeling is unpleasantness. When situations have in them evidences of danger, the emotion is fear. If the experience is thrilling, we may experience ecstasy, and so on.

These emotional tensions may or may not gain complete control of our behavior. When they do, we describe the experience as one of emotional instability. Ability to keep these emotions under control can be called emotional stability, and requires very wise development in our educational growth.

We can recognize at least two types of emotional instability. The first has to do with the intensity with which we experience emotions. The infant expresses his emotions in an all-or-none fashion. He cries as lustily for a minor irritation as for a violent pain. Gradually he learns to differentiate in his responses and respond more violently for the more significant causes. Some people never develop this very far and respond violently all of their lives, no matter what the reason. Temper tantrums should probably never appear after the Kindergarten level, but even some adults exhibit them. Fear becomes terror only in the emotionally unstable. The development of emotional control is difficult for anyone. It is more difficult the more emotional the individual is by nature.

Another type of emotional instability has to do with the irrationality of the intensity of responses in terms of their causes. An individual who is unstable in this way may respond violently to a minor irritation and respond little or not at all to a major tragedy. This is probably almost entirely due to learning. Indeed, we are better able to understand our fellow man if we evaluate situations in terms of the emotion he shows toward them rather than in terms of how we see them or even by some objective evaluation. If a woman thinks a beautiful hat is a source of ecstasy and its absence a source of temper, then for her it is.

PS (Situation As Perceived): The Most Important Factor; Life Is How We See It   What is the meaning of life? It is hardly an exaggeration to say that every individual is giving his answer to the question, or to some aspect of it, all of the time. Though his answer may be highly irrational and change every five minutes, he is always in the process of giving meaning to his life and behaving accordingly.

Here is the very center of understanding human nature, whether that of other people or of ourselves. What the external world is really like is not very important. What meaning we attach to it is everything. One of the hardest lessons to learn in life is that what we see when we look at the external world is always PS far more than S. Can you believe your own eyes? I should say not. When a man stops saying, "This is the way things are," and begins to say, "This is the way things look to me," then he has some chance of understanding himself and his neighbor.

The traditional definition of perception is "the interpretation of sensation." Because the meaning which one gives to his daily experiences is a dynamic interrelationship between his environment and himself, we have chosen to call this integrating process in personality the PS, the perceived situation.

There is a fairly recent systematic "school" of psychology, known as Phenomenological Psychology (128). Put in terms of our CRP concepts, its authors propose that what we are calling PS is the central factor in mental life and therefore the focus about which psychological problems should be organized. Basically, the same point of view was set forth in *Their Future Is Now* (73:4–10), published in 1939. To understand what meaning an individual gives to his experience is to understand the individual.

One result of this concept is the flood of Projective Technique tests that has come during recent years, of which the Rorschach ink blots are best known. The assumption is that an individual's interpretation of the ink blot—or whatever stimulus is put in front of him—tells more about him than it does about the stimulus. And indeed this is true. Furthermore, we are finding that children's answers to many kinds of questions will do the same thing.

A Perception Is the Most Complex Phenomenon in Nature For the most part in our daily experience we are accustomed to making perceptions so quickly and easily that we are unaware of their enormous complexity. It is possible that a perception is the most complex phenomenon in nature. All of the dynamic interrelationships among all of the other factors in personality are integrated into a single Gestalt or meaning in this one process. While most of us are aware of how differently two people can look at the same thing, we probably do not see the full significance of this fact.

Look at the major components which enter into this integrating experience, the PS. In CRP we have found that we need to put them into five categories for our dynamic frame of reference. These include: the physical component, the mental component, the social component, the emotional component, and the self component.

How we interpret our environment depends in part on the efficiency of the sense organs, for these determine which of the many energies in the external world we can become aware of. Then, too, our behavior determines which of these energies we are going to expose our sense organs to. The color-blind individual cannot respond to certain light energy differentiations nor will the color-sensitive individual be able to do so if he doesn't look at them. Then, too, how an individual will interpret his environment will in part be determined by which of his biological tensions are active and with what intensity. When an individual is intensely hungry and wide awake, he is likely to give a different meaning to the same external environment than when he is well fed and sleepy. Then, again, it is far easier for the physically well endowed to see life with optimism than he who is physically handicapped or ill. It is a lot easier for the pretty girl who is bright and healthy to believe in a Father God than the physically unattractive and sickly girl who never has any dates.

The very word *meaning* suggests mental behavior. An individual's mental endowments and skills will certainly play a major role in what meaning he gives to his experience. Insights and meanings are limited both by the developmental levels of mental age and by the relative levels of IQ. Some of the great scientific insights of the ages have seemed to come to men in a moment of inspiration, for which they seemed to have little responsibility. The fact remains that these insights have come only to men with sufficient mental capacity to understand the underlying problems and with enough mental skill to manipulate the variables involved in them. One listening to children discuss problems is immediately aware of the influence of their mental levels on the nature of their perceptions and insights. This holds also for all our value judgments and social, political and religious philosophies. A man can use only those aspects of the culture which he has the mental capacity to comprehend. Many a child memorizes verbal formulae which have no real meaning for him at all. Religion for many people never does rise above the verbal level.

What has been said so far about this mental component might imply that our perceptions are all rational—within the limits of our intellectual capacities. Such is very far from being the case. One's mental capacity sets limits on his insights, but it certainly does not make it necessary for him to seek the best insights of which he is capable. While, of course, this is a matter of degree, it would be a safe guess that snap judgments and impulsive decisions are many times more common than careful and rational judgments. This is one of the major problems of democracy as the ideal form of government. Motivating people to use their best abilities in practice is far more difficult in this matter of citizenship even than training those abilities. Our school system has made great strides in teaching us mental skills. Our culture has as yet done little to motivate us to use them. Our political conventions, even at the national level, are little more rational than they would be if we were all illiterate. It is an open question as to which is more important for the survival of civilization, training in skills (the goal of most of our present education) or training in character (ability to use those skills for good).

If it is true that a basic purpose of PS is to interpret life in terms of security and self-esteem, it is certain that our affective tensions will play major roles in determining what meaning we assign to it. We have designated this component as the emotional component, although the feelings are also included in it. It is really the affective component. However, the emotional aspects of our affective behavior are so basic in character research that we have concentrated largely on them.

Perhaps an easy way to show the part our self attitudes play in our perceptions would be to compare the divergent meanings which two individuals with widely contrasting self concepts would give to the same life experiences. Let us suppose that individual A has a confident and accurate self image, sees for himself challenging and rational goals, has self other concepts which involve rational social confidence and adequate social skills, and has the faith and social outlook of the Christian philosophy of life. Individual B has a deep inferiority complex with little insight into his real potentialities, has no goals in life other than self-protection and self-indulgence, is suspicious and antagonistic in his self other relations, and has no religious faith or social outlook. Let us see how the two might interpret some typical experiences.

Suppose each faces great obstacles in whatever he is trying to achieve. Individual A might well see these as challenges, and meet the difficulty with confidence and determination. If the difficulty resulted in ultimate failure, individual A would be able to interpret this experience with far greater personal strength than would B. Then, secondly, suppose they both face a great opportunity for achievement. Individual A could be counted on to see it as something to be grasped and to be made the most of. Individual B would be far more likely to be afraid of it and decide to let it slip by untouched. If each faced danger, A would meet it with confidence and skill. B would face it with fear and depression, and would be far less likely to meet it successfully. Again, consider how each would look at suffering. Individual A would transcend it and see beyond it, and partly because of it would achieve a radiant and inspiring life. B would see life as dark and dismal. Finally, if each faced injustice, it would be A who could love his enemies and overcome evil with good. B would see his fellow men as evil, not to be trusted, and to be responded to with revenge and bitterness, suspicion and hate.

There is one more aspect of personality which must be considered in this process of perception. This is the social factor. The meaning one attaches to any experience has to be arrived at from some frame of reference. An inch has meaning only when it is related to a foot. So it is with the social aspects of our behavior. Social judgments can be made only in terms of one's social experience. For example, suppose a child can jump five feet high. Is that excellent or poor? That depends on how old he is and on how high other children that age can jump. Thus in most of our evaluations we use social standards. This refers not only to standards of achievement, but to standards of value and ethical principles as well. Then, too, the prestige value of a job will certainly influence our estimation of it. A sense of leadership is a strong motivation for judging a task worth doing. Leadership has no meaning apart from a social frame of reference. Everyone has a desire to have a feeling of belonging. This, too, entirely social in its basic meaning. The sense of security, which is so much emphasized by some child psychologists, is essentially a social perception. Finally, levels of aspiration are very often inspired by elements of hero worship and other social dynamics.

We have talked about the various components in the PS. In actual experience, however, a perception seems to be a unified experience. That is because it is one. One of the most important contributions of Gestalt psychology has been at just this point. Perception is not a sort of mixture of a great many elements. It is a configuration or Gestalt of them. A triangle is not a mixture of three lines bearing certain relationships to one another. It is an organization of lines having meaning as such and in relation to the background in which they are found, quite independent of the lines themselves. So it is with perception in general. When we look at life and any particular experience, the meaning we give to it is just such a Gestalt, resulting from all these various factors, and yet something in and of itself apart from them.

"Judge not, that you be not judged." Judging others is one of the most common forms of man's inhumanity to man. We see a man's behavior, and because we do not see it in terms of the PS from which it came we misjudge the individual. It is probable that if we knew all of the factors leading to any act of behavior, we might have an understanding of it that would make our dealing with the individual much more sympathetic and effective.

R (Response and Adjustment): How, When, and Why We Behave Like Human Beings The last major group to be described in this Diagram of a psychological event has to do with what the individual does in it; namely, his responses in his efforts to make adequate adjustments.

The quantity of our R's is incredible. I estimate that I have already written more words than are in the *Encyclopaedia Britannica*, said more than in all the books in our Union College Library, walked a distance equal to four times around the world, lost my temper at more people than live in Schenectady, and caused that many other people to lose theirs, inspired a much smaller number to better living, and done enough creditable things to keep my conscience in abeyance.

Furthermore, I become increasingly dissatisfied with the term *adjustment*. It sounds too much as if a human being's life consisted in his being tossed from one situation to another, with his only contribution being to make the most of it. If we interpret the word *adjustment* to mean that we adjust the environment rather than adjust to the environment, we shall be closer to the facts.

A great many different ways of classifying responses have been suggested. This has been especially true in describing various types of adjustment. In our efforts to find an adequate frame of reference for our procedures in character education, at present we include two groups of factors. The first group, which we have designated on the Diagram as A1, A2, and A3, is a traditional way of describing behavior in psychology. These are: A1—overt behavior; A2—mental behavior, and A3—emotional behavior. All actual responses in human behavior include these three elements.

We are suggesting, for the other group, a new frame of reference. It has to do with the adjustments the individual makes in terms of his basic purposes. This is to say that each individual develops a concept of the ideal goal and works toward it. We can designate these as B1—avoidance behavior; B2—group-expectancy behavior, and B3—maximum potential behavior. Everyone engages in all three kinds every day, but in widely varying degrees.

Overt behavior is the response we make with the large muscles of the body. In the case of young children it includes the major portion of their behavior.

Mental behavior has to do with those responses which involve intellectual processes. Usually they are verbal in their nature. In the solution of a mathematical problem, for example, the response is largely mental in its nature.

Emotional behavior involves the smooth-muscle reactions of the body. That sinking feeling in your stomach when you are afraid is an example. One is likely to make at least some feeling-tone reaction to everything he does.

An emotionally unstable individual is one in whom A3 is the dominating element in his response patterns. In this case A2 is often reduced to a minimum—largely serving to carry out the impulses of the emotions more completely. A1 is usually reduced to a poorly coordinated gross type of physical behavior. The athlete becomes far less efficient when he loses his temper.

The mature individual can be conceived of as one in whom A2 is the dominant element in his response patterns. His emotional patterns may be strong, but they give drive to his efforts, never dominating his reactions. His overt behavior will be present, but well coordinated and integrated fully with the mental factor.

The three B factors are more characteristic of our frames of reference in CRP.

Every individual expends a certain amount of energy. We use the term *avoidance behavior* to describe that portion of our energy that goes into avoiding the things we don't like or the consequences of which we wish to avoid. Threat of punishment, if effective, leads primarily to avoidance behavior. In our own research in character education, we have regularly found avoidance behavior to be more characteristic of ineffective lessons than effective ones. This is not to say that punishment can never play a useful role in character education. That would be absurd. "Spare the rod and spoil the child," however, can hardly be regarded as the ideal form of character education. Nevertheless, its long history in the culture is such that it certainly has some values which must not be lost in our efforts to make our procedures more positive and more challenging. For that matter, not many of us, even in adult behavior, are so well self-disciplined that we do not need some such external pressures to make it possible for us to do our best. Note that even in this kind of behavior the individual is deciding what his environment is going to be. He may not have everything to say about what his environmental menu is going to be, but he certainly decides which items he will include in his dealings with it.

Then there is *group-expectancy behavior,* describing that energy which we expend in our efforts to do those things we think others expect of us. I suppose good manners ought to be an outgrowth of our thoughtfulness for others. In practice, however, most etiquette is done because everyone does it. Many young people go to college for this reason. Some vocations carry more prestige values than others. Choosing a vocation for this reason is another example of this kind of behavior. Junior High boys do not usually engage in vandalism because of a real desire to be destructive but because of what they think the group expects of them. Social pressures at the high-school and college age are very hard to resist. Of course, to suggest that the standards of the group ought not to be a factor in what we do would be quite unrealistic. The fact remains that in our CRP dynamics studies so far, group expectancy behavior has been more often associated with ineffective than with effective character education.

Finally, some of our energy goes into those activities into which we throw everything we have. This we call *maximum potential behavior*. Athletics usually bring out such effort. Young people fall in love that way. Inspirational music and art motivate us to our best. When men see their jobs as being more important than their salaries, you have such behavior. We find that our most effective lessons are those in which the goals of our character-education lessons inspire this kind of response in our youth.

Now We Can Look at Our Behavior As a Whole The irregular line drawn through the Diagram divides the major factors into two groups. The first group includes S_A, T, PS, and R. The second group includes S_B, Oi, Om_{Sk}, Om_{Att}, and Om_{Self}. An examination of these two groups will reveal that the first group includes those factors which are actually designed to describe the ongoing behavior of the moment. The second group has to do with those factors which represent the relatively permanent characteristics of the individual, and which play background roles in how the first group of factors operate.

Let us pay especial attention to S_A. This is the area of education. It includes the only variables we can manipulate systematically. This includes our curriculum and our efforts to teach it. All the rest of the personality of the child is his to use as he pleases, and he uses it to evaluate our educational offerings. In doing this he is the chief determiner of his educational destiny.

The final point that needs to be made about this Diagram is to re-emphasize the fact that behavior is a unified integrated experience. It is not just the sum of its parts. In describing it, it is convenient to consider all of these various aspects of it separately, but it would be a mistake to think of it as a sort of mixture of a number of independent elements.

Remembering that trait concepts are for the purpose of bringing order out of apparent chaos, you will discover that many seeming inconsistencies in behavior will be seen as completely consistent when examined with the framework of this Diagram.

Now you can see why character education is so difficult. We prepare a curriculum. We expose the child to it. The more naïve writers say, "If you do this, the child will do that." He seldom ever does. There is far too much child between this portion of his S and his response. With all the forces operating within him, one of which is he, himself, it is small wonder that our efforts at character education have not been as effective as we would like them to be.

In Search of Dynamic Traits Never Known Before   Now that you have seen the Dynamics Diagram, what can we do with it? It has given us some of our most significant findings, as pointed out in Chapter V. We can find consistencies in behavior which would be completely impossible without it or some frame of reference like it. Every psychologist would probably do it somewhat differently. Let me show you what I mean.

Modern research usually starts with some hypothesis which is to be tested. But where is that hypothesis to be found? Usually some scientist considers a problem on which he wishes to do research. Using the best judgment he can, he sets up a tentative hypothesis. Then he constructs a suitable experimental design and tests its validity. The difficulty is that there are countless hypotheses which could be set up with regard to almost any significant problem in the field of personality. This makes the procedure a very costly one unless the scientist is brilliant enough to hit upon the right one very early in the process. A few great scientists have done just that. Undoubtedly the greatness of such a figure as Freud is due to an innate brilliance most of us do not possess.

In the process to be described here, we are able to discover some consistencies in human nature with preliminary and exploratory research on which fruitful hypotheses can be built. Since the dynamic patterns are determinable on the basis of objective evidence, the scientist need not depend on his own brilliance entirely; he can start with an effort to interpret these identified dynamic patterns. Furthermore, note that none of them could possibly be observed directly by watching behavior even by the most brilliant of minds. Such tools as this one, then, make possible a lever of scientific progress, previously restricted only to the genius.

Our most outstanding use of this Diagram in our CRP research up to now has been in the Home Dynamics Study, to which I have referred several times before.

Using a questionnaire based on this Diagram, a large number of parents tried to estimate the influence of each of the sixty-three factors on his effectiveness in teaching a CRP lesson to one of his children. For example, one of the questions had to do with the child himself. If the parent answering the questionnaire had had good relations with the child during the week in which the lesson was taught, this relationship was likely to be a positive factor in the parent's success in teaching the lesson. If the child and he, on the other hand, were at odds with each other all week, this was likely to have been a negative factor in the success of the lesson.

Let us consider the questionnaire the fathers filled out about how they thought these sixty-three factors influenced them in their efforts to teach the CRP lesson to a particular child. In this case, those cases were used in which the lesson had been effective.

The scores for each father on all of the questions were transferred to IBM punch cards. Distributions were computed and all of the intercorrelations were obtained. (This was done on one of the large IBM computers.)

Then any one of the questions would be chosen for analysis. Every other factor in the sixty-three which correlated with it significantly was noted. (A correlation of .16 in this study was found to be high enough that its occurrence by chance was only one in a hundred.) All of these factors were listed in a column. Then the same factors were used as headings for a series of columns, and a matrix of coefficients was constructed, so that by reading from rows to columns it was possible to discover how every one of these factors was related to every other one.

Some of these correlations were likely to be low. Gradually factors with low correlations were eliminated from the matrix until finally there was left a group of factors, every one of which correlated significantly with every other one. This is called a cluster. Two actual clusters from this study are included below.

CLUSTER A

	1	2	3	4	5	6	7
1. The child's activities and interests	—	.49	.40	.34	.28	.28	.25
2. Father's activities and interests	.49	—	.28	.28	.22	.25	.22
3. The school which the child attends	.40	.28	—	.22	.19	.25	.28
4. The cultural influences on the father	.34	.28	.22	—	.31	.19	.25
5. Neighborhood and community influences	.28	.22	.19	.31	—	.28	.22
6. Father's evaluation of the social signifi- cance of the situation	.28	.25	.25	.19	.28	—	.25
7. Father's special aptitudes	.25	.22	.28	.25	.22	.25	—

Note what this cluster tells you. The correlations indicate that these seven factors were tending to operate together. There must be some reason for this. We proceeded on the hypothesis that there was some dynamic force resulting from the interaction of these factors which caused them to behave as they did in this cluster. Now is the time for formulating a hypothesis.

A committee of eight attempted to interpret the cluster. At first each person, working independently, tried to formulate such a hypothesis. Then we compared notes. In many cases all eight came up with substantially the same hypothesis, adding considerable confidence in its validity. You might like to try your own interpretation of this cluster before you read the next paragraph.

Our interpretation of the cluster was that this is a "family projects father." That is, when the community or school initiates a project in which families are asked to participate, this father can be counted on to participate and to inspire his family to do so. No great enthusiasm may be evidenced, but there is a great deal of dependability.

That sounds reasonable, you say, but not startling. But had you thought of this as an important parental trait before? If this interpretation is correct—we shall have to test it in actual experience—then we have objective evidence that such a trait, on the one hand, actually exists consistently enough to result in such a cluster; and, on the other, is influential enough to be found associated with effective experiences and not with ineffective ones.

Let us try one more of these clusters. We obtained more than 250 of them from the four questionnaires used in the Home Dynamics Study.

CLUSTER B

	1	2	3	4	5
1. Harmony with wife	—	.25	.31	.40	.37
2. CRP lesson	.25	—	.37	.28	.22
3. Effect of wife on his efforts	.31	.37	—	.22	.22
4. Harmony between children and parents	.40	.28	.22	—	.22
5. Special aptitudes of father	.37	.22	.22	.22	—

We interpreted this cluster as referring to the father who has special talents which result in creating harmony with his wife and children. He is very much interested in the CRP lessons and has skills which can be used in teaching them in the home. Again we have a hypothesis which can be tested in experience.

Here, then, is the Dynamics Diagram and an illustration of how it can be used to discover consistencies in human nature which could not possibly be ascertained by any other method. We propose to apply it to many problems. In a later chapter I shall show you the necessary statistical tools and how to use them. You will need someone with statistical competence to guide you, but with such consultation this procedure is within the reach of every character-education agency existing today.

SOME IMPORTANT CONCEPTS DESCRIBED IN THIS CHAPTER

A dynamic is any force within the personality which accounts, in part, for the intensity and direction of his actions, thoughts, and feelings. Some dynamics, such as the drives, are inherent parts of the personality. Others arise as dynamic interrelationships among various aspects of the individual and his environment.

It is the individual who decides to do something and does it. The environment may help or hinder him, but his decisions and purposes are his own. As far as the environment is concerned, he is in part at least the captain of his soul, the master of his destiny. I can think of no physical analogy, for only human beings have this kind of purpose. Here, then, is dynamic in which the environment is pretty much determined by and interpreted by the individual and in which the environment is the servant of the personality, rather than the person being the slave of the environment.

Most character traits, if not all, are interaction dynamics. To talk about them independently of persons is an abstraction. To try to teach them apart from the experience of individuals is futile.

If we are to study interaction dynamics experimentally, we must have a suitable frame of reference, consisting of aspects of the personality and his environment among which to discover such dynamics. The validity of such a frame of reference is determined by how well it can be used by those who must participate in the research and how fruitful are the results of the research in terms of important findings.

The situation (S) in which the individual adjusts may be in part imposed upon him. In far greater part, however, he chooses his own S, and decides what it means to him.

Any kind of educational methods are parts of the S of those whom we are trying to teach. They are the variables which we can manipulate. Their effectiveness, however, lies in how effectively they get themselves chosen by the learner, and how fully he assigns meaning to them which corresponds to the meaning intended by the teacher.

Much of the basic dynamic of personality is a part of the innate nature of the individual (Oi). His native endowment in terms of aptitudes and physical constitution, his basic needs and drives are in this factor. Probably, there is great potential power far beyond the limits of the basic needs on which the individual can call.

As far as the nature of the self is concerned, no one will question that much of it grows out of experience by such a process as the interiorization of social experience. There are some, among whom is the author, who believe that there is in human nature a basic self, to which religionists refer as the soul, which is more basic than experience itself, and which is the chief determiner of the individual's destiny.

Understanding human nature, therefore, consists first and foremost in knowing and predicting what the PS is to be. Most social and educational success potential lies in this fact.

Our behavior (R) is a function largely of how we perceive our environment (PS), what reaction patterns we have available to deal with it (Oi and Om_{skills}), and what energy resources (Oi) we can use in this reaction.

CHAPTER VII

DIMENSIONS OF PERSONALITY—EVERY INDIVIDUAL IS UNIQUE

ONE OF the reasons that religion has been so superficial in many men's lives is that we have held so many of its basic elements as faith to which we give only lip service, and have other sources of faith to which we really dedicate our happiness. We pray, and believe that we are sincere, "Thy will be done." In practice, however, we think in terms of the prestige values of the task, how important it seems to be, how interesting it is, and especially how it compares with the tasks the other fellow has. In most of us, such values vastly outweigh any feeling we may have of God's will for us.

"What about this man?" It was Simon Peter, burning with jealousy of John, who asked that of Jesus. Jesus' answer could contribute enormously to the happiness of most of us if we could obey it. "What is that to you? Follow me!" However, saying that is not as simple as it sounds. Knowing what is the will of God for us is a difficult thing to find out. Our next dimensional frame of reference is an effort to provide a tool to make that possible. It is our Personality Profile.[1]

HAPPINESS AND AN ACCURATE SELF IMAGE

Each of us has a picture of himself. Unless he has had some pretty thorough psychological tests, it is not likely to be a very accurate

[1] On the following two pages is an illustration of the *Personality Profile* we use in the Union College Psychometrics Laboratory.

PERSONALITY PROFILE

Name _____

Date of Birth _____ Month ____ Day ____ Year

Age in Years _____ On Last Birthday

Age in Months _____

No. _____

Sex _____

Date of Test _____ Month ____ Day ____ Year

Number of Times Tested _____

School Grade _____

Department _____

I—PHYSICAL DEVELOPMENT

Scale	PHYSICAL GROWTH (1)	(2)	(3)	BODILY CO-ORDINATION (4)	(5)	(6)	APPETITES (7)	(8)	(9)	SENSORY EFFICIENCY (10)	(11)	(12)	(13)
100–93	Very tall for age	Very high vital capacity or stamina	Very much over weight	Excellent physical coördination	Very much right handed	Can work rapidly under pressure	Unusually strong healthy physical appetite	Unusually high visual acuity	Visualizes things very vividly	Excellent auditory acuity	Auditizes things very clearly	Not at all sensitive to pain	Very high degree of social perception
84–70	Above average in height	Good vital capacity	Above average in weight	Good physical coördination	Right handed	Can work fairly rapidly	Good normal physical appetite	Fair visual acuity	Visualizes fairly well	Fair hearing	Auditizes fairly well	Not very sensitive to pain	Above average social perception
30–16	Below average in height	Somewhat deficient in stamina	Below average in weight	Below average in physical coördination	Left handed	Works somewhat deliberately	Tendency for physical appetites to be weak	Deficient in visual acuity	Has difficulty in visualizing	Poor hearing	Has difficulty auditizing things	Sensitive to pain	Below average social perception
7–0	Very short for age	Complete lack of endurance	Very much under weight	Unusual lack of physical coördination	Very much left handed	Works slowly; cannot work under pressure	Very weak physical appetite	Very deficient in visual acuity or blindness	Cannot visualize at all	Very poor hearing or deafness	Cannot auditize at all	Very sensitive to pain	Very poor social perception

Column numbers: 1 2 3 | 4 5 6 | 7 8 9 | 10 11 12 13

II—INTELLECTUAL DEVELOPMENT

Scale	USE OF LANGUAGE (14)	(15)	(16)	(17)	(18)	(19)	(20)	CAPACITY FOR LEARNING (21)	(22)	(23)	(24)	LEARNING ATTITUDES (25)	(26)	(27)	INTELLIGENCE (28)	(29)
100–93	Very high facility in use of language	Unusually good articulation	Very large vocabulary	Very high reading & spelling ability	Advanced in school more than one year	In highest quarter of school grade	Excellent rote memory	Unusual ability for solving practical problems	Unusual range of information	Very high mathematics proficiency	Unusual ability to concentrate	Very keen interest in school work	Very efficient study habits	Very strong healthy curiosity	Very high I.Q. on language tests	Very high I.Q. on performance tests
84–70	Language ability satisfactory	Good articulation	Good vocabulary	Above average in reading and spelling	Advanced in school one year	In second quarter of school grade	Good rote memory	Solves practical problems satisfactorily	Good range of information	Mathematics ability satisfactory	Concentrates rather well	Well adjusted to school work	Satisfactory study habits	Curiosity above average	Above av. I.Q. on language tests	Above aver. I.Q. on performance tests
30–16	Not very good language ability	Some lack of distinctness of speech	Vocabulary below average	Has difficulty in reading & spelling	Retarded in school one year	In third quarter of school grade	Rote memory below average	Has difficulty with practical problems	Limited range of information	Has some difficulty with mathematics	Has difficulty in concentrating on work	Rather indifferent or antagonistic to school	Inefficient study habits	Curiosity below average	Below av. I.Q. on language tests	Below aver. I.Q. on performance tests
7–0	Very poor language ability	Very poor ability to speak distinctly	Very deficient vocabulary	Marked deficiency in reading & spelling	Retarded in school more than one year	In lowest quarter of school grade	Very poor rote memory	Has great difficulty with practical problems	Very poor range of information	Has great difficulty with mathematics	Very distractible, almost impossible to concentrate	Very badly adjusted to school work	Very bad study habits	Almost complete lack of curiosity	Very low I.Q. on language tests	Very low I.Q. on performance tests

Column numbers: 14 15 16 17 18 19 20 | 21 22 23 24 | 25 26 27 | 28 29

III—SPECIAL APTITUDES

IMAGINATION

Good constructive imagination	Very strong imagination
Somewhat unrealistic imagination	Above average imagination
Excessive day dreaming	Poor imagination
Strong tendency to abnormal fantasy	Little or no imagination

(scale: 100 – 93 – 84 – 70 – 50 – 30 – 16 – 7 – 0)

Columns: 30 | 31

ARTISTIC ABILITY

Unusual ability for perception of forms	Unusual ability for discrimination of colors	Unusually high drawing ability	Very high capacity for appreciation of art
Good form perception	Good color perception	Good drawing ability	Above average capacity for appreciation of art
Below average in form perception	Color weakness	Below average in drawing ability	Not very much aptitude for art appreciation
Very poor in form perception	Marked color blindness	Very poor drawing ability	Very little or no aptitude for art appreciation

Columns: 32 | 33 | 34 | 35

MUSICAL ABILITY

Very keen tonal discrimination	Excellent tonal memory	Very fine sense of rhythm	Unusual musical performance
Good tonal discrimination	Good tonal memory	Good sense of rhythm	Above average musical performance
Little tonal discrimination	Tonal memory below average	Inefficient sense of rhythm	Below average success with musical performance
Very little tonal discrimination	Very poor tonal memory	Very bad sense of rhythm	Very little success with musical performance

Columns: 36 | 37 | 38 | 39

MECHANICAL ABILITY

Unusually high mechanical imagination	Unusually high mechanical information	Very high degree of manual dexterity	Unusually high mechanical analysis
Good mechanical imagination	Good mechanical information	Above average manual dexterity	Good mechanical analysis
Below average in mechanical imagination	Below average in mechanical information	Below average manual dexterity	Below average in mechanical analysis
Very little mechanical imagination	Very little mechanical information	Very poor manual dexterity	Very little mechanical analysis

(scale: 100 – 93 – 84 – 70 – 50 – 30 – 16 – 7 – 0)

Columns: 40 | 41 | 42 | 43

IV—CHARACTER AND PERSONALITY TRAITS

EMOTIONAL MATURITY

Very great initiative	Very mature for age	Very great emotional drive	Very high degree of self-confidence in work	Unusually even tempered & good natured	Has wide variety of hobbies & play interests	Very dependable	Very purposeful & efficient
Above average initiative	Above average in maturity	Above average in emotional drive	Not often afraid faces danger with courage	Does not lose temper often	Has several hobbies & play interests	Reasonably dependable	In general works toward some purpose
Lacking in initiative	Below average in maturity	Below average in emotional drive	Has several fears & tries to avoid difficult situations	Loses temper rather frequently	Rather few hobbies & play interests	Not very dependable	No very definite purpose in activity
Almost no initiative	Very immature for age level	Very emotional	Unusually fearful/lack of self-confidence	Constantly losing temper, very irritable	Almost no hobbies & play interests	Not at all dependable	Lack of purpose & inefficient

Columns: 44 | 45 | 46 | 47 | 48 | 49 | 50 | 51

SOCIAL ADJUSTMENT

Very marked social skills	With peers
	With other age levels
	With opposite sex
	With same sex
Very marked lack of social skills	

Columns: a 52 b | a 53 b

Very high degree of social aptitude	Wholesome coöperation with authority	Can profit by all criticism	Very marked capacity for leadership	Very high degree of social self-confidence	Highly developed philosophy of life for age
Above average in social aptitude	Can coöperate with best authority	Can profit by some criticism	Occasionally acts as a leader	Above average in social self-confidence	Rational outlook on life
Below average in social aptitude	Cannot coöperate with strict authority	Somewhat sensitive to criticism	Seldom acts as a leader	Below average in social self-confidence	Somewhat irrational attitude toward life
Total lack of social aptitude	Very negativistic or submissive	Very sensitive to all criticism	Never acts as a leader	Total lack of social self-confidence	Total lack of philosophy of life

(scale: 100 – 93 – 84 – 70 – 50 – 30 – 16 – 7 – 0)

Columns: 54 | 55 | 56 | 57 | 58 | 59

one. He may see himself as more or less well endowed than he actually is. Furthermore he has some strong value attitudes about how this picture looks to him. He may see it as high or low, good or bad.

Our evaluation of ourselves in this regard may very often be determined by how we see the endowments of others. We are especially likely to see those areas in which others seem to surpass us in ability. Our value attitudes toward them may be envy and jealousy, or happiness in their abilities and a spirit of helpfulness toward them.

We also live in some environment. To be sure we have a great deal to do with determining what it is. But some aspects of it we are helpless to do anything about. We may see this environment as filled with opportunity for achievement. We may see it as characterized by frustration keeping us from achieving our best. There are, of course, obstacles in every environment. We can see these as frustrations or as challenges.

We also see the environments of others, as Peter did that of John. We can envy them as Peter did, or we can rejoice in them and turn to doing the task assigned to us.

Now, note some of the religious concepts involved in the Christian philosophy of life. They will be discussed more fully in the next two chapters. One of them we call our *Child of God* concept. It is the faith that because each of us is unique, each of us has a unique and important task to perform. If we fully believe that, jealousy of the endowments of others would never occur.

The other is faith in a Father God. If God is good, we shall never find ourselves in an environment which does not provide challenge for the best we have to give. If we really believe this, we shall not envy the jobs assigned to others nor see frustration in our own, for we shall find full challenge in the one we have. Its very obstacles usually represent opportunities.

Such religious faith as this, however, is not made real by emotional decisions alone. If we are to find out what is that unique task for us, we must know ourselves. What are our assets and liabilities? In the Personality Profile we have endeavored over a period of many years, and through thousands of tests, to find a practical set of dimensions by which to make such an evaluation.

Yes, the kingdom of heaven is within us. Whether we find happiness in our world is far more a function of ourselves than of our environment. But to make such a concept real, we must know ourselves. That is why we have found it necessary to develop such a frame of reference as that represented in our Personality Profile.

A teen-age girl is speaking to the counselor in a vocational-guidance interview: "I can't do anything important in the world. I am not bright or attractive. Let's just find some job where I can make a living if I ever have to."

In this statement Mary Ann is expressing the belief of many people that an important task in the world depends on native endowment. As was stated earlier in this volume, it is a basic concept of CRP that everyone is put here to do something of importance, and has the necessary endowment with which to do it. Let's put this in terms more comfortable for the psychologist who shies away from a theological frame of reference. The social order of the universe is so constituted that no matter what one's native endowment is, he can do something of great value in the world.

Our second CRP trait frame of reference, and our oldest one, is our Personality Profile. It is designed as a tool with which to help the growing youth get as accurate a picture as possible of his native endowment. Native endowment does not set definite limits on the level of one's achievement. It does have a great deal to say about the nature of that achievement.

A book could be and is being written about this second trait frame of reference, the Personality Profile. It was described in some detail in *Their Future Is Now* (73: Ch. III). There is also a chapter dealing with the Personal Equation in *A Greater Generation* (82: Ch. IV). We also publish a small pamphlet for use in our Psychometrics Laboratory, which describes the most recent revision of the Profile (118).

In this chapter, therefore, I shall discuss only its significance in the problem of dimensions. It has played a very important role in the history of the Project, and has been the basis for most of our systematic studies concerning the nature of individual differences.

Character Is an Individual Matter It is much easier for one with high native endowment and with an abundance of this world's blessings to believe in the friendliness of the universe and the fatherhood of God than for one whose endowments are mostly inferior to those of his fellows, and whose material advantages are few and far between. Our years of research have resulted in a steadily increasing conviction concerning the importance of this principle.

Literally thousands of tests have been developed in psychology. They are designed to measure hundreds of personality characteristics. From among all these, how can one know which ones to include in a measurement program? You will recall that on the chart in Chapter V, six requirements were indicated as governing our choice of traits for the Personality Profile. They had to be consistent with the nature of human nature. They were not retained unless experience proved them to be of value in personal-social adjustments. They had to be acceptable to psychologists and educators. At the same time they had to be meaningful to parents and youth. Of course, they had to be quantifiable to be useful in either guidance or research. They needed to be such that many observable indicators could be found for measuring their strength.

In actual practice, the Profile has been used most extensively as a tool in our testing program at Union College. The program was originally designed to discover and measure the individual differences of the children in our CRP program of character education. Children in our first participating church were tested every two years, and the test results made available to parents and teachers for their use in adapting the character-education program to the individual children involved.

As the CRP program expanded to other parts of the country, such individual testing became impossible, and alternate tools for discovering and evaluating individual differences were developed. At the present time the testing program is devoted mainly to vocational guidance, based on the concept of an individual's unique and significant contribution to the world. Since 1948 we have tested from two to three hundred individuals a year, mostly high-school youth from our participating groups all over the country.

Personality is more than—yes, something far different than—the sum of its parts. You can't predict what picture a child will draw from the paper, crayons, and even a knowledge of his drawing ability. Neither can you predict the quality of his behavior from knowing his height, weight, IQ, and mechanical aptitude.

How Many Ways Do People Differ from One Another? The sixty-one variables on our Profile range from traits like height and weight, which are pretty much in the basic nature of the individual, to social aptitude and leadership, which are convenient frames of reference with which to describe how some of his constitutional characteristics make possible certain types of performance commonly needed in our culture. For example, leadership is not an absolute quantity but a relative one, best described by answering the question, "Whom can he lead to do what?"

Going back to the Dynamics Diagram, it will be recalled that some of the factors in it are relatively more stable than others. For example, most of the aspects of Oi come in that category. Though all of our inherited traits are in a constant state of maturation, nevertheless they can be regarded as fairly stable. Furthermore, when we describe these inherited traits in terms of the individual's rank in a group (percentile scores), they are still more constant. For example, a growing child is changing in height all of the years of his growth. The fact is, however, that if he is taller than the average of his fellows in early years, he is fairly likely still to be taller than they when he reaches adolescence.

The skills group, too, while not as stable as the Oi group, must be included in such a profile. As the child adjusts to his environment he acquires many such skills: motor skills, intellectual skills, social skills, emotional skills. These have some stability, and therefore, in describing his personality, appropriate dimensions for stating them quantitatively are placed on our Personality Profile.

While these two categories include a large majority of our Personality Profile traits, there are a few fairly stable attitude groups which need to be described. For example, the child forms some pretty well defined reaction patterns which grow in part as a result of his temperamental endowment as he selects and evaluates his environment. Thus he may tend to be aggressive or submissive, introverted or extroverted. Another attitude group on the Profile includes those of a fairly permanent nature which are related to the educative process: study habits, interest in school, curiosity, and ability to concentrate. Anger habits, self-confidence and social confidence, purposiveness, and adjustment to authority are still other attitude-based traits included. The Profile, then, among its sixty-one traits, must also have variables for describing these aspects of the personality.

It may occur to you that some, if not all, of the self factors should be included on the Profile. Some of them are included indirectly.

The last trait, "philosophy of life," probably has the self as its chief constituent. In future revisions of the Profile we may very well add one or more self traits. At present, however, we can characterize the Profile as containing those aspects of personality with which the self has to work. One method of measuring the self, then, will be to see how the individual uses the sources of power described on his Profile in his life adjustments.

Finally, I want to point out one more characteristic of the Personality Profile. You will note that all of its traits are meaningful to the layman. If you go through the psychological literature and examine proposed psychographs, you will find many traits not included here.

It may also occur to you that a great many other traits could have been included. This is, of course, true. But here is another principle of trait construction. We have chosen only those traits which have frequently been found to be important in the kinds of guidance adjustment with which our research is concerned.

Testing to Determine Man's Strengths, Not His Weaknesses A very important determiner of the make-up of the Profile has been our emphasis on positive rather than on negative guidance. Our approach has regularly been challenge rather than therapy.

I believe that the level of native endowment is far less important than the nature of character traits as a predictor of the power of a personality. I do believe that a positive approach of challenge is probably "more socially useful" than the negative task of the clinical psychologist. I consider it unfortunate that the psychology taught in many theological seminaries is more concerned with psychotherapy than with positive guidance. I believe it is as much or more the task of the minister to challenge the youth of the church as to give comfort to the sick soul. Jesus himself spent far more of his energy training a group of young men for the ministry than he did healing the sick.

When we first started our psychometrics program at Union College, many parents refused at first, on the grounds: "There is nothing wrong with our children. Why should they go to a psychology laboratory?" It took us a year to change this point of view and give them a vision for positive guidance. The Profile, as well as our whole educational procedure, was not constructed from the clinical point of view. Its whole background is positive.

"As He Thinketh in His Heart, So Is He" I should like to call attention to the last trait on the Profile, *Philosophy of Life*. Here we rate the individual in terms of the answer to this question, "Considering all of his attitudes toward life, himself, his work, and his social environment, how effectively is he living his life?" Fears, angers, suspicions, hates, pessimism, feelings of inferiority, insecurity, and frustration are certainly among the evidences of an unwholesome philosophy of life. Confidence, magnanimity, faith in others, optimism, self-confidence, a sense of security, and the inspiration of challenge—these are the evidences of wholesome personality. When these latter are achieved in the face of handicaps, difficulties, social problems, and adversity, they are the evidences of the highest potential of human nature. This does not mean running from these problems, but transcending them with courage and skill.

This is the trait for which in the next few years we shall probably see the largest expansion. Everyone has a philosophy of life, part of it verbalized, part of it implicit in his behavior; in part consistent, in part inconsistent. The fact remains that his system of values has much to do with his happiness and usefulness.

Consider, for example, one criterion which might be used in evaluating it; namely, his ability to hold on to his idealism in face of the often stark realism of the world around him. Many a youth becomes bitter and disillusioned as he runs into life's increasingly difficult problems. Unless he has a very solid philosophy of life as a framework into which to fit these problems, his adjustments become increasingly difficult. This is where religion comes into the picture with great force. The next two chapters will show how significant a role religion can play in this phase of the youth's development.

Then, too, there is the matter of growth in spiritual potential. Parents are inclined to protect their children from most of life's tragedies and frustrations. Yet it is clear that the child ought to learn to face them as rapidly as he is able. When we have mapped out the growth of spiritual potential from age level to age level, as we are now doing in CRP, we shall be able to guide parents more intelligently in this problem. Much work has been done in psychology on frustration and the individual's reaction to it (28, 122). We need to make careful developmental studies of the capacity of the growing child to face blocks between him and his goals as challenge rather than with frustration-aggression or surrender.

It will be obvious that this trait is one of the most important dynamics in personality. It does not depend upon the native endowment of the child, nor even on the environmental problems he is asked to face, but on how he integrates his endowment assets into dynamic forces with which to meet and solve these problems.

SOME IMPORTANT CONCEPTS DESCRIBED IN THIS CHAPTER

An individual can see himself in terms of how he sees his fellows. He can also see himself as a unique individual, with a unique task to perform, our Child of God concept. Every individual has an environment in which he lives, some of which he chooses for himself, some of which is there in spite of his choosing. He can see the difficulties of this environment as being frustrations, especially if he sees the environment of his fellows as better than his own. He can also see in that environment opportunities which challenge the best he has. This he must believe if he has faith in a Father God.

The personal equation; that is, the profile of one's native endowment and acquired skills, is important to learn as one decides upon his life work. The quality of achievement possible for each individual, however, is largely independent of the nature or amount of this endowment. It is our concept that the universe is so ordered that every individual can achieve something of significant importance in its social order.

In character education, then, the teaching of traits, or, more properly speaking, the learning of traits, must be related to the unique nature of the individual. This in turn means that in any effective education we shall need to know the range of individual differences and the particular make-up of each individual in the group.

A mental testing program has little value in and of itself. It is a tool deriving its value from its integration into the program of which it is a part. The configuration of traits included on such a profile is largely determined by the purposes it is expected to serve in this program.

The role which a trait plays in the individual's life is in some part a function of how the individual measures in that trait, but even more his interpretation (PS) of his measurement in that trait. Believing that there is something tragic about having a low IQ is far more disastrous than having a low IQ.

CHAPTER VIII

DIMENSIONS OF PERSONALITY— RELIGIOUS FAITH AND HUMAN POTENTIAL

The selection or discovery of the particular variables to use in an investigation is a major problem confronting any scientific investigator. . . . The major concern of scientific pursuits seems to be the discovery of new and important variables (17:4).

Because value judgments do play so important a role in scientific thinking, every effort must be made to discover ways and means of making value judgments themselves the subject matter for scientific inquiry (17:8).

THROUGHOUT HISTORY men have been devising value dimensions by which to describe, predict, and control man's behavior. Thousands of trait names have been used. Most of them have proved to have some shortcomings, with the result that they have been discarded—the good in them as well as the bad. The end of the process is not in sight. It certainly will never come as long as we find use for the scientific method in man's search for truth.

Why is "the discovery of new and important variables," especially value dimensions, of such central importance? To the casual observer it may seem little more than an academic game of no practical value. Let us look at some of the potential results of creating new value dimensions. In other words, let's examine some of the dimensions of dimensions. Of what value can they be to us? Here are some of their best possible fruits.

OF WHAT VALUE ARE VALUE DIMENSIONS?

Here is a father who recognizes that his relations with his children are in a state of constant tension. He is doing the best he can and feels bewildered and helpless. In our Home Dynamics Study we have been able to isolate a number of dynamic characteristics of father-home relationships which are favorable or unfavorable to such relationships. He immediately recognizes one of these dimension-characteristics as relevant to his problem. Recognizing this dimension is a big step forward, but he asks, "What can be done about it?" Analysis of the factors whose interrelationships were the source of this dynamic showed that there are twelve of them. Among these were his "emotional interpretations of the children's behavior," "his lack of family interests," "his harsh methods of discipline," even "his concept of himself." Now he sees how he can tackle his problem. He has insights which he could never have got without some appropriate dimensions by which to take stock of the situation.

How to See the Whole Problem in Our Moral Decisions Most of us make many of our judgments with very incomplete data. We see a few seemingly relevant facts and then draw our conclusions, often completely unconscious of vast areas of knowledge whose existence we do not even suspect. For example, here is a chapter from a book on religious education. In it man is described in terms of a single dimension, or at most two of them. In so simple a picture of personality, the author leaves his reader largely unaware of the ever enlarging store of scientific knowledge, indicating that we must describe man in terms of many dimensions. A one-dimensional concept always involves a black-or-white evaluation which results in throwing out much good with the bad. Personality is much more like Ezekiel's vision than like any one-dimensional concept of it.

Or again, here is a book on personality which describes man entirely in terms of his needs and his maladjustments. The book would lead the reader to believe that it has exhausted all of the possibilities. The many religious and moral qualities which have challenged the heroic in man are never touched in it because the author included no dimensions by which to observe them.

I remember my first course in botany. The instructor almost daily pointed out to us aspects of plants which we had never seen before because we had never known the dimensions by which to observe them. Many an ethical theorist has confined his concept of the good life to negative ethics because he had no positive dimensions by which to observe anything else.

From Frustration to High Performance For the man in the street, appropriate dimensions can lead from frustration to high performance. I remember as a child being told, and being deeply intrigued by the thought, that if I just knew what the fourth dimension was I could get out of the most solid steel vault. The fact is, many of our most frustrating experiences would be unnecessary if we knew the right dimensions by which to guide our efforts. Mastering most skills consists first and foremost in knowing the dimensions of those skills. Fast reading is easy, once we learn such dimensions as scope of perception, speed of perception, and continuity of perception. Even mastering a good golf stroke requires the knowledge of its constituent characteristics.

In the pages which follow I shall try to show some of the potential in human personality made possible by religious dimensions, which are not possible without it. The unquestionable fact that Jesus has influenced world history far more than Tiberius Caesar, who was emperor when Jesus was crucified, means that some forces were operating which we ought to be able to make a part of man's striving toward a greater social order. But this will be possible only when we discover and utilize fruitful dimensions by which that power can be described and observed.

From Mediocrity to High Performance Challenging dimensions point the way to many a man from mediocrity to high vision. Not only can new dimensional concepts lead to insights for seemingly insoluble problems; they can make us aware of levels of human achievement of which we were totally unaware before. Most of us are satisfied with a life of respectable mediocrity. Almost every student who enters our colleges each fall has the capacity for distinction. Only a very few ever achieve it. Why? One of the reasons is that they never have dimensions which lift their sights to such achievements.

Here is a high-school girl bemoaning the "drip" with whom she must go to the season's most important dance. In a youth-group discussion she sees a new dimension, one implied in the concept of vicarious sacrifice. She decides to "treat him like a king." The results in this case were that a very discouraged young man got the inspiration to work harder toward a splendid goal which later he actually achieved.

"You can't change human nature." It is true that we cannot change basic human nature, but consider its unusual potential. Consider it in light of some relevant dimensions. What about our potential for learning? Could students learn more than they do? The fact is, probably they could learn ten times as much if they mastered what we now know about study skills. Or consider the dimensions of emotional power. If we could channel the emotional energy we now use in anger and fear into magnanimity and courage, would this contribute toward a greater generation? Or again, consider our social skills. Almost none of us wants to make our associates angry. We would like to be liked and respected by everyone. Suppose that we could master adequate skills of social effectiveness capable of translating this social conflict into co-operative endeavor. Would this produce a greater generation? Finally, consider our spiritual stature. Suppose that men in general actually did attempt to apply the philosophy of Jesus to daily living. Would we have a greater generation?

These are just a few illustrations of dimensional concepts which can and have picked up men's visions and led them on to new levels of human endeavor.

New Vistas of Tolerance　Finally, sufficiently comprehensive dimensions ought to show us new vistas of tolerance. It is one thing to condemn intolerance. It is quite another to change it. Most intolerant people—and that includes all of us at times—are unaware of the fact that we are being intolerant, and we rebel when accused of it. Appropriate dimensions could lead most of us to new levels of wholehearted acceptance and tolerance.

THE CHRISTIAN HYPOTHESIS—DIMENSIONS ROOTED IN RELIGION

Now, let's come to the climax of this chapter—for that matter, the climax of the book. Can a man's religion be measured scientifically? Does it make any great difference in the strength of his personality and character? Psychologists are becoming increasingly agreed that value dimensions are indispensable to any complete study of personality. They are not agreed that some of these dimensions must involve religious faith. Some of them would insist that as they look at their fellow men, they do not see any great difference between those who profess religion and those who do not, in terms of height, depth, breadth, or length of personality and character. As far as they can see, ministers, too, cut each other's throats as do some businessmen who profess no religion. They observe religious leaders sometimes using shady methods to protect vested interests. Religion to many psychologists, then, seems not much more significant in personality than fashions or ethical mottoes hanging on the wall. In making such judgments they are violating the first rule of science, an unbiased sample. It is still inconceivable to me how psychologists have been able almost to ignore a force which has exerted such power in society as has religion.

Down through the ages there have been religious giants who have changed the course of history. Moses, Jesus, Luther—name a trio outside religion who have even approached this one in terms of influence on history.

It is not within the province of this book to deal with the purely theological aspects of this question. Our problem is, when we study the life and teachings of Jesus: Can we discern some dimensions of character and personality, presupposing religious convictions—quite apart from questions of his divinity—which distinguished him from such other men as Tiberius Caesar? And do these religious dimensions account, in part at least, for his greatness? If such dimensions can be formulated, and if they can become the ideals of growing youth, then there is more than wishful thinking to Jesus' prediction, "Greater works than these will he do."

Fortunately, Jesus himself on more than one occasion provided a basis for such a set of dimensions, in the form of his Beatitudes. Then, too, scientific psychology within the last half-century has made enormous strides in providing both methods and systematic data for attacking such a problem. If we examine the history of trait theory, we find that many important lessons have been learned. Such scholars as James, McDougall, Hartshorne, May, G. W. Allport, and R. B. Cattell are only a few of the significant scholars in this progress. Many pitfalls, which made numerous earlier trait concepts sterile, can now be predicted and avoided. Powerful methods and tools are available to us for constructing dimensional concepts of far-reaching value. We ought, therefore, to be able to do a far better job than has been possible in the past.

If you have read the fifth chapter, you will realize that there are many qualifications which are essential to the development of any trait dimensions which utilize what we have learned in the past. In the following presentation of the eight dimensional concepts which we are proposing as a reasonable formulation of the Christian Hypothesis, let us examine each in terms of eight of the most important of the qualifications presented in Chapter V.

The eight dimensional concepts to be described in this and the following chapter are expansions of those presented in earlier writings (67: Chs. II and III; 73: Ch. II; 82: Ch. XII). During the twenty years since the publication of *The Psychology of Christian Personality*, a million dollars, tens of thousands of hours, on the part of parents, teachers, and staff workers, hundreds of thousands of Parents' Reports, and the courageous efforts of many thousands of children and youth have gone into exploring the hypotheses set forth there. The development of child psychology and the psychology of personality has been great during that time. The result is that, while those eight dimensional concepts still seem adequate for describing the Christian personality, the dimensions themselves have grown enormously in their breadth and challenge. I want you especially to note what these twenty years have taught us about the potential of religion in human personality.

Criteria for Choosing Value Dimensions of the Christian Hypothesis These dimensions ought to be Christian and significant. We need to ask then, if one examines the life and teachings of Jesus, are these dimensions reasonably adequate for describing not only the stature of his personality but his own teachings on the subject? Or to put it another way, when all eight dimensions have been applied to the personality of Jesus, will we have made a worth-while beginning toward exploring some of his greatness? Or again, if these dimensions were applied to him and Tiberius Caesar, would we have a better understanding of why the ultimate influence of Jesus on the world was so incomparably greater than that of Tiberius? You see, we could probably compare the two in scores of traits, such as height, weight, intelligence, special aptitudes, education, mental and physical health, without having touched upon any characteristic which would explain the incredible difference between them. If our dimensional picture is to have any value, it ought to show such differences.

Even value dimensions must be psychologically valid. If our children are to be challenged to seek to grow in regard to religious dimensions, the attributes of personality implied in them must be an inherent part of human nature. For example, it would do little good to urge our children to sprout wings, no matter how desirable; for man does not inherit the biological capacity to do so. The fact is that in religion we have often demanded impossible things of men, admonishing them, for example, to repress some of the principal dynamic forces in their natures, or expecting them to show personality qualities completely outside the range of possibility for human nature. Our value dimensions, therefore, must be humanly possible, as well as socially and ethically desirable.

Value dimensional concepts must make full use of achieved scientific progress. The progress of psychology during the last two decades has been especially great in studies of development and personality structure. Our third question, then, can be: Do our religious dimensional concepts take full account and make full use of the findings and insights, especially in these areas, of modern psychological research? Fortunately for the purposes of this chapter, at the White House Conference in 1950 the leaders in this field attempted to describe the growing personality in terms of eight qualities (146). They were set forth out of a full appreciation of this enormous body of scientific endeavor. For purposes of comparison, then, we shall examine each of our eight dimensions in terms of the dimensions formulated at the White House Conference. The purpose of this is not to defend our particular CRP formulation of dimensions, but to demonstrate the important role a religious philosophy of life can play in strength of character.

Significant dimensional value concepts ought to point out new levels of human potential. It is a central thesis of this book that man has levels of potential far beyond what most men have thus far achieved. Furthermore, it is proposed that most men can hope to approach what thus far only a few great men in history have done. Indeed, what useful purpose could be achieved by simply setting forth a set of dimensions which accomplished nothing more than to provide convenient descriptive categories into which men could be pigeonholed, but actually which led them nowhere beyond where they already are?

Useful dimensions must describe qualities of personality which can be learned. No sensible teacher confuses teaching and learning. If he suffers from such a delusion, he needs only to look at his next examination papers to discover the gulf between the two. Our amiable habit of not giving examinations in religious education may, of course, be one place in which ignorance is bliss, for the studies thus far made to test the effectiveness of religious and character education have given us discouraging pictures. We would, however, be doing a far more effective job if we had continually tested our results, and not just assumed that if we expose children to what we think they ought to learn they will learn it. Not the least important reason they do not learn what we ask them to is that we have set up learning goals which cannot be achieved. Our goals must be capable of integration into all the child's other learning experiences, formal or informal, and subject to the teaching abilities of parents, teachers, and other youth leaders on whom the child must depend for guidance.

Is growth in our proposed dimensions attainable throughout the whole normal range of individual differences? Many psychologists would say that the concept of individual differences is the most significant one in psychology. For those who believe in a good God, it is even more significant in religion. It would not seem to be religiously valid, certainly from the Christian point of view, if any of our traits, in the nature of the case, presupposes high intelligence or great art ability or outstanding muscular coordination. People vary too much in the level of their possession of these qualities. In other words, our dimensions must be such that by use of such methods as implied in our CRP adaptation procedure we can make any of them a dynamic part of every kind and variety of personality.

Such dimensions must constitute measurable variables with infinite capacity for growth. If God is infinite, we shall never exhaust any important aspect of his truth. "My child already has this trait," says many a parent about some of our proposed character-education goals. If this is true, then such a goal is of little value for the kind of dimensional concepts which we are seeking. They must be infinite variables. Nevertheless to make our most rapid progress, we must be able to evaluate growth in them with increasing accuracy. They must, therefore, be both measurable and infinite. Our seventh question is, then: Are our dimensions, potentially at least, measurable variables and at the same time infinite?

Such dimensions must reveal the power of religion in personality and character. Finally, then, let's ask a very old question, but the most significant one for this section: What can religion add to the stature of a man's character and personality that he could not achieve without it? Even religious people nowadays sometimes ask: "Shouldn't character education be done in the schools and through the Scouts and other similar organizations? Is it really a part of religious education?" It is a central hypothesis of this book that human potential with religion is far beyond human potential without religion. With respect to each of these eight dimensions, then, let's see what they would mean with and without religion. Fortunately, the White House Conference developmental traits, previously mentioned, can be used as a good basis for exploring this question.

For those of you who use this book as a guide to research design, these eight essentials of a good value-trait theory will be found valid for whatever dimensional concepts you decide to use. There can and probably will be dimensional concepts which go far beyond these I am about to describe. Note that these criteria are not guides for all-or-none acceptance or rejection of proposed dimensions. They are exceedingly useful tools for revising and enlarging such concepts. In CRP we still use eight dimensions. They have, however, grown and changed enormously during the years, and will again in the future. Creating such dimensional concepts represents perhaps the most difficult task in research design. The thirty years of effort which have brought this frame of reference to its present stature are indicative of how difficult it is. Its rewards, however, repay this investment many times over!

CHRISTIAN VISION IS A DIMENSION OF CHRISTIAN CHARACTER

If you have thought that it matters little which dimensions you use by which to measure a man's character, or if you doubt the potential power of religious faith in personality, examine carefully this first dimension: the stature of a man's vision.

Here are two statements by High School seniors dreaming of their future. One says, "I'd like a good soft job, in which I can make lots of money and retire at forty and have a good time." The other, in a youth discussion group, says: "This idea of creative conflict makes me see things I never saw before. What if men really could learn to make their conflicts creative instead of destructive. That could become the basis for eliminating war! . . . I want a job in which I can dedicate my life toward making this idea a powerful force in our nation, and in the world!"

These two High School seniors are the same boy! One depicts him before he first took sight along the outreaches of this dimension. The second describes him after he had begun to measure life in terms of it. Let's take a closer look at this dimension of vision, in terms of our criteria.

Jesus' Concept of Personality Always Involved Vision Is it Christian? Is it significant? Its original inspiration came from Jesus' Beatitude, "Happy are the poor in spirit: for theirs is the kingdom of heaven." A recent commentary makes this statement about the Beatitude: "The word 'poor' covers also all who would learn, who come like children to the great book of life; and who, like Newton, know at last that all their knowledge is but a handful of pebbles on an illimitable shore" (55:280).

With such a dimension as this one it is possible to comprehend a little more fully some of the great reaches in the stature of Jesus. Note, too, how he dealt with most of those with whom he came into contact. "Follow me, and I will make you fishers of men." "Go, sell what you have, and give to the poor." "Arise, take up thy bed, and walk." He not only had vision himself, but one of the ways in which he changed men's lives was to fire their imagination with it. It is possible to interpret the term "poor in spirit" as a sort of intellectual and spiritual inferiority complex. It is possible also to see it as lifting one's eyes to great vistas compared to which his past dreams become small indeed. Our High School boy's idea of a soft job and great wealth looked small when compared to changing the world. It is this latter interpretation on which we have built this dimension.

Man's Unused Imagination Potential and the Concept of Vision Is it psychologically valid? Is there the necessary potential in man's basic endowment? If you will examine human nature, you will find in it at least four clearly inherent characteristics which certainly are suitable for developing such a trait as this one. They are curiosity, imagination, a tendency to hero worship, and a natural sense of right and wrong. A step in developing vision is that of recognizing the inadequacies of one's present dreams and envisioning higher ones.

Does this dimensional concept take account of scientific progress? How does such a discussion fit in with the general nature of our present-day psychological thinking about personality development? The White House Conference report, which came from the combined thinking of most modern scholars in the field, suggests an important stage in the wholesome development of a child which ought to come about around the ages of six to eleven. They referred to it as a "sense of accomplishment." "This is the period in which preoccupation with phantasy subsides and the child wants to be engaged in real tasks that he can carry through to completion. . . . Children need and want real achievement" (146:17, 19). Here is evidence of the psychological validity of such a dimension, for surely a man of vision will gain a sense of accomplishment. Note in particular that phantasy is expected to decrease. Imagination does not decrease. On the contrary, it increases rapidly. But it need not be wasted in phantasy. It can far more effectively be channeled into vision and thence accomplishment.

Lives of Dissatisfaction or of Vision Will it add to man's potential? Let's picture a youth in a series of relevant steps.

a. He has a sense of dissatisfaction about life and his experiences in it. Left on his own he does not even know what is the matter, much less what to do about it. Without any outside suggestions, he usually looks for pleasure and appetite satisfactions as the answer. He finds that they are not very good answers in the long run. He still feels a deep sense of dissatisfaction and futility.

b. Then along comes a teacher who says that he needs a sense of accomplishment. It is interesting, by the way, that none of the White House Conference traits, of which this is one, have to do with pleasure or appetite satisfaction. And yet, left on his own, this is what youth seeks with the greatest enthusiasm. The idea of a sense of accomplishment commends itself to him at once. What youth does not want to improve his basketball prowess, his social skills, or his ability to learn? Here then we have a value dimension which opens new doors of happiness he never suspected before.

c. Let's go a step further. He is told that he is a unique individual (our Child of God concept) and that therefore he has unique potential. I have never seen a youth who was not inspired by this seldom considered truism. Yet, obvious as the idea is, he usually has never seen it before. It has to be pointed out to him.

d. Then he is urged to search for the particular nature of his uniqueness, so that he can discover his own unique potential. This may take him to the psychometric laboratory or, at any rate, to a careful assessment of his assets and liabilities in terms of what can be done with them.

e. Then let's suggest that he look at the world's need and that he tackle some portion of it which challenges him and for which his unique endowment fits him. Again a new door is opened, which he would never have seen on his own, but which he enters with enthusiasm when it is shown to him.

f. Finally, let's urge him to work out careful plans of preparation and progress toward achieving that goal. He must choose a vocation in which it can be done, and plan his further training to fit himself for it. What a far cry from the pleasure-appetite satisfaction theory of happiness with which he began! Note, however, that none of it would have been possible except for this value-dimension concept which we are calling Vision!

Can it be learned? As for man's capacity to learn the things which he must learn if he is to become a man of high vision, consider two major facts. No one will deny that the four inborn capacities previously referred to—curiosity, imagination, tendency to hero worship, and sense of right and wrong—can be expressed either for good or for evil. Curiosity, for example, can become morbid or the motivation for the search for truth. Imagination can become phantasy, destructive gossip, or creative planning. Hero worship can motivate youth to be gangsters or good citizens. Even one's sense of right and wrong can be negative and inhibiting or positive and challenging.

In the second place, many studies in education, including our own CRP experience with the vision concept of vocational guidance, have shown how strong a motivation vision can be in the growing youth. Learning seems to be one native capacity which usually has to be motivated, if it is to be used to even a fraction of its maximum potential. To be sure, there is often pleasure in learning just for the sake of learning, but very few people seek this pleasure without some strong outside encouragement. In our CRP experience, however, it has been a fairly common experience to find children's school marks going up significantly after the unit based on this dimension has been taught. Our best explanation of this is to suppose that vision is one of the strongest motivations for learning.

The question as to the learnability of a dimension is not fully answered until it can be shown that it lends itself to the successive developmental levels in the life of the growing child. We have identified almost fifty such steps relating to this dimension. They have been revised and validated by the study of a great deal of experiential evidence over a period of years. This included many hundreds of parent and teacher records, as well as the findings of developmental research in general. Let me point out a few key developmental facts which relate to this trait.

The child starts in the Nursery by developing a growing enthusiasm for learning about the world in which he lives. In the Kindergarten he begins to absorb inspiration which at this age only his parents can give. In his first school years he begins to learn to use his imagination creatively toward social insight, through dramatization of the lives of others. As he becomes increasingly aware of individual differences in ability, which he does about the third- and fourth-grade level, he can begin to sense the potential in his own endowments, whatever they are, for meeting his ever enlarging responsibilities. At the Junior level (fifth and sixth grades) we can inspire in him the faith that everyone can do something important in the world. At Junior High we need to help him develop the determination to see his future life in terms of the world's needs, on the one hand, and, on the other, in terms of his own abilities. In the early High School years he can sense more fully that he has the power to make a unique and significant contribution to society. And then in the final years of his High School life, he can bring his vision to relative maturity and plan for his further preparation and the vocational choice by which this vision can become a reality. Note that throughout the steps in this process, the religious basis is the undergirding force that gives them strength.

A Youth's Vision Is a Far Better Predictor of His Future Than Is His Native Endowment   When we come to the question of individual differences, the religious factor begins to show itself especially strongly. "Children need and want real achievement . . . despite differences in native capacity . . . one of the school's most serious challenges" (146:19). This from the White House Conference report just quoted. In a culture in which modest endowment is usually regarded as evidence of inferiority, how will you fill this need? If, however, the child is given the faith that everyone can do something important in the world, no matter what his endowment is, that is a different story.

Or, again, consider such an item of faith as this: One of the ways of discovering what God wants us to do is to find out what he made us able to do. Here again we have the foundation for achieving all that is involved in the White House Conference concept of sense of achievement, and at a much higher level. As I think back over the hundreds of vocational guidance interviews I have had, a disproportionate number of the most thrilling ones have been with youth of astonishingly modest endowment. I think this is because they are suddenly confronted with a challenge for levels of achievement they had previously believed were reserved for a favored few.

Is it a measurable variable? Does it have the characteristics of being a good variable by which to measure? Try this experiment, not only with this dimension but with the others as well. There is a technique for preparing rating-scale points, known as the man-to-man rating scale (134). Applied here, you would proceed as follows. Think of the person you know whose personality is most completely described by saying that he is a man of vision. Then think of someone who seems to you to have no vision at all; then of a third in between the two. If you wish, divide each of these steps and thus make a five-point scale. Then rate a number of people you know on this scale. That is, think where they belong among your five "scale point" personalities. You will be surprised how accurately you can do this. In fact, if two or three other people prepare a similar scale, each using his own "man-to-man" points, you will find that all of you rate your common acquaintances remarkably alike.

Does Religion Contribute Something Unique to a Man's Vision? It would be absurd to suggest that a desire for achievement is the product only of religious motivations. The fact is that by nature most men crave a sense of achievement. And history shows that some of them have high ambition and make great contributions to society. But how many do this? Probably not one in a thousand.

Most people settle for very minor achievements or even vicariously for the achievements of others.

For one thing, most folks think of high achievement as being limited to those who have high native endowment. It is common to consider low IQ as evidence of inferiority. This, of course, is not a book on theology, but suppose that our growing youth all accepted the following tenets as a part of their religious faith. Suppose that they believed that the universe is so ordered by a good God that every individual can find a divinely inspired and worth-while destiny. No matter what a man's endowment, he can make an important contribution.

Let some of our youth gain their sense of vision and achievement from our normal social culture, seeking only the values which characterize so large a proportion of our modern society. Where do you think they will end in choice of vocations, and in social influence; in short, in making the world different because they have lived in it? Let us inspire others with the kind of religious faith which I have just set forth. How do you think they will choose their vocations? What will they strive to do in the world; and what impact will their lives make on our social order?

So whether one be concerned with the healthy personality, or with seeing it achieve its maximum potential; or even with the health of the social order in which we live with such uneasy apprehension, I offer religious faith as a power indispensable to the future. Compare, then, the best that can be hoped for in a philosophy without religion, as exemplified perhaps in the White House Conference report, with the increased possibilities when these forces in religious faith can be added.

DOMINATING PURPOSE IN THE SERVICE OF MANKIND

Make a list of half a dozen people you know who would rate high on the dimension of vision. The chances are that some of them have vision, all right, but accomplish little. This means that we are going to need another dimension, related to this one, to be sure, but accounting for this difference among people of vision. A concept to which we refer as dominating purpose is the one we propose. Don't confuse it with good intentions. That is the reason we use the word "dominating." We are talking about the kind of purpose which dominates one's actions. You can measure it by observing how much of what a person does, on the one hand, consists of rather aimless behavior, as contrasted, on the other hand, with how much of it goes into achieving some definite objective. It takes both dimensions—vision and dominating purpose—to describe adequately the forcefulness of a man's behavior. One can have vision and be a visionary, accomplishing little. By the same token he can exhibit much ado about very little, or even about too many very big things, bustling about in a hundred directions, getting nowhere very rapidly. It is the man who gains a high vision of what he wants to achieve and bends all his efforts to that end who can be rated high on both these dimensions.

Christian Leaders of All Ages Have Had Dominating Purpose, Usually in the Service of Mankind   Is this dimension Christian and significant? The inspiration for it came from the teachings of Jesus in the Beatitude, "Happy are the pure in heart, for they shall see God."

Let me quote again from *The Interpreter's Bible* as to the meaning of this Beatitude:

"Heart" in the Bible usually means the whole personality. . . . The word "pure" occurs twenty-eight times in the N[ew] T[estament]. . . . Two meanings are perhaps dominant—rightness of mind and singleness of motive. . . . As for singleness of motive, that meaning is more central (55:285).

It is clear, then, that our statement of the dimension is in the spirit of this Beatitude. The fact is, if one goes through the teachings of Jesus he will see that an astonishingly high percentage of them have to do with purpose and action: "Be doers of the word." "He who does the will of my Father." "As you did it to one of the least of these." It would be difficult, if not impossible, to conceive a set of dimensions by which to describe the Christian philosophy of life without a purpose dimension standing high in the list. And yet, it is at this point that the Church has frequently failed most. Being a Christian has too often been defined in terms of what one does not do rather than as being doers. Growing youth have often found far more challenge in antisocial behavior than in what the Church has held forth to them. Yet in Jesus' own dealings with men, he usually began his ministry with them by asking for very difficult, often seemingly impossible, achievements of them.

Scholars Agree That Purpose Plays a Major Role in Strong Personality From the point of view of its relevance to the nature of man, a trait of purposiveness hardly needs to be defended. Purpose is so intimate a part of human behavior that psychology has sometimes been defined as "the study of purposive behavior." The desire for achievement is one of the strongest, if not the strongest, drive in normal human nature. Athletic sports, mountain climbing, hobbies—for that matter, most of the projects we undertake—gain much of their meaning from the opportunity they provide for achievement. Purpose is a common characteristic of men whether that purpose be financial, political, athletic, social, or any of many other things. Dominating purpose in the service of mankind is much rarer, but has been found in enough men to make it clearly within the range of human potential. To be sure, most of us have so many purposes we accomplish very few of them. Singleness of motive is not a common characteristic among us. Nevertheless all our behavior is purposive. This is true of even the seemingly random movements of the newborn infant. Purpose, then, is not only psychologically valid: it is a basic motivation for all behavior.

How does such a trait fit into the thinking of modern psychology? The White House Conference report included a trait described as "a sense of initiative." "The ability that is in the making is that of selecting social goals and persevering in the attempt to reach them" (146:16). Occupational therapy has long been a central method in psychotherapy. Modern education attempts to achieve much of its results by stimulating the child's motivation for achievement. When the Gestalters describe field structure, the integrating factor is the goal, and all other factors are perceived as they facilitate or inhibit progress toward that goal. It would be difficult to find a trait more solidly indicated by all of our research and theory in developmental psychology.

Man's Maximum Potential Cannot Be Described Without Such a Dimension This is an ideal concept with which to demonstrate how important it is to choose such dimensions so that they provide, not only a personality variable by which to measure it, but also an inspiration and guide to youth in achieving his maximum potential. We have a great many descriptive traits in psychology: coordination, energy, intelligence, the special aptitudes, emotional drive, for example. Measuring a youth in terms of each of these traits tells him something about the quantitative limits of his maximum potential, but gives him little direction as to how to achieve it. We do test all these things in our efforts to guide a young person into the job for which he is best fitted. When, however, we can help him find a vocational goal which dominates his every act, then almost automatically he integrates all his endowment into one purpose.

Finding a job in which the youth believes that he can make a significant contribution to society is usually a greater motivation for dominating purpose than just aptitude and interest patterns, even plus financial and prestige rewards. I have seen industrial workers, for example, engaged in very monotonous and routine tasks, become enthusiastic and eager about them once they had got a vision for the results of their work. One of our own staff said, not long ago, "We would be willing to number 50,000 Parents' Reports backwards if we could see the ultimate value of doing so."

Purpose Must Be Developed by the Person, Not Forced upon Him Few will question the value of purposiveness in personality. The problem is: Can a curriculum be so conceived that youth exposed to it will be challenged and able to acquire the attitudes and skills relevant to it?

Growth in this dimension usually comes about as a result of a number of things, some inside the individual, some outside. If we examine the curricular procedures which have proved to be most effective, we find that they vary in nature from direct, rational attacks on the knotty philosophical and even theological problems involved, to so indirect an approach as simply creating a favorable climate in which growth can take place. If you will examine the illustrative steps for growth in this trait listed below, you will see how dangerous it is to limit your teaching techniques to one learning theory.

In the Nursery, for example, we try to create situations in which the child will find constructiveness to be more fun than destructiveness; that it is more satisfying to build blocks up than to kick them down. At the Kindergarten level the child can learn the first stages of perseverance. We achieve this by placing before him increasingly long tasks, requiring persistence to complete.

It is not until the Junior age, however, that he can be challenged to persist in activities he does not enjoy. It is the Junior High who can acquire the determination to carry out his contracts, once he has made them, no matter how difficult this proves to be. During the latter years of High School, he can acquire a very important and seldom recognized attitude skill; namely, recognizing the effectiveness of continual short accomplishments in reaching difficult goals. This is a very important skill most of us never learn. "Give us this day our daily bread." To do big things is the desire of almost everyone. We seldom realize that this end can usually be best achieved by small daily tasks, allowing no exceptions to occur. Then, finally, the Senior High needs to choose his vocation, plan his preparation for it, and set out to achieve it with all his heart and soul. This is a very direct, rational process. In the past our vocational choosing has been unbelievably blind. Choosing fishing instead of the ministry was not the unique experience of Simon Peter. Unfortunately, most of us do not have Peter's good fortune in having someone come along and hold before us the high vision of what we really ought to do. As a matter of fact, it is not improbable that as many men who set out to be fishers of men ought to be fishers of fish as is true in the opposite direction. It is my guess that Jesus would have urged them to do so with the same enthusiasm he used with Peter the other way around.

There Are Individual Differences in the Nature but Not in the Quality of a Man's Sense of Purpose It requires little proving that this dimension of purposiveness obviously takes into account individual differences. Indeed, it would have only superficial meaning except in terms of them. There are many different kinds of jobs and as many different kinds of individuals. The problem here, however, is not only the obvious one of finding a job to fit individual differences, but it is even more important to inspire the individual with the challenge of the job that fits him. Many a person aspires to a vocation for which he is not fitted and feels inferior when he fails in it. Our Child of God concept is our answer to that. If each individual has a divinely inspired destiny, it follows that he has the ability to achieve it. One way to discover what that destiny is, is to discover what our native endowment makes us able to do.

The measurement of purposiveness is not so simply accomplished. At the extremes, to be sure, it is easy to distinguish between the man, on the one hand, who has no purpose at all beyond the exigencies of the moment, most of whose abilities and energies are wasted in useless activities; and, on the other, the man who is pure in heart, who has singleness of purpose, who directs every energy toward that purpose, and whose achievements are limited only by his capacities and opportunities. Between these extremes, the smaller gradations are not so easily described. However, it is obvious that there are such gradations, and that we shall be able to evaluate many stages in man's stature according to this dimension. Possibly the key to a valid scale for measuring youth's growth in this dimension is the degree to which he exhibits singleness of purpose. If his energies are expended on many things, he will rate low. If he achieves a dominating purpose he will test high.

What role has this concept of dominating purpose to play in religion or religion in it? Certainly we see around us many men of purpose who are not conspicuously religious, and also men who profess religion who exhibit no evidence of having any dominating purpose. Is this a trait which is not the special responsibility of religious education? Vocational guidance may not sound like a religious concept.

There are a considerable number of people whose purposes have to do only with the satisfaction of their various felt needs. They satisfy their appetites as well as they can, seek pleasure, and look for a measure of social approval and perhaps a sense of achievement. There is certainly nothing of a distinctively religious character at such a level of purposiveness.

Then, too, there is a considerably higher level, characterized by the White House Conference report concept of a sense of initiative. It is to be taught at the ages of four and five, at which time the child is encouraged to work toward social goals which he can achieve. Youth who reach this level of development may well become community leaders, gain social approval and prestige, perhaps also a sense of high achievement. They may contribute to a better social order and become recognized as the pillars of our society. This level, too, can come about without the power of much religious faith entering in.

Now, let's go on to what I conceive to be the religious faith end of our purpose variable. In the first place, what of people with modest endowment? Levels of achievement, as seen by those who do not have the orientation of faith in God, are usually judged by high IQ, strong personality, and spectacular accomplishments. Those with less endowment think they must surrender to accomplishments of which they are most ashamed. Of one high-school student body, 85 per cent wanted to go into the professions. Less than 10 per cent of them could. What of the other 75 per cent? If, however, one believes in a Father God whose universe includes roles of importance and dignity for everyone, that is a different thing. Then youth can seek his place in the universe by finding what his endowments are, not by envying those whose endowments are larger than his.

Perhaps an even stronger role of religion in a man's purposiveness comes about when he faces persecution. A youth begins to serve men with eagerness and enthusiasm, only to discover that all too often they do not want to be served. Many a religious leader has become embittered as he has discovered that those who fight him most are other religious leaders and the very persons he wants to help. In all history, religious persecution—that is, persecution in the name of religion—has probably been the most violent and the most ruthless. Jesus was not the only prophet who ran into Pharisees. A very deep faith in God is required for a man to "rejoice and be glad" instead of becoming cynical and bitter. Dying for a noble cause is often much easier than living for it, especially when those you serve are your most severe persecutors.

Then, again, if one comes toward the end of his life and senses that his youthful dreams are to become achievements only of a future generation, that he is to live to see almost none of it come about— what then? It requires an even greater religious faith to rejoice in what on the surface looks like a life of futility.

IN SEARCH OF THE RIGHT WHICH IS MIGHT

As a third dimension of the Christian personality we propose love of right and truth. This dimension is one of the easiest to define. It means just what it says, seeking with all one's heart for right and truth. However, it becomes apparent at once that such a love is not inspired in our youth simply by admonition; nor by just any conceptions of right and truth. One does not search vigorously for anything unless he considers it of value and something he does not already possess. Teachers can usually convince their students of their relative ignorance, but this brings about learning only when the students themselves want to learn. When we turn to religion, where all too often goodness has been depicted largely in terms of negative ethics, it is not astonishing that our children are not much challenged to discover simply what it is wrong to do. This is especially true when this often seems to include practically everything they really like to do. One man stated that everything he really wanted to do seemed to be childish, immoral, or fattening. How, then, shall we undergird such a dimension? We can compel children to do some learning and to obey a code of ethics whether they want to or not, but we certainly can't compel them to love either. The answer must consist in a burning faith that there are great universal laws of right and truth which men have sought to learn through all the ages. Perhaps one great "heritage of the ages" is man's faith that the search for ever increasing insights into right and truth will forever grow in scope and magnificence. For generations men of science and other scholars have been driven by a love of truth. Those who have worked in research know that it is a thrill of great proportion to stand before a body of data and see meaning in it which no one has ever seen before.

"Seek and You Will Find" As you will have guessed at once, this dimension was inspired by the Beatitude, "Happy are they who hunger and thirst for righteousness: for they shall be filled." Its meaning is obvious. In speaking of it, *The Interpreter's Bible* includes such statements as: "There are . . . hungers which . . . are . . . fulfilled through further enhancement to eternal life. Such is . . . the hunger for highest truth" (55:284). One does not have to search long among the teachings of Jesus to find abundant reason for the creation of such a dimension: "Not my will, but thine, be done." "Why do you call me good? No one is good but God alone." "You will know the truth, and the truth will make you free." There can surely be no doubt that such a dimension is entirely congruent to the spirit of the teachings of Jesus.

Is Human Nature Really Interested in Knowing the Truth? Is such a trait one which is realistic in terms of human nature? To be sure, no experienced teacher can be persuaded that love of truth is a universal characteristic. Nor will any minister accept the suggestion that love of right is an innate part of human nature. It would be easy indeed to make out a case for the belief that man seeks only to satisfy his own selfish needs, with little concern for right or truth except as they contribute to this end. The fact remains that many do seek truth with all their hearts and minds. Many also are willing to die, a few even to live, for what they conceive to be right. Such a trait, therefore, is not foreign to human nature, even though it may be rare. •

Does such a dimension make use of our best thinking in modern developmental psychology? Again, let us turn to the White House Conference report. One of the developmental stages suggested there is described as the "sense of identity." It is thought to be appropriate for adolescence. A few sentences from that report will indicate its general nature.

The adolescent seeks to clarify who he is and what his role in society is to be. . . . If . . . personality development [in this regard] . . . has been healthy . . . a feeling of self-esteem has accrued . . . the child has come to the conviction that he is moving toward an understandable future. . . . The sense of identity is the individual's only safeguard against the lawlessness of his biological drives and the autocracy of his over-weening conscience (146:19, 21–22).

I think most psychologists will agree that this sense of identity is possible only against a background of some philosophy of the universe. How can he clarify who he is or how can there be an understandable future without such a faith? The important thing here is that when psychologists try to define wholesome personality growth they include a step like this one which presupposes just such a faith. Many a youth finds it difficult indeed to find a moral code which is neither the road to the repressive neuroses of an over-weening conscience nor the psychopathic selfishness of lawless biological drives. Such a concept as this one, then, is not only in tune with modern psychology; it is indispensable to its application to personality development.

The Search for Truth Has Inspired Some Men to Great Heights
Does such a dimension widen the horizon of man's aspirations? Of all the eight traits, probably more people have striven toward the ultimate reaches of this one than for any of the others, once they have dedicated themselves to it. Large numbers of scholars, for example, seem to exemplify it in large measure. And there are others who love right and truth enough to seek it with enthusiasm.

Over against that, however, note some very clear facts, which demonstrate dramatically how far we are from our maximum potential.

In the first place, most of those who have exhibited this trait to a high degree have in general been those also whose intellectual endowment has been near the extremes. On the one hand, the very bright have frequently chosen to become scholars. At the other extreme, the very dull, even the feebleminded, have often been challenged to their best by our great concern for them to achieve their best. In between the two extremes, however, and probably including at least 80 per cent of society, only the rare individual would rate high in such a trait.

Beginning about the Junior High School level and going through the College level, a large proportion of our youth seem to be bent on keeping their intellectual development almost at a minimum. Vacations, holidays, cut classes, easy assignments, snap examinations, and undeserved high marks stand much higher than real learning among the acknowledged blessings for which they are most thankful.

Finally, and perhaps most significant of all, most of us seem to be content to set the limits of our learning on a plateau the height of which is determined by our obvious adjustment problems, such as passing our school courses, reading the newspaper, taking care of our business and social obligations, and such skills as are necessary for our pleasures. Crossword puzzles probably stimulate more diligence for learning vocabulary—much of it useless—than any genuine interest in the great thinking of the ages. If we can inspire in youth a desire for right and truth which goes out beyond man's daily felt needs, we shall certainly have vastly increased his potential.

What about the very pertinent problem of teaching and learning such a trait? It will be clear here that our main task is that of motivation. How can we instill in youth a genuine hungering and thirsting for righteousness of any sort? Advertisers do a highly effective job of making us hunger and thirst for foods, cars, television sets, and toothpaste. Can we do as well for righteousness? As a result of our work in CRP we have become reasonably sure that one of the reasons youth does not do so is that no one has ever convinced him that some of life's greatest satisfactions lie in this area.

Development in this trait is twofold. On the one side, it has to do with truth as such, and, on the other, with concepts of right and wrong. The two are closely interrelated, but I think you will agree that in general children are not easily inspired either to love negative ethics, or to search for truth in which they can see no values. Here are a few of the steps we take in helping the child grow in this trait.

The Kindergartener can come to discover that goodness gets more and better results than does badness in terms of happiness and life's best satisfactions. If he has achieved this first step, in the Primary he can acquire the intellectual insight that goodness is something one does, not something one does not do. At the Secondary level, we try to teach the child that right, in the best sense of that term, consists in part in striving toward our highest potential; and even more important, that it is wrong not to. At the Junior level, we try to expose him to the inspiration of the lives of those men and women of history who have found real enthusiasm in discovering right and truth. It is at this age level, for example, that a Bible course can be presented showing the development of some of the great truths of our religion in language and concepts he can understand. The Junior High can begin to sense the concept of universal law and to discover that there are great spiritual laws as well as natural laws. For example, he can see that it is quite as impossible to build a good social order on fear and anger instead of courage and love, as it is to build a skyscraper in violation of the laws of gravitation. In his early High School years he is challenged to do things which most generations before him would never have attempted. He tries to find a concept of social and personal morality which is realistic as well as idealistic. In the past we have operated largely on the implied assumption that morality could be one or the other, not both.

This search for a philosophy of life is carried to still greater maturity in later adolescence. Not only can he reach for the White House Conference goal, sense of identity, in which he seeks "to clarify who he is and what his role in society is to be"; he also begins to discover how he can help society find new concepts in which that sense of identity is possible for everyone.

Is This Possible for Everyone or Just for the High IQ's? We may well ask whether such a trait as this one is suitable for the whole range of individual differences. Is it perhaps only for the upper levels of intelligence? Here we find our greatest challenge for such a dimension as this one. However, we have much experience to go on. Probably no area of our American educational philosophy has been more fully explored than our training of the feebleminded, the retarded, and the handicapped. We have been much less effective in our efforts to utilize the full resources of the gifted, and to a large extent have been satisfied with "good enough" for the middle ranges. We have far to go in developing curricula which challenge youth to his maximum potential, no matter what the nature of his own personality as it differs from that of his fellows.

Surely no one can question that this is a dimension, nor that it is a dimension with infinite proportions. Youth can give his best thinking and enthusiasm to this task and still find untouched reaches toward which he is beckoned. Intellectual humility is certain to be a natural outcome of learning this dimension. What better way could there be to make youth aware of the greatness of God in his truly infinite wisdom? What we are measuring here is not youth's possession of a knowledge of right and truth, but youth's desire to seek it. We shall then not be so concerned as to how much Bible he knows except as that is an indication of his eagerness for exploring the riches of its truth.

Religion Has Usually Been a Great Motivation for Seeking Truth
I suggest that here is a trait which most psychologists would agree is highly desirable in human character. On the other hand, I submit the following evidence that it can only be achieved in the framework of a religious philosophy of life.

Consider a few excerpts from the White House Conference report. "The adolescent seeks to clarify who he is and what his role in society is to be . . . the conviction that he is moving toward an understandable future" (146:19, 21). Well, who is he? What is his role in society? What future does lie before him which is understandable? Perhaps for a small minority of the more fortunate, reasonably satisfying answers can be had outside religion. But what of the great masses of mankind? The countless millions of poor, hungry, oppressed, diseased peoples of the world? What kinds of answers can they give to these questions, unless they have a religious faith on which to base such answers? Faith ought to be an opiate for neither the fortunate nor the unfortunate. Neither should life be hopeless and meaningless for anyone.

And how shall the youth find in his sense of identity a safeguard against either "the lawlessness of his biological drives" or "an overweening conscience"? One leads to psychopathic personality; the other to the hell of the neuroses. I suggest that the Christian philosophy of life not only provides such a framework of faith but can bring about to the fullest extent the very results which the White House Conference report urges.

Whenever man starts searching for truth he finds it, but along with it an ever increasing sense of its infinity. The more he learns, the more he enlarges the scope of his known ignorance. What more healthy way to gain a genuine humility for his own sins of ignorance and the infinite greatness of God than through such a trait as this one? The sins against which Jesus preached with the greatest vehemence were those of the Pharisees, the self-righteous. Dogmatisms proclaiming final knowledge of an infinite God can never be convincing to one who searches with humility for insights into greater and more creative moral visions.

Few hungers perpetuate themselves as does this one. Once let the growing child catch the vision of the unknown in the unexplored areas of right and truth, he will seek for it with quite as much enthusiasm as for space ships to travel to other planets.

FAITH IN THE FRIENDLINESS OF THE UNIVERSE

Our fourth dimension is probably the most difficult to describe accurately. We call it an indomitable faith that the universe is friendly; namely, the fatherhood of God. Our concern here is not with defending the theological implications of this concept, but with the effects of such a faith in personality and character. Surely no one will question that faith in God can be a powerful force in personality. The tendency among psychologists to ignore such a force in their study of personality is difficult to understand. No matter what their personal concepts of the nature of the universe, the fact remains that faith in God or the lack of such faith has played a major role in the lives of millions of people and, through them, on our social institutions.

For example, here is a young couple who through a tragic accident lose their only son, in whom they have centered most of their dreams and affection. Shining through our sympathy for them was the inspiring experience of seeing the young man, a doctor, change from a good doctor to a great doctor, from a doctor who could cure the body to one who could cure the soul. It was equally moving to see the young mother grow in the breadth of her sympathies and understanding, and correspondingly in her influence in the community. It is clear that their faith in a good God was not confined to verbalizations, but had become a source of great strength in their innermost personalities.

No one questions that there are great forces governing the universe. As to what these forces are and how they operate, there are thousands of ideas. Certainly it is not strange that when men look at an infinite God, they see him in many different ways. When, however, they face the problem of evil—sin, disease, deformities, poverty, injustices, pain, hate, disasters due to storms, drought, cold, and so on—that is when they decide what faith they really hold. Many maintain their faith in a universe which is friendly, a God who behaves as a good father, in spite of these violent forms of evil. It is this kind of faith with which this dimension is concerned.

Actually, the aspect of personality we are trying to describe with this dimension can perhaps better be described by two dimensions, closely related, but yet with some independent characteristics. One of these dimensions is a fear-faith dimension. It varies, at one extreme, from the personality whose life is dominated by fear to the one, at the other, whose fears never gain control of his personality. If he is normal he will often experience fear. But he is its master.

The other dimension is also a faith dimension. At the one extreme it is complete lack of faith in goodness in the universe. It may range from belief in a cold, impersonal, mechanistic universe to one in which the universe is actually evil. At the other extreme is the quality of faith Jesus demonstrated at Gethsemane in God as a father, when, facing crucifixion he said, "Not my will, but thine, be done," with the obvious assurance that that will would be good.

"Fear Not, for I Am with You"   When we turn to the teachings of Jesus for the inspiration of this trait, from among the many relevant things he said, we can select the Beatitude, "Happy are the meek: for they shall inherit the earth."

Because "meekness" is one of the least understood words in the New Testament, let us turn again to *The Interpreter's Bible:*

> The Greek word means good will toward man, and reverent obedience toward God. . . . In a world where our knowledge . . . of the forces of nature may well at any time, because of some absurd and tragic impasse, threaten the very extinction of human life, genuine meekness becomes man's one hope. . . . God made the earth, and his sovereignty is never usurped (55:282–283).

As Jesus described this quality in a man's character, it is surely not an attitude of abject and weak submission, but an indomitable faith that God is good. It has been an inspiration that has put steel into the hearts of most of the heroes of the ages.

Fear Is the Greatest Single Cause of Man's Unhappiness Psychologists are disagreed on many things. On one, however, I think that they will almost all agree; namely, that fear is undesirable in personality from almost any point of view one can look at it. Fear is an important force in most mental disease. It surely underlies much of our most abject unhappiness and misery.

Another fact goes along with this one, however, which some psychologists probably would question. Faith in God has overcome more fear than all of the other forces ever conceived put together. During the last war Einstein pointed out that the churches were the only group in Germany which had consistently resisted the Nazis. Their faith made them able to stand while others were falling prey to fear.

Lest this imply that psychologists have ignored this aspect of personality entirely, let us turn again to the White House Conference report to seek a relevant "stage of development." To be sure, psychologists have spent far more energy studying fear than studying courage. The fact remains that in the White House Conference report the very first developmental stage described is stated as a "sense of trust":

The component of the healthy personality that is the first to develop is the sense of trust. . . . Studies of mentally ill individuals and observations of infants who have been grossly deprived of affection suggest that trust is an early-formed and important element in the healthy personality (146:8–9).

Which Is More Powerful Among Men, Fear or Courage? Does this dimension suggest new levels of human potential? It hardly seems necessary to discuss whether or not such a trait will increase a man's potential if it becomes the quality of his character. One needs only to look at the power of faith in men's lives through history to see that. Most heroes have had an indomitable faith in something which gave them strength for their work. Everyone will think of the faith of those who die for their country, or the faith that has made the religious prophets of all time actually able to rejoice despite their persecutions.

The concept involved in this dimension is difficult to describe simply. Meekness to some suggests a weak submissiveness. A creative faith can hardly be built on such a surrender attitude. It is rather a faith that God is good, and that even in evil, therefore, there must be the secret of good. This implies a determination to search even in evil for the good it can reveal. Just as medical research men look for the secrets of health, in disease as well as in health, so men who stand high in this dimension search for the will of God in evil as well as in good. In practice this means that faced with disaster, injustice, disillusionment, failure, disappointment, hate or tyranny, we certainly will not like them nor ever give up our fight against them. On the other hand, neither will we let them destroy us or even slow down our efforts.

Even scientists have such a faith that the universe is lawful. It is this faith that makes them approach a problem over and over again in spite of repeated failures, never doubting that there is an answer. The great achievements of science during the last century testify to the power of such a faith.

Faith that the universe is friendly as well as lawful is the faith of the Christian. It is as difficult a conviction to hold as one could ask. The forces of sin and evil in the world make it take strength of character indeed to hold such a faith. Yet men have done so, and are they not the ones on whose shoulders most of the advances of civilization have been made?

How shall we go about making it possible for our youth to achieve such a faith? Certain types of physical courage are easy to inspire. Indeed, heroism means physical courage to most men, and it is one of man's best traits. For example, some men do go to pieces in a combat situation. Most of them, however, have the necessary courage to carry out their assignments, and many rise to levels of courage of great proportions.

The more difficult kinds of courage, however, are those which involve years, not moments; indefatigable patience, not bursts of heroism; continued faith in the face of endless discouragement, not courage growing out of obvious strength, and especially ability to face ridicule and misunderstanding, not moments of popular acclaim.

Most of our research in child development seems to indicate that parents play the first and perhaps the critical role in a child's growth. This is what is behind the White House Conference "sense of trust" concept. During the Nursery years the child needs to find a growing confidence in his parents, not only as the basis for this sense of trust, but also to increase his awareness of how they can help him grow. It should not be difficult for the Kindergarten child with this sense of trust as a background to begin to develop a rational confidence in those situations so commonly associated with fear. It seems probable not only that children never inherit shyness, but that they need never to learn it. During his Primary years, he can take another step and come to recognize that it is possible to learn lessons of value from difficult and frightening experiences. Owing to his natural sympathy, which now matures rapidly, he can also sense the fears of his friends and help them grow in a similar way, thus giving and getting strength from them. At the Secondary level, he should begin to be able to comprehend the role faith in a Father God plays in this problem. He can understand, for example, how even things which seem at first glance to be unhappy experiences can be the will of a good father. At the Junior level, physical courage first comes to maturity. Our task in this growth is to see to it that this courage gives him strength to carry out his responsibilities instead of becoming, as it so often does, simply a manifestation of foolish bravado—the "I'm not afraid of anything" variety. At the Junior High level he can add substantially to his concept of faith in a Father God. Now can come the realization that the will of God constitutes the basis for the great spiritual and social laws that govern the universe. In the early High School years, he can gain a sense of security which will persist in the face of great danger or even suffering. It is this quality of security that constitutes another stage in the depth of his faith in a Father God. Finally, as he approaches maturity, we teach him our Child of God concept, and he finds his role in the universe. He gains strength from faith that, as a child of God, he has an important place in the scheme of things.

Courage Can Be the Possession of the Bright and the Dull, the Strong and the Weak In a social structure in which high IQ is "rather to be chosen than great riches" by most parents, how shall we give a "sense of trust" to those who do not have such an environment? In a culture where minority-group status automatically carries with it social limitations and frustrating prejudices, how can a child from such groups acquire a sense of security? I submit that the answer can be found in a faith of this sort. It makes possible a sense of security in light of individual differences, and I doubt if one will find any other approach which can possibly do so.

Can a concept like this one be represented as a dimensional

variable? In practice we have found it necessary to describe it as a sort of double variable, one which relates specifically to fear, the other to faith. The two might be described as follows.

Let us consider the fear dimension first.

1. The lowest scale point relates to the individual who lives a fear-filled life, given to hopeless panic whenever danger arises.

2. The second level is primarily social fear, based on the belief that all men are evil, and that each individual must fend for himself.

3. The midpoint has to do with the man who takes life as it comes. He does not show excessive fear nor certainly much courage.

4. Here is physical courage, the courage of the soldier. He may need the motivation of hate to give him this courage, but at least he does not let fear dominate his personality.

5. At the highest point is the characteristic of the man who moves steadfastly toward his goal, no matter what the cost or danger. He may experience conscious fear, but he transcends it without hesitation, actually using its energy in courageous performance.

The other dimension is the one which deals with faith in God as such.

1. God is regarded as cold, impersonal, natural law, in a universe ruled by survival of the fittest, or even as a cruel, despotic, vengeful God, who demands only fear and trembling.

2. Then there is the true mechanist. He does not believe in personality in the universe; but neither does he doubt its dependability. He is, however, essentially pessimistic.

3. This is the person who can say, "I accept the universe." He may believe in a personal God in a rather abstract fashion, but lives his life without such faith playing much role one way or the other.

4. Here is the person who has faith, as long as things go well, but whose faith will not carry him through a crucifixion. The scientist has faith of this sort, which makes him persist, for example, in the search for the physical laws.

5. Finally, there is the indomitable faith in a Father God, which persists no matter what the turn of events from prosperity to poverty, from blessing to tragedy. This humility, however, is inspired by the faith that out of such tragedy can come blessing, and a greater world order.

These two dimensions are clearly related, each interdependent with the other. Faith can hardly exist in a fear-filled life.

Does Faith in God Give a Man Unusual Courage? Does such a dimension as this one reveal evidence of the power of religion in personality? First, let us look again at the White House Conference trait, "sense of trust." Here is the best that psychology can offer in this regard, without religion. Consider how it alone is to be made a part of the child's development. No one will question the value of affection for the infant, nor the significance of this early stage of development in regard to this sense of trust. It undoubtedly does provide a strong foundation on which to build even the higher levels of religious faith. A sense of insecurity in the early years will result in a fundamental weakness that is difficult indeed to repair in the later years.

Yet, such a sense of trust, even if well developed, is far from giving sufficient strength for meeting such tests of a man's faith as losing a son, destruction of one's life work, or facing the frustrations of being a part of an oppressed minority group. Only a religious faith such as the one we are describing in this dimension can do that. Consider the young doctor and his wife who lost their only son. Will a sense of trust gained from the affection of their parents during their own infancy give them strength to meet this tragedy? On the other hand, people with genuine religious faith in a good God meet just such tragedies every day with just such creative growth in strength of character.

SOME IMPORTANT CONCEPTS DESCRIBED IN THIS CHAPTER

Psychologists are placing increasing emphasis on value dimensions in the description of personality. Such dimensions bring order out of chaos in regard to moral and social problems. They make it possible to see the whole problem at once. They often point the way from frustration in one's personal life to high achievement. They make a genuine tolerance more possible. They can constitute infinite dimensions which lead us ever to higher visions.

The Christian Hypothesis consists of a set of dimensions by which it is possible to describe personality in terms of the Christian philosophy of life. Other dimensional systems could be created for the same purpose. The value of such a system is determined by its results in Christian education and character.

Eight criteria are especially pertinent for the evaluation of such a dimensional frame of reference. They must be Christian and significant. They must be psychologically valid. They must make it possible to take full advantage of scientific progress. They must inspire men to new levels of achievement. They must be capable of being learned. They must be relevant throughout the whole range of individual differences. They must be infinite traits. They must demonstrate the power of a religious philosophy of life.

High achievement is possible for the whole range of individual differences. This level of achievement is determined far more by finding the particular task for which one's native endowments fit him than it is by how large those endowments are.

In this chapter the first four dimensions in our CRP frame of reference for the Christian Hypothesis have been set forth. They are all based on faith, and include: vision, dominating purpose in the service of mankind, love of right and truth, and faith in the friendliness of the universe.

CHAPTER IX

———•—•———

DIMENSIONS OF PERSONALITY—THE
CHRISTIAN CONCEPT OF *AGAPE*
IN PERSONALITY AND SOCIETY

ONE YOUTH group was entertaining another. The home group drew names from a hat, each boy a girl's name from the visiting group; each girl a boy's name. Jim drew Mary S——. Jane drew Tom W——. When the visitors arrived, Mary S—— and Tom W—— proved to be far from being the most attractive members of the visiting group. Jim, classifying his choice as a "drip," quickly left her to shift for herself, while he found more glamorous company. As a result, Mary had a miserable time, went home completely crushed, and cried herself to sleep. But with Jane and Tom, it was a different story. Jane, sensing Tom's shyness, set out to make his visit a mountaintop experience for him, hanging on his every word, and paying those little attentions by which the weaker sex have charmed men from the beginning of time. To Tom it was a great event. He never saw Jane again, but she left a spark in his life which went far toward making him able to overcome his shyness, hold up his head, and reach for bigger goals.

What shall we say of Jim and Jane? Surely they stand poles apart in their levels of genuine Christianity. If we were selecting the extremes of a man-to-man rating scale on social sensitivity and good sportsmanship, we could hardly find a better person for the top of the scale than Jane nor for the bottom of the scale than Jim. What dimensions, then, can we postulate by which to describe the quality of Christian love in a human personality?

FOUR DIMENSIONS BY WHICH TO DESCRIBE *AGAPE*

You will recall that the first four dimensions have one characteristic in common. They all presuppose some basic aspect of faith. They were designed, therefore, to evaluate the role of faith as it is exemplified in personality and character. Their validity depends on their usefulness in education and research.

Our other four dimensions have a second basic factor in common; namely, Christian love. The word "love" is used in so many different ways in the New Testament that it needs to be more precisely defined for our purposes here. This difficulty arises because of the almost forgotten word *agape*, the word for "love" used by Jesus in such sayings as, "Love your enemies." There are several Greek words which we customarily translate as "love." We have English equivalents for "Eros," physical love, as in our word "erotic"; for "philos," love of truth and beauty, as in our word "philosophy"; and for "charis," love of people in need, as in our word "charity." We have, however, no English equivalent of *agape*, probably because we have made so little use of it in our social order. The four dimensions centering around this concept have been set forth on the hypothesis that the central core meaning of this word is closely related to the spirit of parental love. Such parental love is shown at all age levels. It is exhibited in childhood, for example, in love of dolls and pets and, of course, in later life in the love which parents show to their children. It becomes a part of character when its basic spirit becomes an inner motivation for a person's dealings with all his fellows.

The complexity of such behavior is very great. Choosing dimensions by which to describe it was an ambitious task. The four which were finally chosen have, however, served us well.

The first two dimensions are complementary to each other. The first has to do with our sensitiveness to the needs of our fellows. It is the spirit which has brought about our hospitals, medical research foundations, social service, and so on. The second has to do with our belief that man ought to be given full opportunity to develop his maximum potential. It has given rise to our schools, our basic concepts of democracy, and our American dream of "from a log cabin to the White House." Jesus demonstrated the former in his healing ministry. He showed the other in his efforts to inspire a group of young men to the ministry.

THE RANGE OF SYMPATHY, WHERE HUMAN NATURE IS AT ITS BEST

This is our first proposed dimension for describing *agape*. It seems probable that this aspect of the Christian philosophy is the one which has been most fully achieved in our culture. The Parable of the Good Samaritan would hardly happen today. Few would "pass by on the other side." There would be more danger of a traffic jam. Human nature is at its best when we are in need, especially physical need. There is still, however, great unexplored potential in it, so let us examine it carefully.

Jesus Vastly Broadened the Social Values in Sympathy "Happy are they that mourn; for they shall be comforted," is the Beatitude most closely related to this concept.

In the discussion of this Beatitude, *The Interpreter's Bible* includes the following statements. "Blessed are they that voluntarily share their neighbors' pain. . . . They expose themselves to the world's misery. . . . They agonize over slums and become leaders in civic righteousness" (55:281–282).

Of all the eight traits, this one would probably be most universally recognized as Christian in its spirit. At least no one will question that it is completely in accord with the teachings of Jesus.

Sympathy Is an Innate Part of Man's Native Endowment As for the relevance of such a trait for human nature, one needs only observe two obvious characteristics found almost universally in human nature: sympathy and parental love. Sympathy is one of the earliest emotional reactions found in the young child. By the time he reaches school age it is a strong drive, and remains so throughout life.

As for the parental drive, it is found not only in parents but in children of astonishingly early years. In CRP we have used it effectively as a basic motivation in Nursery groups with children as young as eighteen months of age. Even in children of this age, one sees interest in younger children and concern for their problems.

The most comparable trait in the White House Conference report is called a "sense of intimacy." It is described as, "The surer he becomes of himself, the more he seeks intimacy, in the form of friendship, love and inspiration" (146:22).

In passing, let me mention another quotation from this same section, which reads as follows:

American adolescents are likely to get too little support from their parents for their desire to sense intimately the full flavor of the personality of others and to find too little confirmation of this desire in story and song. . . . There is some evidence, however, that a change in conventions and customs in this respect is in the making (146:23).

In our modern search for new concepts of morality, this dimension of personality, especially as viewed in light of this part of the White House Conference report, is highly significant. Consider, for example, the role that sex has played in human affairs. Powerful as it is as a human drive, it has nevertheless been more often associated with immorality than with morality. It has so frequently been expended on man's selfish side, that even in marriage it has probably been more commonly associated with getting than with giving. Its maladjustment has very often indeed been a central factor in marital difficulties. Even its "normal" adjustment has seldom achieved the kind of inspiration for great marriages which by right it ought to do. When, however, sex and all the other forms of social intimacy are built around such a dimension as sensitiveness to the needs of others, then we shall have taken a long step toward a greater and more positive morality.

Note that the concept of a "sense of intimacy" is essentially a selfish one; that is, it is conceived in light of the needs of the person experiencing the intimacy. Our concept, on the other hand, is concerned with the needs of others. There is evidence that when people seek their own happiness, they seldom find it. When they seek the happiness of others, however, they find their own. In Jesus' words, "Whoever would save his life will lose it, and whoever loses his life for my sake will find it."

Man's Natural Sympathy Gains in Power Through Christian Application of It Note that human nature in general demonstrates this quality of being sensitive to the needs of others in astonishing degree, especially when the needs are dramatic. Everyone who has suffered a bereavement, or lost a home by fire, or experienced serious physical injury, can vouch for the overwhelming sense of human kindness, as aid and sympathy come in great abundance. If a great catastrophe should happen today either in Russia or the United States, the other would, by tomorrow, be rushing to its aid with food, clothing, medicine, and whatever else was needed. When needs are great, we see human nature at its best.

It is the less dramatic needs in others that are unnoticed and unsatisfied by most of us. Some of them are felt needs: the need of the less popular for friendship, the need for achievement by those who do not experience it, the need of all of us for feeling needed, the need of all of us for belonging, the need for whatever kind of security we want—these are just a few of our needs for which responsiveness is not always so apparent in our social order. Then there are the unfelt needs: need for full development of our endowment, need for wholesome food, and plenty of sleep during most of childhood, need for opportunity to express one's aptitudes during the growing years, need for mastering self-discipline, need for mastering one's emotional energies, one of our greatest needs— these we hardly notice at all.

Will all this increase human potential? Make a list of the next hundred instances of human unhappiness and misery you observe. Then count the percentage of them which are a result of lack of just this trait in our personalities. People who hurt us seldom do so intentionally. Yet we find an astonishing number of ways to be unhappy, most of them unintentional on the part of those responsible for the unhappiness. Suppose we could teach our children the skills of observing all of men's needs, what would be the result in greater human happiness, both on the part of those who give and those who benefit by this level of sensitiveness to our needs?

Can such a dimension be taught and learned? Perhaps I can answer this best by again describing the steps we have found effective during the developmental stages of the child's growth.

In the Nursery we try to create situations in which it is possible for the child to discover that one can have a good time in the process of helping others. This obvious truism, like many aspects of Christian morality, does not look true to the child until he has tried it. When the innate quality of sympathy first begins to mature, in the Primary years, for example, then the child can discover the values of social vocabulary and social manners, not as arbitrary forms of right and wrong, but as forms of thoughtfulness to others. By the Secondary age level, the child can recognize that he has the capacity to make contributions to some of the most important needs of his social group.

The Junior can learn that fair play, which is very important to him, is as meaningful to the happiness of others as it is to him. He can also be challenged to search for types of social skills for gaining social recognition which are more effective than bullying, shyness, teasing or ridicule. When children of this age use these latter forms of behavior, it is usually because they do not know what else to do.

Junior Highs can learn skills for showing inspiring friendliness to children who are concerned about their modest athletic ability, physical attractiveness, and the like. It is far easier to do the opposite— not from innate cruelty, but from sheer thoughtlessness or lack of such skills.

At Senior I, it is possible to learn, for example, one thing most of us never learn—a dynamic sympathy for those who consider themselves unpopular. Many a wallflower has suffered untold agony; many a boy lacking social confidence has spent years in suffering; when some thoughtful skills on the part of his fellows could have made life many times more worth living for him.

The Range of Sympathy Among Men Goes from Selfish Cruelty to Christian *Agape* It seems hardly necessary to discuss the appropriateness of this dimension throughout the range of individual differences. The problem is a vastly different one for the natural and popular leader than it is for the youth whose native endowment usually places him in follower positions. However, in general, this dimension is a great leveler. It is one trait in which native endowment does not limit one's achievement. Indeed, the modestly endowed man gains more from the trait than the highly endowed. To be sure, those who inherit a keen social sensitivity may find such skills easier to learn and to carry to a high degree of perfection than others. The fact remains that it is within the range of possibility for all who wish to learn it.

Few will argue that it is not a genuine dimension. It is obvious that men demonstrate it over a very wide range. At our present level of knowledge, we cannot be sure that it is a simple variable, however, or that it is linear, or even that its various levels are causally related.

Sensitiveness to the needs of others may be simply a name which we can apply to a number of psychologically unrelated habits.

In Religion, Sympathy Finds Its Most Powerful Role   Most people sense that, in general, love resulting from a religious maturation is better than selfish love. The extent to which this is so, however, is amazing as we look at this dimension of the Christian Hypothesis.

There are three methods of dealing with these needs of ours, and the resultant personal and social effects in our social order.

Perhaps the most common approach is the selfish one. The right of every man to pursuit of happiness is often interpreted as his right to be sensitive first to his own needs and only then to the needs of others. One of the oldest truisms in our philosophy is that happiness is never found that way. Social conflict is an inevitable result. Most of the energy finds its way into a deep sense of frustration and conflict with others, thus not even satisfying the needs themselves.

It is easy to see why this is so. For one thing, the primary needs differ from individual to individual. One feels most the need for security, another the need for status, another for achievement, another for love, another for self-confidence, and still another for satisfaction of his physical appetites. Consider the presence of these needs in any social group. Even a small family is large enough to show that these needs inevitably conflict with one another from person to person. For that matter, they conflict within the person.

But now let's take a look at a second level, that implied in the White House Conference report. "The surer he [the adolescent] becomes of himself, the more he seeks intimacy . . . to sense intimately the full flavor of the personality of others" (146:22–23). This is still a somewhat self-oriented philosophy, but shifts the emphasis to "sensing intimately the full flavor of the personality of others." To be sure, it becomes tangled with our concepts of morality as the report points out. The full flavor of the personality of others is surely deeper than just their physical needs. One could hardly gain this goal without sensing many needs to which most of us are usually not very sensitive: needs for self-respect, for being needed, and for being a real member of his social group, for example.

But now let's bring in the ingredient of religion. For example, when Jesus told the parable of the Good Samaritan, he introduced a new definition of the world "neighbor." It became not merely the people who live in our block, but whoever needs our help, wherever he is. When this ideal began to permeate our society, hospitals, children's and old people's homes, charity organizations, medical research, and the like, sprang into being. In earlier days asylums were the order of the day, places in which to isolate the undesirables, primarily to protect society. But parents recognize no undesirables. So when the spirit of *agape*, parental love, began to be felt, these other things became a natural harvest.

CHALLENGING EVERY MAN TO HIS MAXIMUM POTENTIAL

Our proposed second dimension, by which to explore the Christian concept of *agape* is the extent to which an individual exemplifies a determination to do everything he can to make it possible for every man to get his full chance at happiness and success. Note the relationship between this and the preceding dimension. The first dimension had to do with being sensitive to the needs of men; this dimension goes beyond that. It is over on the positive side of the picture. It is a desire to challenge men to strive toward their maximum potential. This is certainly characteristic of parents. They often do things to and for their children—sometimes even when the children rebel against it—to make as sure as they can that the child shall have every opportunity to reach his best. The fact is, owing to his immaturity, many a youth enthusiastically and determinedly cuts his own throat in this regard during his early years. His elders would be far more merciful to him in the long run if they refused to let him do so.

Jesus Challenged Most of the People He Met to Do Seemingly Impossible Tasks   Let us turn again to the Beatitudes to look for a concept giving us a clue as to whether Jesus' philosophy included a comparable dimension. The most closely related Beatitude is, "Happy are the merciful: for they shall obtain mercy." *The Interpreter's Bible* has this to say about its meaning. "It is no true mercy to restore a man's body and neglect his spirit. . . . What of the morally crippled? . . . What of those diseased by greed? What of the wicked in the world? . . . The practice of mercy . . . *is* practice, not mere feeling or sentiment" (55:284).

When this is put in more positive terms, such a dimension as this one seems to be implied. There is in each of us a sort of divine spark, which, if encouraged, makes us want to live our best, to achieve our maximum potential, and to feel guilty unless we do. It is no true mercy on the part of our parents and teachers, for example, which permits us in ignorance due to immaturity to do those things which are detrimental or leave undone those things which are essential if we are to reach that goal.

The Desire for Achievement Is the Strongest Drive in the Normal Personality In the process of teaching this trait we have made central use of the concept of sportsmanship. Is good sportsmanship normal in personality? Sometimes one wonders. Our high-pressure athletic sports are tending to make winning so important that our youth and their coaches are strongly tempted to put that goal ahead of sportsmanship. That is easy to do, for the joy of winning is as natural as breathing. The athlete who would rather lose than to take unfair advantage of his opponent seems to be becoming increasingly rare. The fact remains that when he does appear he commands our respect and admiration far beyond the winner who wins by "fair means or foul." It has been said often that the American ideal is one in which fair play is central. It clearly must be learned, however. It does not come naturally.

When we turn to the research findings of modern developmental psychology, there is a considerable body of evidence which is relevant to the implementing of this trait. It is based on the growth-stage concept described in the White House Conference report which they call "the parental sense." "The essential element is the desire to nourish and nurture in its essence what has been produced. . . . In order that most people may develop fully the sense of being a parent, the role of parent, both mother and father, must be a respected one in the society. Giving must rank higher than getting, and loving than being loved" (146:24).

Note at once that a motivation provides the central relationship between the White House Conference trait and the one proposed here. Because parents do love their children, this concept of mercy comes naturally and finds expression in their determination to see that their children get their full chance at happiness and success.

Education for Maximum Potential Is a Part of the American Dream "From a log cabin to the White House" is a typically American concept. The Horatio Alger books of a few years ago would have been very unlikely except in America. But is it a realistic dream? Only one person has gone from a log cabin to the White House. A great deal of frustration and unhappiness has come from overambition. Surely there must be a third alternative to overambition, on the one hand, and a dead-level-needs philosophy, on the other. What kind of challenge shall we hold before our children?

Any good coach will agree that the thrill that comes from releasing superb skill in a potential athlete is as great or' greater than having mastered the same skill himself. The clinical psychologist who can replace a patient's frustrating fear and inferiority with courage and self-confidence finds the deepest of satisfactions. The physical therapist who gives back muscular control to those who have lost it through disaster has also tasted this same thrill. The teacher, watching young minds become awakened through his efforts, seeing in them the spark of discovery as they gain successive insights, wonders how any vocation on earth can be as thrilling as teaching. The vocational guidance adviser faces a bewildered and aimless youth across the interview table. With his skilled guidance that same youth finds himself, sees his abilities, plans his mastery of skills, gains a vision of how best to invest his life. There can be no greater satisfaction in life than that.

Note, however, that such a dimension of character must be learned and that it is difficult to learn. In competitive sports it is far easier to rejoice in one's own achievements than in those of our opponents. The inborn love of winning is far stronger by nature than this kind of mercy. Once learned, however, the satisfactions for this are infinitely greater.

As in the case of each of the other dimensions, we in CRP have attempted to find developmental steps which the child can be expected to take as he grows up.

In the Nursery about all that we can expect is that he will discover that he is a part of his social groups but not always the center of them. When he has learned to play happily in social games which are not designed with him playing the central role, he has made as great progress as his teen-age brother who begins to develop high social vision. At the Kindergarten age, however, cooperation begins to become a meaningful experience. He can learn to help others as well as himself. Perhaps this is the first step toward "love your neighbor as yourself." During the first school years he will need to learn to do gladly for the good of the group tasks which he regards as uninteresting. Some people never reach even this stage. They will work only if their jobs are interesting to them. At the Secondary level he gets his first lessons at being a good loser. This is a most difficult thing to learn, and can be built only on the motivation of this trait. At the Junior level, fair play becomes an especially important ideal. This is good, even outside the scope of religion. During the Junior High period, he will probably begin to become aware of the large proportions of the problem of conflict and the prejudices which most of us have toward groups who have other economic, social, intellectual, race, and class characteristics than our own. Finally, as he approaches the end of High School, he should begin to develop a mature social vision, which insists on the infinite value of every individual. This he can probably achieve best by making his understanding of people's values apply to an ever broadening group. Beginning with his family, he extends his vision to include his neighborhood, his community, his state, his nation, and even the world.

Our experiences with these and many other similar goals have led us to believe that such a development is entirely possible. Notice, however, that such growth is not a matter of chance. Furthermore, it does not come about suddenly as an act of will at maturity, nor by nature in the growing child. There are important steps which must be taken at each age level, which probably can never be achieved so fully at any later age level.

The Fact That Individuals Differ Does Not Make Some Inferior to Others Does such a dimension as this take into consideration the fact that there are great individual differences? The answer is obvious. The trait finds its deepest meaning owing to the presence of individual differences. A basic concept in our CRP philosophy, based on faith in a God of love, is that everyone has the capacity to do something important in the world. It is very easy for youth, even of considerable native endowment, to lead lives of minimum achievement and filled with feelings of inferiority, unless someone imbued with this ideal can point the way to releasing his potential in some form or other. Helping each youth to find what that is for him is mercy of a high degree.

Highly reliable and valid scales for measuring in terms of such a dimension do not yet exist. It should be clear, however, that people do vary widely in their possession of this quality of mercy and that, therefore, such scales are quite within the range of possibility for the future.

The Christian Contribution to the American Concept of the Importance of the Individual When we read the White House Conference report, and find such a statement as "giving must rank higher than getting, and loving than being loved," we must admit that here the report reaches its highest stature. The point is, can such an ideal be reached without religious faith? I doubt it. But once we have added the full leaven of the Christian faith, then we begin to see the breath-taking potential of such a concept as this one.

"Whoever would save his life will lose it." This is a basic spiritual principle. Watch the fruitless efforts of the millions who strive so desperately for their own happiness. The harder they try, the less they succeed. This spiritual law seems as inevitable and powerful as the laws of gravitation. Even the White House Conference report admitted this by implication.

Good sportsmanship is one of our American ideals. But take religion out of it and what is it like? Winning becomes more important than fair play. Booing the poor player becomes louder in our grandstands than applause. Without the religious faith involved in this dimension of being determined to see that every man gets his full chance at happiness and success, such progressive deterioration of our American sports is as inevitable as the weather.

This trait is the spirit of democracy and, probably, the spirit without which democracy must eventually fall. Our public-school system has arisen out of faith in the value of everyone. To be sure, one hears people speak as if the value of democracy rested in giving each of us the right to be selfish. This is a shortsighted view, however, for this is the weakness, not the strength, of democracy. In the last analysis the power and even survival of democracy will depend on the degree to which the electorate holds the burning determination to see that our political decisions guarantee for every man his full chance at happiness and success, even when those decisions involve sacrifice of some of our own selfish desires.

A BURIED TREASURE—THE IRRESISTIBLE FORCE OF MAGNANIMITY

Let us add a third dimension, in our efforts to evaluate a man's behavior on the basis of *agape*. We call it *magnanimity*. *Webster's*

New International Dictionary defines this as follows: "Loftiness of spirit enabling one to sustain danger and trouble with tranquillity and firmness, to disdain injustice, meanness, and revenge, and to act and sacrifice for noble objects."

In a vocabulary test given to six hundred children and youth through the high-school age, we found not one who would even attempt to define this word. One explanation of this could be that it is the quality of character which is the most difficult to achieve.

In our Character Research Project frame of reference, this trait may be defined as the determination to make the conflicts among men creative instead of destructive. The ability to rise above injustices and personal grievances is not easily attained. Among its most common exemplifications are: the ability to work with those who are difficult to work with, the ability to take criticism objectively, an objective attitude toward hate and injustice.

The Christian Concept of Peace Is Positive, Not Just the Absence of Conflict   We have related this dimension to the Beatitude about the peacemakers. This term "peacemaker" also is descriptive of very few people. Even when one looks through the list of distinguished men, successful warmakers outnumber successful peacemakers many times over. Loving enemies, preventing social conflicts, transcending bitterness and hate themselves, making conflicts creative instead of destructive—these are achievements possible only for men whose character can be accurately described as magnanimous.

The Interpreter's Bible among other things has this to say about the Beatitude.

What is this work of peace? It is the task of reconciliation between groups and men at odds. . . . Peacemaking is also a preventive task. If poverty embitters the masses of men and thus tends to war, the peacemaker enlists to banish unmerited poverty. If insecurity or maladjustment in toil makes a man fractious in his home, the peacemaker strikes at that root of the problem (55:286).

Probably no one will question the fact that this dimension is clearly Christian. Note that our common-sense definition of peace as the absence of war does not hold here. Peace is something positive. In fact, making conflict creative is not as impossible a task as simply trying to avoid it.

Conflict Is a Part of Human Nature, but Must It Be Destructive? Among the eight concepts describing the mature personality set forth in the White House Conference report, the one most closely related to this dimension is called a "sense of autonomy." Quoting from the report:

What is at stake throughout the struggle of these years [second and third years] is the child's sense of autonomy, the sense that he is an independent human being and yet one who is able to use the help and guidance of others in important matters. This stage of development becomes decisive for the ratio between love and hate, between cooperation and willfulness, for freedom of self-expression and its renunciations, in the make-up of the individual. The favorable outcome is self-control without loss of self-esteem. The unfavorable outcome is . . . doubt . . . and shame. . . . Personal autonomy, independence of the individual, is an especially outstanding feature of the American way of life. American parents, accordingly, are in a particularly favorable position to transmit the sense of autonomy to their children (146:12, 14).

The development of this sense of autonomy during the second and third years is certainly an important step in the child's growth. To suppose that this is the end of the matter, however, is not justified. At best this is one way of preventing an unwholesome personality. It does no more than begin to explore the child's unused potential. Furthermore, it presupposes an ideal social environment for the child. His adjustment to the injustice, tyranny, and selfishness which he will surely find in his real environment, will be helped very little by this sense of autonomy, except as it is a favorable mental attitude on which he can build.

Let us look more closely at this concept of autonomy. To be a mature individual, it is proposed, the child must come to recognize himself as an "independent human being." But how can he give complete obedience to the many inevitable forms of authority to which he must adjust and still be independent at the same time? Granted that he ought to have the kind of freedom which makes it possible for him to maintain the dignity which is the right of every individual, nevertheless in his daily life he will need to practice both self-expression and self-renunciation many times. He ought to be free but at the same time must be wise enough to decide which to practice and when. He will need to learn, as one biologist put it, that to satisfy his deepest desires he will often have to deny his more superficial desires. In other words, he needs to discover that his most ruthless master may come to be himself, unless he can achieve full command of the sources of power in his own personality. To do this he must learn that self-control not only does not imply loss of self-esteem, but is an important part of it. In his real social environment he must distinguish between cooperation, on the one hand, and submissiveness or rebellion, on the other.

Magnanimity, a Force Representing Some of Our Most Unexplored Potential Let us look at the relationship between peacemaking and magnanimity. It does not take much insight to realize that one must have the qualities of magnanimity to become a successful peacemaker. For example, the spirit of anger and revenge are not effective stimuli for peace. Go through history. Name one great peacemaker who had not achieved such peace of mind that he could very literally love his enemies. We may win wars with anger and hate, but in the process we may also lose the peace for which we strive.

If a man grows in terms of this dimension, probably his greatest increase in potential will be in becoming master of his emotions. His parents and teachers will probably not be masters of theirs; at least, few of our generation are. Nor will they fully know how to guide him in this important phase of his growing up. When we look at great men, however, most of them have been able to make positive use of their emotional power. Of those that could not, their greatness was achieved in spite of their emotional weaknesses, not because of them. Temper tantrums are never admirable. It has been said that "the measure of a man is the size of the thing it takes to get his goat." This may not be the whole truth, but it has some validity. The man who expends most of his emotional energy in anger, "standing up for his rights" and "the principle of the thing," is seldom highly admired by his fellows. Nor, on the other hand, are doubt and shame qualities of greatness. Emotional drive can make us able to do the impossible, but not if wasted in behavior which can only be described as being emotional. If, then, in mastering this trait, a man gains control over his emotional energy, he will certainly have improved on our generation.

Magnanimity, at the level of significant social effectiveness, is within reach of a thousand times as many people as show it. Even this is probably an understatement. This means, then, that if we hope to bring this dimension of character within reach of our growing youth, we shall need to find methods of character education more effective toward this end than we have thus far been able to produce.

Man is instinctively a social animal. He obviously does not, however, inherit ready-made the social structure by which he can live with his fellows without friction. Anyone who can help us gain control of our appetites, give us courage to meet our dangers, and teach us magnanimity with which to replace our angers is a real peacemaker. The fact is that a child can as readily learn to be characteristically courageous, magnanimous, and unselfish as to show fear, anger, and greed. But let us see how this is to be brought about.

At the Nursery level, let me point out a trait which is one of several which have to do with the concept of the family team. The Nursery child can learn actually to try to help make the family mealtime happier. This may not seem of world-shaking importance, but it takes great self-denial at times to make this contribution. And if he learns this lesson, he has made a very significant amount of progress. By the Kindergarten age he can extend this desire to wanting to learn the things he must do to make people happy in a variety of social situations. It may sound strange to speak of a child showing magnanimity toward his schoolteachers, but this is precisely what the Primary child must do. The point is, whether an act is unjust or not, as far as the child is concerned, depends on how the child sees it, not how it actually is by some objective standards. If, for example, the child sees the teacher's criticisms as unfair punishment, he will find it much more difficult to engage in the educative process at the level of creative participation which is easier to do if he learns to see this criticism as coaching. During the Secondary years he must learn to broaden this concept to more and more kinds of criticism. If he concentrates on finding whatever values there are in criticism, he will have learned to make creative use of one of the commonest areas in which we waste our emotional energy in useless anger. At the Junior level, when fair play is so important in his philosophy of life, he will often lose many values from the guidance of teachers and other adult leaders whom he does not like for one reason or another, usually because he sees their actions as unfair. If he can transcend this personal dislike and learn all that they can teach him anyway, he will have mastered a level of self-control most of our generation never achieved. Anyone can learn with enthusiasm from a good teacher. It takes the superior youth to learn from a disliked teacher. The Junior High youth finds the idea of "turning the other cheek" a little hard to swallow. He is usually pretty sure that "sock him back" is more realistic. When, however, he discovers that there are skills relevant to this "turning the other cheek" business, which are neither cowardly submission nor bullying aggression, he faces a challenge of high attractiveness. His chief problem is in finding anyone who knows these skills among his adult advisers. The Senior I (ninth and tenth grades) begins to develop his abilities for being a creative member of the groups to which he belongs. What is more important, he can do this even when his own role is low in prestige value and when the group leadership seems to him to be unfair and highly arrogant. Now, we can put these two things, autonomy and magnanimity, together. The youth wants freedom, but must learn that true freedom has to be earned and carries with it proportionate responsibilities. The dignity and importance of the individual is guaranteed only when he accepts his role in society with all its restrictions as well as its privileges.

Men Are Born Free and Equal in Their Potential for Magnanimity Probably among all of the qualities ascribed to men, this one also deserves the role of being a great leveler. Men of outstanding ability achieve very little when they lack the quality of magnanimity. On the other hand, recall all of the Lincoln stories you can remember. How many of them have to do with his native endowment? How many of them, on the other hand, have to do with his magnanimity? I suspect that you will find the latter outnumbering the former several times over. Furthermore, when you think of his greatness, it is the latter which mark him more clearly as a great man. Magnanimity may very well be the most important single characteristic of great leadership.

The physically unattractive girl often becomes beautiful in the eyes of all who know her if she possesses this trait. The reverse happens, too. The beautiful girl becomes unattractive if petty anger is an outstanding quality of her nature.

The name "Magnanimity" is certainly well chosen for the trait. Great-minded indeed is the person who can achieve high levels in it.

Are there people who show more of it than others? Of course

there are. From a socially effective point of view, then, it is a legitimate dimensional variable. At the same time it is obvious that magnanimity is not a psychological entity in personality.

When we consider adjustment to the educative process, this simplicity of trait structure probably ceases. There are many independent attitudes toward education which the individual can exhibit in varying amounts. The same is even more true of "creative membership in society." These are socially desirable variables, which probably relate to psychologically unrelated characteristics of personality.

Future research will tell us more about the complex personality structures which underlie such a concept as magnanimity. We shall, at the same time, learn better how to teach and learn it. The fact remains that it is likely to be a highly complex aspect of character, which will be achieved by growing youth only with wide and varied experience and the wisest of sympathetic guidance.

It Is the Religious Ingredient Which Raises Magnanimity to Its Qualities of Greatness   If one is to show genuine magnanimity, he must have faith in its ultimate value, and this involves religion. For some years we called the curricular unit involving this dimension the "Adjustment to Authority Unit." No man can be a law unto himself. Neither he nor the social order of which he is a part finds happiness when he attempts to be. To what law or authority, then, shall he adjust? To be sure, in his daily life he finds rules at home, on the playground, at school, and in the community, to which he is strongly urged to conform. However, just as anarchy leads to social disaster, so does weak submissiveness result in social sterility. What then shall he do? Here, again, is where religion comes into the picture. If his faith leads him to accept the will of God as his authority, then in his growth he searches to discover that will for his life and for his living. One aspect of the Christian faith leads to the conviction that he can learn God's will everywhere: in good and evil, from friend or enemy, under good or bad teachers, in success or failure. This is one of St. Paul's greatest insights, that "in everything God works for good." As the scientist seeks laws to obey in nature, however chaotic it appears, so in his social environment he seeks to find the will of God.

The child recognizes that his parents are not infallible, but that they do have wisdom usually far beyond his own. He seeks to learn all that they can teach him first, and then to surpass it. The mores and social customs and legal institutions in his community are far from perfect. Yet they represent the best man has been able to achieve up to now. So he determines to master them first, and then seeks to make them better.

WHOEVER WOULD SAVE HIS LIFE WILL LOSE IT!

Our fourth dimension of *agape*, and the most uniquely Christian of all the dimensions, is the one to which we refer as *vicarious sacrifice*. A tentative definition of it is: the courage to carry through one's social vision, especially those aspects of it which can only be achieved through personal sacrifice. Jesus, in his discussion of this phase of human behavior, pointed out that the prophets have regularly been persecuted. At the same time he pointed out also that they have just as regularly been happy. Probably his best statement of the principle is found in the quotation, "Whoever would save his life will lose it, and whoever loses his life for my sake will find it." This is regarded by many as the central core of his whole religion.

This is the most difficult of the eight dimensions to describe psychologically because it has been used so little that we have no large body of experience on which to base our inquiry. To be sure, the pages of history are studded with inspiring examples of its effect on behavior and the resultant enormous influence on history. But most of us have been far more concerned with financial security, freedom from fear, and a high standard of living than with sacrifice of any nature. Note at once, however, that these things are not incompatible with this principle. Indeed, they may become powerful means for its application. On the other hand, however, neither can they ever be the chief goals of life. The concept can easily be misunderstood and distorted. It must certainly not be confused with a martyr complex, in which people gain a morbid sense of satisfaction from self-torture. Probably most of the prophets, except for a few understandable low moments, were so intent on their visions that they were almost unaware of the sacrifice involved. It is not without significance that the word "sacrifice" by derivation means "to make holy."

The fact of the matter is that life confronts us with many situations—including some of the most crucial ones—in which sacrifice is clearly the normal response of the man of courage. This dimension, then, has to do with the extent to which people have the courage and skill to carry out these challenges of their Christian faith.

Jesus Won His Greatest Victory on a Cross　This trait is at the very core of the Christian philosophy of life. Furthermore, it is generally conceded to be the aspect of Jesus' philosophy which is most nearly unique. The Golden Rule, for example, is found in one form or another in almost all religions and was stated centuries before Jesus was born. This concept of vicarious sacrifice, however, while found in some other religions, is given the central role only in Christianity. The experience of the Cross is its most supreme example. Does any other religion use the death of its founder as exemplifying its greatest strength? Jesus achieved in his death what he had not been able to achieve before that, even with his disciples. Peter's behavior at the trial and then later, ranging from cowardice to indomitable courage, illustrates this effect. The whole course of history has demonstrated its basic validity ever since.

You see, the significant thing about Jesus' statement of this principle does not lie in merely the courage to sacrifice, even die, for what one believes. This has been exemplified in the lives of many men throughout history. The difference lies in the fact that Jesus saw in vicarious sacrifice, not a burden to be cheerfully and heroically borne, but the most powerful force in the universe.

"Happy are they who are persecuted for righteousness' sake." This is the Beatitude which most closely describes this trait. Quoting again from *The Interpreter's Bible*, "Persecution awaits the honest politician, the tradesman who will not compromise for profits, the teacher who cleaves to the truth. . . . The persecuted have the stamp of courage . . . in their hearts" (55:287–288). Of all the eight traits, then, this is the most characteristically Christian and the least achieved by the great majority of those who strive for Christian living.

Martyrdom Is Not a Normal Human Trait, but Christian Courage Is　At first glance, any sense of enjoyment being related to persecution might well seem to have a taint of morbidness. And there have certainly been many people whose behavior can be aptly described by the term "martyr complex." This kind of "sacrifice," however, is totally unrelated to the Christian concept. In fact, the two are contradictory to each other, as you will see if you examine them carefully. The martyr complex type of behavior is self-centered, "saving one's own life." Vicarious sacrifice is centered outside one's self in one's vision.

Let us see if there are some normal characteristics in human nature which can constitute a favorable basis for such a dimension in personality.

In the first place, the willingness to sacrifice for some unselfish purpose is an almost universal quality of human nature at its best. The athlete is heedless of his bumps and bruises in his desire to play the game hard. If injury comes, it is not unlikely that he will find a healthy sense of satisfaction rather than to be depressed because of it. Lovers daydream of fantastic ways in which they can risk life and limb for their beloved. A very small percentage of soldiers fail to find the courage to face death on the battlefield. You are, of course, familiar with the many heroic examples of such vicarious behavior.

Then, of a somewhat different type, are the sacrifices which parents make for their children. The gladness with which they do this differs from parent to parent and from child to child. Nevertheless they do so countless times. None of us would survive our childhood except for this quality in our parents. Indeed, much of it is almost unconscious. For the most part they would not even consider it sacrifice.

What about such a trait in children and youth? We frequently think of young people as being basically selfish. In a preliminary examination of approximately two hundred Parents' Reports at each level from Nursery to High School, chosen pretty much at random, we found so many examples of vicarious sacrifice, even in the Nursery, that we were astonished. Furthermore, as we read them we sensed that they were describing these children at their wholesome best, with not even a hint of morbidness.

If you are still in doubt as to the normality of this concept, just try one more thing. Imagine a social order in which no one willingly made any sacrifices. Eliminate from it sacrifices made by parents for their children, by lovers for their loved ones, by friends for one another, by heroes everywhere, by statesmen and patriots. Let all of these seek only their own personal gains. Surely, when you contemplate the results, the normality of such a trait as this one will be as obvious as it is difficult to achieve.

The growth stage described in the White House Conference report which is most closely related to this concept of vicarious sacrifice is what they call the "sense of integrity." Quoting from that report:

The final component of the healthy personality is the sense of integrity. In every culture the dominant ideals—honor, courage, faith, duty, purity, grace, fairness, self-discipline, . . . —become at this stage the core of the healthy personality's integration. . . . "It is a sense of comradeship with men and women of distant times and of different pursuits, who have created orders and objects and sayings conveying human dignity and love. . . . The possessor of integrity is ready to defend the dignity of his own life style against all physical and economic threats. For he knows that, for him, all human integrity stands or falls with the one style of integrity of which he partakes." (146:24–25) [1]

The two most interesting things about this concept are, on the one hand, its implication that one must have the courage to defend his ideals in the face of threats if necessary; and, on the other, the fact that it describes the normal individual as thinking not primarily of himself but of others and of ideals which he considers more important than himself. Keeping in mind, then, that this White House Conference concept was formulated as a result of a general consensus of opinion among experts, it is clear that modern psychologists consider sacrifice not only as normal, but that willingness to face it is an essential part of wholesome personality development.

What Has Learning to Do with Sacrifice and Increased Strength of Character? If the level of human achievement is increased in terms of this dimension, will man's personal and social potential be any greater as a result? Every time I try to answer this question I am sure I will be accused of exaggeration, for here is the central quality of Christianity. The longer I observe our social efforts, on the one hand, and study the effects of religion in personality, on the other, the more I am convinced that in this concept lies the best hope of our civilization.

[1] The quotation within the extract above is given in Witmer and Kotinsky as being taken from Erik Erikson, "Growth and Crisis of the 'Healthy Personality,'" *Problems of Infancy and Childhood*, Supplement II, Josiah Macy, Jr. Foundation, New York, 1950, p. 143.

When such an ideal as the one implied in this vicarious sacrifice dimension becomes the guiding spirit of a man's behavior; when, that is, he seeks a vision bigger than himself—the will of God—and works toward it at whatever personal cost, then both personality and society achieve their best. The nature of the evidence to support this principle is obvious. Make a list of all the illustrations you can discover that demonstrate the principle, "Whoever would save his life will lose it," and then another list which illustrates the other half of the principle; namely, those who have followed their visions regardless of the cost, and you will see clearly the power of vicarious sacrifice.

Efforts to teach concepts like this have sometimes resulted in distorted and morbid personalities. A person who prides himself on his sacrifices is hard to include among the healthy-minded. Then, too, the full power of such a trait as this requires more exacting skills than perhaps any of the others. For example, many who try to love their enemies find their efforts backfiring, leaving them with the feeling that they have failed. Here we are, then, with probably the most powerful social law in the universe, and with the least equipment to carry it out. Perhaps this is why *agape* has never been really translated, and why for the most part even in religion we relegate the power of the Cross to liturgy and Easter ceremonies.

Let me describe briefly a few of the steps we take at the various age levels, from which we have had highly encouraging results.

Among the attitudes relating to this dimension which constitute our goals for the Nursery child, a characteristic one is stated, "Learning to adjust to the fact that others will sometimes have the things he wants and will not give them up." Consider the child's need at this age level to discover that he is not the center of the universe, then the significance of this attitude will be evident. At the Kindergarten level, among other things he can learn the value of making sacrifices for his family and playmates. It takes some wise guidance on the part of parents and teachers to keep such an educational endeavor from backfiring and doing more harm than good. His early school years, even if he has attended public kindergarten and especially if he has not, are certain to be filled with social problems and he should come to see them as challenges to social growth. At the Junior level he comes to grips with the more central aspects of the problem. What does one do when faced with injustice and persecution, even in such everyday garb as ridicule and teasing? He can discover, if we are wise enough to teach him, that when faced with such apparent "evils," one can choose whether he will grow smaller or bigger. At Junior High, the opinion of one's peers comes to be of great importance. The determination to stand for the right even when there is strong social pressure to the contrary is a form of courage, stamping him as one likely to play an important role when his generation takes on the world's responsibilities. He can even develop some of the skills by which this is accomplished. Then to the Senior II can come a vision of the full power of this dimension. He can trace intelligently the growth of people's attitudes toward the problem of evil through the Old and New Testaments. He can gain a realization that he has social responsibilities which are more important than he is.

Is It Possible to Measure the Caliber of a Man in Terms of This Dimension?   To be sure, much of the effectiveness of vicarious sacrifice is a spiritual quality, not a physical one. Here is an embittered old man whose spiritual and mental health is revitalized by his four-year-old grandson giving him his favorite toy gun, so that "he can be happy again." Our staff has been inspired to supreme efforts on several occasions on receipt of a ten- or twenty-dollar gift to the Project from a grandmother who earns her living doing housework, but who "wants this [CRP] for her grandchildren."

You can probably list many instances of a similar nature which went unnoticed or were ignored primarily because of the humble status of the doer. Some of the well known heroic sacrifices which have altered the course of history have done so in part because of the prominence of the one sacrificing. The fact remains, however, that usually it is the spirit of the act, rather than the status of the actor, which makes it so powerful.

Can such a concept as this be regarded as a true dimension? There can certainly be no doubt that people differ in regard to it. We see around us some people who spend most of their energy at the futile task of seeking "to save their own lives." They are seldom happy, but they are always sure that they will be, if only they can find what they are looking for in terms of pleasure, wealth, prestige, status, and the like. At the other extreme, there are other people who seem to be so dedicated to their social visions that they hardly think about themselves at all.

Here Is the Pinnacle of the Power of Religion in Personality If we may judge the validity of a trait concept by its effectiveness, we certainly can defend this one in light of our experiences with it in CRP. As one reads history, for that matter, he will be impressed with the large proportion of the most inspiring stories in it which are about men whose stature was great in this dimension.

Note that the "sense of integrity," described in the White House Conference report, is also based on values greater than the individual which he must defend against all threats. Patriotism is essentially such a force. The same report points out that the culture includes concepts of dominant ideals to which the individual also gives strong loyalty. If religion is defined as consisting of one's universal values, this is religion. But let's add to it elements of faith characteristic of the Christian religion and estimate the effect in human personality.

Consider, for example, the influence on history of a little nation like Judea in the centuries preceding and including the life of Jesus. Most conquered nations continue for generations later to have bitterness and a desire for revenge against their conquerors. The prophets of Israel, however, were able to make this natural bitterness subordinate in the minds of their people to faith in God. As a result, such concepts as the suffering-servant ideal of the second Isaiah came into being. Hosea, taking on himself the punishment due an unfaithful wife, introduced another mighty lesson in vicarious sacrifice.

As we face the problems of this present atomic age, it may be true that a stockpile of atomic bombs is an indispensable force for our national security. Such a situation, however, can never bring permanent peace to the world. At best it can only prevent war for a while. Probably a greater world need is a leadership dedicated to the use of this force which we are here calling vicarious sacrifice. Thus far in history, including that of our own country, nationalism has certainly not led any of us to any far-reaching use of vicarious sacrifice toward other nations. When the history of this era is finished, I predict that such an event as our returning the money to China during the Boxer Rebellion or our sending wheat to famine-stricken India will prove to be a greater influence toward world peace than our winning the first and second world wars.

But let's be more practical and consider this dimension in the daily lives of our children and of most of the rest of us in our own communities. Does it work there?

A superficial examination of our hundreds of thousands of parent and youth reports seems to indicate elements of vicarious sacrifice in at least a third of them, whether they are from the Vicarious Sacrifice Unit or not. I have asked one of our research committees which is working with these reports to give me a number of them which do just this. From that group I have selected a few for each age level, disguised them so as to protect the confidential nature of the reports, and listed them below.

These are not unusual. We could have presented hundreds as good or better. You may not agree with all of their solutions, but you will sense the sincerity of their efforts and the caliber of youth who are doing them.

Nursery (Two- and Three-Year-Olds)

Teresa (three years old) had quite a list of Christmas wants. I tried to explain to her that Santa couldn't bring her *all* the gifts or he'd have none left for other children. Days later Grandma asked her what she would like for Christmas. "A doll house." "And what else would you like?" "That's all. Santa wouldn't have money to buy me *all* the toys because he has to have some for other boys and girls."

Kindergarten (Four- and Five-Year-Olds)

I heard Tom (four years old) tell his friends in the garden, "If you want me I'll be at Mrs. Evans'." Later I asked Mrs. E. (neighbor) if he went to her house, and this was her reply: "He knocked at my door and said he'd come to clear up the building blocks the children had left strewn over the living room floor. I let him in, and in no time at all he'd put them away on the play shelf, and said goodbye."

Her goal was: Being brave and understanding, when the doctor gave her the vaccination so that the whole group would remain in a good, wholesome attitude. (If one cried, the others might cry.) Nancy (five years old) approached the vaccination with confidence and knowledge that she must be brave so that the group would remain intent on its purpose.

Primary (Grades I and II)

Martin (grade 2) very shortly came out beaming and said, "I've got a wonderful idea—and it's thinking of others! I'm going to buy Laddie (friend's dog that had been hit by a truck, and was quite sick) a toy bone!" He was perfectly happy about buying that toy and was overjoyed at delivering it to the dog's house. Usually Martin is very fussy about his money.

When Manny's father went out to work on getting our car out of the alley where it was stuck, he (grade 1) said: "I'll go out and help Daddy. I don't feel good staying in the house while he's out there working."

Secondary (Grades III and IV)

I feel Eddie (grade 3) really responded to this lesson. I believe he gained a new sense of contribution, that we really need him and what he has to offer, and that he is appreciated. He did his chores much more readily and gave up a TV show right in the middle to go to the store for me. He also raked the neighbor's lawn just for the reward of pleasing her and using the leaves for a marshmallow roast.

Junior (Grades V and VI)

Four or five days elapsed, and I was taking Wendell to school and he passed Kim who was on patrol duty at the corner, without any sign of ever having known him. I said to him, "Didn't you wave at Kim?" and he said, "No," very emphatically. I suggested he ask Kim to come over, but he seemed very reluctant and said, "Well, I would have to make friends with him first." I told him that Kim had been very timid and shy just last year and now he was trying to get over that, and that was why he teases.

Wendell came home from school and had Kim with him. Wendell just beamed all evening, and each time would ask Kim what he wanted to do next. They had a very happy time during supper and the evening, and this morning I said to Wendell, "What do you think of the way you handled your problem with Kim?" and he replied, "It makes me feel awfully good."

Junior High (Grades VII and VIII)

Roberta (7th grade) told of sitting in front with Mary instead of back farther with her special friends—on two occasions when the class went to the movies. The reason was that the "kids don't like her." They say that two kids they don't like are Mary and (a boy). Roberta said that "Mary was so happy that she sparkled."

Tilly told of the usual fight over the "kick ball" at noon one day between the boys and the girls in her class. One afternoon at recess one of the boys struck Sue, her girl friend. "Why don't you turn and let him hit you on the other side," Tilly suggested to Sue. Sue did. The boy struck her, but then he went away and caused them no more trouble.

Senior I (Grades IX and X)

A spastic child had been ignored by most of the children until Jane (grade 9) bothered to be friendly, and to her surprise and joy found an amazing sense of humor and intelligence and friendliness. Many others in her group are now following suit and enjoying something they didn't dare risk finding for themselves.

(Grade 10) "I was to help my brother with his reading. It is very hard to help him because he can't read the words. I tackled the job of helping him. I have a short temper that is hard to control and by holding it back I helped him to read his lesson. I also learned how to help hold my temper back. I think it worked because it helped my brother to read better and I have helped myself."

Senior II (Grades XI and XII)

The high-school team was playing in the finals for the state championship. Everyone wanted to see the game. No one would tend the coat room. John (grade 11) finally agreed to do so, even though it meant missing the big game. Everybody told him he was crazy, but after that it was noticeable that when similar situations arose, many were willing to do that kind of thing.

The local high school was going to put on an operetta. Robert (Negro) has a beautiful baritone voice. His classmates suggested him for the lead. The supervisor said "No," because of misunderstandings that she felt were certain to arise. The students came to his defense and threatened to boycott the operetta. Robert, however, sided with the supervisor, suggesting that his participation might actually hurt race relations. Instead he coached the boy who did sing the lead. The news got around, and at the time of the operetta Robert received a great ovation for his wonderful spirit. (Grade 12)

This, then, is our final dimension. Will religion give us stronger character and more effective personality? On these eight dimensions, I rest my case.

THE DEVELOPMENT OF DIMENSIONAL CONCEPTS

If it is true that dimensions are frames of reference used by the scientist to organize his data, not necessarily or even ever, organic parts of the very nature of things; then their validity is determined by the purposes they are designed to serve. In our case it is measurement of growth of character. Let me show you at least three ways in which dimensions for a Christian Hypothesis could be formulated.

The first one might be called the method of exegesis. This would be a task for theologians and Biblical scholars, not psychologists. It would involve the study of the teachings of Jesus, to discover by methods of Biblical research exactly what he meant by his various teachings. It is not impossible that New Testament scholars could produce just such a set of dimensions. So far as I know they never have. While it is desirable for the psychologist to have a reasonably sound background in this field if he is to attempt such a dimensional system, exegesis is not his basic methodology.

A second method can be called the logical method. We can bring together all of the research-determined attitudes which seem relevant to the Christian philosophy of life and sort them into logically related groups. Thus a number of categories could be set up, studied for their basic nature, and used as dimensional concepts for research purposes.

The frame of reference which I have just described is a combination of these two. I first examined the literature of Biblical exegesis to find an adequate set of dimensions based on the teachings of Jesus. Then attitudes were sorted into the dimensions for educational purposes. With some changes, these have served us well for twenty years.

A third method is now being explored in our laboratory by Koppe (63). It is a search for consistencies of co-variant attitudes in behavior itself. Behavior items, selected from our parent and youth reports, are examined by a group of judges as to their probable motivation by various attitudes. Because behavior is seldom motivated by a single attitude, pattern groups of attitudes may frequently be found to be present in the same behavior items. This would indicate that these attitudes tend to go together as a co-variant group, at least as far as our every-day experience is concerned. Studies of these consistency patterns should result in a considerable reorganization of our attitude clusters and possibly even a reformulation of some of our dimensional concepts. This would certainly have obvious merit as far as educational methods are concerned. When attitudes consistently go together in behavior, it would certainly be easier to learn them that way and to prepare effective curricular materials in terms of such patterns.

SOME IMPORTANT CONCEPTS DESCRIBED IN THIS CHAPTER

The power of a religious philosophy of life in strength of personality and character can be demonstrated in dimensions related to the *agape* concept of Christian love. The potential, both in terms of personal happiness and in terms of the social order, is awe-inspiring in its magnitude.

Such dimensional concepts as set forth in these chapters are frames of reference, not objective realities. If a sample of all of the types of behavior, inspired by the spirit of *agape*, were given to a number of scholars, each might categorize them into a different set of dimensions.

Such a formulation, however, is an exceedingly difficult task. Years of study and testing by many criteria, of which eight have been used in this presentation, are prerequisite to any useful dimensional system. Its validity will be tested in the long run by usefulness in terms of educational effectiveness.

If the Christian Hypothesis of a Father God is true, then native endowment and individual differences ought not to be the deciding factors for levels of happiness and achievement. Those with modest endowment should be able to achieve just as much as those with high endowment.

In this chapter the last four dimensions in our CRP frame of reference for the Christian Hypothesis have been described. They are all based on *agape*, and include: being sensitive to the needs of others, being determined that every man get his full chance at happiness and success, magnanimity, and vicarious sacrifice.

CHAPTER X

---•‑•‑•---

DIMENSIONS OF PERSONALITY—
TESTS OF VALIDITY AND
EDUCATIONAL GOALS

DO CHILDREN LEARN ANYTHING IN CHURCH SCHOOL?

ARE SUNDAY schools worth their cost? Many people, some of them Sunday-school leaders, have serious doubts. Many a religious educator loudly protests his faith in the Sunday school. But his very vehemence sometimes indicates that he is whistling in the dark.

The fact of the matter is, we really don't know whether we are accomplishing anything or not. That holds for our other character-building efforts too. Here is a foundation which has received a request for funds from one of its local character-building agencies. The foundation asks, Is this movement worth the investment? The answer is, No one knows. In that city alone, the movement has available to it about 250,000 child hours per year. However much or little it has been achieving, its potential is large indeed.

The foundation asks, Is it possible to set up evaluational procedures to measure its effectiveness? The answer is, Not only can that be done, but what is far more important, it is possible for these same evaluational procedures to guide the leaders of this agency to the level of effectiveness which ought to come out of an investment of 250,000 hours.

The first step in such an evaluation, however, is to set up some dimensions in terms of which to measure. Up to now the dimensions used have been attendance and hopeful thinking on the part of its well wishers. Our last two CRP dimensional frames of reference are designed for just such a purpose.

We have found increasing evidence to show that wherever there is home participation, religious education does make observable impressions on our growing children. Following are two short essays written without previous preparation by two Junior Highs. Before I tell you about them and the study of which they were a part, read them carefully. Decide which one is best getting the kind of religious education you think a Junior High should have. I have tossed a coin to decide which one to quote first, so that is a matter of chance.

The essays were written in answer to the question: "What are your ideas about Jesus? Why is he important to you?" Here is the first of the two essays.

Jesus is God's son. He was born on earth through Mary and Joseph. Before Jesus was born Mary was told by angels that the baby Jesus came from God. Jesus' teaching lasted only three years but in that time he accomplished much more than anyone except God knew. Only a few people believed in Jesus when he was alive but after he died people began to realize why he was sent to earth. Jesus taught people to love thy neighbor as thyself and that if you did something wrong God would forgive you if you prayed and asked forgiveness.

The priests and Pharisees did not like Jesus' teachings. They were always saying that he shouldn't cure people on the Sabbath. Jesus cured sick people. Sometimes when the people saw Jesus make a blind man see again, they wondered how the miracles came about. The people were told that if you honestly believe in God, He will cure you.

When Jesus was crucified he asked that the people who crucified him be forgiven. Not until long after did the people realize why he gave his life up for them. Today we know that Jesus wants us to be strong believers in God. If we were, the world would be much better off than it is.

The second essay reads like this.

Jesus was born in Nazareth, the son of the carpenter Joseph, and Mary. When he was old enough, he was taken to Jerusalem. Here he met the wise men, and became very interested in their teachings. He decided to become a teacher of God, preaching as a Christian.

Jesus is very important to us all. Without him we would have no Christianity, no brotherhood. He started us in learning God's works, taught us to be followers of "Our Father." He taught us how to pray, and how to love each other, even those that hate us. He taught us how to build the other fellow up, not to break down our neighbor, and to be forgiving of all ill done to us.

Jesus died on the Cross, and left his disciples to go on teaching us the love of Christ. He could have been spared; he could have had God save him the agony which he suffered carrying his Cross to the hill, and then hung on it by his hands and feet, with a crown of thorns upon his head. But instead he stuck through it all, to teach us the pure unselfishness of Christianity; the help and guidance prayer gives us; that by praying in a time of poverty, doubt, sadness, or trying to solve a major problem, we can be consoled; problems will disappear.

Following is a brief description of the study from whence these essays came and the judgments concerning each of them. Do not read the following, however, until you have judged the relative values of the two essays yourself. Then see if the results we found conform to your own.

These two essays were among some fifty-six written by the children in two Junior High departments. One of them was a church using only the CRP curriculum. The other was from a church, comparable in size and general educational and economic level to the first, in which another curricuum was being used. The CRP essay is the second of the two.

Judges from CRP and from the other church ranked the entire set of essays according to this criterion: "How well they are getting the kind of religious education I think they ought to have." The second essay was ranked first, according to the pooled rankings of all the judges. None of the judges knew from which church the essays came. They were given code numbers and shuffled before each judge saw them. The first essay was given a pooled ranking of sixteenth by the CRP judges, but first by the other group of judges. The second essay was ranked first by the CRP judges and twelfth by the other judges. These differences are statistically significant.

I wonder if you see the full import of these findings. They reveal several things of importance.

In the first place, they reveal that some religious education learning is taking place in both curricula, at least at the insight level. Note that this was an indirect examination. That is, the children are not asked to repeat what they have been told, but are given an open-end topic on which to write. It is so formulated that if they have learned with any degree of real insight it will be reflected in their answers. If the curricula themselves, having somewhat different objectives, were not getting across these objectives at all, judges would not be able to differentiate among them in this manner. We can therefore say with some confidence that we are doing some religious education in our church-school programs. Our specific objectives are being learned well enough by at least some of the children to be measurable. It is to be noted, however, that in both cases teachers did need to know what these objectives are and to seek to give them forthrightly to the children.

Note in the second place that it was possible to distinguish between the two groups only in those cases where a high level of home participation was known to be taking place. We can say, then, that the church school *plus* the home can give religious education. We are much less likely to do so when there is no home participation.

Three Approaches to Evaluation of Educational Programs You can approach the problem of evaluating educational objectives in three ways. You can ask the question, "What results, if any, are coming from our educational efforts?" Our method of characteristic differences, to be described fully in Chapters XI and XII, is an effective procedure for answering such a question.

You can also approach the problem in terms of some general objectives. For example, in the case cited above it is hoped that the efforts of this particular agency will make better citizens. Our Definition of Character dimensions are set forth to serve just such a purpose. I want to show you how to use them that way.

There is still a third method of evaluation. This has to do with determining how successful you have been in achieving your specific objective. This means of course that you must know what your specific objectives are. Certainly, it is improbable that you will succeed with your general objectives if you fail with your specific ones. Our last dimensional frame of reference is set up for that purpose. You may not want to use it, but you will certainly have to use one like it.

A DEFINITION OF CHARACTER—CROSS-VALIDATION DIMENSIONS

Let us now turn to the CRP frame of reference which we call Definition of Character. Unless one has some yardstick independent of his educational hypotheses against which he can test his educational philosophy, he is almost as likely to make regress as progress. It is clear that when the various judges mentioned above ranked the two essays, they had certain criteria by which they judged them. The CRP judges had a fairly common group of criteria and so tended to agree with one another. The Curriculum X judges did not agree nearly so well, probably because their criteria were less clearly defined or because they differed more among themselves as to what these criteria ought to be. As a result their judgments were far less consistent with one another.

In the case of this frame of reference, we were seeking an essentially psychological definition of character, which could be used as a cross-validation measure of the psychological soundness of our religiously oriented trait concepts.

Cross-Validation Is a Valuable Tool in Evaluation Cross-validation consists in setting up a set of variables, as independent as possible of the set being tested but designed to measure the same general phenomenon. For example, let two psychologists each independently create a test of social skill, both designed to measure the same thing but including different variables and different test items. These two tests are then given to a large group of individuals. If the correlation between the scores obtained by the members of this group on the two tests is high, this tends to prove the validity of both. This is the method of cross-validation.

Our CRP trait theory, which we call *A Definition of Character*, has been designed to serve such a purpose. It includes six definitive variables of a different type than those of the Christian Hypothesis, by which strength of character may be measured. These include: two ethical variables (sense of ethical values, and ethical consistency); two social variables (social effectiveness, and temporal and social orientation); and two personality variables (personality integration and maximum potential). These will be defined more fully a little later.

Note that these are entirely different variables than those constituting the eight dimensions suggested for the Christian Hypothesis. You will admit, however, that if a person testing high in regard to the traits of the Christian Hypothesis should test low according to these criteria of strong character, we would certainly be forced to question the validity of the frame of reference we have used to describe Christian character.

How does one go about constructing a cross-validation frame of reference? Probably you will already have guessed the first step. Education is for the purpose of training youth to become the kinds of adults we want them to be. All right, what kinds of adults do we want them to become? When we have spelled out the answer to this question in terms of meaningful characteristics, we have the rough outline of the dimensions needed to evaluate our educational methods for inspiring our youth to become such adults.

You can do some good exploratory research even with this crude framework. You can do a more effective job, however, the more carefully you refine these objectives. During the period of psychological research characterized by the Character Education Inquiry (23) many criteria relevant to our purpose began to emerge. The *Tenth Yearbook* of the Department of Superintendence suggested a more basic approach to the problem, in their discussion of the objectives of character education (26:50):

The objectives shall (1) correspond to the structure of human nature, (2) point to the real drives involved in conduct, (3) center attention upon the observable consequences of acts, (4) recognize the need for concrete and specific experiences, (5) take account of race experience as experience rather than as absolutes handed down from the skies, (6) induce whole-sightedness in facing moral problems, and (7) stimulate the creation of new moralities in accord with our changing society.

In choosing our cross-validation dimensions, then, we have tried to describe character in terms of certain criterion variables, which can serve as a basis for the constant revision of all of our other dimensional-trait concepts and thus help to divorce character from the realm of individual opinion.

A Cross-Validation Set of Dimensions of Character Character, as we use the word, can be described in terms of the following frame of reference. Character is the total effect of one's evaluative attitudes on the social influence of his personality. Six variables or dimensions are proposed in this scale for describing it. As already indicated, the first two are basically ethical, the second two social, and the third two personal.

1. *Extent of ethical values.* It is important that this variable be clearly understood. We are not concerned here with what particular ethical code is held, but that one is held. In abnormal psychology we speak of the psychopathic personality as one which seems incapable of learning moral principles. This is the low end of this variable. At the other extreme are those who conceive of moral principles as among the greatest values of mankind. Items (5) and (7) of the above list from the Department of Superintendence are certainly implied in this dimension. It is as absurd for an older generation to imagine that it can impose upon youth completely its ready-made moral and ethical codes, in which so much fallibility is to be found, as it is for youth to fail to take into consideration the progress of their elders in their search for new and better ones.

2. *Moral consistency.* The other ethical variable is the consistency with which one lives his moral principles. One man is so consistent that his moral decisions are almost perfectly predictable. Another is so inconsistent that it is difficult to know whether he even has a moral code. The man who is described as having the courage of his convictions would be high in this dimension. The man who is so weak that he is the pawn of whatever impulse is at hand is at the other extreme.

To be sure, moral inconsistency is usually ascribed to a person in regard to traits by which observers evaluate him, or even by which he tries to evaluate himself. It is probable that everyone's behavior is consistent if we can discover the way in which that consistency expresses itself. A man who tells the truth one minute and lies the next may be inconsistent when judged from an external point of view. If each act, however, is done to help a friend, he may be perfectly consistent in regard to loyalty to his friend. Nevertheless, moral dependability is certainly a mark of strong character.

3. *Social effectiveness.* If two men have the same moral principles and one adjusts well with his fellows and is able to influence them for good, he can be regarded as having the stronger character. By the same token, if character education leads to social maladjustment this can surely be regarded as evidence that the concepts used

are faulty. It becomes obvious that many traditional moral concepts would be invalidated by this criterion.

4. *Temporal and social orientation*. This variable is measured by the length of time and number of people involved in one's moral decisions. The man who lives only in terms of the present impulse and who considers only those with whom he comes into direct contact is at one extreme. At the other extreme is the man who has longer past and future perspective and whose social judgments are in terms of all mankind. Many moral decisions are reached which bring great unhappiness to others because of limited character in regard to this variable.

5. *Personality integration*. This is the first of the personality variables. It is implied in the study made by the Department of Superintendence. If among a number of possible moral principles, some of them lead to neurosis and personality maladjustment whereas others lead to integration and dynamic personality, the latter are more characteristic of strong character. This, for example, certainly involves the formation of accurate and confident self attitudes and self other concepts. Here, by the way, is another criterion variable by which to distinguish among possible moral codes on a more objective basis than opinion.

6. *Maximum potential behavior*. Maximum potential behavior is to be distinguished from avoidance behavior (being motivated only by the desire to keep out of difficulty) and group expectancy behavior (desiring to keep up with the Joneses). It is that behavior which we exhibit in which we desire to express the best of which we are capable. Some moral codes have been largely negative— goodness being defined in terms of sins not committed—and these have been essentially avoidance adjustment. Other codes have been built primarily around respectability—the sin against which Jesus preached with the most vehemence—and these have resulted in group-expectancy behavior.

The Method of Cross-Validation in Action   How can such dimensions be used in actual practice? Let me describe two of our own uses of this frame of reference. The first of them anyone can use with considerable confidence. The second is more technical and requires more investment of trained personnel and time.

A group of ten High School young people wrote essay answers on the topic, "The kind of a person I would like to be like." Six judges were asked to rank these essays according to three criteria, which were based on this Definition of Character: breadth of social vision, persistence in carrying it out, and depth of Christian insight. When a ranking of these essays based on the pooled ranking of the six judges was made, it proved to be highly reliable. This was checked against other criteria, giving cross-validation to the scores. Now, you will see how this can be used in local situations such as the one described above.

Suppose that you want to find out whether some effort of character education in which you are interested is getting results. First choose two groups of children or young people, one of which has been exposed to your educational procedure, and the other of which has not. Make sure that they are comparable groups in as many ways as possible. Have them write similar essays on this topic or some other one, which will reveal their basic philosophy of life. Then have a group of judges rank them according to these or some other criteria upon which you may decide. If there is consistency in the ranks assigned to them by different judges, then the pooled ranks will have a high level of reliability. Then find the average rank of those who have been exposed to the educational procedure and compare it with the average rank of the others. If the first is higher than the second, you have evidence of its effectiveness. In Chapters XI and XII, I shall describe statistical methods for determining how large such a difference must be to be meaningful. This procedure, which we call our *Method of Control Ranks*, is easily learned and very effective in such exploratory research as this.

THE FORMULATION OF SPECIFIC CREATIVE EDUCATIONAL GOALS

The Need for Educational Objectives Consisting of Chewable Bites From the point of view of practical educational procedures, it is important to find "chewable bites" which children can use as levels of aspiration in this matter of character growth. Our Attitude Goals consist of some 250 such goals, some of which have already been listed in the discussion of the eight general dimensions.

During the last few years we have done research which demonstrates beyond all reasonable doubt that we are actually stimulating learning in the children who use our curriculum. The leading role in making possible both the fact and our ability to measure it is played by this attitude-goal set of concepts. Our particular attitude list has frequently been criticized. Indeed, we ourselves have been by far its severest critics. It has nevertheless become increasingly certain to us that an indispensable factor in effective religious education is definite objectives. The more specific they are, the more certain we are to be able to challenge children to seek them and to be able to determine the effectiveness of our methods.

Such a frame of reference makes it possible for us to test our procedures quickly and accurately. It is when you set out to achieve a very specific purpose that it is easiest to find out whether or not you have done so. Our own set of specific objectives, evolved over a period of twenty years, makes this possible in our procedures.

How Does This Attitude-Goal Frame of Reference Differ from the Christian Hypothesis?   The first thing we need to do is to distinguish these specific goals from our general Christian Hypothesis dimensions. Such a distinction is essential for understanding our educational concepts.

Possibly I can make it clearest with an illustration. Here are six boys who have been caught lying by their parents. Let us suppose that each of the six believes fully in honesty and by any reasonable standard must be described as honest. Yet here he is lying. How can that be? When we learn all the facts in the case we discover the following picture. One of them lied because all of his crowd lied and he didn't want "to let them down." Another lied pretty much because his wild imagination gave birth to a far more thrilling story than the dull facts in the case. Another lacked social skill and lied to win a friendship. Another one had bragged about what he would do and lied to make people believe that he had done it. Another felt a deep sense of inferiority among his fellows, and lied to make them think that he had done things he thought would win their admiration. Finally, one of them lied to avoid the punishment that he was certain would come from telling the truth.

If you will recall the factors in the Dynamics Diagram, you will note that the first case had to do with the S; the second, the Oi; the third, a skill; the fourth, a self goal factor; the fifth, a self other concept; and the last, a tension. Yet each of these boys had an attitude of honesty. When we were talking about the dimensions of the Christian Hypothesis, we were talking about the ultimate effectiveness of the individual's total personality. Here we are talking rather about some of the personality dynamics which underlie such behavior. One of these groups of dynamics factors consists in his attitudes. In the cases listed above, however, the behavior was actually in contrast to the attitude. Attitudes, then, are important forces in personality, but they are parts of the total personality and their expression is influenced by all the rest of personality, including the other attitudes.

Most human beings are people of good will. They mean well, want to be friendly with others, are basically generous, and by and large pretty fine. If this is the case, where do all our conflicts arise?

A Few General Negative Attitudes Can Destroy Civilization   To answer this question, let's do a little experiment. Take your morning newspaper and check off all the items which relate to conflict among men—whether between individuals, groups, or nations. Assume, however, that all men are basically unselfish, generous, and have good will. However, assume that each of them has also been taught the following eight attitudes in the process of growing up. Note that none of the eight is based on fact but that all of the eight could be and often are held by "good" people. Now consider how many of the newspaper items you have checked would never have been there except for the fact that too many people have one or more of these eight attitudes. In other words, let us consider the hypothesis that if we want to continue having a world filled with conflict and chaos, even with all of us wanting peace and harmony, all we need to do is teach each child, as he grows up, the following attitudes.

1. "If anyone criticizes me, he is insulting me; therefore, I shall respond in kind." The child says to a scolding parent, "You hate me." As adults we hardly dare criticize any of our friends because usually they cease then to be our friends. Furthermore, we are suspicious of their friendship if they do criticize us.

2. "Anyone who disagrees with me dislikes me." Just go into a church—almost any church—and see whether the differences of opinion found there result in stimulation, inspiration, and growth, or in church fights and destructive dogmatisms.

3. "My philosophy of life is right. All others are wrong and dangerous." Note that superficially this is the very essence of sincerity and conviction; but also of the conflicting ideologies which, on the international level, threaten to destroy civilization.

4. "Human nature for the most part is selfish. If everybody else would just start practicing the Golden Rule tomorrow, so would I, but I can't stand against the world alone. If I do so, I'll get my throat cut in this highly competitive, dog-eat-dog society of ours."

5. "Other races, classes, national groups, even other age levels have certain black or white characteristics in common." "Teen-agers are all wild and self-centered." "All Russians want war." "All colored people are lazy." "All Republicans (or Democrats) are crooked politicians." Obviously, none of these is true, but millions of people think and act as if they were.

6. "I don't want to be bad, but other people all demand that I be if I am to be popular." Each in a group of Junior High boys can be a fine boy and yet, when in a group, engage in destruction because each thinks all the others want to. Adults do much the same thing.

7. "Justice consists of 'an eye for an eye and a tooth for a tooth,' with me as the judge as to what is just. It is cowardly to permit an injustice. I won't let people run over me." Of course, in nine cases out of ten the other person did not intend his behavior to be unjust, nor did he realize that it was.

8. "The way to influence other people is through fear and anger. Tell other persons or nations what you will do to them if they do such and such. Ascribe to them all the bad names you can think of." Actually, history shows that at best fear and anger are usually momentary motivations, whose most permanent effects are bitterness and hate.

There they are, then. Note that people could, in general, be sincere, honest, generous, and basically kind, and still have these eight attitudes. Now examine your undesirable newspaper items and consider how many are there primarily because of the prevalence of one or more of these attitudes. Though they are all negative attitudes, they can cancel out much of the existing good will among men.

How Are Attitudes, Traits, and Dimensions Related to One Another? One thing which ought to be made clear at once is the way that attitudes, traits, and dimensions relate to one another. There are many traits which are not attitudes; for example, the constitutional traits of "height" and "weight." There are attitudes which are not traits, because they are not consistent; for example, one's dislike of a sermon to which he is listening. Character traits, however, are always based on attitudes. Since traits are the consistencies in human nature, then an attitude is a trait or a part of a trait when it becomes a consistent characteristic of one's personality; for example, one's love of children. Furthermore, a cluster of attitudes may operate much as a dynamic unit, in which case also it can be regarded as a trait; for example, all of the attitudes which underlie a quality of behavior which we could describe as "dominating purpose in the service of mankind." Completely generalized traits of this sort probably never exist in personality; but they do serve as goals toward which to strive, and some people demonstrate them to so high a degree that they become fairly accurate ways of describing their personalities.

The Choice of Attitudes and a Character Education Program
Since there are literally thousands of attitudes which one might choose as objectives, criteria must be established for determining what your objectives are to be. Note the conditions which an attitude must fulfill to be included in our list of objectives. (1) It must be socially effective. (2) It must be at least apparently capable of being learned. (3) It must be positive and contain challenge for the child. (4) It must be applicable to the child's real daily-life problems. (5) It must fit his age level. (6) It must make his adjustment to his peers as well as his elders satisfactory. (7) It must be capable of being integrated into the rest of his basic philosophy of life. (8) It must be at least apparently mentally healthy. (9) It must be so adaptable as to be a wholesome expression of his own personality. (10) It must be consistent with the Christian philosophy of life.

The formulation of our attitude list has certainly been by far the most time-consuming task we have ever attempted. In a later chapter I shall describe in some detail how we went about the development of the original list, which we published in the original chart (45). Then, after almost ten years of exploratory work, the first complete attitude list was published (79). Since that time, many of the factors have been restated and even combined in different groupings. Almost all of the attitudes have been revised, some of them several times.

How Are Specific Attitude Goals Organized into Curricular Units?
It is difficult to formulate systematic attitude clusters. Not only

must the individual attitudes meet all the requirements which have been described in this chapter, but the organization of the attitudes into curricular sequences sets up a whole host of new problems. Are they related psychologically as well as logically? Do they appear in consistent groups in daily life experience? Do these organization principles change as the child matures? These are just a few of the problems involved.

The nature of this dimensional-trait frame of reference will be clearer if you can see one illustrative development.

Our Vision Unit, based on the Beatitude of the poor in spirit, is a case in point. You will recall the general nature of this concept from its description in the discussion of the Christian Hypothesis.

You will recall that vision is a descriptive term which we apply to the quality of an individual's behavior. It can be understood best in terms of the Dynamics Diagram of behavior. If we are to produce individuals who demonstrate this kind of behavior, we must develop methods in terms of the dynamics of this Diagram. This means that we shall need to consider such things as the situations in which the child finds himself. We must also take into consideration the individual differences which distinguish him from others, which indeed make him unique. We shall need to teach him many skills. But above all we shall need to inspire him to accept certain attitudes as a part of his working philosophy of life, since they are the prime movers of behavior.

Our first task will be to think of the kinds of attitudes which will result in such vision. In our efforts to develop vision, we have come to use four general attitude groups which we call factors. These four factors are: curiosity for truth, development of creative imagination, growth in inspiration, and vocational vision.

Each of these, however, must be spelled out in terms of manageable attitudes as specific goals. They must represent a series which can begin in the Nursery and continue until adulthood.

Take one of these, for example, and see what kinds of goals can be used. Consider the factor of creative imagination. The following steps are involved in our conception of how this is to be achieved. In the Nursery, we try to create situations which will help the child to gain enthusiasm for activities which help him explore his environment. In the Kindergarten, we stimulate him to develop his imagination through discovery of the things he can do with it. In the early grades he will be discovering that using his imagination can develop new resources for living; and gaining new social insights through the medium of dramatization. Later he is made aware of the wonder and power of words and language; and he begins to dream of mastering the skills for building a better world. Still later we encourage him to apply his imagination to discover a level of "goodness" which is more adventurous than "badness." By Junior High, we are challenging him to apply his imaginative power toward acquiring the courage and skills to exceed his present peer standards. In the first years of High School, we want him to discover that he has the power to make a unique and significant contribution to the world, gaining the conviction that he has the power to contribute to a more Christian future.

Some may wonder whether we are not structuring the ideals of the child too much; giving him too little opportunity to choose his own goals; in a word imposing our own ideals on him. I suggest that you examine these goals, which are typical of the ones we do use. Note that almost every one of them is a challenge to creativity. Note, too, however, that very few of them would occur to him if he had been expected to create his own goals. Visualize whether a generation which had mastered these objectives would be "like ours," with our limitations imposed upon them—or truly a greater generation.

AN OVERVIEW OF THE PROBLEM OF DIMENSIONAL-TRAIT THEORY

The really significant trait theories are those which set forth dimensions of personality by which man can further explore his role in the universe. The whole history of science has been highlighted by the discovery of new dimensions by means of which man has been able to escape from some form of the tyranny of ignorance to which previously he had been a slave. When, however, scientists have become content with the dimensions they already have, sometimes simply because they could measure accurately with them, their findings have regularly approached sterility. Only as they have pushed out into new directions have scientists progressed, never losing their faith that an infinite God will have increasingly powerful aspects of his will which he is willing to reveal to those who seek, ask, and knock with sufficient courage, skill, and persistence. Hardly a single great insight in scientific history has been simply a logical deduction from experimental evidence, but always a daring induction that occurs when a brilliant and humble mind dares to look into the infinite for new dimensions to explore.

But you ask, "Can't these new concepts be spectacularly wrong as well as spectacularly right?" That is where the principle of pragmatic eclecticism plays its major role. To be sure, if we just toss out all existing concepts and create new hypotheses from scratch, they can be and indeed usually are spectacularly wrong. Unfortunately, this kind of panacea faddism is very common in our American culture. But if we make sure that we hold on to the values of the older hypotheses in the creation of our new ones, such serious errors are far less likely to occur. That is where the difference between prescientific and scientific trait theory is greatest. We may actually construct almost as many dimensional concepts in the latter as in the former. But they will grow out of objective evidence, be strengthened by pragmatic eclecticism, and tested at once by evaluative research.

Consider the field of personality. Who can contemplate man for even a moment and not sense the enormous potential which he seldom even approximately realizes. The few great personalities of history have not been more highly endowed by nature than millions of others. Why have these others not also achieved great heights? The answer is not so much in good intentions as in ignorance. We do not need to surrender to the evils of war, to poverty, to social strife, to unhappy family life, to wasted potential in youth, to frustrating group dynamics, any more than we are willing to surrender to cancer, drought, destruction, or famine. And the principal key to all these is finding the right dimensions by which to understand the secrets of the universe.

If the factors involved in the individual personality are numerous and complex, they are child's play as compared to those to which one must adjust in finding his role in the social order and his meaning in the universe. From the beginning of time prophets and sages have proclaimed dimensions of the good life which they have urged man to live.

Among the prophets who have attempted this task, Jesus has influenced human history more than any other. It seemed desirable, therefore, in our search for such far-reaching dimensions, to attempt to find an adequate frame of reference which could be accepted as descriptive of his philosophy of life. This we have done, using the Beatitudes from the Sermon on the Mount as a suitable outline to follow.

The test of these concepts for our purposes, however, is not to be found in exegesis and historical scholarship, but in their effectiveness in personality and the social order. Unless they are in tune with the universe, they will need to be replaced with still more adequate concepts.

Having set forth a set of value dimensions, such as those we have included in our Christian Hypothesis, each of them must be interpreted to the growing child in a whole series of dimensions of these dimensions. They must give practical meaning to his religion as he faces life itself. They must include dimensions which have potential for him at each age level as he grows from infancy to maturity. They must be psychologically valid, socially effective, and spiritually challenging. They must have sufficient range for the most modestly endowed to achieve and yet for the most highly endowed to explore with all the richness of his inheritance.

There is one more way in which we can begin to search for new dimensions. It has been made possible by our method of characteristic differences. Leaders in the field of character education have long known that we are probably accomplishing many things with children with whom we work which we did not know we were doing, as well as failing to achieve many of the goals we had set out to achieve. This method of characteristic differences now makes it possible for us to study groups of children and to discover what changes we have brought about in their lives, regardless of what we set out to do. The method is not very technical and I predict that it will be used by hundreds of our co-scientists. Every church-school teacher, camp director, club leader, and any other youth leader can learn to use it and contribute to our store of knowledge about what we are doing. The dimensions that can grow out of this kind of research may well lead to totally new concepts about education in general and character education in particular.

I first started writing these last six chapters seven years ago. During those years I have made three series of lectures on various phases of the subject: the Earl Lectures at the Pacific School of

Religion in Berkeley, California, in 1950; the Robert F. Jones Lectures at the Austin Presbyterian Theological Seminary in 1951, and the Mead-Swing Lectures at Oberlin College in 1952. Again and again baffling problems have forced me to turn to other problems before I could proceed further. At long last, however, here is the first complete statement of where our explorations in character research have led us in this all-important area of dimensions and traits. I have the fullest sympathy with Ezekiel in trying to describe to you a dazzling vision of what is possible as we make increasing progress in this task. I hope never again will any of you say of any serious effort to formulate dimensions by which to describe personality, "This trait theory is good; that one is false." Each of them will have values and inadequacies. No progress is made by destructive criticism. Only by holding on to the values of each and trying to add to them can we find the greater adventures to which more adequate dimensional vision can lead us.

Here, then, is the adventure of dimensions, some of them dimensions which no one suspected before. Each one points out directions to new adventures in living, which may at last bring our spiritual growth to a par with our growth in technical progress. Our atomic age demands such insights. Here are a few roads toward that order of insight.

SOME IMPORTANT CONCEPTS DESCRIBED IN THIS CHAPTER

When our objectives in education are sufficiently specific and clearly defined, then we can readily test the effectiveness of our educational procedures. By the use of indirect methods, we can observe the children's thinking and action to see whether our objectives have become a part of their basic philosophy of life. Learning can be defined at the level of verbal repetition, insight, and conviction, and application and skill. We can test it at any or all of these levels.

Methods of evaluation are now available which will not only measure present achievements of an educational venture, but which will point out directions by which that organization can achieve its potential accomplishments. These methods are based on the discovery of appropriate dimensions for the purpose.

Practical educational procedures can be developed only if their objectives can be stated in the form of "chewable bites," levels of aspiration which are on the one hand challenging to the child, and on the other possible for him to attain.

Much of the evil and conflict in the world comes not from vicious intentions, but from attitudes commonly held by men of good intention. These effects show how powerful attitudes can be and how important it is to find philosophies of life based on Christian principles.

Attitudes, in the very nature of the case, can never be "imposed" upon children. Only if their presentation stimulates in the child challenge and meaning will they produce effects in his personality and character.

New dimensional concepts need to be developed. If they are based on objective evidence and if the principle of pragmatic eclecticism is rigidly adhered to, we need not fear serious error. We can proceed with considerable confidence that we are making progress. We must, of course, evaluate continually to detect at once our successes and failures.

CHAPTER XI

---•••---

THE TOOLS OF EXPERIMENTAL DESIGN
"I WAS BLIND, NOW I SEE"

MILLIONS OF dollars are spent every year on church-school buildings, summer camps, YMCA's, and the like; on personnel, curricula, and programs for religious and character education. In 99 per cent of the cases we have no objective evidence as to whether or not they are doing any good. It may be that in some cases they are actually doing harm. This is all the more tragic when it is not only possible to evaluate our efforts; it is also possible at the same time to set up a process of continually strengthening them.

Let us throw out at once a conception of science as a way of critical evaluation which results in vicious comparisons, wasted energy in competition among the character-building agencies, and even in the possible destruction of some of them. Actually, whatever you have in terms of money, leadership, vision, and children's participation is to be regarded as potential power. Here are some tools which, if built into the very core of your procedures, can help you make the greatest possible use of that potential. Even when all of our resources in religious and character education are put together, they are only a drop in the bucket, compared to the other influences which are exerted on the child. It behooves us to integrate and strengthen them with every skill we have available. It is my honest opinion that if we master and use these methods we can make the combined strength of our resources the major factor in the lives of our children and in the world they build tomorrow.

288

In these next two chapters I am going to describe a few tools, some concepts, and some simple experimental designs, which anyone with a high-school education can master. If all those interested in the problems of moral and social values in our educational procedures will master these tools, everyone from parents, older youth, directors of religious education, Scout leaders, and YMCA secretaries, through professors in our seminaries and teachers' colleges, denominational leaders and leaders in our character-building agencies, we can test and refine our methods with a speed which may yet save our present civilization. Furthermore, these two chapters can be learned by the average college student within a period involving seven hours of instruction and study, plus twenty-one hours of practice. From the point of view of the future of our youth, these two chapters may well be the most important in this volume.

A Simple Experiment Which Could Revolutionize Religious Education   You will recall the simple experiment referred to in the beginning of the last chapter, from which two essays were quoted. They were Junior High answers to the questions: "What are your ideas about Jesus? Why is he important to you?" Let's examine that study a little further, because it was an experimental design which every one of you could learn and use with comparative ease, and by which you can test and continually improve the effectiveness of your educational procedures, whether in an individual Sunday-school class, a Scout troop, a summer camp, a denominational curriculum, or a theory of learning. Lets call the experimental design which it illustrates *the method of control ranking*.

You will remember that these essays were written by Junior Highs from two church schools, in one of which CRP methods are used, and in one of which another curriculum is used. Let us call it Curriculum X. The two church schools were so selected that they represent about the same size churches, the same general socio-economic and educational level of people, and the same general emphasis on and enthusiasm for their church schools.

These essays—in this case 32 from the CRP group and 24 from the CurX (Curriculum X) group—were carefully edited to take out any references, names, or other identifying statements by which they could be recognized as coming from one or the other of the two churches, except in terms of their ideas about the problem question itself. They were then retyped on cards, and given code numbers which were completely independent of the groups from which they came. This step is very important; namely, to delete every clue which could identify the group to which items belong, except such differences as may have resulted from your educational procedures.

Next it is necessary to find two groups of judges. In our case we secured four CRP judges and three CurX judges. The CRP judges were instructed to rank the cards in terms of how well the children were learning the concepts which are emphasized in the CRP curriculum. The CurX judges were instructed to rank them in terms of how well they were learning CurX objectives. Note that this is not a comparison of the two curricula as such. In each case, one of the groups simply acts as a control group, by which it is possible to determine whether the other group is achieving the objectives it is setting out to achieve.

Thus, the CRP judges were actually getting evidence by which this CRP church could find out whether it is making any progress toward achieving its objectives. In this case the other church is acting as a control group. The reverse is the case when the CurX judges were trying to find out whether the church using their curriculum is achieving their objectives. Note that each group is testing only its own effectiveness, although both are using the same data.

The four CRP judges and the three CurX judges ranked the 56 essays independently, and their independent rankings were pooled and re-ranked. Then the number of CRP essays and CurX essays in each quarter of the pooled CRP rankings was determined. The same thing was done for the number of CRP essays and CurX essays in each quarter when they were ranked by the CurX judges. In the table below are the results of that tabulation. Note that in each cell are two numbers. One of them, for example, in the upper left-hand corner of the CRP table, is the number of cases that would have been there by chance. This was 8. The other is the number of cases that actually were there, in this case 12. If the actual numbers had approximated the chance expectancies, we should have concluded that we had no evidence that we had made progress toward achieving our objectives. You can see that the chance expectancy for the top quarter was 8 CRP and 6 CurX. What actually did occur were 12 CRP and 2 CurX.

Below each table are the chi-squares and levels of significance.

Ignore these for the present. You will learn how to compute and interpret them later on in the chapter.

POOLED RANKS OF CRP JUDGES

		TOP QUARTER	2ND QUARTER	3RD QUARTER	BOTTOM QUARTER
CRP	Actual	12	6	10	4
	Chance	8	8	8	8
CurX	Actual	2	8	4	10
	Chance	6	6	6	6

Chi-square = 11.66
Significant at .01% level

POOLED RANKS OF CurX JUDGES

		TOP QUARTER	2ND QUARTER	3RD QUARTER	BOTTOM QUARTER
CRP	Actual	7	8	7	10
	Chance	8	8	8	8
CurX	Actual	7	6	7	4
	Chance	6	6	6	6

Chi-square = 1.75
Significant at 63% level approx.

I have not cited this experiment to compare one curriculum with another. The major importance of this experiment is that here is a method by which religious educators, even at the level of the local church, can discover quickly and easily whether or not they are making progress. This has never been possible before. It ought to speed up the progress of religious and character education, as well as education for moral and social values in our public schools, at a tremendous rate.

EXPERIMENTAL DESIGN FOR CO-SCIENTISTS AND PROFESSIONAL SCIENTISTS

"Only three men who were members of this organization when they were boys are in the prisons of this state today!" said the state commissioner of crime, in a speech at a convention of the lay leaders of this particular boys' organization. This sounded impressive enough. The only trouble is that in terms of the proportion of the membership to the male population of the state, there should have been only one! Countless faulty generalizations of this sort are given in public speeches every day because of ignorance of even the simplest statistical concepts.

Or again, one of the great psychologists of all time made many extensive studies based on a questionnaire technique. The amount of work he did is almost incredible. His published materials run into the thousands of pages. Yet most of his findings were invalid because he did not know one of the simplest principles among our modern statistical procedures—indeed, it was not known then.

In these two chapters, then, I want to talk primarily about statistics. I hope none of you will at this point just turn over to the next section of the book, no matter how little interest you think you have in statistics. If I have done my job of writing well enough, these should be among the most exciting chapters in the book. Statistics is providing us with some of the most powerful tools we have today in our search for truth.

Not very long ago, in a conference session on experimental design, a friend of mine who is doing some exploratory research said to me, "There is a lot of groundwork exploration one can do in valid research, without all these highly technical forms of experimental design." I suppose I ought not to object too strenuously to such a statement, for we have certainly been forced to do a great deal of just such exploratory work in the history of CRP. The fact remains that if some of our new statistical tools had been available when we started, our studies would have shown greater progress than they have because they could have been more effectively designed. There are no kinds of research which cannot be well designed! A clinical study can be planned according to these principles as well as a learning experiment; the revision of a lesson plan, as well as an experiment in animal motivation.

The term *experimental design* to most scientists implies the use of certain statistical tools which have been created for the purpose. They are very powerful tools, if experiments are so designed that they can be used.

Probably one reason that so few people have an active interest in statistical methods is because of a widespread misconception of the nature of statistics and what it can do. The layman's concept of statistics and, for that matter, of research, far too often consists in counting a number of things and then constructing some tables of the results, or of finding the average of a number of scores. Statistics is a form of logic, and constitutes one of the most effective ways in which to think straight. It makes possible clear thinking about highly complex bodies of data, which could not be studied without its help. While statistics cannot in and of itself create new hypotheses or dimensions, it is of immeasurable help in detecting their strengths and weaknesses, and thus makes possible the discovery of better hypotheses. Surely in this day when the making of theories is as rampant as it is, that is of great value indeed. I believe that every minister, every educational leader, of course every research worker and, for that matter, every lay leader ought to know enough about statistical reasoning to evaluate critically the ideas with which he comes in contact.

In a book like this, it would be impossible to describe in detail all of the powerful statistical tools which are now available to us in such a program research as that of CRP. I do want to show you, however, how we can use these tools in our research, and the implications this has for the way in which such research can be designed. Furthermore, I want to select from among these tools a few basic ones which you can learn to use yourself. They will constitute a sort of basic minimum equipment with which you can refine your thinking far above the usual level of logic.

The Five Major Problems of Experimental Design   Perhaps the best way to give you an outline preview of what to look for in these chapters is to show you the kinds of tasks these statistical tools are designed to accomplish.

The whole subject of experimental design can be divided into five sections.

1. The first section has to do with a brief history of how statistical methods have grown up through the years. The story of man's ingenuity in doing mathematically what would be almost impossible experimentally is one of the most thrilling in the history of science. In our own work, the invention of new tools which can be used by the nontechnically trained educator is even more significant. When psychologists, or scientists in any other field, find a need for certain kinds of statistical tools to deal with their data, the statisticians endeavor to create them. Especially for those of you who have be-

lieved that the method of science is out of reach of the layman, this history will prove to be an exciting one indeed.

2. The second section will deal with the all-important sampling problem. It was only a few years ago that an experimenter needed huge numbers of cases to do any legitimate research. Now tools are available which sometimes make even the very selectivity of your sample a door to significant insights. If you want to do a piece of research to find out what six-year-olds are like in some respect, you don't expect to measure all the six-year-olds there are. You measure only a relatively small number—this is what we call a *sample* —and hope that what you find out about this sample would hold true if you had measured all the six-year-olds in the world. The sampling problem is, then, how can you know how good (representative) a sample you have? That is very important if you are to draw any general and valid conclusions from your findings. There are statistical tools for helping you answer such questions as these. I will mention a number of these tools and describe fully a few of them which you will find it profitable to learn to use.

3. The third section, which will be described in Chapter XII, has to do with *analysis of variance*. In almost any social research, the careful experimenter can see a number of factors which could have caused his results instead of the one he hopes he is measuring. Not many years ago he would have had to be content to list them as possible "sources of error," and hope for the best. With the tools of analysis of variance he can test for any or all of them with comparative ease. Let's consider that sample of CRP and CurX Junior Highs again. We have tried to measure them in regard to their assimilation of some of the religious concepts to which they had been exposed. You will note that they were not alike in this regard. The range in each group was very wide indeed. Variance is one of the commonly used measures of the amount of this variation among them. But our major question is, What brings about these differences? It obviously was not just the curricular materials, or the members of each group would have all been alike. A number of factors undoubtedly played a part in the observed differences. We need tools to test these out to find out which ones did or did not contribute to this variance.

4. The fourth section deals with the most important of all statistical tools, *correlation*. I think it can be safely asserted that if the concepts and tools of correlation had not been discovered, we

could never have had a science of psychology, or at least we would not be able to deal with such complex phenomena as those of personality. Do character and church-school training correlate with each other? Helping us to get accurate answers to questions like this is only one of the many uses of the *correlation coefficient*. There are many different kinds of correlation coefficients. I shall list a number of them and describe two of them which you can actually learn and use in the many relevant educational problems you are sure to meet in your own work.

5. The last section of Chapter XII deals with *units*. This topic may surprise you. You may think you know what units are, but you will soon discover that you cannot always be sure that two and two do make four. In fact, in everyday life, we very often assume that this is true in places where it is not. What good are the other statistical tools if we do not have data which can be reduced to quantitative form? Suppose you are teaching a Sunday-school class. You will recognize at once that your pupils are not equally enthusiastic about your efforts. But just how enthusiastic is Jack, or Bill, or Jim? Can you count the units of enthusiasm which each has, so that you can say confidently that one has three such units of enthusiasm, another six, and another ten? Unless you can do just this, you are not likely to get very far with statistical procedures. But don't give up too quickly. There are tools for doing just this sort of thing. You can develop such units for even so abstract a commodity as enthusiasm.

I can only hope, now, that I have sufficiently whetted your appetite for what is to follow that you will be willing to study each section thoroughly enough to understand its concepts and to learn to think in terms of its principles. If you will, you will have at your disposal some powerful new tools with which to meet many of the problems that confront you.

EXPERIMENTAL DESIGN—FROM LABORATORY TO DAILY LIFE

The history of experimental design from our point of view can be described as having gone through three periods during the last half-century.

In the Day When Research Was Only for the Highly Trained

Specialist The first one was the era during which physics dictated the procedures by which valid experimentation could take place. These procedures made personality research impossible. The classical definition of an experiment during this period went something like this: "Hold all factors constant except one. Vary that one systematically, and measure the results." Mathematicians tended to lean strongly toward physics, and those of us in psychology had no choice except to follow, unless we chose to face the charge of not being "scientific." Such a concept of research was all right for physics, where the materials being studied could usually be brought into the laboratory and manipulated at will. But psychologists are concerned primarily with human personality, and it can't be dealt with that way.

Most of our major problems cannot be attacked under such restrictions. Such problems as those found in the study of learning, motivation, and personality involve the consideration of many variables, none of which can be held constant while we measure any one of them in an experiment. The result was that the so-called psychophysical problems, dealing mostly with sensory perception, were about the only ones attempted during this period.

Then a Statistical Tool, Correlation, Made Personality and Social Research Possible But then the second period came into existence. It was ushered in by the creation of a great statistical tool, the correlation coefficient. It then became possible for us to let the many facets of personality keep right on behaving normally—they would do that whether we liked it or not—and still find it possible to study them scientifically. Looked at statistically, it is the name of Karl Pearson which is most prominently associated with this second period. The great tool was first invented by Galton and brought to maturity by Pearson. Statisticians have been enlarging its usefulness, until today there are many kinds of correlation measures and numerous ways in which they can be used. This concept of correlation was like a pardon from prison to the psychologist. He could now let the people in his experiments behave naturally, and still study their behavior scientifically. Many other statistical concepts grew up during this period. But almost all of them were derived from this basic one. I'll give you some idea of what can be done with these tools in the section on correlations in Chapter XII.

Small Sample Statistics Gave Research to All of Us Then came the third period. The name of R. A. Fisher stands high above all others in its development. The term which designates its significance is *small sample statistics*. That doesn't sound very thrilling— unless you know your statistics! But in research like ours, it probably increased the possible rate of research by tenfold or even a hundredfold. You see, during what we have designated as the "correlation" period, we had to have large numbers of cases for the results of any experiment to be very conclusive (large sample statistics). In fact, they had to be large enough that the differences in the statistics we got from them would vary very little from the differences obtained from an infinite number of cases. Oh, to be sure, there were a few tools which did not depend on large numbers of cases. But for the most part, we were confined to the use of large N's. (N represents the number of cases in an experiment.) It is still a common experience to hear someone say: "That experiment doesn't mean much. There weren't enough cases." On the contrary, some types of research can be done far better with small N's. The value of research is determined far more by the nature of the sample than it is by the number of cases in it.

The possibilities of exploration opened up by this statistical revolution are great indeed. If the second period for the psychologist can be likened to being let out of prison, this third period is like a trip around the world, in the breadth of its horizon.

This is not to suggest that we have now attained statistical heaven. Far from it! There are many new tools yet to be discovered, which will broaden still further our search for truth. There are still statistical restrictions which unduly limit the scope of our experimental designs. There can be and are being found mathematical tools with which to interpret confidently any meaningful data.

THE CHARACTERISTICS OF A WELL DESIGNED EXPERIMENT

Now we can look a little more closely at this term *experimental design*. Just what does it mean? Someone has said that many of the experiments done in the field of social problems are so badly designed that no conclusions can be drawn from them. A great many studies are proposed for dealing with important problems. Some of them are worthless because of the omission of one or more basic rules in experimental design. Actually, good experimental design is not as difficult as you might expect, at least for moderately well controlled experiments.

A Badly Designed Experiment Which You May Have Seen I am going to start by describing an experiment as badly designed as I can conceive it, and then show you how it can be re-designed to be scientifically valid. Actually, five principles applied to its original design would have been sufficient to make it a respectable piece of research.

Let us consider a hypothetical "experiment." Our problem is: Which is better, Curriculum A or Curriculum B? So we will go into Church A' which uses Curriculum A and into Church B' which uses Curriculum B. Each of them has an enrollment of two hundred children. On examination we find that there is considerably better average attendance in Church school A', and that a larger number of the children there say they are interested in the church school. Therefore, we conclude that Curriculum A is better. How is that for an experiment? I imagine that even if you have never taken a day's work in science in your life, you know that this cannot, by the longest stretch of the imagination, be considered a scientific experiment. It violates all of the basic principles of experimental design.

If a person with no training in this area should sit down to "design" an "experiment," it would almost certainly not be a good experimental design. Similarly, the chances would be negligible that such a person could find anything of value in the search for truth.

Let us note the major things that are wrong with the "design" I just described. The two churches may represent two different socioeconomic levels from the population. The children in the two groups may differ from each other in age level, one being made up mostly from the lower age levels, the other mostly from the upper age levels. They may differ in sex distribution, one being mostly boys and the other mostly girls. The two schools may differ in the quality of the teaching staff, or in the level of home cooperation they get. Even the popularity of the two ministers may differ widely, or the quality of social program each church has for its youth. One may be a downtown city church and the other a neighborhood church. The two curricula probably do not have the same objectives—and whatever these objectives are, "attendance" and "interest" probably have little or nothing to do with them. Furthermore, this difference in attendance and interest could be due to any one or any combination of these factors which I have mentioned. In other words, such an "experiment" has so many extraneous factors which could and probably would influence the results, that it can in no sense be regarded as scientifically fruitful; that is, it has not been so designed that its data can be interpreted without reference to factors outside the experiment itself. This sort of experimentation is certainly not rare. Fisher himself emphasized its commonness: "The waste of scientific resources in futile experimentation has, in the past, been immense in many fields" (39:84).

A Good Design, the Self-Contained Experiment The concept of the *self-contained experiment*—which is one well designed—simply means that an experiment must be so planned that no interpretations have to be brought in, based on evidence outside the data of the experiment itself.

The first principle is that the experiment must contain its own *controls*. This does not necessarily mean that one must use the traditional "control group," although that is one way of doing it. It does mean that the experiment must be so set up that the results you wish to interpret can be adequately interpreted by comparing them with other results in the experiment. For example, just plain scores on a test seldom mean much in themselves. If John makes a score of 120 on some test, you have no way of knowing whether this is good, bad, or average, unless there are other scores with which to compare it.

Probably the most useful form of "control" in research like that done in CRP is achieved by using some suitable measure of *probability*. This, put simply, means finding out by statistical methods what the probability is that your results could have been brought about either by pure chance and not the factor whose effectiveness you are trying to measure, or by the factor you are studying. Here is a class of eight boys. Suppose the teacher wishes to determine whether his use of the adaptation procedure is of any value in making a lesson effective with them. He decides to use the adaptation procedure on four of them and not the other four. Which four shall he use? If he selects the four whom he likes the best, or with whom he gets the best parent cooperation, then even if the lesson turns out to be effective with these four and not the other four he has no way of knowing whether or not the adaptation procedure had anything to do with it. It may have been the adaptation procedure, but it also may have been personal relationship with the four, the parent cooperation, or some combination of these. The experiment is uninterpretable because it is not controlled. But suppose he chooses the four by a process of random selection. For example, he might put the names on slips of paper and choose four from a hat. There are seventy ways in which a group of four can be chosen out of eight. He uses the adaptation procedure with these four. Now, if all four of the boys so selected are influenced positively by the lesson and none of the others are, the probability of this happening just by pure chance instead of the adaptation procedure is only 1 in 70. We state this as a probability level of .014. Statistically this is significant. That is, we can say that the probability is very great that the adaptation procedure has played a measurable role in the effectiveness of the lesson and that the results have not come about by chance. This procedure may well become one of our most useful methods for conducting exploratory research in religious and character education. Note, in passing, that this experiment can be done with as few as eight cases, and yet fairly confident conclusions can be drawn, especially if it is repeated a time or so with similar results.

We ask ourselves whether our experimental results are statistically significant or not. This has nothing to do with the importance of the experiment itself. It is simply a way of stating what the probability is that our results might have been due to chance instead of being evidence of the factors we are measuring. Usually there are three ingredients in a measure of *statistical significance*. For example, if we are comparing two groups as in our CRP, CurX study, the first ingredient is how big a difference we observe. Of course, the larger it is, the more likely it is to be statistically significant; that is, that it is not the result of chance variation. The second ingredient is the range of the scores in the two groups. The greater the spread between the high and low scores, the bigger the difference you must have to be significant. The third ingredient is N, the number of cases. The more cases you have, the smaller the difference has to be, to be significant. Ordinarily this varies with the square root of N, $\sqrt{N}$. This usually ends up in a fraction something like this:

$$X = \frac{\text{Diff } \sqrt{N}}{\text{some measure of scatter}}$$

X is a ratio which can be looked up in an appropriate table to see whether or not the difference is significant. Later on, I'll show you how to compute one such measure of significance, and mention two others.

Now, let's see how this works out in practice. For example, suppose that only two boys had been enrolled in the above class. If one of them is taught, based on the use of the adaptation procedure, and the other is not, any difference observed (or its lack) could be ascribed to any characteristic in which the two boys differ from each other. On the other hand, if four boys were in the class and two were used in each group, these other possible causes of variation would already begin to equalize themselves. The larger the number in each group, the more this would be likely to be true. This is where the N comes into the picture. Note, however, that if your difference is large enough, you need very few cases. So don't decide that an experiment is no good just because it has a small N. If the differences are large enough, even groups of less than ten can give reliable results. Suppose, for example, I want to test the relative value of two stories at the Kindergarten level. I tell one story to Child A and the other to Child B. Let's suppose Child A learns the most. Does that prove that Story A is better than Story B? No; Child A may have been brighter. In fact, one of the two is very likely to have been brighter than the other. But if I use four children, the average intelligence of one pair is likely to be a little more like that of the other. How many cases you need will, also, be determined by the care the experimenter uses in choosing the subjects for the experiment in the first place. The fact is, the use of large numbers of cases is a poor substitute for careful sampling.

ON FINDING POPULATIONS AND SAMPLES THAT GO TOGETHER

This brings us to two more principles in a well designed experiment, the first of which is *randomization*. This consists in "choosing" subjects from a "population" to constitute a "sample." The population is the total group you are studying—six-year-olds, for instance. The sample is the group of six-year-olds you actually measure to find out something about this population. The selection of the four boys from a class of eight has already been described. Randomization, then, is a process by which a sample is pulled out of a population in such a manner that no selecting factors have operated. For example, even if you take every third name in an alphabetical list, you still have the selecting factor of "alphabetical order." This might or might not influence your samples. If, on the other hand, you put all of the names in a hat, mix them well, and pull out the number you want for your sample, you have more closely approached the ideal conditions of randomization.

Complete randomization is not always possible or even desirable. The attempt to obtain matched groups by selecting pairs, each member of which is like the other in every significant way except in terms of the experimental conditions, is called *stratification*. In the actual everyday work of a research project like ours, very often some combination of stratification and randomization is better than either alone. For example, in testing a whole church school, we may begin by selecting one or more pairs from each age level. One member of each pair can then be put in one of the two experimental groups, but which children are chosen from the age-level populations and which member of each pair is put into each experimental group may very well be determined by randomization.

In our work in CRP, it would probably be—practically speaking—impossible to select subjects from our total population by complete randomization for each study we do. On the other hand, the churches which are included in a particular experiment may be selected in this way, and the parents who are included in each church subgroup may also be so selected. In any case, the principle of randomization cannot be omitted, because so many of our statistical procedures are based on the operation of the laws of chance, and our tests of significance are based on chance probabilities.

Now, let us redesign that experiment with which we started out this section. The first thing we had better do is to employ a large measure of stratification. We will choose similar churches, in terms of type, socioeconomic status of its membership, types of teachers, parent interest and cooperation, and so on. Then, we can select from each age level in each church a number of possible subjects for the study. We can match these in terms of age and sex. Having thus created two stratified population samples, we are now ready to select our actual experimental samples by randomization.

Next, we need to prepare measuring instruments which are designed to test progress in terms of the objectives of both types of curricula. These tests are then applied at the beginning and end of the training period in both churches. Now we really are in a position to test the effectiveness of each curriculum to achieve each objective. We may very well find that each curriculum will be found to achieve the objectives for which it was set up better than the other. In that case, the problem becomes one of deciding which objectives you want to achieve. To be sure, we may also find that one of the two curricula achieves both sets of objectives better than the other.

Having Chosen and Measured Your Sample, How Can You Determine How Good a Sample It Is? We have a number of statistical tools—some of them fairly simple to use—by which you can choose a good sample in the first place, and/or determine how good your sample is after you have it.

A lot of people think that the larger your samples, the better, and that that is all there is to it. I can cite research done with thousands of subjects in which the sampling was bad. I can cite other research in which less than thirty cases were used in which the sampling was good. In fact, nowadays, it is becoming far more common to use good small samples than dubious large samples. Don't be fooled by research reports based on the fact that large numbers were involved. Some such research is very bad indeed. Let's look, then, at some of the interesting tools and concepts used in our sampling problems.

If I tell you that individuals differ, you won't be much surprised, for you know that already. But did you know that these differences are so regular in almost any large group that you can predict in advance what they will be?

Let's start with a very simple illustration. Go to the nearest neighborhood school. Measure the height of a hundred seven-year-old boys, chosen at random. List these heights in order, from the tallest to the shortest. This list, by the way, constitutes a *distribution*. Now, if you will tell me the height of the sixteenth child in line, the fiftieth, and the eighty-fourth, I will tell you the height of all the others. There may be some minor errors, especially at the extremes, but such predictions can be astonishingly accurate. This is because all such random distributions are pretty much alike. In other words, individuals differ, but groups are astonishingly alike, unless they were deliberately chosen to be different. Give an intelligence test in any average elementary school. You will find that about one-sixth will be below 85 or above 115 IQ. About two-thirds will be between these two figures. This will vary somewhat, according to the educational level of the population from which the students come, but not as much as you might imagine.

Let us take one more important step. If you found the mean (average) height of your sample of a hundred seven-year-old children and then found the mean height of another sample of one hundred, it ought to be about the same as the average of the first, but would probably differ a little from it. If you did this a hundred times, you would have a hundred averages. If we put these averages in order, from the largest to the smallest, they, too, would constitute a distribution. Again, if you tell me the sixteenth, fiftieth, and eighty-fourth, I'll tell you what all the others are with fair accuracy. Now, since each of these averages (means) was obtained on a sample, this kind of distribution is called a *sampling distribution* (that is, a distribution of samples).

Perhaps some of you are saying: "This all looks pretty dull to me. I don't see anything very exciting about it. I am interested in children, in people, not all this technical jargon." But if you are really interested in children, that is just the reason why you should be interested in this. These statistical tools will make you able to be of many times more service to children. Why? The answer lies in the fact that all these distributions conform to certain definite mathematical laws. As a result, when you ascertain just a few facts about a group of children, you can at once predict many other facts—often more far-reaching—about that same group. If you will secure for me about a dozen particular facts about the people in your church or community or school, I can—without ever having been there—tell you a great many things about them that you probably don't know at the present time.

Now, let's look at some different kinds of sampling distributions and see what interesting things they can tell us.

Individuals Differ but Groups Are Very Much Alike Most of our useful statistical tools, including these sampling distributions, would never have been developed if things in nature had not conformed to the normal probability curve. This curve is descriptive of how almost every variable in nature is distributed when we choose a large number of cases at random, measure them, and put them into a distribution. Just because nature is this way, we can do some interesting things. For example, let's go back to that sample of one hundred seven-year-old boys. Line them up as before, in order of height from the shortest to the tallest. Then pull out the third, the sixteenth, the fiftieth, the eighty-fourth, and the ninety-seventh. Have these five stand side by side, and put a straight edge on top of their heads. You will discover that it will touch each head almost exactly, slanting up from the shortest to the tallest, because they will be about the same difference in height as you go up. Try it, and see if you don't find the heights of these five boys to be about as follows: 43.75, 46.25, 48.75, 51.25, and 53.75 inches, respectively. Note that each one is 2.5 inches taller than the next shorter boy. Does that seem almost like magic because I have not seen your boys? It isn't. That is just the way nature behaves. This is of great significance for us in character research.

Now, all this is important in our efforts to find out how good our samples are too. If they are good, they ought to conform to this normal curve. When we choose a sample at random from a normal population, it usually will. That is why *random selection* is a technical term. Choosing a sample "at random" is reasonably difficult to do. It consists of selecting cases for each sample in such a fashion that "every individual in the population being studied has an equal chance of being chosen in the sample."

That is not always as simple as it sounds. For example, in the population which we study in CRP, it will often, if not usually, be impossible to achieve this idea completely. What do we do then? Are we completely blocked? No, the nature of the normal curve also makes it possible for us to know what conclusions we can draw from non-normal samples, and how we go about it. Guilford (47:175–180) describes several types of samples.

A *biased sample* is present when there is a *systematic error*. The most common example of a systematic error with which we would come in contact in CRP comes about when we must depend on a "voluntary" sample. If, for instance, we send out a number of questionnaires—even to a random sample—and if only a part of them respond, the chances are that the factors that determine which people answer the questionnaire and which do not, constitute a systematic error. Such samples are tremendously important in exploratory studies where we are looking for fruitful hypotheses. Furthermore, there are ways of minimizing this type of error. In CRP, for example, we are attempting to get a description of our entire CRP population. This will involve a description of the parents and their families—including some facts about them which were used in the 1950 United States Census. This makes it possible for us to compare our CRP population with the population of the country in general. It also makes it possible, when we are forced to use this voluntary kind of biased sample, to ascertain its nature and see whether and how it differs from a representative sample.

The most common way by which we can improve our CRP sampling is based on the principle of stratification. For example, suppose that when we have finished our CRP population study, we discover, as we almost certainly will, that we have parents with different educational backgrounds in proportions quite different from that of the population at large. Then, for any particular study we can select a proportional number of people from our population from each educational level like that of the whole CRP population. Then we can generalize for this level of society. If we want to generalize for the whole national population, we must choose from our CRP population a number at each educational level proportional to its frequency in the national population. Usually we can do this by a statistical selection in the data, and achieve both purposes with the same data. (This may be especially desirable if we have reason to suspect that education is an important factor in the use of our materials.) When we choose people in any subgroup, however, we do so by randomization. This result is what is called a stratified-random sample. Guilford says, "A stratified-random sample is likely to be more representative of a total population than is a purely random sample" (47:179).

It should be obvious, now, that if we can obtain a complete description of our CRP population we shall be in a position to generalize with considerable confidence from the studies we make on various samples. All we need to do is to use the principles indicated in this discussion.

The main point is that perfect random samples are highly desirable, but that we are not defeated when they cannot be achieved. The pioneering search for promising hypotheses is seldom done with pure random samples. We must, however, know what kind of sampling we are using in order to use our statistical tools and to correct for our sampling errors.

WILL OUR EXPERIMENTAL RESULTS STAND UP?

"The differences obtained are significant at the 1 per cent level." This is a sentence which now appears frequently even in our religious literature. If you don't have a measure of significance in an experimental article, your scientific readers will want to know why. So let's look more closely at just what this means and how it is measured.

Three measures of significance are most commonly used: t, F, and chi-square. Chi-square is the most widely used of the three, is easily computed, and ought to be learned by all educators. You ought to know the nature of the other two as well.

The t-Distribution Made Research Possible with Small Groups Possibly the most significant event in the development of this new era in statistics was the invention of the *t-distribution*, by an unknown statistician who called himself "Student." This distribution is the tool which more than any other has opened up the whole area of small sample research.

The t-distribution is a distribution of samples, or rather of means of samples. Let us suppose that we wish to measure the effectiveness of one of our lessons, which is used with 2,000 children. Now, if we could measure its effectiveness on the whole 2,000 and compute the mean, we could be certain what the effect was on the 2,000. Even if we took 1,000 of them chosen at random, we would guess that the resulting mean (mean of the 1,000 sample) would not be very far from the true mean (mean of the "population," in this case the whole 2,000 children). If we measure them in groups of 500, we would expect a little more variation among the means of the various samples, but still not very wide ones, especially if we have used random selection in choosing our samples of 500.

If we used samples of 250, we could expect more variation in the successive means. If we used groups of 100 we could expect still more variation from sample to sample; and with groups of 25 we would anticipate some wide variations in the means of our successive samples. The amount of variation would increase rapidly with samples of 16, 4, 3, 2, or 1.

If we made a distribution of a number of means, each based on a sample of 500, it would probably have a very narrow range. But if we made a distribution of the means of the samples of 100, the range would be a little larger, and the distribution of samples of 25 would be still greater. When, therefore, we study two groups, actually samples of two populations, and wish to know what the probability is that the difference we observe between them would hold if we had measured the entire populations, we need to take into consideration the size of the samples we are using as well as the size of the difference. The smaller the samples, the more the probability is that a fairly wide difference could be observed between them and yet have occurred by chance, and therefore the larger our difference must be for us to be sure that it is a significant one statistically.

The t-distribution takes all this into consideration. If we use a large number of cases, the t-distribution and the normal curve will be about the same. But the smaller the sample, the wider becomes the distribution of sample means and the less it fits the normal curve. This means that in looking up the significance of our differences in a table of the t-distribution, we must take into consideration the number of cases in the sample. This fact is included in a concept which we call the number of *degrees of freedom.*

I won't introduce any more technical terms into this discussion than are absolutely necessary. The concept of *degrees of freedom,* however, is essential. All of the small sample statistical tables include degrees of freedom as one of the variables which you must know in order to use them. You don't have to understand fully what it means, but you do need to know how to find out how many degrees of freedom you have. That is simple enough. If you are dealing with a distribution, your degrees of freedom are one less than the number of cases. Thus if you are studying 20 children, you have 19 degrees of freedom. But if you are putting your data into diagram groups, then your degrees of freedom are the number of lines in your diagram minus one, times the number of columns in your diagram minus one. For example, in the diagram of the control-rank problem described at the beginning of this chapter, the data was set up for computation of chi-square into four columns of two lines each. This means that there are three degrees of freedom in it: the two columns minus one, which is one, times the number of lines, four, minus one, which is three. Here are a few illustrations of such diagrams and the degrees of freedom in them.

	Top half	2nd half	T
CRP	18		32
CurX			24
T	28	28	56

$$(K - 1) = (2 - 1) = 1$$
$$(L - 1) = (2 - 1) = 1$$
$$df = 1 \times 1 = 1$$

	CRP	CurX	T
1st Q	12		14
2nd Q		8	14
3rd Q			14
4th Q	4		14
T	32	24	56

$$(K - 1) = (2 - 1) = 1$$
$$(L - 1) = (4 - 1) = 3$$
$$df = 3 \times 1 = 3$$

(Note: K = Columns, L = Lines)

If you are like me in wanting to understand the reasoning behind such a concept, let me show you just a little of what this concept of degree of freedom means. Let's take the CRP CurX 2 x 2 table on page 310. We know the totals. We have chosen 32 CRP and 24 CurX, so the subtotals of our lines are 32 and 24, respectively. We have divided them in terms of the first half and the second half, so our column subtotals are 28 each. The grand total is 56. Now, suppose the four cells are blank. I am "free" to put any number in one of these cells as long as it is less than the subtotals. That gives me "one degree of freedom." I put 18 in the upper left-hand corner.

But as soon as I do that, if the lines and columns are to add as indicated, the numbers I put in the other cells are already determined. I have no freedom in the matter. Try this with the 4 x 2 table above. You will find that you can put numbers by choice in three of the cells, but no more. The rest are determined.

	1st half	2nd half	T
CRP	18		32
CurX			24
T	28	28	56

It is almost impossible to overestimate the importance of this concept involved in the t-distribution and degrees of freedom. Without it, we would have been confined to the use of the normal curve, with an increasing error whenever we use small samples. Especially in research in which, during the exploratory phases, we wish to examine many possible hypotheses, we can do so easily with small sample techniques.

The F-Distribution Tells Us How Many Populations We Have Now, let us turn to the second of our sampling distributions, the F-distribution, named in honor of Fisher himself. I'll say just enough about it to show you the kind of problem for which it is especially useful. Let us suppose that we measure the heights of one hundred children in each of two groups. After computing an average for each group, we then find out how far each one of the children in one of these groups differs from this average. This we call a deviation. We square each of these deviations and add up these squares, thus getting for each group a sum of the squares. We divide this sum of the squares by one less than the number of cases. This answer we call *variance*. Then we compute the variance of the whole two hundred. We divide this variance by the first variance. This ratio is F. The larger this ratio is, the less likely are the two samples to be from the same population. Let me show you how it is used.

Suppose I go into one of our churches and measure some characteristic of a fair-sized sample of children chosen at random. I may be suspicious that it is not a representative sample of that church, or I may just want to make sure that it is. So, I draw at random another sample and measure the same characteristic of its members. I compute the variance of one of the two samples and then the variance of the two samples thrown together and divide the larger variance by the smaller one. The resulting ratio is the F. If they are true samples, these variances ought to be alike. I shall not discuss the computations of F further than I have done already. But if you do get F by the process I have described, your F ought not to be greater than 2, if you expect to assume that your groups are true samples of your population. This is an over-simplified rule, but a fairly safe one.

But, you may ask, what value can F have in this kind of research? Well, let me show you. One of the most common types of loose reasoning done in the area of character education can be illustrated in this statement, "A much smaller percentage of youth who have had Sunday-school training end up in prison than of those who have not had this training." It would be a safe bet that if two considerable samples were chosen, one from each of these groups, and measured in any one of a dozen characteristics—socioeconomic status, intelligence, education, and the like—the F-ratio computed as above would show that they were from vastly different populations. This would mean that differences in their behavior that might seem to be a result of their Sunday-school training cannot be confidently assigned to that because of the different natures of the respective populations.

On a somewhat less dramatic scale, we are constantly meeting the following type of problem in CRP. In Church A, children who are actively interested in our program and whose parents will co-operate may be put in one class, with those not giving such co-operation in another. Then, suppose large differences are found between the two groups in terms of growth in Christian character. The problem is, Has this increased growth come about because of our CRP training methods, or is it due to the different kinds of people who chose the two groups? If samples of the two groups are measured in a number of such other characteristics as those previously mentioned, and F-ratios computed, we have some evidence to answer the question. If the F-ratios are significantly small, then we can have some confidence in assuming that the training has been effective. If the F-ratios are large, then we know we are dealing with two different populations, and that the reason for the growth differences cannot be determined without making sure that it is not due to some of these other differences.

Do you see, then, the value of this tool? It gives us an attack on a problem which possibly has caused as many fallacious judgments about the value of various kinds of character training as any other cause.

The Chi-Square Distribution, Our Most Useful Small Sample Tool
Let us come, then, to the last of these sampling distributions, and the one we use the most often; the *chi-square distribution*. Actually, chi-square is a fairly old concept in statistics, but many new uses of it have come about as a result of the rise of small sample statistics. Let us take an example. We may wish to know whether one of our lessons is equally well adapted to boys and girls. We can try it on two groups: one of fifty boys and one of fifty girls. Let us suppose that of the hundred children the lesson succeeded with 60 and failed with 40. If the lesson is equally effective with boys and girls, how would we expect the 60 and 40 to be distributed between boys and girls? Obviously, the number of successes ought to be about 30 boys and 30 girls, and the failures 20 boys and 20 girls. Of course, small differences from this chance expectation would not be at all surprising. But if the 60 successes turned out to be 40 boys and 20 girls and the 40 failures were 10 boys and 30 girls, we could be quite sure that the lesson was very much better suited to boys than to girls. But suppose that the successes were 35 boys and 25 girls, and the failures 15 boys and 25 girls; is this chance or a real difference? This is where chi-square comes into the picture.

First, let us find a way to get these differences from "chance expectation" into a ratio. You will recall that we did this with the experiment cited at the beginning of this chapter. What we actually do is take each contingency (that is, boys succeeding, boys failing, girls succeeding, girls failing) and find the difference between the expected answer and the actual observed frequency. (In the case of "boys' successes expected" [40] and the "boys' successes observed" [30], there is a difference of 10.) We square this (100) and divide this by the expected frequency (30). We do the same for each of the other three contingencies, and then add these quotients. The resulting sum is chi-square.

The formula looks like this:

$$\text{chi-square} = \Sigma \left[\frac{(\text{fo} - \text{fe})^2}{\text{fe}} \right]$$

This means that in each cell we determine fo (obtained frequency) — fe (expected frequency); square this, and divide by fe (expected frequency). The Σ means summation, which simply means that chi-square is the sum of the results we obtained in this manner from all the cells.

Consider those examples I just described. Here is how they would look in computing the chi-square:

(a)

	Success	Failure	Totals
Boys	fo 40 fe 30 (a)	fo 10 fe 20 (b)	50
Girls	fo 20 fe 30 (c)	fo 30 fe 20 (d)	50
Totals	60	40	100

Fo—Fe = 10 in all four cells
(Fo—Fe)^2 = 100 in all four cells

In cells (a) and (c)
$$\frac{(\text{Fo}-\text{Fe})^2}{\text{fe}} = \frac{100}{30} = 3.33$$

In cells (b) and (d)
$$\frac{(\text{Fo}-\text{Fe})^2}{\text{fe}} = \frac{100}{20} = 5.0$$

Total of all four cells 16.66 = Chi-square

(b)

	Success	Failure	Totals
Boys	fo 35 fe 30 (a)	fo 15 fe 20 (b)	50
Girls	fo 25 fe 30 (c)	fo 25 fe 20 (d)	50
Totals	60	40	100

Fo—Fe = 5 in all four cells
(Fo—Fe)^2 = 25 in all four cells

In cells (a) and (c)
$$\frac{(\text{Fo}-\text{Fe})^2}{\text{fe}} = \frac{25}{30} = .83$$

In cells (b) and (d)
$$\frac{(\text{Fo}-\text{Fe})^2}{\text{fe}} = \frac{25}{20} = 1.25$$

Total of all four cells 4.16 = Chi-square

Now, we can look up our computed chi-squares in a table [1] to find out how probable it is that so large a discrepancy between expected and observed results could be obtained by chance. In this particular illustration, the resultant chi-square in Case (a) is 16.66. We find in the chi-square table, that for one degree of freedom (which is true of this problem), a chi-square of 6.65 is significant at the 1 per cent level; that is, that it could occur by chance only one time in a hundred. Since this is much larger than that, we can be almost certain that the difference is not accidental and that the lesson actually is better suited to boys than to girls. But let us see what the results would look like if we had taken the less extreme differences as in Case (b). Here you will recall that we had five more boys and five fewer girls who succeeded and five fewer boys and five more girls who failed than chance expectancy. Is this a real difference or could it happen by chance? In this case the computed chi-square is 4.16. A chi-square of 3.81 is significant at the 5 per cent level, and this is a little larger than that. We can still be fairly confident that we have a real difference, but not as much so as before.

Now let us return to the experiment described at the beginning of the chapter. You will note that chi-square was computed for both the CRP and CurX judges' pooled rankings. The chi-square for the ratings of the CRP judges was significant at the .01 per cent level. That of the CurX judges at approximately the 63 per cent level. This means that the CRP judges, ranking on the basis of CRP objectives, could do so far better than chance. This would indicate that for the top quarter, CRP objectives are being achieved. The CurX judges could not distinguish between CRP and CurX essays appreciably better than chance, when judged in terms of CurX objectives. This means probably that the CurX objectives were being achieved as well by children using CRP curriculum as by children using CurX curriculum.

You will probably want to own at least one elementary statistics book. It will contain the table of chi-squares. However, I am listing here a few of the chi-squares you will most often need in research in character and religious education:

[1] A chi-square table is included in most standard statistics texts.

PRACTICAL TABLE OF CHI-SQUARES

SIGNIFICANCE LEVEL

	df	1%	5%	10%	20%	50%
2 x 2 table	1	6.635	3.841	2.706	1.642	.455
4 x 2 table	3	11.341	7.815	6.251	4.642	2.366
4 x 3 table	6	16.812	12.592	10.645	8.558	5.348
4 x 4 table	9	21.666	16.919	14.684	12.242	8.343

In the chapter I have illustrated both 2 x 2 and 4 x 2 tables. You might also use 4 x 3 and 4 x 4 tables, so I have included those also. Note that if your obtained chi-square falls into the 1% or 5% column, you can be pretty sure that you have a significant finding. If it is the 10% or even the 20%, you have a finding worth following up. If it falls below this, your chances of having anything of value are quite poor.

You will find that these measures of significance will help you a great deal in clear thinking. To be sure, some people take them almost as a cult, and use them blindly. They are tools, not slave-masters. The fact remains that they are effective tools. You will make many fewer false judgments if you can learn to use them well. Especially when we are dealing with small samples, these tools keep us from making untenable assumptions in either direction. Nevertheless, we no longer need say, "The number of cases is too small; I can't tell anything from this." With these tools, you can. This makes possible hundreds of previously impossible experiments.

There are many other uses of chi-square. We can measure the normality of our sample by this technique, when it is important that it be normal. Very often the purpose of an educational method is in effect to skew a curve, so that we can use chi-square to discover how skewed we have succeeded in making it. Put in the jargon of the statistician, that doesn't sound very exciting, does it? But let's take a closer look. How many times have you heard people say, "People have always been that way; they always will be." This is usually a surrender reaction given as an excuse for not making any effort to change things. If you take a sample of the American Army in the First World War and find the frequency of illiteracy; then, using that as the expected frequency, do the same thing for the Second World War, you will find a highly significant chi-square. We have changed the literacy level in the United States a great deal. If you should do the same thing for the role of education, social service, and health service between the day when Jesus preached and today, you would almost certainly discover very high chi-squares. The religion of Jesus has made a difference.

Finally, let's take our Vicarious Sacrifice Unit. In it we are trying to challenge our growing youth to test the central teaching of Jesus in "loving one's enemies." If we choose a representative sample of the population today and find the frequency among them in this regard, it will probably not be very high. Does that mean it never can be? At least, we will be trying with all our skill to make it otherwise. Suppose we take a sample of our CRP youth after they have worked on this unit and measure them in this regard, and then compute a chi-square of these observed measures, using the population at large as expectancies. If that chi-square is even the slightest significant, that might mean a turning point in world history.

SOME IMPORTANT PRINCIPLES ABOUT EXPERIMENTAL DESIGN WHICH THE CO-SCIENTIST SHOULD KNOW

All of us make sincere statements and sincerely believe others which are seen as obviously false by those who know even the simplest tools of experimental design. Anyone with a high-school education can master sufficient statistical methods to avoid many such errors in judgment, whether he considers making these judgments himself or wishes to evaluate the ones he hears others make. He is able to judge propaganda in terms of its rational values and to avoid being swayed only by its emotional content.

Experimental-design statistical tools are now available which make it possible to do good research with small numbers of cases and with modest technical training, and which can be used in natural situations. Historically none of these were possible. Now, however, although experts ought to be consulted occasionally, the co-scientist can learn and use them.

The greatest difficulty in educational research is knowing whether changes observed in the children exposed to our procedures have come about because of our procedures or because of other factors. When a group—usually a sample which we hope is representative of the total group (population) we are studying—is measured in terms of some test of performance, the individual differences within it (of which one measure is its variance) are caused by all these factors, including the educational influence, if any. We can test the significance of differences between groups who have and have not had the educational influence by a statistical tool known as t. If the educational procedure has increased individual differences within the group, the best statistical tool to test its significance is F. If we want to check as to how representative our sample is of the population of which it is a part, we usually use chi-square. The main point is that such tools as these, reliable with very small samples, make us able to do good research even in everyday educational work.

CHAPTER XII

THE TOOLS OF EXPERIMENTAL DESIGN—INTEGRATION AND THE TOTAL PERSONALITY

IS PERSONALITY TOO COMPLEX TO STUDY SCIENTIFICALLY?

WHEN I was a graduate student, professional scientists in other fields were insistent that psychology was not and could never be a science. Their reasoning was that you cannot isolate the separate aspects of personality, nor for that matter of the environment, for valid experimental attack. Furthermore, they believed that there could be no measuring rods for measuring most personality factors, because they are qualitative in nature and it seemed impossible to quantify them. These were formidable difficulties, and psychologists readily admitted their presence. However, to a man, psychologists had faith that the hurdles constituted problems to be solved, not insoluble frustrations.

As a result of an incredible amount of intensive work in experimental design, there is hardly an area in the psychology of personality which cannot today be successfully attacked with valid scientific methods. In this chapter I want to describe the nature of some of the tools which have been developed for this purpose. With a few exceptions I shall not try to teach you to use them. You would need extensive training in advanced experimental design to do that, but I do want you to know what they are like and what can be done with them. They can literally perform miracles. Therefore let's look at the three major aspects of this problem of studying the total personality in its normal environment with scientific methods.

In the first place, it is true that we cannot control the environment. When we have children in our church-school classes, they come from different homes and schools, with widely different neighborhood influences, belonging to different clubs, and so on. Out of all these S (situational) factors, how can we hope to evaluate the influence of any one of them? You may wonder whether perhaps the best we can do is to develop the most intelligent curriculum we can create and just hope for the best.

Fortunately, that is not the best we can do! A whole new set of statistical tools, in general referred to as *analysis of variance,* have changed all that. We can now study simultaneously various influences on our children, and determine with a fair degree of accuracy the influence of each one of them. So let the S be as complex as it will, with experimental designs based on analysis of variance we can still deal with them. No longer must we create artificial and unreal laboratory situations to measure them, two at a time; we can let them vary normally and measure them even more accurately.

Then, too, and probably even more important, the personality itself is a complex phenomenon. We cannot ask a child to learn today, have an emotion tomorrow, hold a different philosophy each day of the week, experience one appetite at a time, be the same weight, height, and have the same intelligence as everyone else for the purposes of our research. All of these things are operating all of the time. Even if we could control these factors systematically, the number of possible permutations and combinations, each requiring a separate experiment, would be fantastic.

The greatest statistical concept of them all is suitable for this task; namely, *correlation.* With correlation, and all of the tools which have grown out of it, we can let the individual behave normally, and study the relevant factors which are interacting and varying in outwardly bewildering complexity. The layman will not be able to use all of these correlation tools. (I shall teach you a couple of simple correlation methods which will be of great usefulness to you.) For the most part, however, you will need to consult the professional statistician in the designing of your research. The point is, you should know that such techniques exist and what they can do, so that you will not abandon, as hopeless, research for which techniques are available for thorough scientific study.

Then, finally, what about this business of measuring abstract concepts, such as a mother's love? As I have said, we often give up as impossible things which can be measured fairly easily, and then turn around and use units which are totally incomparable. Making sure that two and two make four in personality research is both possible and necessary. I'll show you how that is done. Some of these tools you can use with a minimum of expert advice. Others are much too complex. But you ought to know of their existence.

In the pages that follow, then, I shall describe two kinds of statistical concepts; a few that you ought to learn to use but more about which you need primarily to know that they exist. I have heard many an educator assert that certain problems he was facing could not be solved, simply because he did not know of the existence and uses of some of these statistical tools. This is especially true of the various types of correlation and the various methods of quantifying seemingly abstract phenomena.

ANALYSIS OF VARIANCE—DO OUR CHILDREN CHANGE BECAUSE OF OUR GUIDANCE OR IN SPITE OF IT?

It would be my guess that *analysis of variance* techniques will one day be as universally used by educators of all sorts, from research experts to just plain teachers, as is the multiplication table or the dictionary. It will do more to replace "subjective opinion" about our educational procedures with "objective evidence" than any other technical device now available in the field of science.

In our work in CRP, we know that there are a great many environmental factors besides our curriculum influencing the children in our participating groups. How can we possibly know how much our lessons have had to do with their performances?

For some years I taught a very difficult and time-consuming advanced course in Union College. The students who took that course have, as a group, distinguished themselves far beyond the general level of college students. Was that because they took the course? In this case I know that they were already distinguishing themselves before they came into the course. The course was so difficult that they would not have elected it unless they had been outstanding students. But let's extend this to education in general, including our religious and character education. If those who participate in it do stand out among their fellows, is it because of, in spite of, or independent of what we have done for them in our educational efforts with them? Analysis-of-variance techniques make it possible to begin to answer just such questions.

But let's go a step further. Probably my course had little to do with the later performances of the students who took it. But suppose that I had known what factors did account for their outstanding characteristics, even before they came into my class; do you not suppose I could have made that course far more valuable in their lives? Probably our religious- and character-education programs up to now are not major influences in the development of our children and the quality of their later performances in our social institutions. But suppose that we can discover what factors do account for the differences among them in this regard, do you not imagine that we can make our character and religious education become an important force in their development? The solution of just such problems is being brought within our reach by such techniques as analysis of variance.

Or again, we may wonder whether one church is doing a more effective job than another. To be sure, we could conduct some extensive research and probably arrive at fairly solid answers. But here, too, we would take a couple of dozen Parents' Report ratings, chosen at random, from the two groups, and in a short time find out whether there are any very extensive differences between them in this regard. We could do the same for the effect of "men teachers" as opposed to "women teachers," for different lessons, for the "level of home cooperation," for the use of the "adaptation procedure."

Just what do we mean by analysis of variance? When you measure a number of people according to some variable, they differ from one another. Why? There must be some reason or, usually, a number of reasons. Now, when you make a distribution of their scores and find an average, the individual scores scatter on both sides of that average. Variance is a measure of the amount of this scatter. Analysis of variance, then, is a technique by which we try to find out what has caused this scatter. For example, we may hope that some of it has been due to our educational procedures. What we do in analysis of variance is to test a number of other possible things that might have accounted for much or all of the variance.

Perhaps this illustration will clarify the principle underlying this method. Let us go into some community and literally count the number of acts among its citizens which could be classified as Christian in their nature. We assign a score to each man in the sample we study, which is the number of such acts he performed in a given period of time. We do this for two groups. One of these groups consists of a hundred people chosen at random from the total population of the city. We find that their scores vary from 0 to 75, with an average of 40. We compute the deviation of each individual from this average and square it. We add up these squared deviations and divide by one less than the number of cases. This is the total variance of this group.

Now we take a second group. This time it is composed only of those people in the original group who have had Sunday-school training behind them. We find that their scores range from 30 to 75, with the average at 52. When we compute the variance for this group, it will obviously be less than the other. This is clearly a more Christian-acting group than the total group, although it does not account for all the Christian behavior.

Now comes the major question. Was the superiority of the second group due to their Sunday-school training? Or could it be accounted for by their socioeconomic level, their educational background, or the kinds of homes they came from? We can measure the group in terms of all of these other factors, throw them into an analysis of variance equation, and find out at once whether any or all of them also entered into the results.

The assertion, then, that *analysis of variance* is potentially one of the most useful statistical tools available to use in such problems probably would not be seriously challenged.

In one of our studies we came to a point in the analysis of the data in which there was the possiblity of having to divide it into 128 different sets of material. By the use of the technique of analysis of variance, with less than two weeks' work, we discovered that at most we needed only two groups and that the errors would be small if we used only one. We used only one. It took us six months to analyze that. To have analyzed the whole 128 different sets would have cost us literally hundreds of thousands of dollars. Such a decision would have been impossible to make with any confidence at all without this tool of analysis of variance.

As you read over the next few pages, you may think the process sounds complex. Actually, it is not very difficult; and although I shall not include actual computational methods, you ought to have an adequate understanding of its theory.

I shall describe four aspects of the problem: (1) You ought to see the basic theory for simple analysis of variance when we use only two groups. (2) Then, we can see how to handle cases where a third variable influences the relationship between the two you are studying, with the use of the method of *covariance*. (3) Then we will turn to the most valuable applications of the tool; namely, when we are dealing with more than two groups. (4) From there it will be relatively easy to see the value of analysis of variance in *factorial design*.

The Process of Simple Analysis of Variance Is Easily Done   Let us suppose that we have scored two sample groups of Parents' Reports and computed the mean of each group. These means will, of course, be almost certain to differ to some degree. The problem is, Do they differ enough to justify our trying to find out what brought about the difference? We may have been using two different teaching methods in the two groups, and want to know whether it makes any difference which one we do use. Or we may want to study the effect of different kinds of parent motivation. The analysis-of-variance technique is often the simplest way to attack such problems.

Here, roughly, is the way we go about it. Remember, we have the scores on two groups. First, we find the mean of each of the two groups. Then we combine the two groups to form a composite group. We then find the mean of this composite group. Next, we compute two variances: one the variance of the composite group—this we call the "total variance"—and then the variance of each of the two sample groups. This we call the "within groups variance." Now, notice what will happen. If it makes no difference which of the two teaching methods we use; that is, there is no difference between them—then the means of each group and the mean of the composite group of the two of them will fall at almost the same point. The cases will scatter about the same amount, and when this is so, these two variances—the total variance (of the composite group) and the within-groups variance (variance of the samples)—will be almost the same. But suppose the two samples are very different from each other, and their means far apart. The mean of the composite group will be about midway between them. Of course, then, the scatter of the individual scores about the mean of the composite group will be larger than the scatter of the individual scores from the mean of the sample in which they occur. The total variance (of the composite group) will be larger than the within-groups variance (the variance of the samples). The greater this difference, the surer we can be that some factor or factors are operating differently in the two samples, perhaps our teaching methods.

But, of course, we want a test of significance. This, you will re-member, is the measure which helps us to tell how great a difference could have come about by chance. We do this by computing a third variance. We can get it by simply subtracting the "within groups variance" from the "total variance." The "within groups variance" is a result of the fluctuations within the groups and there-fore cannot be ascribed to our experimental conditions. It is a meas-ure of the fluctuation of scores within each group due to individual differences and other factors we cannot control. What is left of the "total variance" can be ascribed to the effects of our educational procedures.

The larger this "between groups variance" is in proportion to the "within groups variance," the more confident we can be that we have a significant difference. So we divide the larger by the smaller, look it up in the F-table of probability, and estimate our level of significance.

If we had only two conditions such as in this illustration, then other methods which are simpler are available. They might involve t or chi-square. But consider this situation. Suppose we measure a number of people in regard to Christian acts performed in a given period of time. Some of these people have one curriculum, some an-other; some are in one socioeconomic level, some another; some have one kind of education and some another. We could keep on adding these different conditions. We could compute the within-groups variance for each one, and by appropriate methods find out whether any of them had anything to do with the results in

Christian behavior. In a single computation we could test a number which would require a prohibitive number of experiments by other methods. In educational fields, where there are so many factors that might enter the picture, we can find out quickly how many of them actually do.

There Are Some Factors Which Can Obscure Our Vision for the Real Factors Let's look again at the data concerning the CRP and the CurX Junior High's described at the beginning of Chapter XI. We ranked the youngsters of the two schools from best to worst. We were almost implicitly assuming that the order in which they came was due to our teaching and their learning. But let's take another look. Most of them were twelve, thirteen, and fourteen years of age. Don't you suppose that the fourteens on the average did better than the twelves? That is, chronological age may have made the difference, not learning. They undoubtedly differed in IQ. The brightest in general probably learned more than the lowest in intelligence. Probably the educational level of the homes from which they came made a difference too. We know that the level of parent cooperation was a very important factor. It is possible that because of their greater maturity the girls did better than the boys. If you lined these young people up in order of each of these factors, they might come in somewhat the same order as they do when we rank them according to the criteria we are trying to measure. These we call factors of *covariance*.

Of course, we try to equalize the presence of these factors in our two major groups by methods of stratification and randomization described in Chapter XI. In this study that was probably done fairly well. Nevertheless you can see that each of these factors would probably tend to widen the distance from the best to the worst. And because analysis of variance involves comparing the amount of scatter with the amount of measured difference, these factors would increase the scatter and therefore decrease our F-ratio, until we could not be sure whether or not there were any differences due to what we were trying to observe; namely, our curriculum. What can we do about that? The answer to this question is another of the statistical tools that transforms some of our research difficulties from virtual impossibilities to relatively easy problems.

Notice this. If we tried to correct for all these factors experimentally, we should have to try to find experimental groups all the same age, the same IQ, from the same educational background, with the same parent cooperation, and all of one sex. I doubt whether you could find sufficiently large experimental groups if you had all the children in all of the church schools in the United States at your disposal. For all practical purposes the study would be impossible.

Fortunately we don't have to do that. If we can measure these factors, which we usually can, we need only to determine the amount of correlation each has with our experimental variable. And this is not difficult, as you will see when correlation is described. We can then simply put a correction factor in our formula for obtaining F, and have the same results as if we had got that mythical sample! Quite a tool, don't you think?

Factorial Design—A Method of Testing Several Educational Methods at Once The value of the analysis-of-variance techniques can be demonstrated most dramatically in its applications in *factorial design*. This is a procedure in which we put all possible combinations of several different variables into the same experiment.

In our recent study of Home Dynamics, one of the factors studied was the influence of the child himself on the parents in their effectiveness in helping him develop character strength. This influence was studied on both fathers and mothers for both sons and daughters. As might be expected, this factor was highly effective for both parents and for both sexes. Indeed, the difference was significant at the .001 per cent level. What is more interesting is that for mothers there were no significant sex differences. Sons and daughters affected mother alike. But for fathers, the influence of his relationship to his son was a far more significant factor in dealing with him than was the case for his daughter. To have studied these variables separately would have been a long task. The use of these statistical tools did the job in a fraction of the time.

This has been a very superficial discussion of this powerful tool, analysis of variance. You will need to turn to some good statistical textbook and/or bring in competent statistical consultants if you wish to master the skills necessary to use it. Here I have simply tried to give you a vision for its possibilities.

CORRELATION—THE GREATEST STATISTICAL TOOL EVER INVENTED

From the point of view of science, the study of personality is essentially the study of the interrelationship among the variables by which personality is described. Probably the most important factor in productive research in personality, especially in a field like ours, is the selection of a set of variables which are sufficiently accurate and inclusive to be able to do a fair job of predicting behavior. The statistical tool which has made this possible is *correlation*.

In any research in which a number of variables are permitted to vary simultaneously, some measure of how these variables vary together is indispensable. It is not the purpose of this section to extol the virtues of the correlation coefficient, but rather to show you how it can be used in different types of problems characteristic of research like ours. Fortunately, too, there are a number of methods for computing correlation coefficients, depending on the nature of the data to be correlated, each of which has its own uses. In other words, we need to know what correlation tools are available, when we can use them, and when not to use them. A knowledge of the assumptions made in the use of each method will help us so to design our research studies that we know which one to use with the data we have obtained. In fact, we need to know in advance which one we plan to use, so that we can gather the data in such form as to make its use valid.

For those of you who have had no previous acquaintance with the concept of correlation, I have drawn three simple diagrams which ought to indicate what is meant by the concept. In each diagram two variables are plotted. In each case imagine that you have been given a score in one of them and, with no other evidence to work with, want to predict what the corresponding score would be on the other. For example, if you know how tall a person is, how closely can you predict his weight?

Look at the A Diagram. Suppose that each of the small x's had been located by finding out some person's height and going up the "height" axis to the correct point between "very short" and "very tall" and then going across a distance that represents his "weight" from "very light" to "very heavy." Suppose that every time we grew an inch in height we gained five pounds, then this is what the graph would look like when we have "plotted" a number of cases. Of course, "height" and "weight" are not related as closely as this, so I have used two other variables for Diagram A. In everyday life, we do assume a perfect correlation between "temperature" and the "height of mercury" in our thermometers. These are the variables shown in the A Diagram. We also assume a perfect correlation between "time" and "the distance the hands on our clocks" travel. We don't actually see the "temperature"; we simply see a measure

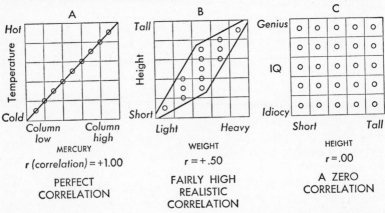

A	B	C
r (correlation) = +1.00	r = +.50	r = .00
PERFECT CORRELATION	FAIRLY HIGH REALISTIC CORRELATION	A ZERO CORRELATION

of the expansion of mercury in our thermometers. We don't actually see the "time"; we see how great a distance the two hands have traveled around the face of the clock. In each case, we assume a correlation of +1.00.

Now turn to B. This may well be about what the case actually is in the matter of height and weight. In general tall people are heavier than short people, but the fact that some are stout and some are slim keeps the correlation from being perfect. You will note that the cases form a sort of elongated elipse, but not a straight line. If you know the score on one axis, you can predict only roughly what the score will be on the other.

Then look at C. You don't expect, of course, to be able to get a good IQ by measuring a person's height. You know that short people range from dull to bright, and so do tall people. This, then, is likely to be an order of zero correlation. The cases form almost a circle. You can't predict at all from one axis to the other.

Now, do you see what correlation means? It goes from ±1.00 to .00, and tells us what relationship there is between the two variables. The coefficient can be either plus or minus, but a —1.00 correlation is quite as predictive as a +1.00. It is the .00 which is nonpredictive. When there is any appreciable correlation between two variables, you can be sure that they have some element in common. You can estimate the amount of common element in the two variables by squaring the correlation coefficient between them. If two variables correlate .40 they have a common factor (or factors) which constitutes 16 per cent of each. When the correlation is lower than 1.00 (which in psychology it almost always is), you know that some other factor or factors not common to both of them enter the picture. In the case of a .40 correlation, these other factors constitute 84 per cent of each variable.

A Simple Method of Computing the Correlation Between Two Variables The basic method of correlation, from which all the others stem, is called the *Product-moment coefficient of correlation*. A majority of research studies making use of correlation have employed this method of computation. It is essentially a large sample method and is subject to increasing error as the sample becomes smaller.

There are many others, depending on the kind of data you have. A few of the best known are: bi-serial r, point bi-serial r, the phi coefficient, and the tetrachoric coefficient.

The rank-difference coefficient is one of the simplest coefficients to compute, and it is very useful for small numbers of cases. You will find it easy to learn and useful in a great many situations. Suppose, for example, we have a class of ten boys and we wish to determine whether their "intelligence" is related to their "popularity with their classmates." We could administer an intelligence test and then rank them according to "IQ." Then, with perhaps a sociogram technique, rank them for "popularity." Suppose, for example, these were the results. Boy A ranked 1 in IQ and 3 in popularity; B ranked 2 and 6 respectively; C, 3 and 1; D, 4 and 2; E, 5 and 4; F, 6 and 7; G, 7 and 5; H, 8 and 9; I, 9 and 8; and J, 10 and 10. I have computed the rank-difference coefficient in this problem—in less than five minutes—to be +.54. (If there are ties among the ranks, you use the average of the ranks included in the individuals who have the same score. Thus, if two boys tied for 2 and 3, you would rank each 2.5.) If the number of cases becomes very large, the arithmetic gets prohibitively cumbersome. But for the thousand-and-one questions which arise in the exploratory phases of studies like ours, this is a very convenient tool indeed. Here is how it is done.

We can use the simple data just described in which we want to determine whether and how much relationship there is between how intelligent a boy is and how popular he is. We start by listing the boys in order of their IQ ranks. Then beside this we put their corresponding popularity ranks. Then in a column beside this we list the differences between the two ranks for each boy. We call this d. Then we square this in the next column, d^2. Then we sum these d^2s which we designate as the summation of the d-squares, Σd^2.

Boys	IQ rank	Pop. rank	d	d^2
A	1	3	2	4
B	2	6	4	16
C	3	1	2	4
D	4	2	2	4
E	5	4	1	1
F	6	9	3	9
G	7	10	3	9
H	8	8	0	0
I	9	7	2	4
J	10	5	5	25
n	10		Σd^2	76

Now we have all the facts we need for computing the rank-difference coefficient which we call rho (ρ). The formula is:

$$\text{rho} = 1 - \frac{6 \text{ times } \Sigma d^2}{n(n^2 - 1)}$$

$$= 1 - \frac{6 \text{ times } 76}{10(100 - 1)} = 1 - \frac{456}{990}$$

$$= 1 - .46 = .54$$

In this case, then, your correlation coefficient is .54. If this data had been obtained in actual research, this would mean that there is some relationship between IQ and popularity. The common element between them constitutes 29 per cent of each of them, the square of the coefficient. It also would mean that 71 per cent of popularity is due to something else than IQ.

In Research You Ought Always to Test the Reliability of Your Measures   In making any sort of measurements, you need some estimate of *reliability*. This means that you must show some evidence that you have made your measurements accurately. For example, consider a ranking procedure. Suppose you rank a group of children in terms of their popularity. What evidence have you that that is how popular they really are? Usually in research such measurements are made at least twice, preferably independently, by two people. Then you can correlate (obtain rho) the two sets of measurements. If your correlation is high, you can be reasonably confident that your measurements have some accuracy. In any experiment involving ranking or rating, you should never depend on only one set of measurements.

It is possible to estimate how many judges you need before their pooled ranks have a high reliability. Here is a reasonably satisfactory method. Compute rho between two judges. If it is .40 you would need 11 judges to have a satisfactory reliability. If it is .50, 9 judges would be necessary; if .60, 6 judges; .70, 3 judges; for .80, 2 judges are enough.

Factor Analysis—the Master Achievement of Correlation   Finally, there is the instrument for which many scientists have such great hope, *factor analysis*. If a number of variables are measured in a population, and all of the intercorrelations are computed, they can be listed in a two-way table which is called a *correlation matrix*. If we find that a group of these variables all tend to correlate highly with one another and much lower with the other variables in the matrix, we may well suspect that they represent a sort of homogeneous group or *cluster* which can be treated as a unit in some ways; or, more precisely, that some "common factor" runs through all of them.

Factor analysis is certainly one of the most important tools ever developed for the service of psychologists. Like all tools, however, and perhaps more than most, it is no better than the skill of the person using it. Because of its complexity, it requires more skill than most, and can easily be the road to fantastic conclusions if used blindly by persons not prepared to use it. Every educator ought to know of its existence and general nature, but probably only the skilled research worker can use it with confidence.

Correlation, then, is the statistical tool which has most changed the course of science. It makes possible the precise description of functional relationships, which could not possibly be observed by the experimenter in the process of an experiment. Unless you are engaged in actual research, you will not need to master the use of all these correlation methods. A few of them are very simple, and can be very helpful to anyone. The rank-difference coefficient is probably the best for this purpose.

If you have learned to use the tools I have described so far, you are in a very good position to evaluate your hypotheses with considerable accuracy. You can find out which are true and which are false. In other words, you can be intelligently critical. You will no longer swallow whole every new theory that comes along. What may be even more important, you won't reject them on the basis of opinion and existing prejudices.

SOME CREATIVE TOOLS IN SCIENCE

Tools are available which reveal the creative side of the scientific method. It is finding new and fruitful hypotheses to test that is the great thrill of the scientist. Until you can do that, you are a laboratory assistant—very important and valuable people, by the way. Until very recently most of us had to be just about that. The great advances had to be made by the Newtons, the Darwins, the Pasteurs, and the Einsteins. Out of the thousands of possible hypotheses that can be made, only a handful are of value. Finding them, except by sheer chance, took the intuitive insight of a genius. Most of us could go all our lives and never hit upon one.

Fortunately, that day has passed, too. There are methods now available which place the excitement of significant insights within the reach of a hundred times as many people. One of these tools to which I have referred repeatedly in past chapters is the *method of characteristic differences*. The method can be used wherever we can divide our sample into two groups, on the basis of some logical difference between them.

For example, in a study on data from a boys' camp, Doty tried to find characteristic differences between boys who adjusted well and easily to the camp situation, as contrasted with those whose adjustments were difficult and even unhappy. He sensed that an examination of the boys' interests gave him a clue to this. He therefore made "interest lists" for each boy. He put these lists into the two groups, adjusted and maladjusted. He submitted these lists to judges who had no idea how the groups had been constituted. The judges looked for characteristic differences which regularly described the boys in the two groups. If this can be done, see what possibilities are opened up for anticipating a boy's reactions to camp. This finding could be of great value to the whole camping movement.

Another procedure which we have frequently used very effectively is one which we call our *Pro and Con Technique*. It is also a good method to divide ideas into two groups for applying the method of characteristic differences. We use it especially when we are making some important policy decision, where there are strong points in favor of more than one decision.

For example, we may wish to decide whether or not to change our basic summer-workshop procedure to another one. Instead of just having a haphazard discussion in which the members of the group align themselves with one or the other point of view and then try to defend it, we proceed in this fashion. First everyone tries to think of all the reasons in favor of the change. These are listed until no others can be produced. Then everyone tries to suggest all the reasons against the change. These, too, are listed until no others are forthcoming.

When the method of characteristic differences is applied to these two sets of answers, usually wholly new dimensions are discovered which make it relatively easy to reach the best possible decision. Not only that; usually it is possible for the decision made, whichever it is, to be modified to include the strengths of both points of view.

There are other methods for finding leads to new dimensions. The cluster-analysis method of the Home Dynamics Study is one of these. It, however, requires extensive use of correlation, the construction of correlation matrices, and the isolation of correlation clusters. This level of research you can do only with the aid of skilled statisticians. Nevertheless, difficult as it may seem, it opens up possible hypotheses to most of us which a generation ago would have been attainable only by the genius.

The reason for this is that the human mind, even at its best, can grasp only a very few interacting factors at one time. I would guess that the most brilliant would be sorely pressed to hold six in mind at once. With the tools of correlation matrices, that number is many times larger. In the Home Dynamics Study we used sixty-three.

Even this is not the limit of what man can do with the proper tools. In one of our studies an IBM electronic calculator did in a few minutes what it would have taken us at least five years to do, and at less than a third the cost. The mathematics involved in some of our highly complex intervariable studies would be an insurmountable hurdle if it were not for these electronic computers which reduce our most complex problems, which once would have taken decades to do, to a few days' work. Human personality is a bewilderingly complex phenomenon, but these miraculous tools are opening new doors of discovery which ought to make even international relations as easy to manage as a child's birthday party.

WHEN TWO AND TWO MAKE FOUR

It will be obvious to you that even the most miraculous electronic computer is helpless without numbers. And in religious and character education we are dealing with abstract value judgments most of the time. Can they be stated in terms of comparable *units*? Many a religious leader has shied away from science because it is inconceivable to him that we could ever state these abstract concepts in accurate scales, which can be counted. Let me show you some of the methods which have been devised for this purpose.

Two times two should make four! This sounds like a fact we learned in the third grade; but is it? If we take two "temper tantrums" and multiply them by two "adaptation procedures" what do we get four of? Or again, if we take four people with IQ's of 100, can they achieve as much as two people with IQ's of 200? Or once more, suppose a hundred people all answer "yes" to the question, "Do you want to be happy?" Are we justified in assuming that all of the "yeses" mean the same thing? It is not difficult to get some numbers to substitute for letters in our formulae; but the results obtained from solving our equations are not worth any more than the meaningfulness of the numbers we put in.

It is just at this point that much of what goes under the name of research in such fields as religion and education is worthless. Many a "study" is made in which a questionnaire is "thought up" in a short time, administered to a few people, and the average taken as meaningful. In 99 cases out of 100 this is waste motion. A questionnaire is one of the most difficult of all instruments to construct. I think you'll see why after you have read this section on units. If, however, you are willing to master a few of these concepts, it can be done with considerable scientific reliability.

Let us deal with this problem of "units" in four ways. Let us first distinguish carefully among the words *units, categories,* and *variables.* Then we can see more clearly how we must go about the task of gathering data, so that it can be described quantitatively in terms of meaningful units. Next we need to find out how to count some of the things we observe with such accuracy that if a number of us count them independently, we come out with approximately the same answers. Finally, let us see how we can make sure—or come as close to it as we can—that in our counting two and two do make four.

Units, Categories, and Variables—How to Construct Them   Our first task, then, is to define three words: *units, categories,* and *variables.* It sounds like common sense to say that a "unit" is "one" of something, whether it is an "individual," a "behavior pattern," a "question on a questionnaire," a "group," or a "Parents' Report." But suppose we have eight small groups of people and divide them at random into two larger groups of four small groups each. Are these two large groups equal? Unless the small groups were all equal in the first place, they probably aren't. Many scales, including questionnaires and rating scales—and teachers' examinations—are constructed in such a way that the individual items on any one of them are so different in value that it is impossible to make any mathematical computations which assume that its units are equal. For that matter, many a scale item is twins or triplets, not a unit.

It will be obvious, then, that a major task is to construct scales of units which are units and which are equal to the other units on the scale, so that two and two of them do make four. That is, this sum, four, ought to be approximately four times as large as any one of them. This, you see, isn't true unless they are all the same size.

What about *categories?* In the early stages of one of our own research problems, we collected some two or three hundred different items (not units yet, just items). Our task was to discover some categories—as few as possible—into which these items could be classified. But, you see, ideal categories should be defined so clearly that no item can be classified into more than one of them. A set of categories ought to be exhaustive, so that all of the items will fit into one or another of them. They ought to be homogeneous, so that each one is clearly just one category, not a conglomeration of several unrelated things lumped together. In this study several of us tried to categorize these items, and each of us came up with a different set of categories—few of them completely satisfactory. As we discussed the matter together, some of our categories became clear and well defined, but even then others did not. The fact is, finding suitable categories is necessary, but difficult. And here is the important point. The categories you use may make the difference between new insights and a futile waste of time. You see, categories are much more a result of the way the scientist looks at his data than they are functions of the data itself. Almost any set of data can be categorized in a number of different ways. Most of these are utterly sterile as far as new truth is concerned. Therefore, finding fruitful categories in terms of which to organize your data is a crucial point in your research.

And finally there are *variables.* Perhaps a satisfactory simple definition of a variable is that it is a category in which the items included vary in degree from one extreme to the other. Statistical tools all assume that variables vary. That may sound like common sense, but it is not uncommon to find the contrary. For example, the writer, during World War II, examined some "trait efficiency ratings" in a number of Officer Candidate Schools. In some cases a dozen of the traits would be rated exactly alike for all of the candidates involved. Such ratings are completely useless, statistically speaking. They certainly were not variables, for they didn't vary.

Furthermore—and here we introduce our basic ways of creating comparable units—if a variable is really a variable, a large number of items distributed at various points on it are likely to approximate a normal probability curve. For example, draw a horizontal line five inches long and divide it into half-inch units. Beginning at the left end, write the numbers 0–10. Then erect a vertical line at the 0 and divide it into one-eighth inch units and number this from the bottom up from 0–30. It ought to look like this:

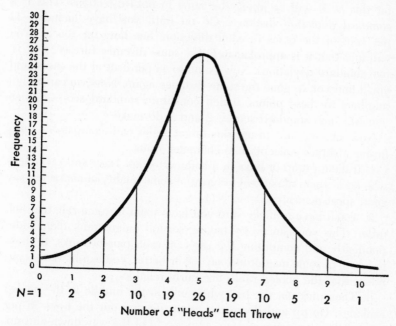

Number of "Heads" Each Throw

Now, take ten pennies; put them in a box; shake them well, and turn them out onto a table. Count the number of "heads." If it is, for example, 4, draw an eighth-inch vertical line up from the number "4." Then repeat the process. If you get "4" again, add another eighth-inch line to the first one. If you get a different number, draw an eighth-inch line at the appropriate point. Shake the pennies 100 times, each time recording the number of heads in the appropriate place. When you have finished, draw a curved line across the top of these vertical lines from 0–10. You'll find that it closely resembles a normal probability curve. In fact, if you do this on the accompanying graph, you'll find that after a certain number of throws you will just about have filled out this curve.

Now let's observe some of the interesting things about this curve. No matter what you measure in nature, you get about the same curve when you measure a large number of them. Construct several such curves if you wish to demonstrate this to your own satisfaction. Now start from the average and go out in each direction until you have included about a third of the cases (34.13 per cent). See how far this is. It will be about the same in both directions. This is a *standard deviation* distance. Go on until you have included 42 per cent of the cases in each direction. See how far this is. You will find that it is approximately the same distance further; that is, two standard deviations. Now go on to 48 per cent of the cases, and you'll find you've gone the same distance again. Now we can assign numbers to these points, which constitute standard scores. When you use such standard scores, 2 and 2 do make 4.

Now let's see how to use this to get scales with comparable units in our abstract concepts like character traits.

1. Take a group of boys in a summer camp. Have several judges who know them rank them in terms of some quality of character, say good sportsmanship.

2. You'll have to make sure you have them in some reliable rank order. This you can do by having several judges rank them independently and computing the rho's on each pair of ranks. If those rho's are of some magnitude, say .60 or better, you can be fairly confident that the pooled ranks are fairly reliable.

3. Then pick out the boy who ranks in the middle in the pooled rankings. Go up and down the group picking out the boys 36 per cent of the way down and up, 42 per cent of the way down and up, 48 per cent of the way down and up, and the distance between them in this quality of sportsmanship as defined by the judges will be about equal. You can assign scores to each boy, thus constituting a scale, in terms of which you can score all of the others.

You can do this for almost anything which can be reliably ranked —essays, behavior items, poetry, skills, or character traits. This is by far the best method for defining comparable units, though by no manner of means the only one.

Getting Evidence That Can Be Quantified Let's take a look at some of the methods by which we can go about gathering data which is meaningful when we put it into numbers.

In the construction of a rating scale or questionnaire, the criteria by which to prepare an item for inclusion are numerous. These vary from making sure that the item is a single fact, not double barreled, to making sure that it is simple enough to be understood and precise enough not to be ambiguous. At least a score of such criteria are listed in Symonds' book on methods in personality measurement (134: especially Chs. III and IV). Scales constructed by the use of such methods show much larger levels of reliability and correspondingly more frequent significant findings than scales constructed without such careful preparation.

Let me point out again that questionnaires or rating scales are among the most difficult and highly technical instruments we use in psychological research. The naïve innocence with which people often do prepare them makes a scientist shudder. People who would shy away from rho, chi-square, and analysis of variance casually attempt the preparation of a questionnaire of sixty-three questions.

Then, again, in our work in CRP we depend a great deal on *interviewing*. We cannot hope to train all of our interviewers in all of the technical skills of interviewing. The fact remains that the closer we can approach this ideal, the more valuable our data will be. We can achieve part of this by a careful preparation of interview outlines. One needs only examine the volume of Bingham and Moore (13)—which is a book you ought to have if you do any interviewing—to discover how easy it is for interviews to bring forth no useful facts at all. Interviewing will be discussed more fully in Chapter XIII. Such principles as gaining rapport with the interviewee, being aware of one's own biases, asking questions which inform the interviewee about the value of the interview are just a few of the obvious principles involved.

How to Count Is Not Always As Easy As You Might Suppose
The third of our objectives is how to count the facts we observe. In the first place, we must distinguish between counting and measuring. Counting is simply determining how many objects there are in a group. This we usually call a frequency. Measuring is applied to a scale and is stated in terms of scale units.

As a result of counting and/or measuring we can produce different kinds of numbers. Frequencies, percentages, proportions, ratios, and ranks are among the most common of these. Which are used depends on the nature of the problem. Each has advantages and disadvantages which make it suited or not suited for particular purposes.

Finally, what can we do to make sure that when we count our

data, two and two come close to being four? For example, one person has better color vision than another. We can be pretty sure about that; but can we determine accurately how much better? Or again, it is not difficult to arrange items of behavior in order of excellence according to some standard, say that of generosity or anger control. But can these be regarded as a scale by which to measure other items? And if we assign numerical scores to them, can we have any confidence that the differences from point to point on the scale are equal differences? A number of methods have been developed for doing just this, of which I have described one, the method of standard scores. Let us look at a few others of them. I think that those of you who have had no statistical training will be amazed at how many different methods we have for establishing equal units in psychological data.

Perhaps the oldest of them in the history of experimental psychology have to do with the so-called *psychophysical methods*. If you had walked into almost any experimental psychology class in the "twenties," you would have heard students talking about JND's. A JND referred to a *Just Noticeable Difference*. For example, let us set two lights side by side which are exactly equal in brightness and then increase the brightness in one of them until the observer can detect a "Just Noticeable Difference." An average of several trials is ordinarily used to make sure of the exact point. Then, the two lights are equalized at this new point and the process repeated. This will result, eventually, in a series of points each being a JND brighter than the one next lower down. From the point of view of the observer, at least, these steps can be regarded as units, and if we keep in mind what they represent they can be accepted as equal units. Units of this sort are not uncommon in physics and physiology as well as in psychology.

Again, suppose we take from our files a number of children's stories and wish to measure the amount of imagination represented in them. One method which can be used to scale them is known as the *method of paired comparisons*. We ask a number of judges to take each story and compare it to every other story in the sample being tested as being more or less imaginative. Now suppose that Stories A and B are compared. If half the judges classify A as better and the other half B as better, the difference can be regarded as too small to be detected by such a method. Or suppose that all of the judges classify A as better than B. Then we know that A is better than B; but we have no way of knowing how much better. But suppose 75 per cent of the judges classify A as better and 25 per cent B as better; then we can establish a degree of difference which is defined as being of such a size that about 25 per cent of people cannot detect it. If, then, we use as scale points, stories which are different from each other by this specified amount, we have some justification in assuming that our steps on the scale represent approximately equal units.

Still another useful technique for creating equal units, somewhat more difficult to use, is the so-called *Thurstone-Chave technique of equal-appearing intervals.* Suppose, for example, that we wish to develop a scale for rating levels of family spirit. A number of thumbnail sketches of various homes are prepared and then ranked by a number of judges. The average ranking of each sketch is computed, and the sketches are then placed in order of this average ranking. If enough of these items are used, we can select scales in which the items have the same intervals between them in terms of average ranks, or they can be chosen on the basis of standard scores, which has already been described.

Still another very useful technique for constructing equal units is involved in the process of *item analysis.* For example, suppose we wish to construct a scale of mathematics problems in equal steps of increasing difficulty. One procedure consists in administering a number of possible problems to a large number of people and then putting them in the order of the percentage of people who failed them. Again, using the method of standard scores on the normal curve, problems can be selected which are equal distances apart, thus forming a scale with equal units.

In the discussion of correlation, the *rank-difference method* was described. It has a useful value in this matter of scaling for equal units. For example, suppose we wish to prepare a scale for children's drawings. We take a sample of such drawings and ask a number of judges to rank them. How many judges we need to make the pooled ranking constitute a reliable score can be determined by rho. Again, equal intervals can be determined by the method of standard scores.

Here, then, is evidence of how we can go about choosing units which we can handle and have some confidence that when we use them, two and two will make four. Everyone who expects to apply the scientific method to any data such as that with which we deal in character research should have a good understanding especially of the normal probability curve and standard scores, for without this tool few of our valuable statistical methods of experimental design would be of any use to us.

THE CHALLENGE OF EXPERIMENTAL DESIGN AND ITS STATISTICAL TOOLS

There are many other principles in statistics which are useful for this kind of inquiry. This has been an attempt only to show you the tremendous implications of these methods for research of this sort. With some care in the setting up of our procedures, we can explore many times as many hypotheses with the techniques of small sample statistics as was possible with the older methods. The fact is that in CRP we face so many problems that we can attack only a few of them at a time even with these simpler methods. This will be true in most educational research programs. But such procedures as these can make the application of the scientific method many times more widespread in such research. Our hope in all our work is to get further and further away from individual opinion as a basis for making decisions (no matter how expert or how dogmatic), and use, instead, objective evidence and valid interpretation of that evidence.

To demonstrate dramatically how practical all this can be, let me show you what statistical skills can be acquired within a week by almost any minister, director, teacher, educator, or other youth leader. It is possible to acquire enough familiarity with (1) the *normal probability curve* and the tables based on it, to construct fairly accurate scales for most of the variables needed. Mastery of (2) the *rank-difference correlation* makes it possible to handle many problems relating to interrelationships among variables. (3) The *chi-square distribution*, with one or two of its more useful applications, will help to test numerous hypotheses. Simple forms of (4) *analysis of variance*, with prerequisite familiarity with (5) the *F-distribution*, can be one of the most useful tools available for clear thinking in regard to many problems faced by every educator.

All these can be mastered easily in a week. As for the computations involved, you will need tables for the *normal distribution,* the *chi-square distribution,* and the *F-ratio distribution.* These can be found in almost any standard text on statistical methods. Aside from these tables, others which will be useful, if available, are tables of *squares* and *square roots, products,* and *quotients.*

Most of the principles which have been set forth in this chapter can be applied to your thinking with this minimum facility in the use of statistical tools, even if you are a layman. Having acquired some competence in their use and the principles behind them, you will find them of great value even in many of your daily problems. This will not make you a statistician; but it will make you able to understand their ways of thinking. More important, it will help you to play a much more significant co-scientist role in the world's hope of achieving, for all forms of education, the advances into new areas of truth which the scientific method can open to us.

Of course, I would not have you think that these methods cannot be misused; they certainly can. If you are not trained in statistics, you will frequently need the counsel and guidance of someone who is expert in their use and interpretation. The fact remains that they do make progress possible at many times the speed of the older methods; and we who are concerned seriously about future generations would be criminal, indeed, if we did not take advantage of these new and powerful tools.

SOME IMPORTANT CONCEPTS DESCRIBED IN THIS CHAPTER

Effective personality research must deal with the total individual. Personality is a highly complex set of interacting forces. This means that major research must use factorial design procedures. That is, all of the factors in personality vary all of the time. Research must study their patterns of intervariation. In determining the major factors involved in any particular differences observed in the performances of two or more groups, the tools of analysis of variance quickly isolate the forces playing the major roles. Because the factors in personality are neither completely dependent nor independent of each other, correlation is the tool for measuring the interrelationship between any two variables.

Fruitful research ought to be creative as well as critical. That is, it ought to provide promising leads to new areas as well as to evaluate critically our past efforts. The method of characteristic differences is a most useful technique for the discovery of possible new dimensions. The pro-con technique is an effective procedure for establishing the pros and cons of any problem (without personal conflict) into a position where characteristic differences can be sought. The search for unknown interaction dynamics is best done with cluster and factor analysis, which are of course beyond the skills of the co-scientist. The great electronic calculators of recent years make possible complex interaction research which was virtually impossible a few years ago.

Such abstract qualities as value judgments, religious beliefs, and differences in basic attitudes can be measured with high degrees of accuracy. There are many tools available in psychology, of which the standard score is the best known and most widely used, with which to establish equal units for such measurements. Questionnaires and rating scales, which are among the most difficult technical tools to construct, can be developed with these techniques. Their reliabilities can be determined by several methods, in many of which the rank-square correlation coefficient is useful. Since this is usable by everyone, many people who have been constructing defective and meaningless questionnaires and rating scales can now learn to make them far more useful and dependable.

The co-scientist can learn within a week a minimum set of statistical tools with which he can soon master the basic elements of experimental design. Doing so opens up vast new areas of research which would be impossible when the persons participating in research do so at the guinea-pig level.

CHAPTER XIII

CO-SCIENTISTS AND RESEARCH CURRICULA IN CREATIVE RESEARCH

It is an American tradition that we never do things by halves. When an idea or movement commends itself to us, we go after it with a will and make it into a national movement overnight. I see research as now coming into just such a focus in religious education. Research committees are being set up in almost every educational group. Designs for large research projects are being submitted by the score to foundations for financial support. Foundations, too, are eager to invest their funds in such research if they are convinced of its value. The dangers, as well as the potential fruits, are great indeed.

In our enthusiasm we may conceive some badly designed research, invest hundreds of thousands of dollars in it, fail with a resounding crash, and thereby set back our faith in research by many years. We may well contemplate the disaster that can result from huge failures in badly designed research programs.

INTEGRATED EDUCATIONAL RESEARCH MUST BE PROGRAM RESEARCH

In this final section of the book, then, I want to talk about *program design*. Program design consists of a whole interrelated program of research designed to investigate some broad general area. What is the effectiveness of our present-day religious education? What are the factors influencing religion on our campuses? Are our summer camps important molders of character? How can we develop Christian character? Such questions as these call for program research. Objective research in simple situations is many times more valuable than opinion in the solution of specific problems. Program research, however, is far more effective for attacking our major problems than restricted individual experiments.

But the possible blind alleys into which program research can be turned probably vary as the square of the factors involved. Even some very good scientists can get lost in them. More than 7,500 articles and books per year are published in the field of psychology. No single individual can possibly keep abreast of the entire field. The wise scientist who is attempting program research, therefore, seeks advice from as many of his colleagues as he can.

Furthermore, there is no area where actual experience is more important than in program design. If that experience does not exist, as was the case when we began in CRP, then accumulating such experience becomes a first step in the creation of fruitful designs.

How Can We Plan Programs of Research with Confidence in Their Validity? Even designs worked out by nonscientists with experience in the field of study and scientists without such experience can be almost incredibly impractical. The following steps will avoid many such disasters.

If you wish to plan a program design in religious and character education, bring in to your conferences at once several competent scientists who know something about your field. Explore these questions with them:

What are the major areas of research likely to be involved in such a study? Who, in the social sciences, are the "experts" in each of these areas? Then consult those listed before you decide on a final design.

What measuring instruments are available which might be used or adapted for this research? Who is experienced in their use and interpretation? Who can help you design your studies in light of them?

What are some of the "realistic" problems which are likely to arise in such research and how can you deal with them without invalidating the research itself? Only scientists with comparable practical experience can answer this.

What actual research projects comparable to this one have used this design? What experimenters were engaged in these studies? Get them to tell you of their actual experiences and what rewards they found in their research.

What statistical tools are likely to be most effective and what restrictions do they impose on the way in which to collect the data? Who has had practical experience in comparable situations and who can help design your studies accordingly?

What dimensions seem likely to lead to fruitful findings? As I have said before, it is possible to measure people a thousand ways and learn almost nothing useful in the process. Find out what dimensions are proposed and what you can hope to learn from them. As you will remember from Chapters V–X, this has been one of our major problems in CRP through the years.

Other questions could be added to these, but these ought to safeguard us from the frustrating futility of research failure due to gross errors in design. This may sound like a formidable program. And so it is. But if large funds and the personalities of our children are the stakes, this investment is small indeed.

Experimental-Control Group Designs Are Seldom Fruitful in Program Research At the risk of seeming dogmatism, let me say that it is my increasing belief that the experimental-control group method is seldom, if ever, desirable or fruitful—except for isolated small segments of research.

For example, the experimental-control group method is excellent in comparing one Kindergarten class with another to determine whether or not some clear-cut objective included in the curriculum has been achieved. It would, so far as I can see, never be desirable to use the same design to determine whether Curriculum A in general is better than Curriculum B.

Factorial designs are much simpler in administration, lend themselves to dynamic analyses, and can evolve as evidence points to new, promising avenues of exploration. In factorial design you can study as many factors as you can measure. Clusters of intercorrelated factors reveal the presence of forces which are otherwise unobservable, and whose nature can be guessed by the factors which go to make them up.

Finally, experimental-control group designs usually result only in Yes or No answers. Your methods are effective or they are not. When so many factors are involved, you have no way of determining the influence of individual factors or of their interrelationships. Factorial analysis points out new directions and makes possible much more rapid research.

I should like to use our experience in CRP as the basis for this discussion of program research. It took us at least fifteen years before we had achieved a reasonably mature over-all design. It is still in the process of change. We have had the counsel of some of the outstanding scientists in the country, and have watched with care the work in the great research centers of child development: Yale, Iowa, Columbia, Minnesota, California, Kansas, the Fels Foundation study, Harvard, and Michigan State, to mention only a few.

INTRODUCING THE CRP RESEARCH DESIGN CHART

We have formalized it in what we call our Research Design Chart. I imagine that it will look reasonably complex to you. When you consider that it took us about fifteen years to bring it to maturity, perhaps it is not so complex after all.

It may be that an almost unique characteristic of CRP is that the research is part and parcel of a character-education program. We believe that we can develop character and we are actually trying to do it. Our central task has been to construct a curriculum for the purpose. Such a curriculum embodies our hypotheses concerning effective character education. This is what is meant by a *research curriculum*. It is being used in churches, YMCA's, schools, and many thousands of homes. The important thing is that such a curriculum includes in its very nature techniques for testing the effectiveness of every part of it. Every educational venture should do this!

A Preview of a Long-Time Program of Research for Character Education An examination of the over-all outline of the chart will show that the general research program method of CRP includes the following steps: constructing a curriculum, which in fact consists of a set of educational hypotheses, designed to achieve our objectives; collecting all of the available evidence as to the validity not only of the curricular methods and materials, but of the objectives themselves, and even of the methods of gathering the evidence for doing so; a qualitative evaluation of this evidence, and relevant methods of revision; and the formulation, in the form of a revised curriculum, of a revised set of educational hypotheses.

UNBIASED EVIDENCE IS THE CORNERSTONE OF RESEARCH

If I suggest to you that in doing scientific research you have to get unbiased evidence, you may think that that is so obviously a common-sense statement that there is no use in mentioning it, much less devoting a whole chapter to it. The fact is that when Jesus said of some of his hearers that they had closed their eyes and ears "lest they should perceive with their eyes and hear with their ears," he was talking about all of us some of the time and some of us all of the time. You see, the Lord didn't make any of us infallible; but neither did he make us sufficiently aware of that fact. For the most part, we take a look at the problems that surround us, form an opinion which seems good to us, then shut our eyes, close our ears, open our mouths, and there we stand.

This matter of evidence is by no manner of means as simple as you might think. The first thing you have to be sure about is that you are honestly looking for it. There ought never to be a scientist or even a layman who is satisfied with today's social order—or even with his own idea of how much better he could run the world if he were in charge—nor a theologian who is dogmatic about even the most thrilling vision he has had of God.

Sometimes unbiased evidence is pretty drastic to our pride. For example, we develop a theory of character education. We try it out, and find that the evidence seems to indicate that what we have done has made no appreciable difference in the lives of the children at all. Or, again, we come face to face with some evidence which seems to upset our most cherished beliefs. It is disconcerting, to say the least. The fact remains that we never need to be afraid of truth. I believe that when all of the evidence is in, and we evaluate it with all of the energy and skill we can, we will always come out with concepts which are better and finer than those we held before.

The Thrill of the Never Ending Search for Evidence That Tells You Something After ten years of arduous search for the best picture of truth we could find in the area in which we were working

RESEARCH DESIGN
UNION COLLEGE
CHARACTER RESEARCH PROJECT
1955

FIRST ORDER PROBLEMS
(EVALUATION AND REVISION OF EDUCATIONAL HYPOTHESES)

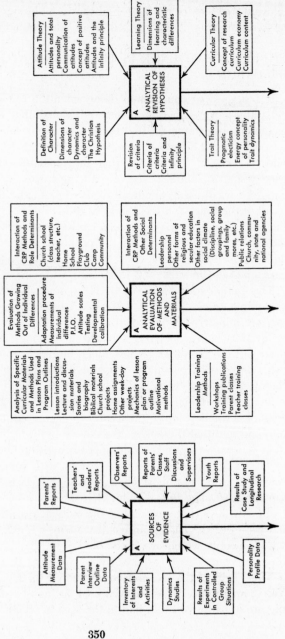

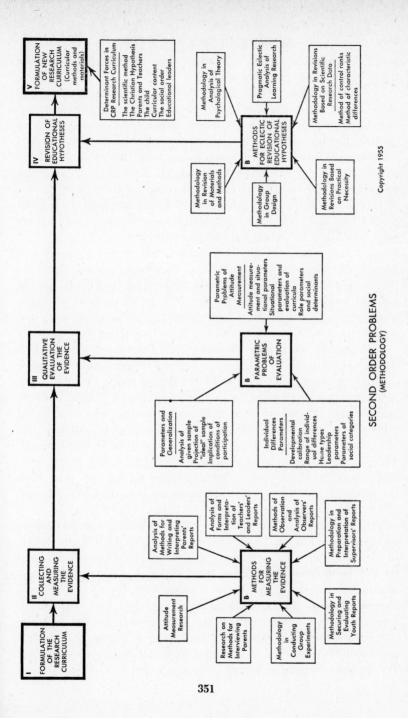

SECOND ORDER PROBLEMS
(METHODOLOGY)

Copyright 1955

I FORMULATION OF THE RESEARCH CURRICULUM

II COLLECTING AND MEASURING THE EVIDENCE

III QUALITATIVE EVALUATION OF THE EVIDENCE

IV REVISION OF EDUCATIONAL HYPOTHESES

V FORMULATION OF NEW RESEARCH CURRICULUM (Curricular methods and materials)

B METHODS FOR MEASURING THE EVIDENCE

Analysis of Methods for Writing and Interpreting Parents' Reports

Analysis of Forms and Interpretation of Teachers' and Leaders' Reports

Methods of Observation and Analysis of Observers' Reports

Methodology in Preparation and Interpretation of Supervisors' Reports

Attitude Measurement Research

Research on Methods for Interviewing Parents

Methodology in Conducting Group Experiments

Methodology in Securing and Evaluating Youth Reports

B PARAMETRIC PROBLEMS OF EVALUATION

Parameters and Generalization
Analysis of given sample
Projection of "ideal" sample
Implication of conditions of participation

Individual Differences Parameters
Developmental calibration
Range of individual differences
Home types
Leadership parameters
Parameters of social categories

Parametric Problems of Attitude Measurement
Attitude measurement and situational parameters
Situational parameters and evaluation of curricula
Role parameters and social determinants

B METHODS FOR ECLECTIC REVISION OF EDUCATIONAL HYPOTHESES

Methodology in Analysis of Psychological Theory

Pragmatic Eclectic Analysis of Learning Research

Methodology in Revisions Based on Scientific Research Data
Method of control ranks
Method of characteristic differences

Methodology in Revision of Materials and Methods

Methodology in Group Design

Methodology in Revisions Based on Practical Necessity

Determinant Forces in CRP Research Curriculum
The scientific method
The Christian Hypothesis
Parents and Teachers
The child
Curricular content
The social order
Educational leaders

351

in CRP, we realize more fully than ever that there are greater truths to be discovered and explored.

But how do you go on? You have made the best guesses you could about the truth. The only way to find better ones is to try these and see what happens. You are, of course, a good deal better off than the boy with his first chemistry set, who just "puts things together to see what will happen." You have the wisdom and experience of the ages behind you. Hundreds of scientists have forged instruments and discovered facts, thousands of them. The greater of the philosophers and prophets have found ideals of such great proportions that men have been unable even to comprehend them fully, much less to mobilize their great power.

But this is not as simple as it sounds. The casual sightseer will seldom discover significant evidence. It usually takes infinite patience, scores of failures, and particularly effective skills to get the kind of evidence which paves the way to new vistas of truth. Furthermore, our greatest achievements presuppose skills on the part of those who give the evidence as well as those who get it.

It Is Quality More Than Quantity That Constitutes Fruitful Evidence Don't confuse data and evidence. It is possible to gather volumes of quantitative data and learn almost nothing from it. I can easily imagine getting ten meaningful scores on a hundred people and learning a hundred times as much as I could from a thousand other scores on a million people. The N (number of cases) is still important, but far from being either indispensable or self-sufficient. The great Swiss psychologist Jean Piaget seldom did research on more than ten children at a time. It is the quality, far more than the quantity, of evidence which determines how fruitful the results of a study are going to be.

But, you say, if this evidence must be of such a special kind to be significant, how can *laymen* be of any help? Indeed, many people in the history of our Project have doubted that they could. "Parents do not know how to evaluate their children." "Their ratings are worthless." "They do not know what to look for to record on a Parents' Report." The same is said about teachers and youth themselves. The fact is that we consider Parents' Reports the best evidence we have. That does not mean that we assume that parents are infallible observers of scientific truth. Of course they are not. We do have to have technical instruments and methods to make it possible for us to measure and refine the evidence we find in such instruments as Parents' Reports. Nevertheless, the more skilled the parents are at reporting, the better evidence this is.

The doctor asks me my symptoms. I tell him in Anglo-Saxon terms where and how I hurt. He translates it into Latin and Greek, pieces together the observable evidence, and can be reasonably sure where my trouble lies. So it is with us. Here is Parent A who experiences a success or a failure. He may even try to guess what are the more important reasons for this result. More often than not, he is far from being entirely right. But if a hundred parents are looking at the same phenomenon in their children and report what they see, we can search for the common elements and thus identify the real factors operating in the experience. Thousands of such reports pour into our laboratory every month. Our analysts search for useful bits of evidence in them, which when put together form the mosaic of another new step in our search for the truth about Christian personality.

If you will examine the current research in social psychology and studies of personality, you will discover that there is an ever increasing use of what we call *open-end data*. This is data in which the informant in the study is not limited to quantitative or "yes-no" answers, but may express himself as fully as he wishes. Essay-type answers come under this category (27).

This is an important change from the day, not too long ago, when psychologists confined their research to those things which they could measure accurately to three decimal places. But it became increasingly obvious that there is almost an inverse ratio between how important a thing is and how accurately it can be measured. As a result, projective techniques began to spring up, and tools for their analysis along with them.

In our own work we have used open-end materials far more than any other kind. Reliability studies show that they can be used accurately (120). As we develop our co-scientist ideal among those who participate in the Project, this material becomes increasingly valuable.

The Curriculum and the Evidence Are Indispensable to Each Other   The value of the curriculum is determined by what our children learn, not by what we intended to teach when it was written. Evidence of what they learn is the basis for measuring that value.

It is not in the content of the curriculum that our problem lies so much as in its methods of teaching and learning, of inspiration and motivation, of conviction and application. Christian educators achieve an astonishing agreement as to content. Note the volume of curricular materials which are used by almost all denominations. We shall not make sufficient improvement here, to save the world. The real challenge lies in getting our curricular materials and challenges learned and accepted and put into action by our youth. Long experience has made it evident that exposure alone will not do the job. Our church schools are crowded, but the world's problems are not getting solved much better than they ever were.

Let's turn to the youth in our culture to find out what we are teaching them. For example, I'd guess that a very high percentage of the religious education our children do get is taught either by the home or by our culture, and much less of it in our church schools and other character-building institutions. Note this, however. I believe that our church schools could become the key institutions of our day for inspiring a new generation to spiritual heights infinitely greater than our own.

I should like to call your attention to a recent report by Spaulding and Haley (130). They supervised a survey of youth work in our Protestant churches, the results of which are very revealing. Let's do a little experiment using the method of characteristic differences. Below are two lists of Christian-education objectives. Study them carefully for characteristic differences, and then I will tell you where this data came from.

First list: teaching knowledge of right and wrong; provide opportunity to contribute financially to the work of the World Church; challenge youth to follow Christ, live as a Christian; teach knowledge of basic Christian beliefs; influence individual's habits, standards of conduct, and so on; provide information regarding world outreach of church; provide inspiration through Sunday worship services; train youth for participation in group worship; develop Christian attitude regarding race relations; prepare youth for church membership; provide opportunities for service in church (ushering, and so on); develop Christian attitude toward alcohol problem; develop relationship to World Church.

Second list: help with personality problems; provide opportunities to know and understand people of other income levels; provide opportunities to carry social convictions into action; teach under-standing and appreciation of other religions; provide opportunities to know and understand people of other races; teach church his-tory; provide opportunities to meet, work with people of other religious faiths; provide counseling in dating and marriage problems; train youth for leadership in general church offices; provide oppor-tunities to meet, work with youth of other denominations; develop Christian attitude toward economic problems; provide opportuni-ties for membership in Scouting, Campfire, and so on; provide help with vocational decisions.

You will see at once that the first group is concerned with per-petuation of the Church as an institution, with knowledge and ac-ceptance of religious beliefs, with what adults can tell children and youth, with a knowledge of what past generations have labeled as right and wrong.

The second group includes objectives for making Christianity become the leaven of our whole society, for challenging our youth to discover for themselves how Christianity can be applied to life's great problems, to profit by the experience of the past but to go on and find levels of achievement in their own.

The first group consists of those objectives which the youth participating in this research said the Church is doing best. The second group are those objectives which they assert the Church is doing least well.

If our curricula had been research curricula, continuously being analyzed by scientists, we would have known this long ago. We would have discovered it as it happened and revised it then and there. Even now we do not know how to remedy the situation. We only know that it exists. Only with research curricula can we make sufficient progress.

Let me illustrate this concept of the research curriculum. Con-sider first the traditional approach. We spend great sums of time and money creating the best curricula we can. Ten years might be a modest period in which to build such a curriculum. We use that curriculum in thousands of churches for five, seven, ten, or more years. We sense that it is far from transforming our youth either spiritually or in terms of their social effectiveness. We as-semble another curricular revision committee and start over again. We have little or no knowledge either as to the strengths or weaknesses of the old one. When the new one is complete, we won't be sure whether it is better or worse than the old one. Progress cannot be made that way. Even a few "scientific studies of evaluation" will do little to help.

Suppose, on the other hand, that the curriculum is so constructed that every lesson in it by its very nature gets the kind of evidence that at once discloses its strengths and weaknesses. We can revise that lesson or the whole curriculum with a wealth of evidence as to how to do it.

ONLY CO-SCIENTISTS CAN PROVIDE THE RIGHT KIND OF EVIDENCE

Factorial design! Research curricula! There is one more major ingredient in this concept of program research. It is the *co-scientist*. I have said a good deal about this concept already. Perhaps I can focus the whole principle in a single paragraph.

People do far more to their environment than the environment does to them! There will usually be more variety in the behavior of a hundred people in one situation than in the behavior of one individual in a hundred situations. A curriculum and our teaching of it is part of the environment of our children. We have hardly begun our evaluation of it, therefore, when we examine it alone. It is what our children do with it that counts. The only people that can tell us that very accurately are the children themselves and those who deal with them every day. What they report—these parents, teachers, and youth themselves—that is the evidence we need. The more they can master some skills of the co-scientist, the more valuable that evidence will be. Factorial design! Research curricula! Co-scientists! These are the ingredients of the educational visions which can produce a greater generation.

Evidence Teachers Can Give Us   The first source of co-scientist evidence comes from the teacher, by means of parent-teacher conferences. Our CRP curriculum calls for the conducting of such conferences at the beginning and end of each curricular unit. Here is a good example of an element in the curriculum which is both an integral part of the curriculum and also a source of valuable evidence. The purpose of these conferences is threefold. They are designed, first, to bring together as much information as possible about the personality of the child; second, to describe the child's position at the beginning and at the end of the unit with respect to the attitude objective of the unit; and third, to provide the teacher with information on which to plan the lessons. The major instruments used in gathering this information are the Parent Interview Outline and the Parent-Teacher Conference Worksheet.

The Parent Interview Outline is a simple form on which can be recorded the parents' estimates of the aptitudes and interests of the child and his level of adjustment to the various role situations in which he lives; for example, home, school, playground, church, and the like. The PIO is the simplest possible substitute for a testing program. To be sure, churches, YMCA's, and schools using the Project materials are encouraged to augment this common-sense evidence by the gradual development of a more adequate measurement program. In the Union College Laboratory we have developed an Inventory of Interests and Activities graded for four levels, which we can analyze to provide a number of different insights into the nature of the child. In addition to being an inventory of the different kinds and number of interests and activities the child engages in, the scale is so constructed that it is possible to discover whether they are common or uncommon activities, active or quiet ones, group activities or solitary ones, and so on. Our most recent revision of the PIO includes, in less elaborate form, many of the features of the Inventory of Interests and Activities. I am sure you can see that we can learn a lot about a child, or adult for that matter, by studying the patterns of his interests and activities.

The Parent-Teacher Conference Worksheet is designed to help parents and youth to set goals in terms of the attitude objectives of the lessons and to work out practical methods of achieving them.

In our curricular research design, the Parent-Teacher Conference Worksheet plays several roles. One is to give both parents and teachers a more comprehensive picture of the attitude and the possible range of children's growth with respect to it. Another purpose is to provide a vision for the character potential the attitude affords the child if it is successfully learned by him. Still another is to help parents distinguish between attitudes and mere overt behavior. A number of attitudes underlie almost every act of behavior. Every attitude can be expressed in many different ways. The same behavior in different children may be the result of entirely different motivations. Sharing, for example, as evidenced by outward behavior, may or may not be unselfish.

In addition to providing a method of attitude measurement, the Parent-Teacher Conference Worksheet contains questions which are used as an outline for the parent-teacher conference. The answers to these questions give the teacher the information needed to adapt the lesson to the individual child. It also provides space for the teacher to record a goal for the child for each lesson, which is decided upon in the parent-teacher conference. The choosing of a goal (something the child will try to achieve for the coming week, in learning the attitude) has proved to be one of the most effective steps in bringing about significant learning experiences for the character growth of the child. It also includes space for the teacher to use in planning motivations and methods which can be used to help the child move toward this goal. All this is what we refer to as the *adaptation procedure*. The adaptation procedure can be defined as taking abstract traits or attitudes, plus the materials and methods designed to teach them, and adapting them to the unique nature of the individual child. It will be obvious that both the adaptations and the evidences of success will be important sources of evidence.

This planning sheet also provides spaces in which the teacher can describe the responses of the children during the class session and record a general evaluation of the success of the lesson, together with recommendations for revision.

The potential contributions to revisions of our curriculum from this source, therefore, are limited by our ability to construct tools which make it possible for these teachers to give us objective evidence, and their skill in doing so.

Is the Co-Scientist Concept Possible in Genuine Scientific Research? Is it not probable that parents may not know what is good evidence, how to report it accurately if they do, or even be willing to do so? We call this the problem of *motivated capacity*. This means that we must find ways, on the one hand, of motivating parents and teachers to report in larger numbers and, on the other, of teaching them the skills of reporting useful evidence.

On the motivational side, we have found three chief factors operating. They must be given a vision for reporting, taught how to do so, and form the habit of doing so. Many of us do not find writing our easiest form of expression. It requires strong motivation to make some of us write anything. However, as parents and teachers understand this co-scientist ideal, and the potential for the next generation that comes from it, they are far more strongly motivated to overcome any personal reluctance about doing so. If they are taught a few skills of reporting, they find the task much more interesting. If they form the habit of doing so regularly, they find it much easier to continue.

On the method side of writing lay reports, the secret lies in the Dynamics Diagram. If we can teach our co-scientists to describe the situation in which behavior occurs, how the child looks at it, what motivations are operating in him at the time, how all this relates to his native abilities and his acquired skills, how it relates to his already existing attitudes, and how he responds, especially in terms of avoidance behavior, group-expectancy behavior, and maximum-potential behavior, we shall have excellent evidence. We are finding this possible for youth themselves as well as for parents and teachers.

Evidence Parents Can Give Us Up to now, the Parents' Report has proved to be by far our largest source of co-scientist evidence. In the Positive Potential Study alone, the parents who through the years have turned in these reports may well have made a contribution far beyond anything they dreamed of. Both secular and religious education will probably be different because of the results of this study. This gradually became more complex as the possible values of this kind of information came to be recognized. These values are of three types. The first purpose is to help the parents do an effective job of planning, teaching, and evaluating at home. The second is to help the teacher to be better able to evaluate the effectiveness of the class procedures and to cooperate more fully with the parents. The third value is to provide evidence by which we can do a more adequate job of evaluation and revision of our curricula materials.

Trained Observers Can See Many Things Others Cannot The field of expressive movements is an old one in psychology. Trained observers are able to perceive, with more and more validity, the underlying personality structures of individuals as evidenced by significant expressive movements. An expressive movement is a form of behavior—such as a smile—which is the expression of a feeling or emotion. A great deal of work in projective techniques is relevant. Projective techniques are efforts to interpret these expressive movements. The use of projective techniques, as thus far developed, however, is restricted to highly trained observers. Observers of the co-scientist variety are being used in many of the class groups now participating in CRP. It is their task to record the behavior and speech of the children involved, and on the basis of this evidence to attempt to evaluate the success of the methods used. They know the plans of the teacher, and what is expected to take place. They are often able, therefore, to make some shrewd judgments. We have not used this observation procedure very extensively and are as yet unable to estimate fully the value of these observers' reports.

The place in which we have developed this method of observation most fully has been in our YMCA summer camp (Camp Chingachgook, the Schenectady YMCA Boys' Camp). One of the instruments used there is known as the Leader's Observation Report. Counselors are asked to record every situation in which they are able to observe a boy's behavior or speech, relevant to one of the attitude goals toward which they are working. Using these valuable sources of evidence, then, we are able to construct measuring instruments and curricular methods which show increasing promise for use in camps.

Evidence Youth Can Give Us   Let me show you aspects of the youth "problem," which have to do with his own inner life and can only be reported by him. There are two aspects of his development to which I want to refer here: first, his immaturity, and, second, his love of fun. In dealing with each of them, we shall have to work hand in glove with him. We can help youth, but he must work out his own salvation. We can't do it for him.

Let's look first at one way in which his immaturity betrays him. Youth, about the time he enters Junior High, is likely to have a sense of infallibility concerning the wisdom of his own judgments. Of course, this is true at all age levels, but especially so here. And usually we, his parents and teachers, are not demonstrating the ultimate in humility in our evaluation of our own ideas. Now, simply telling him that his ideas are immature is not likely to be very convincing in his mind. He has to see proof of his lack of infallibility.

Then, too, I cannot help thinking that in this age of supercolossal entertainment, even the Church has led him to believe that a youth group is to be judged in terms of how much "fun the kids have there." Speakers are often not even treated with courtesy unless they are "interesting." Churches and YMCA's and the various youth clubs too often judge their success in terms of the numbers attracted. Is a church's youth program a success if it draws large numbers and its members are enthusiastic? Many of the ministers I know would say, "Yes." I must confess that few things could be more tragic than for the Church to add its voice to the others that tell youth that the world owes them a living, sugar-coated, and handed to them on a silver platter. In dealing with such problems as this, we will need to have the youth's thinking in the matter.

We won't solve the "youth problem" by a program of entertainment alone, even if accompanied by some pious-sounding worship services and some "interesting talks" followed by "good discussions." We are going to have to dig much deeper than that. Of course, not all of our youth have any feeling of greater need. There are, however, enough youth capable of helping us discover the evidence that such a task demands.

Just as is true of parent and teacher reports, the value of these Youth Reports will vary with the skill with which they are made and our ability to find and construct effective scientific instruments for interpreting them at the level of this skill. We can achieve our best results if we can bring about teamwork among youth, parents, and teachers in this matter.

THE PRINCIPAL SKILLS OF THE CO-SCIENTIST

"You can see cats' eyes in the dark," said the experimenter to the child who was acting as a subject in the experiment. "This cat, whose picture you see here, is asleep. We will turn out the lights and in a little while he will open one eye and wink at you. I want you to see if you can tell me which eye he winks, as soon as you can."

That doesn't sound very scientific, but it certainly was. The experimenter (139) had devised a technique to measure dark adaptation in young children, which up to that time had been believed to be impossible.

You Can Measure Many Things You Might Think You Can't You see, there are two important aspects to this problem of measurement. There are many people saying that you can't measure this or that; when the fact of the matter is, you can. Trumbull's experiment is a case in point. But just as significant is the fact that there are many other people who think they are measuring something who aren't! I'd guess that 95 per cent of the questionnaires and rating scales used don't measure anything worth measuring, don't measure even that accurately, and are tragically misleading when we assume that they do.

In this second half of this chapter, then, I hope I shall be able to show you how you can measure some things you don't see how to measure now. I also hope you will learn some principles which will protect you against a lot of pseudo-measurements, which don't measure anything. In particular I want to show you some of the skills which can be used by the co-scientists in providing meaningful evidence.

Science progresses in proportion to the accuracy and importance of its measurements. In any program research quite as much time must be invested in methodology as in the direct study of the area of investigation. A new insight in this area may be many times more fruitful than the same amount of time spent in studying the central problem as such, with existing methods. Look at some of the outstanding research adventures in the history of psychology. Garrett's (40) book is a very readable story of a number of such studies. Note how often the experiments had to stop along the line to create new tools, which were necessary to further progress. You will note that in our CRP Research Design Chart, the direct measurement problems are above the central line; the methodological problems, below. So let's take a look at the problem of evidence from the point of view of method.

The Tests of Evidence—Reliability and Validity　The ultimate purposes of all methodology in regard to scientific evidence can be subsumed under two terms, *reliability* and *validity*.

The question of reliability has to do with accuracy. We are always trying to measure things more accurately. You have probably noticed what follows an announcement by physicists that they have developed a method of measuring something to an accuracy of a millionth of an inch which before they could only measure to a ten thousandth of an inch. It isn't long after that before a whole new body of breathtaking discoveries are forthcoming. That is the way it is in psychology, too. Whenever we find a greater degree of accuracy, there are characteristics of our data which can be seen which before were buried in the crudeness of our measurements.

Probably all of you have heard the well known statement of the late Dr. E. L. Thorndike, "Whatever exists, exists in some amount, and can be measured." Most of us who got our scientific training in my generation cut our scientific teeth on that dictum.

That doesn't mean that it has been, or that it can be now, but it does mean that if we search hard enough we can eventually find methods for measuring anything that exists in differing amounts. That is quite an assertion and requires some proving. In our work in CRP there are some things which we can measure with a fairly high degree of accuracy; some that we have not yet found any way to measure at all; and all gradations in between the two. But also in our Project, as in all science, our research will progress in proportion to the accuracy of our measurements.

The Different Kinds of Evidence and How They Are Used This methodology problem is not a new one. There have been scientists who have devoted their whole lives to nothing else. You don't have to start from scratch, therefore. When you have stated your problems clearly, you will discover that there are existing methods which will be useful in finding ways to attack most of them. These methods usually have to be refined and adapted to your purposes, but you would be very foolish, indeed, not to take advantage of them.

Probably, at this point, I ought to set forth a reasonably comprehensive description of the more common methods. Instead I am going to give you a few references, which do the job far better than I can do it here. Two books were published in 1931 (43, 134), both of which had to do with methodology. Then in 1937, another classic was published (110), which included still more methods related to the kinds of problems we face in CRP. This book also includes a summary of the results of the relevant research which had been done up to that time. Finally, I would suggest a relatively new book on psychological methods (9). While it discusses psychological methods in general, a number of the chapters—each written by an authority in that particular field—are very relevant to what we are doing. Chapters 1, 3, 4, 13, 18, 21, and 22 are especially pertinent to our kinds of problems.

If you will look at our Research Design Chart at the section designated as II B, *Methods for Measuring the Evidence,* you will see that the various areas included fall into four natural groups. Perhaps it would be useful to list these various technical methods in terms of the methodological problems we face in CRP. For these are likely to be the ones appearing most frequently in any kind of educational research.

In character research our primary task is to measure *attitudes.* These are the most difficult measurement problems we face. Anyone faced with the task of measuring attitudes needs to be familiar especially with the following types of psychological methods: rating scales, questionnaires, ranking methods, inventory methods, and matching methods.

Our second group of problems in methodology for gathering evidence have to do with *interviewing.* This requires familiarity with interviewing methods, play interviews, and case-history methods.

Our third set of problems relates to *group experiments.* One need only glance at the methods developed in the Character Education Inquiry (23) to see the many ingenious devices for direct measurement. Other experimental methods include: standardized tests, total-personality measurements, statistical trait analysis, problem-solving techniques, classification methods, and methods of free association.

The five blocks on the Research Design Chart to the right of the II B heading all have to do with *co-scientist methods.* What scientific skills can we expect the co-scientist to learn? Fortunately, many of the techniques used by the professional social scientist are quite within his grasp. The following are some useful types of attack: methods of incidental observation, diary methods, methods for controlled observation, projective techniques, correlational methods, levels of aspiration methods, action mapping, play analysis, and sociometry.

The Elusive Attitude Is Difficult to Measure Our CRP program is built around the unit of the attitude, and we still do not have sufficiently accurate attitude scales. Oh, we can measure opinions fairly accurately. Furthermore, there are some excellent statistical tools for creating accurate scales. But the attitudes involve the total personality. Often the individual is not even aware that he holds certain attitudes. Behavior is always the response of the total personality, never of a single attitude. How, then, can we measure attitudes? We can evaluate them pretty well in groups, but as yet not in the individual.

"If at first you don't succeed, try, try again," certainly has to be our motto in our search for accurate attitude scales. Let me mention just one of many unforeseen "disasters" we have experienced. We had administered one set of our attitude scales, by means of parent-teacher conferences, to all of the parents in the Project. At the end of the unit we repeated the process in order to measure our level of success. But here was one thing that happened frequently. A parent who had rated a child 5 at the beginning of the unit (5 was the top of the five-point scale) would rate him 3 at the end of the unit, but accompanied by a remark like this: "This has been a wonderful unit. We have accomplished a great deal with Johnny!" What was the matter? Well, in this case it was the failure of the scale to take into account the fact that the parents would learn a great deal about the attitude during the unit. This meant that a parent who saw no deficiency in the child's expression of the attitude at the beginning of the unit vastly broadened his own concept of the attitude during the unit, and although the child had learned much, the relative score was lower in terms of the scope of the enlarged parent vision. This means that if parents are to make successful ratings, they must have an accurate picture of the full range of the possible expressions of the attitude. We are at present constructing "spiritual potential" descriptions for each attitude objective. If parents will study them carefully, they will be far better able to evaluate their own child with regard to these.

We find that up to now we can place more confidence in the evidence given us through Parents' Reports than we can in attitude scales. We use the former as our most confident basis for judging success or failure rather than the latter. The fact remains that eventually we must and will discover how to measure attitudes accurately.

I think you may find it interesting and perhaps informative to see just what steps we have taken thus far in our search for an adequate attitude scale.

We started with a simple *rating scale*. The attitudes were put in the form of questions and the rater was asked to decide, on a scale of one hundred, where his child belonged among a "hundred children" of the same age and sex. The results showed that for the most part parents were completely unable to use the scale accurately. Many of them said so at once. They insisted that they did not know a hundred children of the same age and sex and so could not make such judgments. Indeed, some of them refused to try. This meant that they must be given a picture of the range of behavior in a representative group of children.

The second form was a *graphic rating scale*. This had had a favorable history where used. The scale points were described in terms of typical behavior. Five such points were used from one extreme to the other. This gave better results, but was still far below the level of accuracy necessary for use of the scale as a confident measure of success.

At this time, however, a new feature was added to the scale. Space was provided on the scale forms for parents to describe *typical behavior* of their child in respect to the attitude being rated. This proved to have a number of values. In the first place, it gave us an opportunity to discover wherein the parents misunderstood the attitude. We could also see some of their own attitudes about desirable and undesirable behavior in children. We could also take these typical behavior descriptions and apply laboratory procedures to ranking or rating them when we wished more accurate ratings than the parents themselves could make. Finally, these typical behavior items were used as the basis for an entirely different kind of scale.

To be sure, there were errors in their "typical behavior" descriptions. Memory errors, ego-involvement of the parents, undue emphasis on recent behavior, and, of course, the parents' own concepts of good and bad behavior—all these added doubt to its being typical. Despite all these difficulties, a considerable quantity of realistic behavior items were collected.

Our next attempt was what we now refer to as the Long Scale. It was our thought to select from the behavior items collected an almost exhaustive list of the types of behavior possible for any particular attitude. The possibility of getting together an exhaustive list proved not nearly as unattainable as one might expect. Actually, the final lists collected were seldom over fifty items in length. A few exploratory studies failed to add materially to this number. We expected this procedure to make it possible for us to construct a scale based on the actual incidence of behavior in the population. At the time it was not successful. I am still confident that it has real value in co-scientist research. Almost 40,000 items have been gathered in our Positive Potential Study. It is possible that an analysis of these items will reveal pretty much the whole range of possible reactions in regard to each attitude. Such an extended list ought to make it far more possible for parents to see the full range of possible behavior, in terms of which to judge their own children.

This Long Scale was changed to a ten-item scale, which was constructed by an adaptation of the Thurstone-Chave technique (138). This used the method of standard scores, described in Chapter XII, for determining equal scale units. Even with the use of this scale, parents were still asked to describe typical behavior with respect to the attitude.

The "typical behavior" descriptions reported by the parents again made it possible for us to discover where and how the parents misinterpreted the attitudes. Using these, together with materials from Parents' Reports, it has been possible to add descriptive sentences to the statement of an attitude, which helps to interpret the attitude.

What, then, of the future of parent attitude rating scales? Parents may never be able to make accurate ratings as such. However, we may be able to prepare scales which will make the parents able to give true typical behavior, relatively free from the errors to which such a method is susceptible. Then, for research purposes, these typical behavior items can be rated in the laboratory by several independent objective raters, to whatever degree of reliability is desired.

As this is being written, Koppe, of our own staff, is testing a new approach to the problem. It is his hypothesis that since attitudes are all interrelated in the personality, they can best be described in terms of their relationships with one another. He proposes, therefore, to measure a particular attitude in terms of its presence in a variety of behavior items, each of which may and usually does involve other attitudes. This certainly is far more in keeping with the integrative nature of the total personality.

Many other techniques for the measuring of attitudes have been and are being developed.

The methods used in projective techniques have developed rapidly in recent years. A form of projective technique which we have found very useful in CRP is to have young people write on some topic; for example, "three wishes," "the kind of person I would like to be like," or "my heroes." When groups of such essays are ranked by several judges according to such a criterion as maturity, astonishingly high reliability coefficients have been obtained.

We have not used situational tests as much as they deserve. The project periods in church-school classes, activities in summer camps, and many other procedures commonly used in dealing with children, lend themselves to situational test analysis. Here observers make independent ratings of certain qualities which are expressed in the children's reactions to the standardized situation.

A Questionnaire Is a Highly Technical Instrument, and Difficult to Construct I have repeatedly emphasized the difficulty of constructing good questionnaires. Perhaps I should not leave you with the feeling that it is impossible. So many people have to prepare questionnaires for various purposes that it may be helpful to list a few of the principles which psychologists have found to be useful in developing any kind of questionnaire. These will not make you an expert at this difficult task, but they may help you avoid some of the most serious errors.

Here are six basic principles listed in Goodenough and Anderson (43: Ch. 42): (1) Ask for simple, objective, concrete information. It is clear, of course, that this is ideal for accuracy though not always completely possible. (2) Write the scale so that it both looks and is brief. (3) It should ask for a minimum of writing. This also helps in tabulation of results. (4) Each question ought to be complete in itself. It ought not to depend for its meaning on some preceding question. (5) The statement of the question ought not to suggest the desirable answer. (6) The less emotional tone the question has, the more likely the people answering are to give objective answers. Three others can be added to these. (7) Make sure that each question is a single question. You'd be surprised how easy it is to ask "double-barreled" questions. So simple a question as, "Is he strong and healthy?" is double-barreled—he can be one and not the other. (8) Be sure the suggested answers are actually answers to the question. "Does he always eat his spinach?" With answers—always; sometimes; never. You end up in effect saying, "He always sometimes eats his spinach" or "He always never eats his spinach." (9) Perhaps most difficult of all, make sure that two people giving the same answer to the question mean the same thing. "Do you have stage fright?" might be answered "Yes" by one person who could talk confidently to groups up to a thousand, and "No" by another, who at least experienced no stage fright in small groups.

An Interview and a Conversation Are Very Different Things If you had to choose between losing your sight and losing your hearing, which would you keep? At first, almost everyone answers that question by saying they would far rather keep their sight. In all probability that is wrong. For almost everyone, hearing is far more important than sight. Why? Because language is by far our most important source of social experience and information. And an overwhelming proportion of our language experience comes through our ears. Just test it for a day and see how many words you hear and how many you read.

Interviewing, therefore, is by far our most common method of collecting evidence. Children begin to interview their parents and brothers and sisters as soon as they can talk. Parents interview their children many times daily to gather evidence as to how to live with them successfully. Throughout life almost all of us interview scores of people every day.

But the amount of misinformation we get outweighs the accurate information by a big margin. We probably find out far more things that don't tell us anything than things that do. We listen with biases and prejudices which distort what we hear. Check the accuracy of gossip as a case in point. What we tell to our questioners when we are the interviewees is colored by our own opinions, convictions, and funds of information. No wonder conversations are so hard to convert into meaningful evidence!

Many different kinds of interviewing are done in educational work. The many kinds which we use in CRP range from the highly skilled interviewing done in our Church Dynamics Study, to the parent-teacher conferences which are conducted at the beginning and end of each curricular unit. Needless to say, these are poles apart in terms of the technical know-how necessary. Psychological research in interviewing has revealed a great many problems that underlie our efforts to get reliable and valid data by means of an interview. At the same time, it is probable that if these difficulties can be overcome, more useful evidence can be got in a short time through interview than by any other method. The problems which arise when we undertake the collection of data by means of interview depend in part on the purposes to be served by the interview, in part on the training and skill of the interviewer, and in part by the skill of the co-scientist interviewee to give accurate information.

Successful interviewers in any area must be intimately acquainted with the methods and general philosophy of the study being made. Professional interviewers have certain specialized skills, but for many kinds of interviewing, a background in the philosophy underlying the interview is even more important.

The parent-teacher conferences which are conducted at the beginning and end of each curricular unit require little technical training but have corresponding limitations. The fact remains that they constitute one of the most important aspects of our educational program. This means that methods must be discovered for creating better instruments to be used during the interviews, better methods for training the interviewers and interviewees, and better methods for evaluating the results of such interviews. It should be sufficient here to point out just a few of the specific methodological problems involved.

These parent-teacher conferences are conducted by people who have not had technical training in methods of interviewing. If, therefore, they seek to obtain information which presupposes such technical training, the results can hardly be expected to be either accurate or useful, and may actually be harmful. An important problem, then, becomes one of discovering what kinds of information ought to be sought by the lay interviewer, and what kinds of instruments can be given him with which to obtain this information. In any case, there are some kinds of valuable information which can be secured satisfactorily by this method. There are also discoverable methods for improving the reliability of such information and the range of its scope. The dangers of bad interviewing are not nearly so great as the positive values of good interviewing. I'd guess that if we give our co-scientist interviewers guidance in what kinds of evidence they can get, not many of them are going to run amuck and begin to probe beyond their depth.

Most of our CRP interviewers are church-school leaders, parents, YMCA group leaders, or schoolteachers. They cannot be expected to take graduate-level courses covering months or years of training on interviewing techniques. The fact remains that they can be given some training. We need, therefore, to discover the most effective kind of training which they can be given.

If you are going to do any interviewing, or if you have any responsibilities (such as our lesson writers) in training interviewers, you ought to read with some care the most definitive volume available on the subject, written by Bingham and Moore (13).

A single illustration chosen from that volume sets forth very dramatically the ease with which one can get inaccurate results from interviews.

Two trained interviewers, one an ardent prohibitionist, the other an equally ardent socialist, interviewed a number of destitute men in New York City. They used the same questionnaire form. Yet the prohibitionist reported that the downfall of 62 per cent of his interviewees was due to liquor and only 7 per cent to industrial conditions. The socialist quoted only 11 per cent as blaming liquor and 60 per cent as blaming industrial conditions. Both were honest, well trained interviewers.

Perhaps we cannot make expert interviewers of all our church-school teachers and club leaders. But it is possible to so prepare the interview forms that many of the basic principles of interviewing are taken into consideration. Read the list of principles in Bingham and Moore (13:29–58) pertinent to this kind of interviewing. These constitute a basic minimum for getting evidence which can be taken on its face value, with much confidence.

For example, many an interview report is distorted by the interviewer's own prejudices. He must know what these are and how to discount them. Most interviews are better when they are genuine conferences, rather than situations in which the interviewer assumes the role of a teacher or inquisitor. An interviewer must guard carefully against implying the answers to his own questions. The rapport between interviewer and interviewee must be that of confidence and ease. Embarrassing the interviewee or putting him on the defensive is certain to distort the evidence.

It Is the Procedure, Not the Laboratory, That Makes a Good Experiment I have been a college professor for thirty years. I have "experimented" with all kinds of class procedures. Or have I? I think I could tell you which procedures I, as a teacher, can use best—in terms of class attention and apparent interest. Until this very minute I would have said that they are my best methods of teaching. It suddenly dawns on me that not once during the thirty years have I ever even checked my examinations to see whether parts of the course taught by one method have been better learned than those taught by another. No wonder college students retain so little of what we professors expose them to. I dare say, if I had really "experimented," I could have given my students, through the years, many times what I have given them. Now that is also true with church-school teaching, which uses up a billion child hours every year. It is even true with home teaching by parents. So let's take a look at methods of group experimentation, which can be done in church-school classes and homes as well as in laboratories.

Problems of methodology are not nearly so difficult here as you might imagine. And here is an area in which our co-scientist can conduct actual experiments. And it is in such small groups that experimental-control group experiments can be done. I described some methods for doing these in Chapters XI and XII. Let us set forth here a few principles which underlie most actual work of this nature, if their results are to constitute valuable evidence.

In the first place, group experiments must take place under natural conditions. When artificial situations are created—at least if they are artificial to the subjects who participate in them—the conditions of manipulation almost always introduce so many extraneous factors into the picture that the results are uninterpretable. Even the manipulation of those factors, such as educational procedures, which you vary systematically in the experiment should be made as much a natural part of the situation as possible. For example, one can introduce any curricular methods he wishes into a group situation. To attempt to bring it about artificially, however, that different groups use them each with a specified intensity is far less possible, and probably not desirable. Rather, we should determine how they have been used by the various groups naturally and then study the results statistically.

A second principle is inherent in the nature of experiments. Control-group designs require that a "good" method be tested by using it with one group and withholding it from another to measure the differences. This is guinea-pigism. Fortunately, however, we can always use the best available methods with every group participating in any phase of our educational work—never submitting any of them to inferior methods. In testing any particular method all we need to do is find a comparable group with which the method is not being used. We do not need to create an artificial control group. There will always be natural ones available.

The third principle is of a different sort entirely. In our CRP research, for example, we have such highly selected teachers, methods, and groups of children that they can certainly not be regarded as typical of the total population. The statement is often made, therefore, "This is all very well under these ideal conditions, but what would happen under average conditions?" This is a question which must, of course, be answered eventually. It is our contention, however, that we had better start with the most ideal conditions we can create. Then, having established effective methods there, we can proceed to less and less ideal conditions. In other words, we'd better not try to solve all our problems at one time. Let us learn just how to solve the simplest problems first and then proceed to the more difficult ones. It is at this point that some of our co-scientists can give us invaluable help. Our thousands of teachers can do individual experiments of this sort, which we could never do in the laboratory. If these can be integrated into our broad program design, they will increase the speed of our progress a great deal. Just the other day in one of our research committees, we began by talking about a rather simple procedure we thought we might try out. But someone introduced another element in the picture. That started us off, and in fifteen minutes we had a procedure so complex that it had become a program design in itself. Our executive secretary, who watches the budget among other things, called us back down to earth and we actually did end up with a simple, practical, and highly promising experimental design.

If you are at all familiar with the vast literature of experimental psychology, you will think these few pages on direction experimentation a pretty small token of recognition for the vast literature behind them. Even so extensive a volume as the one by Andrews (9) is a very brief outline of this phase of the growth of scientific psychology. As our knowledge of the forces involved in the growth of character increases, more and more precise experimental work will need to be done. As you look through the literature even now, you will be amazed at how many different things we can measure.

At the present time, however, we find little help in "laboratory experiments" in the sense of carefully controlled situations, precise and accurate measurements, systematically manipulated variables, and all the other characteristics of highly technical laboratory experiments. Only our most superficial problems can be so attacked with any degree of validity. If all our cooperating groups, however, would do a great many of these peripheral experiments, using the methods described in Chapters XI and XII, they could accumulate for us a body of invaluable evidence, which would certainly speed up our insights in our total program design.

SKILLS OF THE CO-SCIENTIST

There Are Technical Ways of Analyzing Incidental Observations

The place of the incidental observation in the advancement of knowledge is likely to be misunderstood both by the layman and the scientific worker. The layman is far too likely to ignore the possibility of chance exceptions to the general rule and to make sweeping generalizations from any event or sequence of occurrences which happens to fall within his own personal experience. On the other hand, many scientific workers fall into the opposite error of "pooh-poohing" all reports of individual observations and of regarding as necessarily worthless any fact whose generality has not been "proved."

While it is true that incidental observations do not warrant general conclusions, they nevertheless constitute the leading source of material for the formulation of scientific hypotheses (43:363).

It is becoming increasingly evident, however, that this open-end material is an expression of the total personality. All of the forces of personality are operating in it. Furthermore, when a number of people look at some of this material, arranged in some systematic order, they see characteristic differences which constitute dimensions of these forces never before suspected, much less measured. I have seen our staff take a set of twenty such items and identify a dozen important dimensions in them.

The other five cells, then, on the Research Design Chart relating to this problem all have to do with methodology concerning the interpretation of the co-scientist evidence. They are, as you will remember: Parents' Reports, Teachers' and Leaders' Reports, Observers' Reports, Supervisors' Reports, and Youth Reports. Each of them presents some methodological problems of its own.

You can think of this problem of using co-scientist reports in terms of three dimensions. One dimension is the sampling problem, which will be dealt with fully in Chapter XIV. In most research using this kind of material, it is difficult to get a sample of reports which is completely representative of the total population being studied. Therefore, your methods must include finding ways of improving the representativeness of your sample, on the one hand, and determining what generalizations you can make from the one you have, on the other. The second dimension has to do with what your reporters report. Here is where the co-scientist ideal comes to its peak. The more objectively your reporters are willing to report, the more valuable the evidence. Any methods are useful which help them eliminate motivations which distort their ability to be objective. Then, too, they need training on what to report. Some factors are fruitful, some sterile. The third dimension is in how you go about quantifying the evidence you get. Counting the frequency with which various items appear in such reports seldom reveals either accurate or useful information. Such methods as that of controlled ranking is far more productive. Whatever methods you use, the other two dimensions must be taken into consideration. As your procedures improve, they improve along the line of all three of these dimensions.

The Teacher Can Teach As a Co-Scientist or Not, As He Chooses

Very few people can do an effective job of teaching or group leadership and at the same time observe what is happening in the group. It is not likely, therefore, that we shall get effective reports from group leaders of the reaction of the group to their leadership. This will have to be achieved by observers whose task it is to do this.

The teacher, or leader, however, can describe a part of the situation with some accuracy, especially if he has had a share in determining it. In our CRP groups, the adaptation procedure is the central technique on which the class plans are laid. Teachers' records, therefore, consist largely of an accurate description of the class procedure. Let's put it this way. A teacher can report accurately what his plans were before the class session began. After the session is over, he can do a pretty good job of evaluating the success of those plans. But during the class, it is almost impossible for him to observe what happens. He is much too intent on carrying out the plans. This other task is for the observer. If only the teacher reports, then, he can evaluate the success of his efforts, but he cannot expect to get fruitful hypotheses as to why they were successful or unsuccessful.

Learning to Observe What Is Worth Observing Requires Some Special Skills   So far we have made little use of the observers' reports, but they will eventually become very important, for the reason just stated. The problems of methodology involved will center upon training methods, efficient report forms, and classroom procedures involving the most efficient and most stimulating relationships among observer, teacher, and the members of the class. It is a basic policy in the Project to avoid methods which presuppose any form of "deception" on the part of one group toward another. If, therefore, the work of the observer sets up conflicts with the teacher or misunderstandings among the members of the class, methods will have to be discovered in which this does not occur, but in which all three are completely aware of and enthusiastic about the function of the observer. Such misunderstandings have arisen very seldom. Teachers and class members alike have usually welcomed the contribution of the observer.

In all probability the best way to make the observers' reports pay dividends involves the method of characteristic differences. Suppose that we select five observers' reports each, in which one group consists of reports taken when the teacher considered the class experience highly satisfactory, and the other group when the opposite was true. Then judges can study the two groups for characteristic differences. Factors influencing the situation are almost certain to be discovered, which could not possibly have been detected by direct observation. Many of our teachers have not seen the great values to them of observers' reports. The fact is, such a design as this could make the difference between having one's teaching experience thrilling and effective, and the reverse. Here is another excellent example of the value of a research curriculum and co-scientist participation. Such studies as these could not possibly be done without such methods.

Can We Teach Youth Some of the Skill of the Co-Scientist?   If it is true that the chief aim of character education is to create the most favorable possible environment to permit youth to develop to his maximum capacity, then it follows that one of the characteristics of such an environment will be that it motivates him to throw all his energy and ability into the task. Surely, it follows that he can tell us much about how favorable that environment is. To be sure, his judgment in the matter is far from being infallible; he is much too immature for that. The fact remains that there is much information he can give us that no one else can. You see, such reports are always based on the PS (situation as perceived). When parents and teachers report, they are reporting youth and his reactions as they see them. To be sure, they can see some aspects of youth's behavior to which he is blind. But in other ways what they report is their interpretation of his interpretation of the way things are or ought to be. This is a PS of a PS. But if youth himself reports, we have insights into his thinking which the parents could never give.

Youth Reports, however, present unique problems. Communication is difficult enough under the best of circumstances. The younger the individual, the more difficult it seems to be. Many of our parents of Junior High and High School youth are continually telling us that their youth don't talk. Parents do not know what they think. The task, then, of getting Youth Reports which will give us scientific evidence is not an easy one.

We have hardly scratched the surface in our research in this matter of Youth Reports. I can only indicate a few directions in which such research has promising leads. In the first place, a study of the reports of numbers of young people will show common and unique elements. It may well be that these common elements will suggest clues as to what youth can and cannot report accurately Then, too, in the construction of report procedures, most of the principles already stated in connection with the construction of questionnaires and interviewing are probably pertinent.

Here is a point at which a most important principle can be pointed out. When a young person reports, the value of that report depends on the stimulus (question or discussion topic) to which it is a response. In constructing a design for a youth dynamics study recently, we tested and discarded literally scores of questions which, when youth answered, gave us little or no useful information. We wanted some open-end data from them which would reveal the differences between those young people who had long-range vision and those who live essentially in the present. It is easy to find samples of the two groups. Finding open-end data which is characteristic of each and not the other, in which we can search for dimensional forces accounting for these differences, was a task that baffled us for a long time. Interestingly enough, we did find just such a topic. It seemed to lend itself to bringing out the total personality of the youth, so that it could be evaluated.

SOME IMPORTANT CONCEPTS DESCRIBED IN THIS CHAPTER

Religious- and character-education agencies can double the effectiveness of their educational procedures every decade for many years to come. The amount of this progress will vary with the level of program research they carry out. If all of them would participate in one well integrated program of such research, their influence in the world could easily become one of the most powerful in our society. Such program research presupposes the principle of the research curriculum, in which every curriculum and educational program is so constructed as to become a part of the research itself, actually providing the evidence for its own development. Such program research must be realistically constructed; involving the counsel of experts in the problems involved, people with wide experience in the fields being studied, the existence of measuring instruments for the purpose, adequate valid criteria by which to measure progress, and fruitful dimensions in terms of which to describe the data.

Experimental-control group designs can be very useful in the study of specific problems, such as the effectiveness of particular curricula elements. Over-all research, however, must be planned as factorial design. Only thus can the interplay of the various interacting forces be observed and the dynamics of such interactions be measured. At this level experimental-control group designs are impossible to control, result in such large variances as to obscure results, and are usually unethical to carry out.

The concept of the research curriculum in which the curriculum is so constructed as to secure the evidence for its own evaluation is based on the assumption that scientific research is creative as well as critical. Its aim is to find methods of improving the effectiveness of any curriculum, no matter how effective it is at present.

The test of a curriculum is in its results in the lives of the children who are exposed to it. Its content, the intentions of its writers, even its goals mean nothing until they are expressed in the personalities of the children who study it. The fact is, children do more to a curriculum than the curriculum does to them. It makes more sense, then, to measure what they do with it than what it intends to do with them.

Co-scientists can do hundreds of small experiments, testing the elements of a curriculum. This may well be the crucial point in program research. Errors at the periphery of a problem get multiplied over and over again as we approach the major problems, which assume their accuracy. Our large research projects can be frustrated unless the co-scientist feeds into the central-program research accurate evaluation of the hundreds of curricular elements. In the last analysis, then, it is in the co-scientists that the hope of our success lies.

All scientific analysis is based on evidence. This evidence must be reliable and valid. At one time it was thought that this presupposed the carefully controlled laboratory situation, large samples, and highly trained technicians. Now we know that even better evidence —in personality and social research—can be obtained in natural situations and from co-scientists. We need to control the sampling errors, and to train the co-scientists in objective observation. Open-end reports are actually better than restricted evidence. We now have techniques for quantifying them reliably. They reflect the total personality better, so that we can discover dynamic interaction phenomena. Even interviewing—which is not uncontrolled conversation—can be made a useful tool for co-scientists.

CHAPTER XIV

———•—•———

WHAT DOES THE EVIDENCE TELL US?

ON FINDING OUT WHAT YOU HAVE FOUND OUT

IN RELIGIOUS and character education in particular and in all education in general, we have had enacted right before our eyes a drama from which we might learn powerful principles about the will of God. All too often we have just carried out our educational procedures, often making our curricula literally a "prescribed course for our children to run," and never looking for these great insights, usually never even suspecting that they are there.

It is in curriculum evaluation that factorial design comes into its own. If we were to attempt to test our curricular procedures by experimental-control group designs, we might, to be sure, learn something about which procedures are effective and which ineffective, but almost never why. Using factorial design, however, we can systematically study the bewildering drama of interacting forces in human nature and society. Then we can discover principles which will open up new doors of potential, if not for us, at least for our children.

There are three major steps in this process. Of course, the first one is that we must get the evidence. That was the task which Chapter XIII was designed to explore.

Now let's turn to the next two tasks. We must begin to organize this evidence, first, to see what it tells us about itself. How effective have our materials and techniques been with the children with whom we have used them? How successfully have we challenged

their strongest motivations? How good a job have we done in enlisting and training the necessary leadership? Have we given our
visions and skills to children throughout the whole range of individual differences? Have we made our lessons meaningful to the child
as he lives in his social setting? Have we created methods which
can strengthen and be integrated with all the other social forces for
good in our churches and community?

The other task, to be dealt with in the last half of this chapter, is
to discover to what extent our findings with a certain group of children apply to children everywhere. It is one thing to say that certain methods will work with a particular group. It is another thing
to know how far we can apply these principles throughout all of
human nature and society. In this kind of research we always have
a selected sample. Can we generalize from it to all men? We will
always be training our children in specific situations. Can they use
the same methods in all their complex experiences? Will what they
learn in church school work in business? As they move from role to
role, from one social context to another, how well will they find that
our educational efforts have helped them to meet the problems
awaiting them? And as they grow up from infancy to childhood to
youth to maturity, will the lessons they learn in the Kindergarten
help them in Junior High school; or the lessons learned during
teen-age help them in establishing their homes and achieving their
later life visions?

HOW DO YOU INTERPRET SCIENTIFIC EVIDENCE?

After curriculum writers have worked for years to create some
effective methods of religious and character education, they are
likely to get a bit ego-involved about them. No wonder we find ourselves somewhat biased when we begin looking at the evidence. Our
pet theories, which we probably have defended from time to time
with considerable enthusiasm—to say nothing of having tried to sell
them in glowing terms of praise—are almost like members of our
families; we cannot see them dissected even for scientific purposes
without experiencing some pain in the process. It takes zest for
truth, faith in the infinity principle, and large amounts of self-
discipline to approach this matter of curriculum evaluation with
complete objectivity. The fruits of evaluation, however, are so great

that no one who has ever tasted them would even dream of not seeking them.

As I write this we are planning for a youth conference. We need some evidence which we can use to determine the relative levels of character of those who come—defining this as persistence, social vision, and understanding of the more profound Christian principles. In a search through some of our existing data, we found a number of essay answers teen-agers had given to some open-end questions (50: Ch. 24). We asked six judges to rank the answers to one of these in terms of strength of character as defined by the three criteria named above. We found that the pooled judgments of the rankers gave a reliability coefficient of .94. This told us that we had available an accurate instrument. The youth leaders of these teen-agers had written personality descriptions of them. We had six judges, completely independently, rank these. The reliability of these pooled rankings was of the same magnitude. We correlated these two measures—the adult leader evaluations and the essays—and found a correlation of .74. In passing, note that all this was done in a few hours. Without the help of simple statistical tools, such a task would have been almost impossible. With them, we solved a problem with comparative ease which we had expected to cause us a great deal of work.

THE FIRST DIMENSION—THE CURRICULUM AS IT REACHES THE CHILD

If you will examine our Research Design Chart again, you will note that in the section designated as III A, *Analytical Evaluation of Methods and Materials,* two of its five major subgroups have to do with curricular methods and materials and one has to do with leadership training. In the evidence that comes to us from the church schools using them, there is plenty of opportunity for us to discover the extent to which they are or are not effective.

The First Half of a Curriculum Is Its Printed Materials The first area of evaluation, then, has to do with our curricular materials themselves. Every element in them should be studied objectively in terms of the purpose it was designed to serve and in light of the available evidence concerning it. In actual practice, such evaluations vary from almost purely subjective opinion with little or no empirical basis to carefully analyzed studies complete with tests of significance. Here is the major point at which our individual churches and the teacher and parent co-scientists can be of real help to us. This is an area in which we need hundreds of "small" experiments. It would be very difficult for us in the laboratory to include the hundreds of specific curricular elements even in an over-all factorial design. But if our teachers and parents will master such a technique as the method of control ranks and test our many curricular elements in real situations, they can be of inestimable help in creating more effective curricula. In a Project like ours, where as many as ten thousand curricular elements [1] may be constructed in a year, without such help it is impossible for us to make carefully controlled studies about all or even a large fraction of them. This is just as true for those using other curricula. If our denominational boards and character-building agencies want to evaluate their curricular procedures, they will proceed much faster with the help of such a co-scientist body of workers, than by a few large over-all evaluations.

Let me describe some typical methods of evaluating curricular materials at different levels of scientific thoroughness. It should be our aim to proceed as far as possible along this scale of objectivity.

The first level, and the least thorough, scientifically speaking, is to read carefully through whatever evidence is available—assuming that it is unbiased—and record impressionistic judgments as to the evaluation of curricular materials under consideration. Let me show you how we have used this procedure in revising lessons in our own laboratory. For example, the Parents' Reports and other sources of evidence are examined: (1) to find out which parts of the lesson were actually used and their apparent contribution in terms of success or failure toward helping achieve its objective; (2) a listing of the reported successes and failures in the use of the lesson as a whole; (3) a listing and evaluation of the motivations appealed to by parents and teachers in the teaching of the lesson and how they operated in the children learning it; (4) an analysis of the snags and misunderstandings encountered by teachers, parents, or children; (5) a listing of the additional materials and methods which were used by parents and teachers, and their effectiveness. With all this evidence in mind, the evaluation is then made.

[1] A curricular element is a story, project, discussion, etc., used in our curricular materials.

A second level of analysis of any particular element of curricular materials is somewhat more quantitative. The method for rating the effectiveness of the lesson on the basis of Parents' Reports has been described elsewhere (120). Since these reports are rated on a seven-point scale, the average rating of all of the reports on any one lesson can be used as a rough measure of the effectiveness of that lesson. Errors due to sampling can be minimized by using stratified randomizations in the choice of groups to be so tested. With all its shortcomings this is the most objective measure we have been able to use extensively in CRP.

A third level method is as follows. Experimental classes are formed similar to those used in the Morse study (104, 105). Then the various curricular elements can be evaluated by the following steps: (1) Using the adaptation procedure, each curricular element is applied to each child in the class. (2) The child is later observed, to determine to what extent he responded positively or negatively to any given element. Since all of the variables involved will probably vary interdependently, the intercorrelations among them in terms of factorial design will give us the basis for finding many valuable insights not only concerning the individual elements in the lesson, but also their integrative effects in the lesson as a whole.

Evaluating the Elements of a Curriculum But now let's take a look at some of the common types of elements which are used especially in religious- and character-education curricula. In a process like this it is very easy to lose sight of the forest for the trees, in our examination of particular elements. But it is even easier for us to leave a great deal of dross in our curricula by comparing two forests and forgetting the strong and weak trees in each. First, then, let's get an integrative framework—which will keep the forest before us—into which to put our analysis of individual elements. This procedure ought to be the first step in revision.

Open-end answers to leading questions asked of parents who have and who have not used a particular lesson can be ranked according to apparent influence of the introduction, using the method of control ranks, described in Chapter XI. Or, each element in the introduction or its effect can be identified as being present or absent in the two groups of essays and chi-square used to test significance of difference.

Lecture and discussion materials are, of course, included in the lesson plans. Recognizing that lecturing alone may be very ineffective, especially if it is looked upon by the pupils as "preachy," and that discussions can become pleasant ways of wasting time by "rearranging our prejudices," our task is to discover how to use these two tools effectively. The technique described above—rating the reports which mention these procedures, and noting whether the mention is positive or negative—is the beginning of a scientific effort to evaluate them.

Stories and biography are among the oldest and most widely used of character-education methods. There is, however, some research evidence to show that they are not necessarily effective (58). One of the hypotheses which govern our use of these two tools is that they must be adapted to the individual child and made meaningful in terms of his daily life if they are to be effective. A careful study of the Parents' Reports or Youth Reports may reveal some evidence of how successful we have been in this regard. Efforts on the part of children to plan modern stories based on them is both a learning technique and a basis for evaluation of amount learned.

Biblical materials are also used extensively. The most frequent complaint we hear is, "There is not enough Bible in it." This may be true in a different way than usually is implied by those who say it. It is a truism, very seldom recognized in practice, that the amount of Bible in the curricular materials is not a final measure of how much gets into the minds and hearts of children. The curriculum which contains the least amount of content today probably still contains much more than the children can learn in the time available for religious instruction. The more desirable we believe Bible learning to be, the more seriously we must consider the learning capacity of children.

Church-school projects have as their aim giving children an opportunity to gain practice in the attitude being studied. We need, then, to examine our evidence to find the effectiveness of such projects in a number of different ways. In the first place, unless the child has some insight as to the purpose of the project, it will have no effect in terms of character education. Second, unless the role played in the project is adapted to his own individual needs and abilities, there is little chance of its being effective. Third, the only relevant measure of the success of a project is that it helps the child learn the attitude. Whether he likes it or not is irrelevant or at least secondary. Observers' reports during the project period, and Parents' Reports, are likely to be our best sources of evidence for such evaluation.

Probably all of the members of our research staff would agree that the most critical element in any lesson plan is the home assignments in it. Problems related to home participation in the process of character education will be found in many portions of our over-all research design. And, although the "Home Guide" in the lesson plan is by no means our only published curricular approach to them, it is by far the most important one. Research designs need therefore to be set up to measure its effectiveness in achieving the purposes for which it is prepared. A sheer counting of the frequency with which it is used and not used is a start in this direction.

Many problems arise in the actual mechanics of the lesson plan or program outline. When I entered school in the early years of this century, we first learned the alphabet, then the two-letter words, then the three-, and so on. Finally we put them together in short sentences. We all did the same thing, including the retarded boy of fifteen who had not yet "passed" the first grade. Who could have guessed then what a totally different experience the first grade of today has in our modern schools? It isn't just a new first-grade reader; it is a completely new way of going about the process. I doubt if there are many first-grade readers today, certainly not in most of the schools I know.

If a man from Mars had come to our planet in 1900 and visited some of our Sunday-school classes and then returned in 1950 to repeat the process, would he have found differences of the same magnitude? He'd have found some differences, all right; but probably not nearly as many as in our secular education program.

When we evaluate the mechanics of the lesson plan, we need to make sure that we do not assume even its over-all validity. Perhaps we ought to go about the whole process of religious education differently than we do. I am almost certain that this is true at the high-school and college levels. We have not challenged our teenagers to even a small fraction of their maximum capacity. We have tried everything we could think of from completely structured courses to the free-and-easy youth group which "chooses its own activities," even when it is completely frustrated in the process. Our colleges are not so fanatically religious that we cannot do some solid thinking about new approaches for them, too. For example, right now we are considering the idea of making use of the college bull session for a new type of character education, for here is where the college student makes his biggest investment of time. The point is, let's keep our minds open to totally new formats in this process of religious education.

To be sure, there are such simple problems as the order in which the various topics should be presented, but also such complex ones as whether the lesson should be written directly to the child or to the parents and teachers, and problems of language difficulties in the presentation of various concepts. Vocabulary difficulties often present us with dilemmas. Technical-sounding words may set up psychological barriers—or challenges—of one kind, and vagueness of concepts resulting from the avoidance of technical terms may set up even more difficult barriers of another kind. Each of these problems suggests its own particular experimental designs. Here is an illustrative study. Setchko (124) measured the readability of a number of lessons and correlated these scores with effectiveness scores as determined by Parents' Report ratings. The study failed to reveal readability as a factor in effectiveness. This is interesting because so often we have heard criticism of there being too much technical language in our materials.

What Ten Thousand Co-Scientists Could Do for Religious Education! Let us suppose that we have one hundred research centers—churches, schools, YMCA's, or independent groups. Half of those might be connected with CRP and half with other curricula. They should be in pairs. Each member of a pair ought to be using a different curriculum. Centers using any two curricula can carry out this research. Each center will need an active research committee. On any one week, one class from each of two age levels in each of the two groups will set up a test; for example, the essay-type method described in Chapters XI and XII. At the lower age levels behavior situations can be created with observers recording what happens. Using the method of control ranks followed by the method of characteristic differences, we could test the three major elements in every lesson of the two curricula. We could determine, with some accuracy, the effectiveness of almost every lesson and every major part of every lesson. Not only that, we could determine what are the important factors which account for the differences in the performances of the compared groups, thus discovering the strengths and weaknesses of each.

Within a period of from four to six years, we could discover most of the factors which determine how effective religious education is and can be. I think that it could confidently and conservatively be predicted that the results of such a study could increase the effectiveness of our educational efforts in the area of moral and spiritual values at least tenfold.

The Second Half of a Curriculum Consists of the Teachers and Parents Who Teach It The most costly and elaborate curricula are produced by our denominational boards. The only trouble is that they have to be transmitted to our children by us. Even the best curricula and buildings are still a relatively small part of the child's total experience.

What director has not torn his hair endeavoring to find teachers who will invest the effort and skill to teach the curriculum as it should be taught? And what teacher has not bemoaned the apathy of many of our homes, when all the evidence shows that the home is the most important factor in the process? Yet, the curriculum must be evaluated partly in terms of how well it inspires good teacher and parent cooperation. It does no good just to say, "If the parents would only do so and so, our curriculum would be effective." The curriculum must produce this cooperation, and should be evaluated in terms of how well it does. It is not difficult to get frequency counts of parent participation and teacher turnover.

For one thing we should find out what kinds of motivational techniques are implied in our curricular materials. The problem of motivation has received very wide study in psychology. We are able to use the results of a great deal of research in this phase of our curricular methods. It becomes necessary, therefore, to test with great care all of the motivational methods used by parents and teachers in character education, and to revise our curricular materials to improve their skills in this regard. Our chief source of data comes from examination of the parent and teacher reports. We look for evidence as to what motivations they actually appealed to in the child and of their effectiveness. One of our most interesting studies in this regard was designed to determine what kinds of motivations, both on the part of parents and children, seem to bring about success in our "family team" methods and what kinds result in failure in the use of that concept.

One of our concepts in CRP relevant to our evaluation of this parent-teacher dimension is called *motivated capacity*. It has grown out of a recognition that no matter how good our curricular materials prove to be, they must be taught by parents and teachers. Unless our curriculum can challenge parents and teachers so that they not only can but also will carry them out, we shall not do effective character education. The limits within which parents and teachers can be so challenged, we call motivated capacity. The word *capacity* is meant to imply what they can do in terms of native endowment and skills. The word *motivated* refers to what they will do.

Parents and teachers differ widely in terms of this motivated capacity. We shall have to discover the range of this quality, and prepare materials which challenge the best in the upper level, but does not eliminate even the lowest levels. In this regard, probably all of us have sinned grievously. Some curricula, especially in religious education, have made sure that people at the lowest level of motivated capacity could use the materials, but have failed to challenge the best. Probably, we in CRP have tended to go to the opposite extreme and challenge the ablest and most determined of parents and teachers, leaving the less able ones in what seems to them to be hopeless confusion. The solution lies in being able to do both. How this is to be done is a problem both of technique and of theory.

The Curriculum the Child Sees Is What the Teacher Presents "So little is given to so many with which to do so much," is certainly true when we regard the plight of many of our church-school teachers. How often an unsuspecting and well intentioned adult walks innocently into a church-school classroom and takes the worst beating of his life. And is that surprising? We often give them nothing more than a quarterly and class list with which to meet the combined energies and skilled destructive imaginations of, say, a dozen thirteen-year-old boys. No respectable adult deserves a fate like that. It is little wonder that our project materials in religious education are primarily weapons of self-defense for distraught church-school teachers. They may not do the children much good, but they lower the mortality rate in church-school teachers by a considerable margin, and I suppose we must admit that justifies their existence. The fact is, the average public-school teacher has a hundred times the equipment with which to cope with the next generation as does the average church-school teacher. Yet, the lesson texts and planned procedures get to the child only through this emissary. Recognizing that we in CRP have barely made a good beginning, I should like to show you some of our procedures for preparing parents and teachers to guide the growth of our children. In general we have thus far employed five. They are: workshops, training publications, *Adventures in Character Education,* parents' classes, and teacher-training classes.

The most important "people-are-human" factor in our leadership problems is their common failing in persistence to "carry through." Staffs are often recruited and trained, only to have large numbers of them drop out for one reason or another. In the evaluation of our methods, we shall need to seek the causes for these "drop-outs." Probably characteristic-differences studies searching for relevant aspects of their personalities will give us our best clues for attacking this problem.

At the present time we are completing a study to which we refer as the Teacher Opinion Study. Using an interview technique, we obtained a large and varied amount of information concerning more than forty church-school teachers in four churches. These teachers varied in whether they were satisfied or dissatisfied with their teaching experience. They also differed as to the extent to which they were using all our materials and techniques. In analyzing the differences among the teachers showing these characteristics, we are learning many interesting things. For example, knowledge of the age-level characteristics and of the individual members of the class seems to be the biggest asset a teacher can have. Such personality factors as optimism, enthusiasm, self-confidence, and sociability are far more common among satisfied teachers than among dissatisfied ones. This is also true for having an understanding and enthusiastic acceptance of the philosophy on which the curriculum is based. In our case, the importance of the attitude in character education is the central principle. On the other hand, such factors as buildings, classroom equipment, and so on, seem to be about the same in the two groups. Interestingly enough, dogmatism or open-minded-ness do not differ between the two groups; nor do use of authoritarian and democratic procedures.

Thus far, one of our most effective leadership training tools has been our summer workshop. The methods used in it ought to have wide applicability. We require all our new churches to have members of their staff get such training, and urge strongly that all the participating institutions regularly have representatives present. The general procedure of the workshop follows this basic pattern: we first describe some methods and techniques and then give actual practice in their use.

Our evaluation of the effectiveness of our use of the workshop technique has thus far been mostly on the basis of the reactions of those who come. For every class a brief evaluation form is prepared on which questions are asked, designed to learn the extent to which its objectives have been achieved—as far as the opinions of the participants are concerned. But the only final measures of workshop effectiveness are the results in terms of trained leadership.

Here is how we would go about such a study. We would select fifty Positive Potential items, twenty-five from churches which participate very actively each year in workshop and twenty-five from churches which participate least actively. Then two forms of analysis can be made. In one, the fifty items can be ranked in terms of Christian-character criteria. The average ranks of the two groups would tell us whether there is a measurable difference between the two. In the other, the two groups of items can be studied for characteristic differences. This should give us clues as to where we are being effective and where we could improve our methods.

Most educational agencies use as one of their training techniques the publication of many training manuals. Little effort has been made to evaluate them objectively. Thus far, we have prepared and made use of very few training publications apart from the lesson plans themselves. The most outstanding ones we have used are the *Parents' Manual* (115) and *The Why and How of Adaptation* (144). It is not difficult to make some fairly objective evaluations of these. For example, parents can be given examinations before and after studying the *Parents' Manual*, to see whether they have gained the information it was designed to give them. Groups of parents who have and have not used the *Parents' Manual* can be studied in terms of the number of reports they turn in and on the effectiveness ratings on these reports.

ACE (*Adventures in Character Education*) (1) is a weekly publication designed to be used primarily with parents and church-school staffs, to keep them abreast of Project "news," findings, and methods. Procedures to be used in particular lessons are discussed. An exchange of ideas from church to church is included.

Everyone knows the many difficulties to which we refer as the problems of communications. ACE is one of the most important, if not the most important, single instrument of communication we have. What kind of job is it doing? Let me describe to you one experimental design we have used to answer this question in part at least.

For a period of six weeks, we mailed ACE to approximately four hundred people. Each issue included three or four main articles, the titles of which were listed in a box on the front page. Enclosed with each issue was a postcard with two questions on it: "(1) As you read the titles in the box on the front page, which ones seem likely to be of interest or value to you?" Then, after they had read the articles, they were to answer the second question, "(2) How fully were your expectations realized?"

Our return on this study was very high. We were then able to compute a ratio score for each of the twenty articles listed, between favorable and unfavorable reactions to it. The twenty articles were then listed in order of their "popularity." We searched for characteristic differences between the top and bottom half of these articles and learned a number of things which are useful to us in making ACE more valuable to those who read it. For example, technical language did not distinguish between them. Research articles were always in the top half. These are two outstanding examples of our findings (53).

Possibly, next to the workshop, the most effective training procedure used in the Project has been the Parents' Classes. Each of our research groups has such a class. Almost always it is held weekly, and has for its objective the training of parents in methods of carrying out the job of character education in their own homes. The attendance varies from church to church from almost 100 per cent of the families being represented each week to a much lower percentage. The methods used in these classes vary widely. We try to bring together the experience of these exploratory efforts, and to set forth clearly defined objectives and procedures, and to create measuring instruments for testing their effectiveness.

Finally, many Teacher Training Classes are held. This is probably the least well defined part of our training procedures. It is a well known fact to anyone who has made even the most superficial efforts to evaluate such classes, that the dividends are discouragingly small. The general philosophy of the workshop technique, in which, during the training classes, teachers are introduced to procedures and then given actual practice in using them, seems to be by far the most effective. Our general procedure, as has already been pointed out, has been to have the local churches represented at the summer workshop, and then to have these representatives in turn train the entire staffs in the local churches.

It is my own guess that the best teacher training is individual. A teacher works out a plan for the coming Sunday. After the teaching experience he discusses what has happened with the director of religious education or some experienced teacher. He plans again and repeats the process. It would be entirely possible to use the methods of control rank and characteristic differences with Positive Potential items chosen, on the one hand, from churches in which this method is used extensively by the directors of education and, on the other, from churches in which this is not done extensively.

THE SECOND DIMENSION—THE CHILD AS AN INDIVIDUAL

The plastic-clay period of education is gone. At last we have come to realize that our children make up their minds as to whether or not they will listen to us and what they will do about it when they do. A teen-ager says, "If everybody at school would start being Christian at the same time, it would work." The trouble is, they won't. So the curriculum must be so constructed that it makes sense to this teen-ager who has to live with his fellows. One of the ways in which it is evaluated is in terms of how much sense it does make to him. An examination of his English themes at school or of his conversation at the dinner table will soon tell us the answer to this.

As we attempt to challenge people to test the Christian Hypothesis, history will assure us that challenges to selfishness are much easier to teach and more readily grasped than altruistic challenges. We are swimming against the current all the time. Yet, it is our conviction that, basically, the deepest drives of human nature are to swim against the current. In any case, our evaluation processes must examine with great care the evidence in terms of this problem.

It has been a basic concept of the Project that social processes must be dealt with in terms of total social groups, and individuals as total personalities. The fact remains that you will recognize that it is absurd and ineffective to treat a social group as if every member of it were exactly like every other member. And it is equally absurd, in dealing with an individual, to suppose that his total personality can be described without qualitative differentiations. It has, therefore, been a basic principle of ours that the most important way to evaluate our curricular methods is to study their effectiveness with individuals.

We have approached this problem from two directions. The first one can be regarded as cross-sectional, and consists in examining the effectiveness of a particular lesson or group of lessons with all of the individuals for whom evidence is available concerning its use. These include evidence from Profiles, PIO's, attitude scales and, of course, parent and teacher reports. Methods used for this evaluation range from the "effectiveness rating" of the reports to an impressionistic evaluation which can be gained from a careful study of all of the evidence. The nature of the child and the result of the lesson on the child are also areas of significant evidence for such evaluation.

The other approach, and one which is coming increasingly into prominence in our procedures, can be regarded as longitudinal. It consists in getting together all of the evidence we can find for individual children over a period of months or years. Careful analyses of their attitude development can be made, and the curricular materials can then be evaluated in terms of these analyses.

THE THIRD DIMENSION—THE CULTURE IN WHICH THE CHILD LIVES

Then finally the child lives in our social order. He is required to play roles at school, at home, and on the playground. His religious education must make sense there too. Furthermore, our social order being what it is, it is not always easy for him to see how Christian methods are possible in our cutthroat world. "So our good little boys are going to turn the other cheek, are they?" says a cynical school-teacher. "What will you do when you run out of cheeks?" Many a father questions seriously whether Christian ideals are possible in modern business. Many a mother gives such high priority to social standing that vicarious sacrifice is hard to learn. Yet, most of these people are sincere and really believe what they say. Our curriculum can be no more effective than the sense it makes to them.

The fact of the matter is, we are asking our children to live lives we could not live. We often preach to them with our tongues in our cheeks. When a curriculum is evaluated, then, it must be studied not only as such, but in the context of the social order of which it is a part. It can be a very powerful part. But it will be that only if we discover the interacting forces in the structure of which it is a part and take stock of those forces in its construction. So in evaluation, we are always dealing with the total picture, never with just the curriculum as such.

Role Determinants in the Experience of the Child We can assume that each individual plays a number of "roles" in his daily life—a role at home, at school, on the playground, and so on—and that his personality patterns will vary from role to role. Thus a boy may establish certain habits and traits which are highly consistent in a summer camp, but which show no signs of transferring to his home life. The significance of this role concept is obvious, in terms of its implications for character education and for the development of generalized traits. The roles which we have studied in our procedures have been the church, the home, the school, the club, and the camp.

The role of the school has been explored in the Park School experiment in Indianapolis. An initial description of this study was included in Chapter IV. A more carefully designed study is now being carried out (123).

Here is a boy who wins prizes for good citizenship at school and behaves in the very opposite manner at home. The degree of inconsistency which most of us show from role to role is astonishing. Such inconsistencies in a person, however, do not mean that we are dealing with a disintegrated personality. What it does mean is that his real philosophy of life results in what seems on the surface to be inconsistent behavior. In religious and character education we are trying to help the child formulate his basic philosophy of life. It is not likely to be very effective unless it is related to the roles which he must play. Conversely, our evaluation of our success can to a significant degree be determined by how much of what we teach him helps him in his performance in these roles.

Evaluation in Terms of Integration with the Rest of the Social Climate   There is another aspect to the cultural side of the problem. In any community there are a great many activities, both inside the church and in other character-building organizations. This means that we must not only prepare materials which take into consideration the total social experience of the child, we must also think in terms of our interrelationships with the other agencies of a similar nature which operate in the community. The overlapping of effort among our desirable community efforts saps much of their effective strength. Furthermore, the total effect of these agencies can be far greater if their efforts are integrative instead of merely additive and even at times competitive.

Sometimes we talk to parents as if they had no other responsibilities than to be parents. They are allowed to live lives of their own only when there are no more parental responsibilities. Probably churches often think that we in CRP expect them to subordinate all their other functions to that of religious education. Finally, the many community ventures may be lost sight of if our interrelationships with them are not taken into account.

No one of these agencies would continue to exist if it did not have some source of strength. In fact, it would not continue to exist if it did not have some unique strength among the agencies in its community. To lose any one of them, then, would mean a loss to the community. When we are realistic, however, we realize that they operate pretty much on the basis of survival of the fittest. They know almost nothing about one another, except when they compete for funds, leadership, or membership. In fact, their board meetings are often spent too largely on these three topics.

Of a completely different nature in any community are the many different philosophies in the social climate in which our children grow up. We have vastly different concepts of discipline, and our children in their social contacts become keenly aware of them. The social groupings in a community, which result in different kinds of people living in different neighborhoods, constitute a significant community social philosophy which vastly influences our children's concepts of moral and spiritual values. The various inter- and intra-group mores in which these groups differ from one another are forces to be dealt with.

PARAMETERS—THE GOAL OF ALL RESEARCH

A woman living near a college campus was heard to say: "College students are a lot of bums. I know, because one of them got drunk and broke a window in my house the other night."

That, you will admit, is quite a generalization; judging all college students in all situations on the basis of the behavior of one in one situation. Yet most of us reach just that kind of conclusion about many things. If we wish to take advantage of the scientific method in our thinking, such absurd judgments must be avoided like poison. The fact is, they constitute a vicious kind of poison. The enormous quantity of intellectual blindness which results from fallacious thinking of this sort is one of our greatest obstacles to progress in this area.

You Measure Statistics of a Sample to Estimate Parameters of a Population The key word in this second half of the chapter is *parameter*. The main purpose of measurement in any form of basic research is the search for parameters. You can grasp its meaning easily if you see it along with three other terms: *population, statistic,* and *sample*. Let's examine in more detail these terms which were introduced briefly in Chapters XI and XII.

A *population* is whatever group you want to study. It can be all six-year-olds; all Methodists; all college students; all women drivers; all of your friends, or, of course, everyone in the world. It can even be other things than people—temper tantrums, situations, or even standard deviations. A *sample*, on the other hand, is that portion of the population which in your experiment you actually measure: two hundred six-year-olds; all of the Methodists attending a particular conference; the student body of some college; a hundred women drivers chosen at random in your city, or the first thousand people you can persuade to participate in your experiment. In only very rare instances does your sample include your entire population. Almost always you hope that what you find out when you measure your sample will be what you would have found out if you had measured the whole population. A large proportion of faulty thinking comes about because we assume that the sample is representative of the population, when actually it is not. The particular group of six-year-olds you measure may be a highly selected group; Methodists attending a conference are probably far more zealous than Methodists in general. Colleges vary so much that even the whole student body in one of them would certainly not be representative of them all. The women drivers in a large city would probably not be typical of those in sparsely settled rural areas. I am sure you will agree that it would be difficult indeed to find a group of a thousand individuals, especially if limited to those whom you know, who would be representative of all mankind. Nevertheless, if you are to do valid scientific thinking you must try to find samples which are representative of the population you wish to study. You will seldom be able to do that perfectly; so finally, when you have measured a sample, you must determine what population it is representative of.

Here is another reason why it is usually impossible to plan extensive program research in as theoretically well structured a way as you can an animal experiment. Human nature just won't be manipulated that way. I doubt if it is ever possible, in extensive social research, to secure perfect random samples, either of subjects or of their behavior. Are we, then, prevented from doing good research? Far from it. We get the best samples we can. But then we examine the ones we actually have and see what conclusions can be drawn from our results. This is not an easy task, but a most important one.

Now let us look at the other two terms, *statistic* and *parameter*. Suppose you compute the average of a sample. That is a statistic. If you could determine, however, the average of your population, that would be the corresponding parameter. Usually you do not measure a whole population—all six-year-olds, for example. What you actually do is to measure a sample, determine some statistic about it—a mean, for example—and attempt to make it identical with the parameter you would have obtained if you had measured your whole population. It is obvious, then, that in most scientific measurement you are really searching for parameters; but actually determining statistics. One of your chief problems in methodology is to look for ways of finding out what kind of parameters you can postulate on the basis of the statistics you obtain.

Now, let us show how important all this is in research like ours, by a few examples.

Let us start with six-year-olds as our population. Let us choose as our sample fifty six-year-olds in a wealthy girls' school, and observe their manners in a class-day program before their parents. Can we assume that the manners they display there are typical of all six-year-olds? Putting it a bit more technically, could the average, a statistic, of this sample be accepted with confidence as the probable average, a parameter, of all six-year-olds? Obviously not. These six-year-olds would probably be very different from a group of fifty boys chosen from a slum area in some large city. Furthermore, what these particular six-year-olds do in a class-day program is not likely to be a good prediction of how they will behave on the playground at recess. Finally, if you state only the average, in all probability some will do far better and some far worse, even on class-day. If, then, the purpose of your experiment is to describe some quality of six-year-olds in general, this is about as bad an experiment as you could devise.

However, note one important point! Are your results completely worthless? Is this statistic (the average obtained) a parameter of any population? The answer is, it is. In the first place, it certainly is a parameter of itself as a population. Furthermore, it is probable that it is a pretty good parameter estimate of what the average would be if you measured all of the six-year-olds in wealthy girls' schools in their behavior in class-days or similar celebrations before their parents or other visiting adult groups. You would probably want to sample another group or so, to make reasonably sure that some other factor had not entered in, such as geographical location. Nevertheless, there is a fair-sized population for which you do have a parameter. If all generalizations in social psychology were made in this same way, we would have much less poor thinking than we do and much more good thinking. Furthermore, there are some ways in which human beings are much alike, as well as ways in which they differ. In terms of the ways in which they are alike, this selected sample may be as good as any other. You see, it is possible to draw more defensible conclusions than you might have guessed from even so selected a sample as this.

Now let's consider the Methodists at the conference. Our population consists of all the Methodists there are. Our sample are those attending a particular conference. Let us suppose that we want to find out how courteous and thoughtful Methodists are. Let us observe these particular Methodists in a reception held during the conference. Would you suppose that these Methodists constitute a representative sample of all Methodists? For one thing, the proportion of ministers and other professional religious workers present in the sample is likely to be far greater than of Methodists in general. Then do you suppose that how courteous and thoughtful this group is at a conference reception is predictive of how thoughtful and courteous even this group will be in the next rush-hour traffic jam they are in, much less the behavior of all Methodists in all kinds of situations? It is obvious, then, that your evaluation of this behavior (a statistic) of this group (a sample) in this situation (also a sample) cannot be regarded as a probable prediction (a parameter) of what all Methodists (your population) will do in all kinds of situations (also a population). Is there a population for which this statistic is a parameter? You certainly would be reasonably safe in assuming that this would be fairly typical behavior (parameter) for Methodists or any other similar group attending conferences during social events held in them. Even this ought to be checked by testing one or two other similar conferences in other parts of the country.

But what about making generalizations about people in general? Will Rogers used to say, "All I know is what I read in the papers." If he really meant that, how confidently could he make his conclusions about people? Let us suppose that we want to study such problems as the success of American marriages, or safety in automobile driving, or honesty in business (parameters). We shall choose as our sample in each case those marriages, those automobile-driving experiences, and those descriptions of business dealings reported in our morning newspaper. On the basis of any statistic of this sample, we should probably decide that almost all marriages fail, that practically every automobile journey ends in a crash, and that a majority of businessmen are dishonest. A less accurate method could hardly be devised for studying such problems as judging by what we read in the papers. Any statistic based on this sample would certainly not be remotely related to the corresponding parameter of the total population. A great deal of mass hysteria comes about because we do come to think of this distorted sample as typical. A vast majority of our current crop of teen-agers are fine youngsters, but you would never guess this—if you judged them by those who make the headlines.

ARE SELECTED SAMPLES SCIENTIFICALLY USELESS?

Having said so much about the desirability of normal and representative samples, it may occur to some that unless we get this kind of sample we might as well close up shop. If scientists through the years had all done that, we would have no science today. Think how much guinea pigs and white rats have contributed to human happiness by way of the research done on them and applied to us. They certainly constitute a selected sample as far as human nature is concerned. Clinical psychologists have learned a great deal about normal behavior by studying the mentally ill. The concept that the mentally ill person shows the characteristics of the normal person to an exaggerated degree is not always true, but it is true often enough to have made contributions from that selected sample of enormous value to us in our understanding of human nature in general. Indeed, these scientists would prefer to study the mentally ill. They say it is like putting a microorganism under a microscope, because our normal shortcomings become so magnified in the mentally ill that we can see and describe them more easily. I would guess that we have learned more about our modern preschool methods of teaching from trying to train the feeble-minded than from any other single source. Here again is a selected sample which has paid great scientific dividends. Then, there is the long-suffering college sophomore. Probably more psychological research has been done on him than on all other kinds of subjects put together. He certainly cannot be regarded as a perfectly normal sample, however you define that word.

Get the most representative sample you can, then. The more representative it is, the faster you will make progress. Perhaps it is the people in our Project who find the going the hardest because of modest native endowment and limited skills who are making the most heroic and the most significant contributions to our research because they improve the representation of our sample where it is most lacking. But never for a moment imagine that all is lost if your sample is not entirely representative. Pioneers out on the frontiers of new truth are almost never run-of-the-mill people. They are indeed a selected sample. That is why they are there. And from them we shall get our first visions of what lies beyond that frontier.

YOU CAN GENERALIZE ONLY ON THE BASIS OF PARAMETERS

"You had better stick to preaching; you can prove more in one sermon than you can prove in a science laboratory in a hundred years." This was said to me by the head of the department of psychology at Yale some years ago when I had finished my theological work and had moved over to the graduate school for advanced training in psychology. Although it was said in a spirit of jest, there is a large element of truth in it. Many preachers every Sunday— and for that matter all the rest of us—draw conclusions on the basis of evidence which is totally inadequate for such conclusions.

If you really wish to draw valid conclusions about human beings, remember that it is possible to observe one group of people and be almost completely misled; and observe another group of the same size and find principles of far-reaching significance. That much I am sure you see from what has already been said. How, then, can you know which individuals to observe?

The whole problem can be summed up in this way. How do you go about getting samples which are representative of the population you want to study? Or, having studied a sample, how do you find out what population it is representative of?

Usually you begin your research with the first question in mind. In social psychology, however, you will seldom achieve perfect sampling; therefore you usually end up trying to answer the second question, before you draw too many conclusions about your evidence. A cardinal sin is to assume that a statistic obtained on a sample is a parameter of a population of which it is not representative.

You Must Know Accurately the Nature of the Sample You Are Studying The people engaging in religious and character education do so in part at least voluntarily. Whatever the factors are which bring it about that only some of the people volunteer, these factors select people who are in some respect different from those who do not volunteer. A voluntary sample, then, is never a true random sample except perhaps of people who volunteer. It does not follow that scientific research cannot be done with them. But it does follow that if you use such a sample, you must know accurately what kind of sample it is. Any statistic you measure in it can be generalized only to a population made up of the same kind of people included in your sample, except for things which are independent of the selecting factors. It is as absurd to judge the emotional side of all human nature on the basis of observations made on people suffering from neuroses and psychoses as it would be to decide on the physical stamina of the human race by studying the squads of the National Professional Football League.

Now let me show you how this problem of voluntary samples operates in our research in CRP and how we deal with it.

When we had completed the testing of the children of the Westminster Presbyterian Church School of Albany, New York, in 1935–1938, our original experimental group, we found that the average child's IQ was nearly 125. This was not surprising for several reasons. In the first place, the church is an upper-middle-class church. Then, too, membership in the church school was on a strictly voluntary basis. Whatever factors brought about the decision to join Westminster were in themselves selecting factors. Then, too, our methods were so difficult that it required a high degree of intelligence and imagination to use them.

We were not disturbed about the selectivity of this sample. Our methods were aimed as much toward tapping the leadership potential among our youth as toward studying the population as a whole. The California study reported under the title *Genetic Studies of Genius* (136) did most of its work on such a sample. Other studies of highly endowed personalities have been and are being made. However, as we were able to make our methods and materials more practical in succeeding revisions, there was a noticeable broadening of the range of our sample. For example, the average IQ in the Westminster Presbyterian Church School is probably now about 112. This is not due to smaller numbers at the top of the range, but to increasing numbers in the lower IQ brackets, presumably owing to our ability to develop more practical methods.

We are at present conducting a Census Study of our CRP population. Each church is asked to make a sampling study of its membership. The report form being used is in part identical with the report
form used in the 1950 United States Census study. A few additional
questions have been added which are basic to the particular needs
of character and religious education. The instructions given to the
census takers are in large part identical with those given to the
national census takers in 1950. The methods used in conducting the
census are also identical.

Why all these precautions? The answer is obvious. If we can
make such a study of our CRP population, we can then compare
this population as a whole or any part of it with the general population of the country, as judged by the factors in common. Furthermore, we can compare any part of our CRP population with any
other part of it.

For example, here is a church in which two curricula are used,
CRP and a denominational one. Parents choose between the two. Is
the CRP sample different from the other? This church conducted our
Census Study. Judged on the basis of education of parents, there
was almost no difference on the part of education of fathers, but
18 per cent more of the CRP mothers had graduated from college
than the non-CRP mothers. I cite these figures, not for their own
value, but to show you how we go about studying the nature of
our samples.

I wonder if you see the importance of this Census Study. In the
past we could often make confident generalizations about our findings only concerning the actual people with whom they were obtained. We could not even compare one Junior High department
with another; much less with the general population of Junior Highs.
We could not be sure in any way how much the evidence obtained
on the Parents' Reports sent in would be like the evidence if
every parent turned in reports. We had no way of knowing whether
the problems described by teachers on their reports were representative of teachers in general. Once such a census is completed, we
can describe the nature of every sample we get, voluntary or otherwise. In turn we are able to generalize with a great deal more confidence concerning our findings.

On Choosing the Best Possible Sample for Your Research   An
analysis of this data, when collected from all of our churches and

other organizations, will make possible several further methods for dealing with our sampling problem. For example, we now have some fifty cooperating groups participating in the Project. They are distributed throughout the country, representing many denominations, in churches of many sizes, urban and rural, and so on. The fact remains that even as a representative sample of Protestantism in the United States, they are far from being adequately distributed.

It is entirely probable that on the basis of this Census Study, we can determine what might be considered an "ideal sample," both in terms of size and constitution. It is our present guess that an ideal sample would certainly not exceed a hundred participating groups. Some of our staff believe that such an ideal sample would be much smaller than this. It is certainly true that the smallest possible ideal sample is the best for research purposes. We would need to describe, however, the nature of those groups in terms of the ways in which they differ, and select for participation only those which contribute to making our sample more representative of Protestant churches in general. The same could be done for schools, YMCA's, and so on. This is, of course, a stratified, as opposed to randomized, selection procedure.

Sometimes Representative Samples Can Be Chosen from Selected Samples   When it is not possible to obtain an ideal sample, we must make progress with the samples we have. When our CRP Census Study is completed, there are several things we can do to correct for our sampling errors. The same principles apply to any selected sample.

A selected sample comes about, for example, when too large a proportion of the population sampled is in one socioeconomic or educational level as compared to the distribution of the general population. It is possible, however, to choose from such a selected sample, a sample which is fairly representative of the general population. This is done by the process of stratification as described in Chapter XI. Let us suppose that we measure our CRP population in some variable on a five-point scale and find that the frequencies obtained show the following proportions: obtaining a score of 5, 16 cases; a score of 4, 25 cases; 3, 45 cases; 2, 12 cases; and 1, 2 cases. It is obvious that this sample is strongly loaded toward the upper end. A normal distribution ought to show about the following proportions: obtaining a score of 5, 8 cases; 4, 24 cases; 3, 36 cases; 2,

24 cases; and 1, 8 cases. Then, following the principle of stratification, let us form a new sample, choosing these proportions from the biased sample we have obtained. Thus we would use all of the lowest category—6 of the 2's, 9 of the 3's, 6 of the 4's, and only 2 of 16 in the highest. When our CRP Census Study has been completed, this technique can be used for many of our problems.

Furthermore, another technique, which I am about to describe, can be combined with the preceding one to make possible still more significant generalizations in regard to our findings. If a questionnaire, for example, should be mailed to the parents of the 14,000 children now participating in the Project, and 7,000 of these were returned, this would be a selected sample, determined by willingness to fill out the questionnaire. It would be difficult to correct for this selectivity. The fact is, we could select a much smaller sample in terms of N (number of cases) which would be a far better one on which to base confident generalizations, and make every effort to have every person in the sample fill out the questionnaire. Results from such a carefully selected sample could be generalized far more wisely than results from a larger sample based on voluntary returns of the questionnaire.

You will not find very much, even in the statistics texts, about this concept of parameters. Peatman (117) has as thorough a discussion as I have found. You see, statisticians are concerned only with the problem of how to arrive at confident estimates of parameters from the statistics obtained. Emphasis is placed on limitations rather than on possibilities. That is all to the good. A great deal of wrong thinking results when we become careless about generalizing wildly on the basis of limited statistics. Nevertheless, there are very important possibilities in this matter of parameters too.

TO MEASURE ATTITUDES ACCURATELY WE MUST DETERMINE SEVERAL TYPES OF PARAMETERS

How Many Different Kinds of Representative Situations Are There? Even if you are able to develop highly reliable and valid methods for measuring attitudes in one situation, it does not follow that you can predict the behavior of the individuals you have measured in the next situation they meet. This is because the attitude you have measured may not be sufficiently generalized to operate in that next situation. A man who controls his temper perfectly in athletic contests may blow up completely in a political campaign. It is educationally significant, therefore, to regard the possible situations a person may meet as constituting another kind of population. The situations in which you observe him practice the attitude is the sample. You can predict his behavior in all situations with confidence only if this sample is representative of the whole population of situations in which he may find himself. When the staff of the Character Education Inquiry first discovered that being honest in one situation did not predict honesty in another, they suggested the doctrine of specificity. This is the hypothesis that all situations are independent, so that character traits must be learned separately in each of them. I do not believe that this is true, but I do believe that effective character education must help the child develop the skills to use the attitude in a representative sample of them. Furthermore, we must be able to describe such a representative sample if our educational procedures are to be of maximum value.

There are at least two ways in which this "population of situations" can vary. One relates to the varying levels of insight required to practice the attitude in them. The other has to do with the presence or absence of conflicting attitudes which are also a part of his personality, and which operate in any given situation.

It might appear that there would be an infinite number of possible situations, thus making prediction of behavior in any new one impossible. It is highly improbable that this is the case. Having learned an attitude in one situation, there are probably other situations enough like it, that prediction is possible for them. In fact, there may well be a relatively small number of situations so representative of all of the other possible ones that having learned the attitude in this representative sample, one can predict the individual's behavior in most, if not all, of the others, using the situations in this representative sample as types.

What makes one situation different from another one? You will guess at once that the principal factor in this is the PS of the individual. Two situations which look very different or very similar to me may not look the same way to you. This means that what makes them look different or alike is more a function of the personality of the observer than of the situations themselves. In learning attitudes, then, I must learn them not only in a representative sample of situations, but also in a representative sample of accompanying attitudes, drives, skills, and purposes of my personality. There is abundant evidence that this is a highly attainable goal.

For example, let us suppose that we are trying to teach an attitude to teen-agers which they may be reluctant to accept because it looks as if it will bring them into some conflict with their peers (their own age level). Here is one teen-ager who has optimistic self other attitudes; that is, he believes that others think well of him. Here is another who has inferiority self other concepts. I think you can imagine that learning such an attitude will look very different to each of the two.

It ought to be obvious how important a role these situational parameters play in the evaluation of our curricular methods and materials. It is possible to plan a lesson which is entirely successful in terms of the situations which are used in its teaching, and still be unable to predict what the individuals learning it will do in the very next situation they meet. Until we have prepared materials which present representative samples in terms of situations and personality integration, we cannot be sure that our efforts are going to be of very wide effectiveness.

We Play Many Roles, but Only a Few Different Kinds   A closely related and overlapping aspect of this task can be formulated in terms of role parameters and social determinants. Each of us lives in a series of interrelated social situations, which are referred to as roles. At present there is no predictable transfer of attitudes from role to role. It is necessary to learn the attitude in enough different roles that transfer to still other roles takes place. We may, then, speak of parameters in terms of roles as well as of situations.

It may be that the PS of the child is determined from role to role by the different insights and skills required to apply the attitude in each of them. When all of the possible insights have been achieved and all of the possible skills learned, then prediction to new roles can be made with greater confidence.

Finally, we must distinguish between contemporary roles and developmental roles. It will not be very productive, in terms of a greater generation, if attitudes learned in Kindergarten roles are of no value in Junior roles. We hope that lessons learned in the Kindergarten will affect behavior even when the Kindergartener becomes an adult. The projected longitudinal study, to which I have already referred in this chapter, should reveal characteristics of the lower age levels which are predictors of the later age levels. Behaving like an adult, however, far too often involves putting away childish things, even in this matter of attitudes. Here, too, we must discover the common elements among these developmental roles and make sure that in teaching the Kindergartener we include as many as possible of the elements which will be in the roles he will play in later years.

INDIVIDUALS DIFFER IN MANY WAYS, BUT IN SUCH PREDICTABLE WAYS THAT STUDIES OF SAMPLES OF THESE DIFFERENCES YIELD PARAMETERS

In educational programs, therefore, we cannot prepare a curriculum aimed at only one kind of child, whether the average, the top, or the bottom group of individuals is to be educated. Nor is it possible to describe human nature comprehensively in such terms as, "Ten-year-olds do so and so." The range of individual differences among ten-year-olds is so great that no single characteristic can be set forth which applies to all of them, except in terms of variations along this range.

Most traits of human personality, of whatever nature, represent a continuous curve with an infinite number of variations. How, then, shall we state an evaluation of our curricular methods, for example, unless we describe their effectiveness with an infinite number of different children. The answer to this kind of question has always been attempted in some form of "type" psychology. When such type categories have been thought of as pigeonholes into which individuals can be sorted in an all-or-none fashion, they have regularly been found inadequate for the purposes for which they were created. If, however, they are conceived of as convenient points along a curve of individual differences they serve a very useful purpose in our work.

For example, consider the commandment, "You shall not steal." I have had occasion to deal with a great many children who have been motivated to steal. It has been impossible to deal with almost any two of them alike. I am sure, however, that we could study a "population" of such children, observe all of the related aspects of their personalities, and follow the procedure just described. Then it would be possible for us to find a useful type theory for classifying the varieties of this kind of behavior. I would guess that if we had such a type theory to work with, our efforts to deal with the problem would be many times more effective. These types constitute, for all practical purposes, then, representative samples which we can study to estimate the parameters of even this kind of population.

Individual Differences in Development Can Also Be Studied with a Representative Sample of Types at Each Age Level One should try to teach at each age level only those things which can be learned at that age level. Among all of the problems which arise because individuals differ, this one has been most extensively studied in educational research. Graded lessons are now the accepted practice in all educational programs. This does not mean, however, that we have nothing else to learn in the matter. The fact is, we still have far to go in terms of ultimate potential.

Very little work has yet been done in which this sort of age-level data was used and which has been analyzed by the methods of factor analysis. Finding the best developmental types by which to classify individuals is far from having been achieved. And as we are now discovering, while a great deal of work has been done to describe children as they are, very little has been done to estimate their potential. The data of our Positive Potential Study points to a whole new area of developmental calibration of this sort. Our data which comes from a selected sample must be evaluated carefully if we are to find general parameters.

The chief shortcomings of studying child development by the cross-sectional method alone can be demonstrated in two ways: an examination of growth curves and the problems of age-level transfer.

Using the cross-sectional method, growth curves have been constructed by connecting average points of the various age levels. A growth curve of height constructed in this manner is a completely smooth and regular curve. No growth spurts are detected. When, however, individuals are followed in their growth in height, a high percentage of them show definite growth spurts. These are all ironed out, however, in averaging a number of individuals together. This means that longitudinal studies must also be made, if we are to detect and describe such individual differences. There is recent evidence that certain types of regression may even be normal and not necessarily undesirable. They would almost certainly not be detected in growth curves based on cross-sectional data.

But far more important than this, in educational work, is the problem of transfer from age level to age level. What evidence have we that teaching a child an attitude in the Kindergarten will affect his behavior as an adolescent? It is a common experience to have two Kindergarteners learn an attitude, and to have the attitude transfer to later age levels in one case and not in the other. Why? That is the kind of question which can be answered only by extensive longitudinal studies.

The now famous study of the Shirley babies (97:199 ff.) shows clearly that there are such transfers; but very little work has been done to predict them. In CRP we have accumulated a number of records in which individual children have been observed over a period of years. We are just beginning to study these records longitudinally, to see if we can discover growth trends of a predictive nature. Consider the effect of such studies on educational methods as we discover what kinds of training in the early years do result in permanent learning, and what kinds tend to be put away with other childish things! Probably there can be described a relatively few characteristic ways in which such transfer does take place, the study of which can lead to general parameters.

There Are Also Predictable Types of Reactions Which People Make, and Which Are Representative of Them All You will recall that the adaptation procedure is one of our most useful techniques in CRP for taking individual differences into account in character education. We learn as much as we can about each child in a class and then try to adapt the lesson in some way to fit him. Is that all there is to the matter; or can there be some short-cut to this process? When Morse (104, 105) did his Kindergarten study, he found that if he did the adaptation procedure for 12 out of 24 children in a group, it was usually already well done for the other 12. This would lead us to suspect that there are fairly definite types of Kindergarten children. This might even indicate that there are not more than 12 of them.

Or again, some years ago, in an unpublished study, we tried to find how many different kinds of response adjustments were made in connection with a particular attitude. It would seem that the number might be almost infinite. The fact is, we found that fifty about exhausted the possibilities for any particular attitude. This again suggests that the bewildering variety of human nature is more amenable to systematic description than might have been suspected. In a current study going on in our laboratory, Koppe feels that less than ten typical reactions to an attitude are enough to describe it.

Every Home Is Unique; but Again There Are a Small Number of Types   When we realize that there are no two homes which are alike, how is it possible to evaluate educational methods and materials in terms of the homes using them? What works in one home with thrilling effectiveness falls flat or proves disastrous in another. This means that when curricular materials for home use are evaluated, they must be evaluated for all kinds of homes.

If we are to do this, we must try to obtain as representative a sample of the population as we can in which to determine these types. We are at present engaged in research designed to produce just such a type theory. An analysis of the sample on which the study was done, however, showed that it was highly selected. While findings of great value and far-reaching applicability were found, eventually this research will reveal even more far-reaching results if it can be carried out with a much more adequate sample in terms of the general population.

Representative Type Samples in the Area of Leadership Can Also Be Found   "He is a natural leader," is said of a majority of youth. The interesting part of it is that it is true. But not in the way that is usually inferred! As has been pointed out, there seems to be abundant evidence to show that leadership is a function of the leader, in relation to those whom he is expected to lead, and in terms of the objectives being sought. When, therefore, we are talking about leadership in character education, or for that matter in any kind of social experience, this problem of individual differences comes in again. Evaluation of leadership training methods can be established only in terms of the various kinds of leadership there are. How, then, shall we establish parameters among leaders and leadership functions?

Probably the same procedures for establishing general parameters on the basis of our selected sample as have been suggested for the home-type study and the individual-differences study will serve here. If we can obtain representative samples of the populations in which we wish to study leadership, sample the kinds of tasks to be accomplished under leadership, and sample the kinds of groups who have to carry out these tasks, we can analyze these data for representative types.

SOME IMPORTANT CONCEPTS DESCRIBED IN THIS CHAPTER

There are many aspects of educational research which can be done and only be done by the co-scientist. For example, in the evaluation of a curriculum there are some basic tasks which only the co-scientist can do. He can perform the countless needed small studies designed to evaluate the various curricular elements. Whether the procedures proposed in a curriculum frustrate or challenge teachers and parents can be tested in local co-scientist experiments. The effectiveness of various kinds of teacher training are also of this sort. How much actual insight the children gain from exposure to the curriculum and how effective it is throughout the full range of individual differences can also be most thoroughly tested at the co-scientist level.

Scientific generalizations are usually stated in the form of parameters. They are the consistent characteristics of the population being studied. Since research is almost always done on samples of such populations, the more representative the sample is of the population, the more confidently we can assume that the statistics obtained on it are parameters of the population being studied. The search for such parameters has both the purpose of making generalizations from observed data and of discovering new dimensions of the population relevant to the purpose of the research.

Dependable parameters (generalizations) can be made from data obtained on a highly selected sample, if one knows the nature of that sample. Generalizations based on the study of the feeble-minded, the mentally diseased, guinea pigs, and college sophomores are examples of important findings from studies of nonrepresentative samples. Nevertheless, the more representative the sample is, the better. A small representative sample is better than a large nonrepresentative sample whose characteristics we do not know.

The sampling methods characteristic of most newspaper reporting are an example of unbridled and irresponsible generalizations, stated or implied, based on the most biased of samples.

In research the word *population* can be used relating to bodies of data other than persons. We can have a population of situations, or of temper tantrums, or of social groups, or of children's opinions. Furthermore, it is possible to find representative samples of any of these, and to derive parameters from the statistics observed on these samples.

CHAPTER XV

———•••———

ON CHANGING YOUR MIND
CREATIVELY

YOU DON'T TEST A CURRICULUM TO PROVE IT
BUT TO REVISE IT

Now WE come to the task of evaluating our original hypotheses, as they were embodied in curricular procedures. Wouldn't it be wonderful if all of them proved to be upheld by the evidence? The answer to that question is that it certainly would not be wonderful. It would be a tragedy! Of course, it would be discouraging if you found that you had made no progress at all, that your hypotheses were entirely wrong. But even that would be preferable to finding them all right. Why?

You have probably guessed the answer to that already. It is the infinity principle. If God is infinite, there are always wonderful insights to be had. If we find nothing lacking with the ones we already have, we are at the end of our row. Read the history of science. Consider, for example, the scientific progress that led to our spectacular increases in medicine. That same thing can be true in Christian character. You don't make progress through final answers. As we evaluate our former hypotheses, then, we shall look for their inadequacies with quite as much zest as we look for their strengths. For it is in their inadequacies that we shall find the secrets of new and greater insights, just as it is in their strengths that we can consolidate our progress up to now.

ON SEARCHING FOR MISTAKES TO PROFIT BY

All this involves some new ways of thinking for some of us most of the time and all of us some of the time. We have had many people reject CRP or even drop out of it because of its "flaws." If its flaws constitute its greatest source of strength, this is an unfortunate reaction. I doubt if it ever makes sense to reach a decision as to what methods we will use or not use in terms of their flaws. Every curriculum has those. It is whether or not those flaws are being made the highroad to new insights that counts.

A curriculum whose creators and evangelists emphasize its values entirely, and try to hide or minimize its flaws, and in which there are no methods for its critical evaluation, is attempting to condemn man to his present stature toward becoming a child of God.

This is almost like a contradiction of terms, isn't it? The weaknesses of a curriculum are its strengths, and its strengths may actually become its most tragic weaknesses if they blind us to its weaknesses. But this is actually the case.

In Chapter XIII we talked about the kinds of evidence that can be secured for the evaluation of educational procedures. In Chapter XIV the emphasis was on how to evaluate our curricular methods in light of this evidence. However, behind every curricular element is some theory on which it is based. We sometimes call them basic assumptions. Actually, they are hypotheses which we are testing and fully expect to revise from time to time. In Chapter XIV we asked, "Is this lesson project, or some other lesson element, a good one?" In this chapter we are asking, "Is the concept of project construction on which this particular project was based still adequate in light of our new evidence?"

This is the climax of the story for the scientist. Here is where new insights replace old ones and he is able once more to penetrate a little beyond the present horizon of truth. This is related to Section IV of the Research Design Chart: Revision of Educational Hypotheses.

Six Areas in Education in Which We Must Have Working Hypotheses In CRP we find that we can list our basic theoretical hypotheses under six headings (Research Design Chart, IV A). You as reader may find that your own educational concepts will include at least these same general categories.

In the first place, you will set up certain hypotheses about the nature of your major objective(s). In our case, our major objective is character education. This means that we must set up some hypotheses about the nature of character. To begin with in our research, we defined character as best we could.

In the second place—and clearly related to this—we must reconsider our criteria. Our ultimate criterion had been pretty much decided when we first defined our objectives. The ultimate criterion of character education is character growth.

Our third area of basic hypotheses has to do with "trait theory." All of us are always setting up hypotheses about personality structure. Psychology is advancing rapidly in this area of research. This means that we must be alert to possible revisions in this aspect of our work. Through the years we have made scores of revisions in our CRP hypotheses involving aspects of personality structure. We shall certainly make many more in the future.

The fourth area of basic hypotheses is that of attitudes or other educational objectives. Because the attitude is the unit of personality we use in CRP, its nature is very central to our research. In the practical job of curriculum building, the attitude is directly related to our concepts of personality structure. Furthermore, one of the most important factors in personality-structure theory is the nature of attitude formation and change.

All education is based on the learning process, which is our fifth area. Although learning has, of course, been going on since the beginning of human life on the earth, we still are far from understanding its nature.

Our sixth area of hypotheses has to do with theories in the area of curriculum construction. Because it is directly related to learning theory, it will need to be modified quite as rapidly as is our learning theory.

WHAT IS CHARACTER? FROM PRIGGISHNESS TO GOD'S WILL FOR US

"He is a good boy!" Ask the next twenty Junior High boys you meet whether they would consider that a compliment or an insult. In all probability their answers will depend on their concept of what is meant by the term *good boy*. Or again, if your son announces some morning that he is going out to "develop a little character," you may have some misgivings either as to the desirability of such a purpose or as to the complete normality of the boy. Religious education ought to be something more than "just character education," insist some of our CRP critics.

These illustrations grow out of a weak conception of character. Unfortunately, the church has played no small part in giving character that kind of reputation, in its "shabby treatment of education as though it were a noble but relatively unimportant sideshow for manicuring the minor virtues of small children" (106:325). These notions are certainly a far cry from the vision Jesus had of human potential, or that of any of the world's great leaders who have insisted that the world's greatest need is for strong character.

In CRP, at the present time, we are presenting to youth concepts of goodness that have to do with the so-called impossible commandments of Jesus. "Turn the other cheek," "Return good for evil," "Be not anxious what you shall eat or wear." The whole concept of vicarious sacrifice comes under this heading. Here are concepts of goodness of a new sort.

As Your Concept of Character Grows, Your Definition of Character Must Keep Pace What methods are there, however, for making as sure as we can that this growth is in the direction of progress, not regress.

To begin with, you must postulate some dimensions by which to define character. You may have to start with the best ones you can conceive, using whatever sources of information you can find. In our own case we used primarily the literature in the field of mental hygiene, social psychology, and sociology. After you have established your dimensions, however, you can revise them on the basis of evidence you accumulate in their use. You will remember from Chapter V that the dimensions you use are very important determiners of the significance of your results. Characterologists of history have used such dimensions as lines in the hand, distance between eyes, color of eyes, protruding chins, even shape of ears, and other anatomical features. Such dimensional concepts have never given us useful results, for none of them correlates with character.

These criteria ought to be internally consistent. Lack of internal consistency among these criteria would be reason for doubting their validity as useful axes of a consistent form of personality expressions, which we call character. You would not expect them to correlate too highly with one another, for then it would be useless to use them all. But neither would you expect them to correlate negatively with one another. If measuring high in one of them tended to bring it about that usually you scored lower in another, then you would most certainly not have a consistent area of study. For example, the results of the practice of some negative-ethics concepts of goodness have caused the individual practicing them to become less socially effective. That is why so many people believe that a child can be too good—"goody-goody," as it is called. The difficulty here is that we are postulating two dimensions of character which correlate negatively with each other. Our cross-validation dimensions could very well correlate zero with each other, if each of them were a completely independent variable ("orthogonal," the statisticians call it); but it is highly improbable that they will until we have done a great deal of research with methods of factor analysis. Even then they might have no practical meaning for the layman, and we would still have to use dimensional concepts which did make sense to him. Probably all of the intercorrelations among our concepts, then, will be positive; thus bringing it about that an increase in any of them will tend to result in an increase in one's total character strength.

Another factor which will influence your revisions is related to the term *eclecticism*. Whatever field of psychology includes the general area of your research—in ours it is child development and personality—progress will always be going on in it. Better frames of reference will come into being. Old frames of reference will be found less adequate for studying some of your problems. You will have to keep up with this field, and make sure that the designing of your own procedures takes full advantage of its progress.

Most important of all, in this process of eclecticism, you must keep in mind the factor of the implications for daily life. For example, no earth-shaking changes are going to occur in our social institutions, if we decide to use Saturday instead of Sunday as our day of worship. But other new hypotheses in religion may produce striking changes. Changing our goals from the level of "manicuring the morals of young children" to the sort characterized by "dominating purpose in the service of mankind" could make quite a difference. Suppose we could challenge a whole generation "to be determined to see that every man gets his full chance at happiness and success"! Consider the results of such a challenge on our problems of race and social prejudice alone.

Finally, there is the sheer problem of measurability. It is of little value to define character in such mystical terms that your hypotheses can be neither proved nor disproved. That simply slams the door on further research and forces you to close your eyes and shut your ears to new insights in this area. We must always be searching for new and more central aspects of the problem, making sure, however, that we can measure them.

I have a friend who is a minister and, I suspect, a good one. But every time I see him he has a new enthusiasm. Some new concept has come along and he has accepted it totally and uncritically, entirely thrown out as useless his former ideas in the relevant area, and now preaches the new one with fervor. This is probably the outstanding weakness of his ministry and his thinking. Never changing your hypotheses is staying in a blind alley forever. Changing them as often as the weather is likely to be jumping from one blind alley to another. Progress toward new truth is a process which takes rigorous and painstaking effort but which pays large dividends in the end.

IN SEARCH OF BETTER CRITERIA OF BETTER CRITERIA

There is probably no other phase of our daily lives in which we do so much superficial thinking as in our choice of criteria for making our most important judgments. Young people let "falling in love" be the sole criterion for marriage. Businessmen use letters of recommendation and pictures as criteria for hiring employees. Colleges use many criteria for selecting freshmen and still make serious mistakes. We accept the advertising exaggerations we read or hear as criteria for buying this or that product. Gossips use behavior minutiae as a basis for extensive character defamation. We choose a minister on the basis of one good sermon. And so on ad infinitum. Some of these criteria are totally unrelated to what we use them for. For example, some of our criteria for judging character have no more to do with character than the number 13 has to do with bad luck.

The simplest method of testing the validity of any criterion lies in the principle of the known sample. In practical research, whenever we have two groups of people, one of which exhibits one end of our scale and the other the opposite, we test for the presence of our criteria in the two groups and look for other characteristic differences in search of better ones. We don't do this nearly as much in education as we ought to.

Our CRP Adventures in Search of Criteria Almost all criteria imply the expression of a logical fallacy. It is an inevitable one; but because it is a fallacy a good share of our efforts to find better criteria consist of trying to reduce it to a minimum. Indeed, some of the statistical tools with which you are already familiar were devised in part for that purpose. Let me illustrate the fallacy. It goes like this:

"All A is B; therefore all B is A." This is perhaps the commonest of all logical fallacies. You can see its fallaciousness more easily if I say, "All dogs are animals; therefore all animals are dogs." You can put another term in this. "All A is B; all C is B; therefore all C is A." Illustrated, this appears: "All dogs are animals; all cats are animals; therefore all cats are dogs." But let's take some illustrations which are not so obviously absurd. "All honest people do not steal; therefore all people who do not steal are honest." "All good Christians know the Bible; therefore all people who know the Bible are good Christians." "If you have a good curriculum children will be interested. Therefore, if the children are interested, you have a good curriculum." Because most of our work in CRP, for example, must be done with lay parents and teachers, we must use criteria which they can observe. It will be obvious that we shall be very eager indeed to revise them as rapidly as we can. Let's see how we go about this.

In the first place, we try to make sure that the criteria are as closely related as possible to the objectives we seek. That is, we make certain that all A is B. You wouldn't look at your watch to see who will win today's football game; neither, then, do you count attendance to determine how much education has taken place. If you will make a list of the criteria used in a number of educational ventures with which you are familiar, you will probably discover that few of them are, at the one extreme, totally dissociated from your objectives, or, at the other extreme, that they will ever be infallible evidences of those objectives. Your task in revision, then, is to keep trying to find criteria which approach more and more identity with your ultimate goal; in our case, growth in character.

The criteria you use ought also to have *differential validity*. This means that they ought, of course, to be indicative of the concept for which you are using them; but, as far as possible, they ought not to be associated with any other concept in the same area. In psychometrics, for example, a good mechanical-aptitude test ought to be related to mechanical aptitude; but it ought not to measure intelligence also, so that you can't tell which one is indicated by a high score.

In personality research we are always dealing with at least two kinds of variables: personality variables and situational variables. Our criteria, then, ought to include indicators from both kinds of variables. When you hear a generalized statement made about an individual—"He is a natural leader"; "He is dishonest"; "He is a brilliant scholar"—ask for the evidence, the criterion used. More often than not, you will find it based on a single act of the individual. This is more likely to happen on the negative side than on the positive. Observers are more likely to see maladjustment than to see good adjustment. Feeling that "a friend has let you down" is usually an example of this fact. Then, too, if you look merely for the obvious evidence, you are far more likely to see the bad than the good.

At the present time the Parents' Report is our best criterion. These include a definite evaluation of the lesson's effectiveness and a statement of the evidences on which the parents base that evaluation. In the laboratory our research assistants rate these reports on a seven-point scale. Seven is assigned when the rater finds what he considers unquestioned evidence that progress has been made by the child in learning the attitude. It is these *number seven reports* which we at present consider our best measures of success. But what about the validity or reliability of these ratings?

As to the reliability of the rating itself, we have little doubt. Each report is rated independently by at least two raters. (The number of raters needed for reliable judgment is determined by statistical methods—see Chapter XI.) The reliability coefficient of these independent ratings is sufficiently high to be regarded as significant.

Laboratory raters have several advantages over the parents in this process. Because they are not ego-involved with the children, they can evaluate much more objectively. They are, to be sure, prejudiced by their own personalities; but training in objective methods plus the use of the pooled ratings of independent judgments makes us able to guard against such personal errors. All this places them in a better position to make valid judgments. To do this we must describe the criteria for which they are to look. For example, using our definition of character, they ask, "Is the behavior described socially effective, personally dynamic, integrated, skilled, consistent, characterized by temporal and social distance?" All this gives us considerable confidence in the use of this criterion.

In our research in CRP there is one more factor which influences our choice of criteria. That is the role of the infinity principle in our research. It is relatively easy to find criteria in purely descriptive research. Here we simply observe a representative sample of children, describe their characteristic performances, and then relate any particular performance to the resultant norms. In our case, however, we are concerned not so much with how children do perform as with what they could do. We are seeking maximum-potential criteria.

"WHAT IS MAN THAT THOU ART MINDFUL OF HIM?"

Every research design involving people implies concepts of personality. What is more significant is that these concepts of personality have a great deal to do with what comes out of the research. An educational program which assumes the plastic-clay concept of personality is not likely to find out much about children except the degree to which they are subject to this kind of adult manipulation. Community surveys which in their designs assume that man is the pawn of his environment are likely to produce an entirely different description of a community than surveys in which man is studied in terms of how far he can be the master of his destiny. In a sense, then, you can say that the concept of personality you use can be determined by the aspects of human behavior you want to study. If you want simply to find out what man is like, as he is, you can use a concept of personality which is purely descriptive. If you want to find out what he could be, you need a different frame of reference.

The second half of this chapter will be concerned with the principles of pragmatic eclecticism. Here is its major role. There are many current concepts of personality. Each of them was derived from a limited sample of people and in terms of limited forms of behavior. In general, theories of personality are of six types.

Behaviorism and most of the cultural theories of personality put the emphasis on the environment. They make the assumption that man is what his environment makes him. They tend to be especially attractive to sociologically minded people because of this emphasis on the environment.

The emphasis of the Freudian school is on internal personality dynamics. Basic drives in personality are striving for expression, and adjustment is determined by the ways in which man works them out in his environment. When research is done in light of this concept of personality, educational procedures are evaluated in terms of how well or how badly they make possible this full expression of the individual's instinct drives.

The Gesell school of developmental psychology goes a bit further in this concept. They assume that man is endowed with the natural capacity to grow up into a normal, well adjusted human being. It is our educational task, then, to make sure that we do not interfere with this normal process. Our role is to create a favorable environment in which the child can grow, just as we feed him healthy food so that his physical growth processes can go on.

A somewhat less extreme position than this, but not unlike it, is one that can be called the mental-hygiene position. It assumes that children have a number of natural needs. These are both physical and social. The need for security is quite as natural as the need for nourishment. The purpose of education, in terms of this point of view, is to help man satisfy these needs. This is perhaps the most widely accepted view of personality in current research.

The Gestalt point of view puts far more of the responsibility for what happens on the individual himself. His perceptions, the meaning he gives to life are the deciding factors. The phenomenologists hold a similar position. When you accept such a concept of personality as this, you vastly complicate your research designs.

Finally, there is the energy concept of personality. We would classify our own here, if in any one place. When you use the basic concept of democracy and Christianity, as to the importance of the individual, you almost have to use such a concept of personality as this. The emphasis on the unique nature of the individual in such personalistic theories as those of William Stern and G. W. Allport, our own CRP concept of adaptation procedure, our Child of God concept, our vision concept of vocational guidance, these are all likely to presuppose such an energy concept of personality.

If you examine our CRP concept, however, you will discover that all of the other five emphases play a role in it. This is another illustration of the fact that it is not necessary to accept completely one or another of the systematic theories. Most of us use eclectic concepts which recognize the strengths of each.

How, then, can you go about revising your concepts of personality? Having decided the ultimate purpose of your research, you will know the area or areas of theoretical position in which you want to work. But as the evidence comes in, you will find a great many data which do not fit into your theory. You will then need to study your theory in light of these facts and revise it to conform more closely to them.

INCREASING VISIONS OF THE PURPOSE OF EDUCATION

If you are to improve your objectives in education, you must know what they are. That sounds like a truism. But the fact is that a good share of education has only the vaguest of objectives. Then you must obtain adequate evidence as to how well you have achieved those objectives.

Where is the best place to start setting up objectives for a curriculum? That depends on where you want to come out. The child usually has, at most, a dozen to sixteen years to learn whatever he is going to learn in this field of religious education. When we know what our objectives are, we must find the most economical way to help him achieve those objectives. He hasn't any time to waste.

There are at least three major ways one could go about deciding on objectives. One is simply to teach the experience of history. A second starts from an examination of the social climate in which he must live. The third starts with his own philosophy of life. The traditional way is to begin with content. The hope is that from his study of this will come the right philosophy of life, and the will and ability to meet his problems as they come to him. Certainly some of his educational experience ought to be of this type, although the evidence for its effectiveness in terms of Christian character is not promising.

Another method is to have him start with the situations he must meet in his life. He interprets each situation in light of the experience of the past, and forms the proper attitudes and skills for dealing with it. I am sure that there are many aspects of his education which can best take place this way.

Finally there is the method of starting with a philosophy of life, one which has grown out of the experience of the ages, and which can be applied to the social problems he will meet. This is basically the approach which we have used. Because most psychologists are agreed that the attitude is the best unit of personality, we have spelled out an appropriate set of objectives in terms of attitudes. Some of these attitudes we teach directly, because our experience indicates that that is the most economical way to teach them. In other cases, we start with the experience of history and let the child derive the attitude from this experience. We teach still other attitudes by helping the child explore ways of meeting various situations, using the principles and skills implied in the relevant attitudes. This is a good illustration of an eclectic procedure.

There is much to be said for all three approaches, and probably elements of all three ought to be included in a well rounded educational program. However, in CRP we have chosen to emphasize the attitude approach to objectives because it places the emphasis on the personality. If we had thought of education as the transmission of content, pure and simple, we would have chosen the first method. If we had thought of the child as the pawn of his environment and of education as helping him to make the best of it, we would have chosen the second. But because we expect him to transcend his environment and search for new truth, we choose the attitude objectives leading to that end.

In CRP we have never thought of the attitude as an isolated element in personality. It is simply one characteristic of the total personality. This means that each attitude can be described for any particular child only as it relates to the rest of the child's philosophy of life; that is, his other attitudes. This is obvious in principle. It is more difficult to achieve in practice. However, we are discovering many new ways to implement this principle in revising our objectives. Education is probably effective in part to the extent that its individual objectives can be integrated into the total personality. You can't start with the total personality, but you still have to teach a specific objective with the full knowledge that the total personality is always in the immediate background and determines whether or not your objective is going to be achieved. This is the area, then, in which we expect to make some of our greatest progress as our research continues.

The statement of the attitudes implies not only hypotheses which are relevant to the general problem of trait theory but hypotheses about ways in which the concepts embodied in each attitude can best be communicated to those concerned in its learning: teachers, parents, and youth. In a practical program of character education it would not matter much whether the statements were logically and technically correct, if the people using them misinterpreted them. As we begin each revision of a unit, therefore, we make whatever revisions are necessary to make this meaning clear to those who use them.

Perhaps this extensive section on attitude revision can be summarized in terms of Jesus' statement, "You will know them by their fruits." I haven't the slightest doubt that the first major task a research team would encounter in a factorial-design community survey, such as I have described, would be to define the objectives of many of the community agencies. It might be difficult to make a list of objectives which are definite enough to be observed by objective methods. Yet if we are to make progress, this is a first step.

THERE IS MORE TO BE LEARNED ABOUT LEARNING THAN WE HAVE LEARNED

In few areas of modern psychology is systematic theory as active as in regard to learning theory. This fact, plus the fact that it is generally conceded that we know very little about it now, means that revision of learning theory needs to be one of the most active areas of our modern educational progress. This is not to suggest that psychologists and educators do not know a great many practical things about learning; they do. It is to suggest that as we discover the underlying principles which run through the learning process, we shall undoubtedly be able to make progress many times faster.

In everyday educational work these systematic theories of learning are as yet of not much practical value to us. When I talk about learning theory here, then, I am speaking of a much more down-to-earth problem. From the point of view of research design, revising our learning theory consists of the following steps: (1) The first thing to do is to define the kind of learning you expect to take place in a given situation. It may be gaining familiarity with the subject matter, being able to recall what is learned, being convinced of its value, understanding its meaning, or being able to apply it in life's situations. Be sure, then, that you decide just what you are going to expect to happen in the process of learning before you start. (2) Then decide what methods of learning will achieve this end. This is your learning theory. (3) Then plan the actual lesson itself. How do you propose to apply your theory in the practice of the actual learning situation? (4) Observe what happens. Collect valid evidence and see how much learning of the type you expected to take place did take place. (5) Then consider how you would revise steps (2) and (3) in light of this evidence. It is at this point that you change your ideas about how to bring about the learning and what your procedures for carrying them out in the particular situation ought to be. This, then, is what is meant by revising learning theory.

There are a great many ways in which learning and teaching are attempted. Conditioning is one of the best known. It is valuable for some types of learning, especially at the lower age levels. Sheer drill is still the most widely used method of verbal learning. While progressive educators look askance on drill, it is not likely ever to be discarded entirely from our educational procedures. Almost all of us find it useful for mastering new tools, whether statistical formulae or swinging a golf club. Problem solving must be gone about in a different way, because here it is insight which is wanted.

Attitude learning involves all types of learning from time to time. Some attitudes are learned best by conditioning. Often in drill, attitudes are acquired which the teacher never intended to be learned. The fact is, you probably form some attitude toward all of your experience. It is when you are concerned with teaching some particular attitude that the difficulty begins.

Attitudes are learned in as many different ways as there are ways to learn. Sometimes an attitude is the end result of a process which begins by severe discipline. The child may be required to carry out certain performances long enough to come to like them for their own sake. This is what G. W. Allport refers to as functional autonomy. The child may practice the violin because he is required to do so, until he achieves enough skill to like it for its own sake. My own suspicion is that all of us require some external discipline from time to time to keep near our best. I have never had a class even of graduate students whose good intentions were enough to keep them on the job without emphatic prompting on my part. Other attitudes are set before the pupils, and they are literally dared to try them out. A great many of the concepts of Christianity, such as turning the other cheek, have to be tried to be believed. They don't make sense to the child until he has tried them out. Still other attitudes ought to be discovered by the child. In this case he is placed in an appropriate situation and challenged to work his way out of it, with a minimum of guidance from the teacher. He arrives at the attitude goal himself. This is especially true when it is attitude skills which we are after.

As a conclusion to this discussion on learning-theory revision, let me describe one method for discovering such insights. It consists in an adaptation of our old friend the method of characteristic differences. We take two groups of children, one of which has been through a part of the curriculum, and the other not. We observe their behavior over a period of time in situations in which the attitudes being learned ought to be applicable. The observers ought not to know which children belong in which group. Then we take the two groups of sketches and have a number of judges examine them for characteristic differences. In these should be the clues to what we have and have not taught and which should give us important insights as to where we need to revise our methods. This ought to give a great deal of insight into the effectiveness of the learning procedures of all of our educational agencies, of whatever nature.

THE CURRICULUM—A PRESCRIBED COURSE TO RUN OR A CHALLENGE TO NEW VISIONS

Why have a curriculum at all? Why should our children learn what we have put in our curriculum? These are basic questions which most of us never think to ask. A large part of Chapter XVI will be used to describe our plans for our next CRP curricular revision. As you read it you will sense much of the theory that underlies them. I shall, therefore, at this point simply sketch in the broad outlines of revising the underlying theory of curricula.

My dictionary says that a curriculum is "a specified, prescribed

course of study." Its derivation comes from the race course prescribed for the chariots of ancient Rome. It suggests a kind of rat
race for children, in which one generation gives the next all of the
final answers. Is that what we want? Probably all of us would
protest with a horrified, No! But that is what we often do in practice.

Let's consider, then, a dimension for evaluating curricula which
at one extreme is just that, a prescribed course to be run by the
children. We tell them what it is, and that is the end of the matter.
At the other extreme it is a challenge for them to work out their
own salvation, with a minimum of guidance. There are some who
would choose each extreme.

An either-or decision is not necessary. I'd say that ideally our
CRP position at the present time would be something like this: As
teachers and parents, we present the following picture to our children: "We should like to show you our assets, which include the
truth that men have wrested from the universe over many centuries. As far as we know how, we should like to teach you our
skills and help you strengthen your will to do right. But then you
are on your own. You will have to reach beyond frontiers that we
never crossed. We shall help you in any way we can, especially by
pointing out some of the problems we never solved, but for the
most part it's up to you from here on."

But, having decided this, another problem arises, to which I shall
refer as curriculum economy. Suppose you agree that you want
youth to have both sides of this dimension. Then if your curricular
writers are given uninhibited freedom to pour everything into it
they choose, your previous decision is canceled out. Consider again
the curriculum to which I referred that would require seven hours a
week for twelve years just to learn the content in it to a level of
verbal recall. Not even the clergy of that denomination could possibly pass an examination on it. No matter what else they say they
want the next generation to learn about Christian living and social
vision, they won't have time to teach them, if this is their content
assignment. Furthermore, the retroactive inhibition operating in such
enormous content is probably so great that if they wanted to make
sure that the next generation shall be Biblically illiterate, they need
only expose them to this curriculum.

It is granted that the same lack of balance can be put on the
other side of the picture, too. We are sometimes accused of erring

in this regard in CRP on this other phase of Christian education. If
we really do not have "enough Bible in it," that is a flaw in the
other direction. What we need to do, then, is to decide what proportions of the curriculum are to be devoted to the two processes:
the heritage of the ages and the challenge to new visions of Christian
adventure. Then we must see what are the child's resources in time
for religious education, and proportion this time accordingly.

Perhaps we shall have to place our content materials into some
rank order and teach as many of them as there is time to teach. This
may also be true of the character-education end of the task. We
have cut down our attitude list from thousands to hundreds, and
may cut still further in our next revision. Space in textbooks is infinite. So long as we look no further than that, the only limits to our
curriculum are our imaginations and money for printers' bills. This
is not the case with what children can learn, and this is where our
final decisions ought to lie.

Textbooks, project materials, and classrooms are only half of a
curriculum—perhaps the least important half. The other half are
the prophets who proclaim it to our children. These, of course, are
our teachers and parents. In this regard, we must decide first whether
we are satisfied with this generation. If we are, then our teachers
simply go before the children and say, "Follow us." If, however, we
dream of a greater generation, then the teacher must usually be
challenging children to go where we have not been able to go.

What is the teacher's role in the process of a religious education
that aims toward a greater generation? In the first place, we tell
teachers and parents what to do, not what not to do. We try to train
them to be coaches, to bring out children's potential, not therapists
trying to cure children's deficiencies. I have referred repeatedly to
our concept that the best way to have children learn these attitudes
is to learn them with them. Then, too, we help them search for problems which we could not solve, and challenge them to try. When
they have done so, we can help them evaluate their efforts and rejoice in their accomplishments. Finally, we can add the elements
of maturity and perspective which the children do not have. The
notion that youth can take care of themselves is dangerous. One of
our finest youth groups in CRP found that their inexperience made
them unable to do a good job even with a church pancake supper
without adult assistance. The same youth group did a magnificent

job when they took full advantage of the resources of the generation preceding them. It is our contention, and one which we practice, that the only way to test a curriculum is in terms of what the children exposed to it learn.

PROGRESS COMES FROM CONSOLIDATING OUR GAINS AND ATTACKING OUR WEAKNESSES

A slot maze will be found in most psychometrics laboratories. This is a labyrinth of paths through which the subject pushes a stylus until he reaches the end goal of the maze. I have seen children get into blind alleys and go all the way back to the beginning. They seem to believe that getting through is a stroke of good luck, and that if they start over they may hit upon the path. This is rarely successful. I have seen other children stay in the blind alley, content with having achieved that distance. Still others wander around haphazardly from one blind alley to another. Finally, there are those who try to learn something from each blind-alley experience, so that they can find the true path more quickly.

Analogies are never more than partially valid, but in education and religious education we have four kinds of people like the four kinds of children working with the maze. There are some who persist in a false hypothesis even though the evidence of its lack of usefulness is bursting out at the seams. Still others simply throw it all out and start over again. Others espouse every new fad that comes along. Only a few have the will and skill to use the painstaking but highly rewarding method of eclecticism, based on research.

"Yours is just an experiment," says a leader in religious education. The implication is that the curriculum espoused by the leader is tried, true, and delivered. Let me repeat: A standardized curriculum is one whose authors have got into a blind alley. Either they don't know how to get out of it, or they don't even know that it is a blind alley. We must recognize that in the field of religious and character education we are still in the stage "where uncharted complexity confronts the inquirer and where the cast of the basic topography is revealed only to men of bold insight" (132).

The concept of eclecticism has great potential, but is one of the easiest to misuse. Let me give an illustration. Suppose that you had ten curricula of ten elements each, and you wished to construct a new curriculum by selecting one element out of each of these ten curricula, do you realize how many possible ways there are in which that could be done? The answer runs into the billions. If we were allowed to choose more from one than from another, the answer becomes even more astronomical. Eclecticism, then, is not just a sort of intellectual tasting process. Furthermore, its methods are difficult and exacting.

If you will look again at the Research Design Chart, at the group of "Second Order Problems" under IV, Revision of Educational Hypotheses, you will see that the central cell reads, *B Methods for Eclectic Revision of Educational Hypotheses.* You will see that there are six cells around this one, each one concerned with some problem of methodology in this area of revision. I think that these fall naturally into two groups, one of which has to do with the process of eclectic revision itself as we use it in revising our procedures; the other with the application of the principle of eclecticism to educational theory. There are hundreds of relevant books and articles being published which we ought to know about. But it does not follow that we will automatically become infallible in our use of them even if we read them carefully.

Three major sorts of problems face us in the process of eclectic revision of our procedures as such. Each is of a different order. There are those which relate to the methods and materials themselves. Then there are those which have to do with our use of group design in revision. Finally, there are those which have to do with revisions which we make out of practical necessity.

Revising Curricular Materials and Methods by Pragmatic Eclecticism   Consider one of our central tasks in CRP, that of revising our curricular materials and methods. How shall we know that whatever changes we make are for the better?

The single most important thing to do is to make sure they are not any worse! But, you say, how do you do that? The answer is the central principle of creative eclectism. Make sure that you hold on to the values of preceding materials. I always regard it as disastrous when a whole lesson must be discarded. This is like the child going back to start the maze over again. *As long as we can hold on to our values, progress is inevitable.* More errors in revision are made at this point than at any other. If a new curriculum is really new, this is not cause for rejoicing. It just means that we are starting over with an unknown quantity.

Two Heads Are Better Than One, If They Use Creative Eclecticism Two heads are better than one, or at least should be. In almost all of our work, decisions are made only on the basis of the thinking of several members of the staff. Our "creative resolution of conflict" concept is one of the proofs we have of the value of group design. And this is another form of creative eclecticism.

It is an interesting experience to observe the process of creative conflict in action. Almost daily one of our research committees will approach some problem, finding as many ideas for its solution as there are members of the committee. If such a discussion ends with their having adopted one or another of these ideas, that is the exception. Indeed, we feel somewhat let down when it does end that way. The far more common outcome of the meeting is for a new concept to evolve which none of the members of the group had thought about in the beginning. All of us recognize it as far superior to our original ideas, and are again impressed with the power of the method.

To be sure, creative conflict is a costly process, and we always need to make as sure as we can that the problem justifies the investment. Very frequently we reach an arbitrary decision on some problems in the interest of research economy.

Decisions of Practical Necessity Are Safer with Pragmatic Eclecticism If you have given more than a passing glance at the Research Design Chart, you will not need to be told that the infinity principle certainly operates as far as the number of our problems is concerned. Furthermore, the curriculum as a whole is bewilderingly complex. We are not able to do all that we should like to do on any of the lessons. This means that hundreds of decisions must be made on the basis of far less careful study than we could wish. I have already referred several times to the objective impressionistic judgments of skilled workers. Here, however, ego-involvement is likely to be a most difficult factor to control. Whether I am a "skilled worker" and whether my judgments are "objective" are qualities not easily assessed by the individual involved. Not knowing what we do not know may often result in self-evaluation of possession of levels of skill beyond that justified by the facts. For example, members of our staff who are not skilled in statistics usually know that they are not. Their evaluation of their understanding of child psychology is not nearly so easy for them to make accurately, resulting sometimes in overconfidence, sometimes in underconfidence.

This method assumes, then, that a person making the judgment is skilled in the field in which he is given such responsibility. It assumes also that he exposes himself to all of the objective evidence he can, as a basis for making such judgments. But, having done this, his judgment is still an impressionistic one. If he has scientific humility, he is not likely to be happy about it. The most excessive tyranny I have to use as director of our Project is to demand that members of the curricular staff meet deadlines. This means that they must submit materials less well done than they would like to do them. In a project like this one, such judgments must be made. The problem in methodology is, of course, that of finding ways for making impressionistic judgments more valid.

It will be clear, then, that the first method involved will be that of making sure that the members of the staff who have the responsibility of such judgments are taught all of the skills which they need for their work. Then we should develop as many practical guides as possible. In Chapter XVI, I shall describe the tools we expect to put at the disposal of our curricular writers when we begin our next revision. The final product, however, will depend to a high degree on their ability to use them in this form of eclecticism.

Probably the most useful skills they can possess for this task involve the statistical concepts set forth in Chapters XI and XII. If our curricular writers can learn the theory and use of the statistical tools available for testing different kinds of hypotheses, they can do far more objective thinking, even when they do not actually have time to use them. It is not always necessary to compute levels of significance to the third decimal place, to sense with considerable accuracy the meaning of the unquantified data before you.

New Theories of Education Can Be Kept Positive by Pragmatic Eclecticism The other three cells in this section of the Research Design Chart are related to the broader areas of eclecticism; that is, those which have to do with educational theory.

The first thing to note is that principles selected for other research were relevant to the conditions which existed when that research was done and may not be relevant in the present conditions. In integrating these principles into another situation, then, a comparison of the underlying conditions needs to be made. Some of the most serious theoretical errors in the history of psychology have been made by scientists who have done all their work on psychotics and psychoneurotics, and then assumed that characteristics holding for these people will necessarily hold for mentally healthy people as well. In fact, a very large proportion of modern psychologists work in the clinical field. It inevitably follows that a disproportionate amount of our theorization is based on this kind of evidence. When their theories are positive, that helps; but we badly need theories growing out of a study of normal behavior and in search of man's potential. Valid eclecticism in the field of character and religious education, in particular, must take into account this distorted characteristic of the available evidence. In religious education we want our youth to do more than just keep out of mental hospitals. We want great homes, not just homes that avoid divorce. We want magnanimity, not just an insipid popularization of the Golden Rule.

In any case the important thing to do is to keep a careful record of the ideas which you accept from other sources, indicating the hypotheses on the basis of which you did so. Then later check the accuracy of these hypotheses. Never accept an idea just because it sounds good. Always have an objective reason for doing so.

Pragmatic Eclecticism in Evaluating the Flood of New Psychological Theories Everyone likes to create a theory about something. Psychologists are no exceptions. In fact, at the present time psychological theorizing is at the peak of its popularity.

A theory is always created to serve a need—to explain something which could not be explained before. If your present frame of reference is satisfactory for your purposes—that is, if you do not have such a need—then a new theory will usually serve no useful purpose for you. Scientists usually develop a new theory so that they can conduct experiments in some new area. For example, when psychology was defined as the study of the mind, experimental psychology was impossible, because the mind, as such, is impossible to get at experimentally. Then functionalism—in its extreme case, behaviorism—was conceived, and we came to define psychology as the study of behavior. You can do something about behavior experimentally. It is for this reason that functional theories have become almost universal in psychology. Be concerned about systematic theorization, then, only if it opens up new research possibilities for you.

Pragmatic Eclecticism in Evaluating Learning Theories The difference between what man is and what he could be is in large part a function of his will and skill to learn. It is incredible how far short of our maximum potential in learning we actually are. It has been estimated that the average college student could learn ten times as much in his four years as he does learn. This is a matter, on the one hand, of study skills, and, on the other, of motivation. Sometimes our youth appear to exert their best energies in the process of preventing learning from taking place.

Much is being learned about learning. This is one of the most active fields of psychological research, and many practical theories are being set forth.

Eclecticism here is probably as difficult as in any aspects of research. In the field of learning theory, a great deal is sometimes based on such simple kinds of learning as that of a white rat running a maze. It is a far cry from that to character education, and we need great skill to use eclecticism wisely in this area. On the other hand, much learning research is of a directly practical sort. This is being done in such great volume that it is difficult to keep up with it (103). Integrating that which is pertinent into our procedures is a real problem.

Pragmatic Eclecticism in the Use of the Vast Reservoir of Scientific Evidence   Finally, in this eclectic contribution to our process of revision, there is the influence of scientific methodology in general. I believe that our greatest progress in the social sciences recently is in the area of research methods. The whole co-scientist ideal has been made a practical possibility because of this progress. These developments are opening up new research possibilities for us every day.

SOME IMPORTANT CONCEPTS DESCRIBED IN THIS CHAPTER

Using the principle of *pragmatic eclecticism*, it is possible to make research creative and positive. The purpose of this procedure is to identify the strengths and weaknesses in an educational procedure, so that when it is revised as much emphasis is put on retaining the strengths as is put on eliminating the weaknesses. A totally "new curriculum" is a discouraging event, for it means the loss of the real values of the old along with its weaknesses. A curriculum in which research revealed no flaws would be a major tragedy, for it would point out no directions for further progress. One imbued with the spirit of science would never say, "This is the way it is." He would always say, "This is the best judgment I can make until further evidence is obtained." It will be clear that the principle of pragmatic eclecticism is a corollary of the infinity principle.

Parents who believe in the infinity principle will be continually revising and enlarging their understanding of their children. This is done best, not by haphazard all-or-none changes, but by this same process of pragmatic eclecticism. They must eliminate the distortions of their ego-involvement without losing their burning desire for the success and happiness of their children. The principle of looking for typical behavior as over against outstanding events is one practical method of doing this. A knowledge of the child's capacity, of the level of his past performances, and of the relative performances of his peer group will help parents to evaluate his performance more accurately. Looking for the implications of the energy concept of personality as over against the plastic-clay concept will help them find a good balance between healthy control on their part and challenging creativity on his. The Christian Hypothesis is more likely to lend itself to this goal than any of the existing concepts of personality now current in psychology.

Children's capacity for learning is far greater than has thus far been achieved. We must therefore be constantly searching for new insights into the learning process. This, too, can best be done in the framework of pragmatic eclecticism. For example, if we ask the child to learn so much of the "heritage of the ages" that he has no time left for anything else, we make the curriculum literally a "prescribed course to run." If we ask him to do enough "creative work" to use all his learning time, he is deprived of the values of the past. A search for the strengths of both learning procedures ought to produce curricular methods which will integrate the two into far more effective curricula. The skills to apply the wisdom of the past to life do not follow naturally the learning of those principles. These skills also must be learned. Interest does not guarantee effective learning; nor does lack of interest necessarily prevent good learning. The organization of curricular materials into learning units ought to be done in light of the child's ability to learn and apply them. Artificial logical or chronological orders may constitute severe handicaps for learning.

CHAPTER XVI

VISIONS AND REVISIONS

OUR NEWS broadcasts shout continually these days about the danger of war. Of all the skills man has mastered, his ability to make war has been developed to the highest degree. We have spent and will spend billions to prevent any other nation or group of nations from taking away what we consider our most priceless possession, freedom. If war comes, every scientist in the country will offer his services to the Government. Our ablest ones will join their best brains and skills in a supreme effort to give all the help they can. And that will be of great proportions.

And yet, we are still convinced that right is might. We spend only millions to develop the moral and spiritual values of our youth. Yet, if we can mobilize all the resources we have at hand for the purpose, I believe that that is sufficient for us to make even greater progress than we have in the art of war.

The longer I try to evaluate the potential of the spiritual inheritance God gave man, the more convinced I am that a level of social order is possible for us, incalculably greater than our present one. To be sure, "vicarious sacrifice" may replace "high standards of living" in our system of values, and "returning good for evil" may be our substitute for "national sovereignty," but those who have faith in the power of Christian principles will encourage our youth to try it.

AN INVINCIBLE TEAM—WHEN IT BECOMES A TEAM

When we look at the many influences that bear upon the child in our civilization, and the billions spent on them, it seems that nothing short of a miracle can make the available resources of religious and character education of any significance at all. How can this numerically small force hope to achieve these results? Yet, I am convinced that they can. But for them to be effective, we shall need a level of teamwork never before even approximated among them. On the chart which accompanies this chapter, I have diagrammed such a team as having seven members. Together they are invincible. I am equally convinced that any one of them or, for that matter, any six of them can have only minor influence on our youth. Under each one of them I have listed a few of the relevant concepts which have been discussed during the preceding chapters.

THE TEAM

1. THE SCIENTIFIC METHOD
   Parameters and statistics
   Differences and significance
   Correlation and dynamics
   Pragmatic eclecticism

2. THE CHRISTIAN HYPOTHESIS
   The infinity principle
   The power of positive good
   Dimensions of character
   Objectives

3. PARENTS AND TEACH-
   ERS
   Home dynamics
   Motivated capacity
   Co-scientists
   Sources of evidence

5. THE RESEARCH CUR-
   RICULUM
   Discovery-prescribed
   course to run
   Learning-teaching
   ratio
   Levels of aspiration
   Principles of calibra-
   tion
   Positive acceleration

4. THE CHILD
   Child of God
   Adaptation procedure
   Positive potential
   The learner
   Personality dynamics

6. THE SOCIAL ORDER
   Social dynamics
   Program design
   Sampling-parameters

7. EDUCATORS CONCERNED WITH THE
   MORAL AND SPIRITUAL VALUES
   Group dynamics
   Creative evaluation
   Infinity principle
   Heritage of the ages in terms
   of visions for the infinite

THE RESULTS

A GREATER GENERATION   and   A NEW SOCIAL ORDER
   Positive potential   The Christian Hypothesis

Let us think of our whole process as a drama of interacting forces. In the diagram above I have set forth a somewhat oversimplified picture of such a concept. Note that there are seven primary roles in the cast. Not one of them has power to bring about the desired end, except in terms of the other six. Research dealing with any of them individually or in pairs is likely to be of relatively minor value. Let me explore this hypothesis a little further.

There are many individual books about the family, and still others on child development. Sociology books dealing with the social order are endless in number. Books on religion, with its theological tenets and its ethical implications, are equally numerous. There are many books on scientific method, and still others on curriculum. I know of none which deal with the seven as an interacting whole. What happens when we deal with all seven at once? Every one of them is indispensable, but the one which has been least used up to now is science. When the method of science is added to the picture, the potential is unbelievably increased. I am fairly certain that we are doomed to only minor success without it.

The Curriculum Must Depict the Plan for the Team's Efforts   If this book achieves its purpose, one of the evidences of that achievement will be a vastly changed concept of the nature and purpose of a curriculum. This is not to say that we shall throw out the heritage of the ages, but we shall certainly make it the beginning and not the end of the child's religious education. The child ought to see this curriculum as the most thrilling adventure story he has ever read or heard. And just as he watches a Western on TV and then goes rushing about the house "shooting it out with the bandits," so the curriculum ought to fire his imagination and inspire him to try out his capacity for adventurous religion—religion that he sees as adventurous. It is significant that no children's play forms are built on a religious motif. Is religion to be excluded from the place where children learn best—in play? Our teen-agers and college-age youth should see in this curriculum the most exciting possible investments of their lives.

We cannot build effective curricula by simply pouring in great quantities of "good material." Such "shotgun" approaches to curriculum cannot hope to succeed. The curriculum, like life itself, must be an integrative process. One can put too much, as well as too little, in it. It is possible to construct a curriculum in which the various elements cancel out the influence of one another, far more easily than to build one which becomes a blueprint for Christian action.

I shall organize this final chapter around the curriculum, for that is the key to the whole problem. Build your curriculum. Let youth take a look at it. Then see what he does, says, thinks, and feels. Then you will know how far you have gone toward helping him find the door to new levels of Christian vision.

You cannot build such a curriculum without dealing with the other six factors. For example, a major emphasis in this book has been on the role of parents and teachers. We often assign roles to them which they cannot or will not play. I do not believe, however, that any considerable number of them are insincere or do not love their children. If we can write parts for them in the script which fit their abilities and capture their imaginations, they can make the difference between success and failure.

The central and deciding role must be played by the child. He is not to be regarded as a pawn in the hands of his environment, even when that environment is a good one, including our curriculum. He may not be completely the master of his destiny, but he certainly bends it this way and that, to his liking.

I can't tell you what the curriculum of the future will be. I can't even tell you what our next CRP revision will look like. I am sure that it will not be a prescribed course to run, in which we urge the child to follow the course we have already run so disastrously. I can describe to you the tools which our CRP curricular writers will have at hand when they set out to achieve it.

Then, I want to turn to the community as a whole, and to educators everywhere who wish to mobilize the full potential of the moral and spiritual forces in our communities for our youth. I'd like to show you some of the characteristics which a factorial-design survey of a community would have.

Whether or not the Christian philosophy of life is to permeate our social order will be determined in large part by the vision of a few thousand men and women who head our religious and character-building agencies. Thus far they have made little use of the scientific method. We need all the indomitable faith that our theologians can inspire in us. We need every practical skill that educators can teach us. But if we leave out the leavening power of the scientific method, our efforts must inevitably be puny ones, for this is the most effective way we can pray, "Thy will, not ours, be done!"

Finally, let us finish where we began, with the infinity principle, and dream dreams which we hope young men will one day transform into visions.

THE SCIENTIFIC METHOD CAN BE A POWERFUL MEMBER OF THE TEAM. IN THE ROLE OF A CRITIC, ITS CONTRIBUTIONS ARE OF MINOR VALUE

During most of my lifetime I have dreamed of a time when the educators concerned with moral and spiritual values would make use of the resources of the scientific method. And now the day is at last approaching when most leaders in the field have great hopes for the value of science. Yet I am discouraged, for I see so clearly how easy it is to waste the values of the method, to expend quantities of time and money and learn little or nothing of value. Every year I have opportunity to examine the proposals submitted by workers in this field for which financial support is being asked from some of the foundations. All of them are submitted in complete sincerity, and with faith in the value of the study proposed. The unfortunate thing is that a great majority of them contain basic flaws which doom them to failure or insignificance before they start.

It Is Very Easy to Do a Vast Amount of Sterile Scientific Research When it comes to program research, great projects can be set up in the area of moral and spiritual values which can be invaluable for the hope of the world. They ought to be high in priority among our tasks in religious and character education. Furthermore, there are many foundations ready and eager to underwrite them. Planning them, however, requires a great deal of skill and experience in the areas concerned.

One of the most common symptoms of an immature design is implied in such statements as this. "We will develop or adapt existing measuring instruments for our purposes." We need to make sure that such tools do exist or that they can be constructed with a reasonable investment of time and effort. Sometimes years of work are required to construct, test, revise, and standardize what seems to be a "simple" measuring instrument. Anything can be measured— if you stay with it long enough. But don't create a design on the assumption that it can be done easily or soon, unless you have evidence that it can!

In educational-research proposals, another common flaw in design is what is sometimes referred to as the "shotgun approach." For example, if it is character education, you just throw at the children as many different forms of character education as possible, and measure the effects. Now, this may work in advertising a commercial product, as can be demonstrated in increased sales. In education, it is far different. You may use educational techniques A, B, C, D, and E. Perhaps A is effective, but the other four may be useless or even negative. Suppose that your total results are positive, what do you do? Do you just go on with the whole program, the bad as well as the good? You must have techniques which can evaluate these various educational procedures individually and in their interrelationships.

What of the uncontrolled social and moral forces in the community? If you are trying to measure the effectiveness of religious education, how can you do that if more than 95 per cent of the child's behavior experience is in nonreligious settings? In the Midwest study (61) previously referred to, it was found that the 120 children in Midwest participated in 100,000 episodes of behavior per day, more than 36,000,000 per year. The chances are that the larger the city, the smaller the proportion of religious behavior would be. Even with the most extensive efforts to make religious influences appreciably greater in one community than in another, they would still be only a small part of the child's total experience. If you could double the amount in one community as compared to another, the percentage of the total in the two communities would hardly be noticeably different. Your design, then, must take into consideration all these other community forces individually and in their interrelationships. Trying to hold them constant by sampling would be impossible and unfruitful.

I have already referred to the experience pitfall. When I think back over the hundreds of mistakes we have made in CRP, owing to inexperience, I realize how important this is. If a design is prepared by scientists, no matter how able, who have had no direct experience in the field, its chances of practical operation are slim.

Many research proposals are also highly unrealistic in the assumptions they make about group participation. One ongoing, successful program research of which I know has two people who just smooth ruffled feelings, both in the staff and in the community in which the study is being made. You can do about what you will with guinea pigs, but people are pretty stubborn creatures in that regard. They lack a great many of the "ideal" experimental qualifications of guinea pigs! Unless the co-scientist principle is an integral part of the design, their participation will be unpredictable, much less effective.

THE CURRICULAR TRINITY—THE CURRICULUM, PARENTS AND TEACHERS, AND YOUTH

The high road of the scientific method is certainly not an easy one. It was a long time ago that we in CRP first set forth a set of educational hypotheses in the form of a curriculum for Christian character education and set out to test them. Now we are approaching what appears to us to be the climax of this long task. We are getting ready to formulate a new set of insight-hypotheses in the form of another curriculum revision. This time, however, we shall have spent seven years laying the foundations, and anticipate a minimum of six for the actual process of revision.

In our case, the curriculum is created as a part of the research design. The research design is part of the educational program. The scientific method, the Christian Hypothesis, the teaching staff, the home, and youth are all integrated into an interacting dynamic force. This is the way in which science can make its real contribution to religious and character education.

Our own research has been largely confined to the character-education side of religious education. The same principles, however, are applicable to the other phases of religious education. It is not sufficient just to list the things you wish youth to learn and then appoint a staff of writers to translate it into their language, adding a sugar coating to make it palatable. It is when you capture their imagination to high achievement that you get their best. We have found this, however, one thing to say and another thing to do.

Some of Our Adventures That Paid Large Dividends But now let's look at some positive guides to writing curriculum. You have high vision for the goal which you have set for your lesson. You are indeed setting your course by the stars. In addition to these blind alleys which you must avoid, there are several important calibrating guides you can use. In fact, such calibrations constitute one of the chief roles which the scientific method can play in the research curriculum.

Taken literally, to calibrate an instrument means to test it to make sure it is measuring accurately. Can you imagine reboring the cylinders of your car engine without checking it with some accurate instrument for size? When you want accuracy, say, of a hundredth of an inch, you certainly cannot determine it by just looking at it with your naked eye. Neither can a lesson writer who would build curricula which challenge the growing youth to his best efforts.

The most obvious such check is the one we refer to as age-level calibration. The three-year-old thinks differently than his ten-year-old brother. To build a lesson for either means that it must be put into ideas which they can understand, which have meaning and reality for their own problems, and which represent levels of challenge which inspire but do not frustrate them. A little later on I shall show you the far more thorough way in which we can go about this task of age-level calibration now.

You could not have read this far without guessing that another of these calibrating instruments would have to do with individual differences. Our typical class concept was a very useful one in former revisions. We now are creating what we call longitudinal typical classes. They, too, will vastly increase the effectiveness of our materials.

A type of calibration in our work, which is due to our dedication to the Christian Hypothesis, represents another type of calibration which our writers have to use in the preparation of their materials.

The last calibration we have used up to now in the formulation of our revisions has to do with the forces underlying the learning process. No one will question that how learning takes place is determined in large part by the potential functioning of the human mind. I have read with interest the volumes prepared by the curriculum committee of one of our denominations in the construction of a new curriculum, which sets forth what they hope the average adult will know about the Bible and other religious materials when he has completed his religious-education experience. It is a very interesting and challenging picture. They have certainly set a high goal for themselves. Achieving it is another matter. They are in for a great many years of arduous research before they will have found out how to bring about this learning; and they will need to examine their procedures in the light of everything we now know or can learn about the learning process.

CO-SCIENTISTS—THE GREATEST POTENTIAL FORCE FOR GOOD IN THE WORLD

Some years ago a rather shy young woman volunteered for the church-school staff for which I was at the time responsible. I promptly appointed her as a department superintendent. Just as promptly her husband called me up and "gave me a piece of his mind." It was not the most attractive part of his mind, but the one best suited to the occasion. I had done what so many of us in religious and character education all too frequently do. Given a willing volunteer, we assign them to an impossible task. Likely as not, the very next day an able, well trained volunteer comes along and we ask him to take tickets for next Friday night's dance.

This is the problem of motivated capacity. We must offer challenges which motivate people to accept them. Our Teacher Opinion Study reveals that teachers whose only motivations consist of a sense of duty usually turn out to be dissatisfied and ineffective.

Perhaps even more important than that is what we ask them to do. They want challenge but not frustration. To ask them to do tasks which are impossible for them is frustration. Many a person's Sunday-school teaching career has been terminated in two weeks because of lack of skills to cope with a group of youngsters blowing off steam. Just as frequently what we ask them to do seems so petty and insignificant that they find no satisfaction in it at all.

It is a part of our co-scientist theory that parents and teachers have both the will and the ability for high achievement, if our curricular procedures utilize both.

Here, then, is the second part of our curricular trinity; namely, the co-scientist parents and teachers. I have emphasized this co-scientist concept throughout the book. It may well be the most important concept in the book and the principal key to the future.

The development of the co-scientist principle is a two-way process. On the one hand, we must create materials and methods which the co-scientists can and will use. Our curricula must be within the capacity and skills of our co-scientists to carry out. They must also present a vision in a way that will inspire their strongest motivations.

Then, on the other hand, the co-scientists must develop the scientific skills which make them more effective in this role. In this book many such skills have been suggested. It will be interesting to see how many lay people are willing to accept the co-scientist challenge and how far they will go toward mastering the skills described, as well as helping us find new ones. I want to bring together in the next few pages the high points of this co-scientist concept which have been set forth in the book.

What Are Some of the Scientific Skills the Co-Scientist Can Master? Let me review for you a few of the characteristics and skills of these co-scientists and the effect they can have on our present methods of distorted thinking.

The first step is the skill of searching for an unbiased sample. When you make a judgment and look for evidence to support it, you are not a scientist. When you make a judgment, gather a body of unbiased evidence, and examine your judgment in light of it, you are a scientist. This is the threshold of science to which I have referred several times.

The second step consists in an acceptance of the infinity principle, with the ability to apply its philosophy to all relevant situations. An example to which I have referred several times is the principle of creative conflict. If I get an insight and then feel an urge to defend it against all comers, the outcome is destructive conflict and, at best, compromise. If the infinity principle and creative conflict are the order of the day, then I am motivated to integrate my insights with those of my colleagues in the faith that we shall be able to find third alternatives better than any of those with which we started.

To say that a belief that God is good is a scientific principle may come as a surprise to many of my colleagues in professional psychology and other branches of science. The fact is, they have implicitly believed it all along. Certainly the whole philosophy of science operates on the hypothesis that the universe is dependable and predictable. But what makes medical research about some disease go on after decades of failure, except the firm conviction that there is a cure; namely, that the universe is friendly? Examine every branch of science and you will find the same principle underlying it. How does this concern the co-scientist? Most of us doubt seriously that right makes might, that good can overcome evil. Most of our fears are based on this lack of faith that God is good. Yet as each of us looks back on the "worst evils" which have befallen us, over and over again we see in them an even larger measure of good. Hysteria, whether in individuals or groups or nations, would never arise if its citizens held firmly to this conviction. Its implications for scientific progress would be a faith to try again and again after repeated failures.

The fourth skill of the co-scientist has to do with the production of reliable and valid evidence. I have spoken of our need in CRP for "typical behavior" of children, and the ability of parents to give it. This is based on an application of the first step in this process, the unbiased sample. As long as we think that the world is actually the way we see it, scientific progress is difficult. When we recognize that whatever we observe about the external world is colored by our own personalities, then we can seek for ways to correct for the bias and give better evidence. Add to this level of objective attitude the concept of sampling, and our co-scientists can furnish evidence which now can be obtained only with the greatest difficulty.

Next, let us turn to the concept of statistical significance. When we look at two groups and detect a difference between them, our next question is, "Is this a real difference, or could it have come about by chance?" One seldom hears a public speaker quote evidence to support his points without violating this principle. Our co-scientists, then, ought to master such a tool as chi-square. It is not a difficult one. With practice it can become as natural for him as the multiplication table. The method of controlled ranks set forth in Chapter XI is the simplest way to implement this concept for many types of problems.

The sixth skill of the co-scientist is implied in the method of characteristic differences. I have referred to it repeatedly in earlier chapters. Here is an educational procedure which we apply to a group of children. Traditionally in science we would then measure its effectiveness. If we find no evidence of effectiveness, we try to think of another process. We continue this until we find one, if ever, that does work. This is very time-consuming and highly frustrating. Let us reverse the process. We take two groups of children who differ in some respect in regard to skills they possess or evidence of growth in some regard which they show. We study these children in every way we can in a search for characteristic differences. As soon as we find these, then we have almost certain leads to the reasons for the changes and can modify our educational procedures in a fraction of the time involved in the other procedure.

Finally there is the principle of correlation. If our co-scientist can learn even the rank-difference method of correlation, he can attack many problems which are closed to him without it. Personality is a highly integrated phenomenon. No two factors in it are related exclusively to each other. They are always influenced by the rest of the personality. When we are asked to state why we did such and such, we are always wrong if we cite one reason as if it were the whole story. When, however, we can measure the correlation between the two factors, then we need only to square that correlation to have a fairly objective estimate of how much the two factors do have in common, and even more important, how great is the effect of other factors in the personality in bringing about the behavior of the two factors. The correlation coefficient makes us able to see what cannot be seen in direct observation. It reveals to us interaction dynamics, which are the kinds of dynamics which operate in daily life. This final skill of the co-scientist, then, opens doors of exploration of which generations before never dreamed.

I wonder now if you can estimate the effectiveness in our search for moral and spiritual values, if our lay people learn these skills of the co-scientist. To be sure, we can make progress by using lay people as guinea pigs. We can even make progress with the destructionists blocking every step of the way. But the day has come when our lay people, by accepting this new role, can make our progress many times greater than we have dared to hope.

WAIT TILL YOUTH GETS THROUGH WITH OUR CURRICULA

Every one of the seven factors described in the beginning of the chapter as being significant in curriculum effectiveness is an indispensable one in this matter of effective religious education. But of one thing you can be certain, youth has the last word. Unless he casts a vote of approval for your curriculum you may as well save yourself the trouble of writing it. This means that the curriculum must be so constructed that it will command in him the responsiveness of his major motivations.

It is not common practice to put youth on curriculum committees, though in local churches we may go to the opposite extreme by giving them the veto power on any one or all of them. As we prepare in CRP for our next revision, we are more and more turning to youth himself for evidence on which to build our unit. This is especially true at the High School and College levels. The fact is, they are giving us a quality of evidence never before available to curriculum writers. They are indeed learning many of the skills of the co-scientist.

One of the most difficult problems parents face has to do with youth's large investment of his boundless energy and love of adventure. Hot rods, vandalism, dangerous moral experimentation— these are only a few of the activities which make parents prematurely gray. We shall not command the full acceptance of youth for our educational visions unless they provide a level of adventure and challenge which seems equally attractive to youth.

This ought not to be difficult, considering the roots of the Christian religion. Jesus certainly experienced little difficulty in finding roads to high adventure for those whom he met. In fact, if we depict Christianity to youth the way Jesus did, in all its stark reality, they will love it in spite of its danger and uncertainty. Recently I listened to a young minister who is investing his life in a ministry in the worst part of our slum population. His wife and children live there, too. He literally made our hair stand on end as he told of the incredible experiences he had gone through. I do not know his parents nor those of his wife. But I'll bet they would say that they would consider the dangers of this level of Christian adventure far greater than hot rods, vandalism, and playing with fire in moral behavior. "Do not be anxious about your life, what you shall eat or what you shall drink, nor about your body, what you shall put on." "Happy are you when men shall revile you and persecute you. . . ." These are dangerous messages.

SOME SCIENTIFIC TOOLS FOR REVISING A CURRICULUM

I live in the central General Electric Company town. I often hear their top research men describe in glowing terms what we may expect in the future. Their production people look to the research laboratory for just such visions. We in CRP have dedicated our energies to this kind of exploration of the vision in the teachings of Jesus. Probably all of you who dream of a Christian social order can envision the wisdom, courage, and persistence it takes to travel such a road into the future. We shall share with you our findings and hope that you will feel that our efforts have not been in vain.

Beginning in 1957, and probably taking at least six years, we propose to bring together all that we have done during the last twenty years. We will rethink our hypotheses, and report to you the best that we can conceive, of how it is possible to give to our children better insights into the Christian philosophy.

All of this will implement itself into what, for want of a better term, we call a *curriculum revision.* The word *curriculum,* however, carries to most of us connotations which are not involved in this one. Perhaps to call it a *research curriculum* helps some, but even that is not adequate to convey our vision for this next adventure in our work.

As we think of this next revision, our first question is: How can we gear our findings into those of the other agencies which are concerned with the Christian education of our children? We certainly can help in the all-important problem of methodology. But we have also got to make our work available to all of the forces of character and religious education. This is not done by just saying, "Here are our findings—help yourself." It is going to take much cooperative work with other educational leaders to find out how it is to be done.

Our job is service, not competition. We believe that we are doing a program of research which can be of great value to the various denominational boards and the other character-building agencies. We hope that they will come to look upon us as at least one of their important research centers.

As you read the remainder of this description of the tools we expect to place in the hands of our curricular writers in the near future, I think you will agree that most of the same tools can be of value to any curriculum or program writers. A careful study of age-level characteristics, especially on the positive potential side; the typical class, especially the longitudinal typical class; learning methods, and teaching methods; home types and teacher types; methods of enlisting and using parent cooperation—such tools can be invaluable for anyone who works with youth.

We expect to develop these tools into a manual which can have as great general usefulness to those outside CRP as possible.

Just as we hope we can help the denominations and other character-building agencies, so we know that they can help us. It is they who can see to it that we have a representative sample of participating groups. It is they who hold the communication key by which our findings are made available to everyone who can use them.

The Major Revision Tools Which Our Curriculum Writers Will Use What kinds of tools, then, can we place at the disposal of our curricular writers, and any others who can use them, as we face our next revision?

Attitudes are being formed or changed all of the time, whether that is the purpose of the behavior or not. In any form of religious education, whether or not for attitude development, attitude change is taking place. This means that it behooves all educators to know what those changes are and to evaluate their curricula, in part at least, in light of them. We have learned much about attitudes during our twenty years of research in CRP. A summary of our findings, then, should be of value not only to our own curricular writers, but to all curricular writers. Here are some of the types of information we expect to place at the disposal of our own curricular writers:

We know which attitudes are hard or easy to interpret and some of the reasons why. We know how the attitudes we use show themselves in behavior at the various age levels. Attitudes toward authority in Kindergarten children are quite different from those at the Junior High level. We can now trace the development of various attitude sequences from Nursery to Senior High. In view of the fact that an attitude is a part of the total personality, such sequences tell us much about the total personality as reflected in the expression of a particular attitude at a particular time. Furthermore, as we examine the forty thousand items of the Positive Potential Study, they give us many dimensions of childhood growth by which to evaluate our success and failure. The same dimensions ought to be useful to religious or secular educators in any kind of curriculum procedures.

For parents and teachers, we are now in a position to describe a wide variety of applications of every attitude in the variety of situations in which every child normally finds himself. This will make it much easier for parents, teachers, and youth to choose goals for themselves which have on them the realistic stamp of experience. I have emphasized several times the fact that in our daily lives we organize our experience psychologically, not logically. As we study the systematic trends in these attitudes, we ought to be able to find organizational principles which can be as useful to curriculum builders outside CRP as to those in CRP. I have repeatedly said that an attitude is an abstraction until it becomes an integrated part of the child's life. From the Positive Potential Study will be found illustrations of what these attitudes do look like when they are so integrated.

From these attitude studies we can learn much about learning. We can learn what can be expected from children of the various age levels, the range of that behavior in terms of individual differences, and the best methods of teaching and learning to be used in mastering it. Consider the old question of direct versus indirect teaching. We can demonstrate that direct teaching is very effective in some cases, and the reverse in others. We should then be able to eliminate this question as an either-or and replace it with, "What is the thing to do in this particular learning situation?"

When we made our first effort to build curricular hypotheses, we brought together everything that we could find about the various age levels. This was summarized in a chart (45) and in *Their Future Is Now* (73). Recent examination reveals that most of that work was well done, especially in terms of the psychological and physical development of the child. However, the character and spiritual potential as suggested in part of the chart had to be based on inference from this body of psychological research. Now, thanks to the abundance of evidence found especially in Parents' Reports, we can prepare pictures of the spiritual potential of our children which are not only accurate and calibrated for the age levels, but which will put in the hands of our curricular writers the raw materials from which many thrilling but practical visions can be prepared in the form of lessons for our youth and their parents.

In 1939, based on our study of the literature of child development, we could say with considerable confidence, "This is what a six-year-old child is like." Now, as a result of our body of data derived particularly from Parents' Reports, we can say with almost as great confidence, "This is what the six-year-old child can be!" In other words, we can put into the hands of our curricular writers a more comprehensive picture of the spiritual potential of the child. Furthermore, this can be described in the language of parents and youth, for that is where it came from. We can now describe the ways in which the child can be challenged to throw his motivational energies into Christian living.

Another thing which we attempted to do in the construction of our original curriculum was the use of a "typical class." As curricular writers, we tried to create a sort of typical class which we kept in mind as we wrote. This was to make sure that our lessons would hold visions for the whole range of individual differences. Since that time, we have tested thousands of children in our laboratory, and we also have great quantities of lay evidence in our files. We can re-do this job many times better than was possible ten years ago. Here are a few ideas:

We shall need to decide what variables we must consider if the class is to be fully representative of the age level. Sex and age (because our curriculum is in two-year cycles); physical, mental, and emotional endowment; socioeconomic status; size of family; attitude of parents toward the curriculum; and the amount of cooperation they are willing to give—all of these factors will be considered in the process of selecting a typical class. Children representing the full range of each of these variables, therefore, will be included. Data from our Census Study and the testing program will help us determine these variables.

This typical class, then, will be given to lesson writers so that they can have the experiences of real children to call upon as they endeavor to create lesson adaptations, with some assurance that these children represent a cross-section of at least the CRP population at their age level.

Then, perhaps even more interesting than this age-level typical class, is a possibility that grows out of the kinds of evidence we now have available. We have many files filled with evidence about children whose parents have written reports for a number of years. We call this longitudinal data. We have long known that some of the bad boys of the seventh grade (most boys in the seventh grade seem to church-school teachers to be bad boys) may become the community leaders of a few years later. How shall we be able to recognize them in the seventh grade? Both in psychology and education we have dealt largely with problems as they occur. It is entirely possible and indeed probable that some of the immediate behavior which we think of as "good" may be predictive of bad in the future. Oversubmissiveness is certain to be like that. Suppose we could see them as they will look a few years later. Suppose our curricular writers not only had a typical class but a good picture of what that class looked like two years ago, and even more important, what it is going to look like in a few years to come. That dream is a real possibility for us, and our Longitudinal Committee proposes to achieve it for us.

For some, we have records of church-school and home teaching for many past years. We propose to examine this additional material and to prepare brief "life histories" of varying lengths which will give our curriculum writers a better idea of what these children were like and are going to be like. Because we shall have background data on all of our typical children at each age level, it should be possible for us to match children of different ages, study types rather than individuals, and finally arrive at a "typical longitudinal class" in which we can describe the development of a group of typical children from Nursery through Senior II.

As we look forward to this next revision, then, we take stock of the evidence we have and of that which we need. Then we consider how much of the latter can be given us by parents and teachers and youth through the medium of co-scientist reports. For example, one of our greatest lacks is a body of data regarding failure. Parents tend to report their successes but not their failures. Such failure reports can be of great value to us in revision, and we are setting out to find ways to get them. I have sometimes thought we ought to appoint a failure reporter in each church, someone who has a vision for thus charting the outer reaches of our knowledge, and for laying foundations for our next great insights. Such a reporter would do nothing but seek for evidences of failure, misunderstanding, or frustration.

When a Sunday-school class, or YMCA club group, or secular education class gets together, textbooks and the other curricular materials are not the only things present. Two far more important things also there are the teachers and pupils, leaders and youth. Furthermore, they differ widely. The teachers differ. What one can do another cannot. A lesson written for one would be a total loss to another. Most of us have, in the past, prepared curricula almost as if every teacher were pretty much like every other one. Just recently, through our Teacher Opinion Study, we brought together our first systematic picture of the different kinds of teachers we have. I think you can guess what values this will have for our curricular writers. Their work can be much more realistic with such information.

I wonder if in all the fields of education there is a more forgotten man (more often woman) than the church-school teacher. There is a church in my town which has just dedicated a $400,000 educational building. It is the fourth to do so within the last two or three years. We are certainly "building conscious" these days. With just the interest on $400,000 the members of that church-school staff could be paid $10 a week (enough for transportation, baby sitting, help with housework, and so forth). There would still be enough left over to invest more than $1,000 a year in teacher training.

Moreover, our Teacher Opinion Study has shown that such external factors as buildings, equipment and organization are certainly not key influences in determining the effectiveness of a teacher. This means that our failure in religious education to provide effective teaching material and helps is all the more serious. From this study, we shall be able to determine the ways in which our effective teachers operate, and provide materials which will be more directly useful to them. For instance, I suppose the most underrated aspect of our lesson materials has been our projects. We have always had great dreams for them. They were the medium through which youth themselves could try out some of our challenges to them.

Someone has said that youth at Junior and Junior High ages try on various personalities: tough guy, student, good sport, and so on, just to see if they like them. We are quite sure that if we can hold before them a picture of the Christian personality that makes sense to them, they will try it on, too. And, having done so, they will call it good and bet their lives on it. But these youngsters differ widely. Projects which form the base for this trial adventure, then, have to be both realistic and meaningful to all kinds of children. Our Positive Potential Study reveals scores of usable project ideas in its findings. We ought to be able to introduce dynamic elements into the projects of this next revision which will be vastly better than any of us in CRP or other forms of education have been able to come up with so far. It is our expectation that from the materials of the Positive Potential Study, we shall be able to list great numbers of project ideas both for class and for home. They will need to be classified in terms of their attitude reference, age-level relevance, and even type of teacher and church-school space and equipment. On the other hand, they will have the advantage of having come from the real experiences of children. There should be no difficulty in providing as great variety as desirable.

If we have acted as if teachers were all alike, we have done much the same thing for homes. "This lesson doesn't fit our home," is a very common complaint. How do homes differ?

The Home Dynamics Study will produce an accurate description of home climates which curriculum writers will want to take into consideration in writing new lessons. These descriptions will include the personalities of each parent, and the descriptions can be accurate and positive enough so that parents themselves will have no trouble in recognizing themselves when they are so described.

An increasingly important part of our curriculum is by way of our weekly publication, ACE (1). The findings of a recent study on it have already influenced ACE very much. They will do so even more in the future as ACE finds more and more of the maximum-potential role it can play.

Because ACE is issued weekly and sections of it go along with the individual lessons to be taught during the week at home, further interpretations of the lesson can be made on the family level, whereas the lessons are committed to a particular age level.

Further exploration and research with our co-scientists, the parents and teachers in CRP, is another important area for our ACE publications. As you can see, then, ACE becomes in reality a vital part of our curriculum. Because of its continuous publication and its flexibility it can be the source by which an important element of adaptation can be added to the curriculum. Curriculum writers need to keep this in mind and write the curriculum in such a way that this potential can be fully used.

Finally, we preach to every curricular writer or board with whom we come in contact: "Evaluate! And if you are going to evaluate, you will have to write the design for doing so right into the curriculum itself." What tools can we provide curricular writers for doing this? This new revision of ours will one day be superseded by another one, far beyond this one. What a tragedy it would be, then, so to write this one that in it we did not lay the groundwork for the next one. But there are many ways in which this task can be done. Our curricular writers must have at their command the methods and information necessary for building this new revision to be a milestone, not an end. Let's see how this can be done.

They should be of such a nature that parents, teachers, and local churches can use them to estimate the progress made by their own individual children. Parents and teachers should be able to evaluate their efforts constantly in order to become better and better guides in the character growth of their children. We can now see definite possibilities of developing scales which describe the dimensions of character in such a way that parents and teachers can know what to look for, and then can measure with confidence what they have seen.

These techniques should be so designed that after parents and teachers have used them, they can be used by our CRP staff (or one similarly trained) to evaluate in more technical ways the effectiveness of our curricular efforts. In this case the measurement of attitude growth in children would provide a valid criterion by which we can divide our data between success and failure experiences. For our purposes, anecdotal reports from parents and teachers about their efforts to teach the lesson, and the results achieved, could be studied by the method of characteristic differences and the simplified forms of factor analysis described in Chapter XI.

So far, we have been describing methods of evaluation based on reports and ratings from parents and teachers. Our experience with

Youth Reports, made by High School young people themselves, indicates that these reports are more useful for some purposes than reports from adults, because they give direct insights into the operation of the total personality. Our evaluative efforts will include increased use of reports directly from Junior High and High School young people.

Praying, however sincerely, "Not my will, but thine, be done," is far easier to do than to bring it about. We have long dreamed of the day when we could prepare curricular materials entirely on the basis of objective evidence, leaving none of it to be the product of our own individual opinions. We have not yet reached that goal. But I think you will agree that we have made some progress toward it.

IT WILL TAKE PERFECT TEAMWORK AMONG THE CHARACTER-BUILDING AGENCIES FOR THEM TO BECOME A DETERMINING FORCE IN YOUTH'S FUTURE

The child has many things to choose from in the community, the social order in which he lives. As yet we know too little about it, from his point of view, with its hundreds of forces trying to pull him this way and that. Some of these forces are good, some bad, and some neither good nor bad, though powerful. Yet, in the beginning of Chapter XIII, I said that I was convinced that although we have only millions at the disposal of the character-building agencies, we can still win youth despite the billions spent in these other ways. But how is that to be done?

One fact stands out in the answer to this question. We must know accurately the forces which are operating in and through these other agencies as well as in our own. Some of them are good and must be used to good advantage. Great inspiration has come from motion pictures as well as incentive to crime. We must integrate our own forces. Nothing is more pitiful than the character-building agencies of a community competing against one another. If we can study our resources carefully and integrate our forces fully, we can become the leaven in the community which will give youth the chance he needs to meet the world of tomorrow. Divided, our efforts are puny indeed.

Fortunately, the methods of science are now far enough along that even this Herculean task can be done. There was a day when a community survey was little more than a counting of noses and organizations. It could almost be done with a telephone directory. A city that had more churches, schools, and character-building agencies than bars, pool halls, and motion-picture houses was a good community. Now, with the tools of factorial design at our disposal and some of the techniques developed in recent years, we can make studies of our communities which are of more far-reaching significance.

If the Forces for Good in a Community Are Integrated, Their Total Strength Is Multiplied Many Times Over Far deeper understanding of the dynamic forces operating in a community is required than we have thus far had to achieve real integration. This means that research techniques are a prerequisite to any such effort. Just as is true in religious and character education, community evaluative research ought to be an integral part of the ongoing processes of character education in the community. An outside study made at some given time to measure some designated over-all aspect of the community is likely to be of minor value. A design such as I am going to portray has educational value in itself as well as measurement potential. I cannot describe the design in detail. That would be a long process. But I do want to go far enough that you can see its potential values.

Such a project should begin with a functional survey of the religious and character-education agencies in the community. The key word here is *functional*. This should include both religious and secular agencies. It should include informal as well as formal ones. A public-speaking club in a high school may be as important to list as the YMCA.

A careful list should be made of their stated objectives in terms of their goals for character and religious education. This should also include a description of the criteria by which it seems possible to determine the extent to which these objectives are being achieved.

Membership lists of these agencies should next be examined. The ages, sexes, and socioeconomic level of the membership should be studied. This would at once indicate what portion of the population is reached by each agency and, for that matter, by all of them. There ought also to be made a more psychological analysis of the membership in terms of such variables as sociability and shyness, possession or absence of various common age-level skills, vocational aims, and the like. It is probable that significant individual differences among the agencies will be found when this is done. This would have immediate practical value for the agencies. Each agency, knowing accurately the nature of its membership, could do a far better job of planning programs to serve that group.

The second phase of such a study is a little more complex. It will consist of a number of interviews with children and their parents. Each socioeconomic area in the community should be sampled by good sampling techniques. The samples need not be large. Two small samples in each area to check against each other will be better than large samples.

These interviews should be designed to seek six kinds of information. In the first place, a fairly good picture of the home should be obtained, including the number and quality of family activities. The second kind of information should be to find out the child's participation in various community agencies, both those which have religious and character education included among their goals, and those which do not. In the Midwest study (12), a useful concept was described as *levels of penetration*. This is a measure of how deeply the child penetrates into the organizations (or, as they call them, *behavior settings*) of which he is a member; whether simply as an onlooker or as a leader in it or even as one having policy-making responsibilities.

Then, by means of interest finders of some kind, the child's participation in and interest in such other influences as TV, radio, the movies, the playground, clubs of various sorts, and the like, should be determined. These, too, were included in the concept of behavior settings in the Midwest study.

Still another kind of information to be obtained in these interviews should be a description of the child's objective performances: marks in school, success in athletics, citizenship activities, any other behavior which might indicate the quality of the child's character. The criteria suggested by the various agencies as evidences of the effectiveness of their programs could be sought here. These data form the basis for our criterion variables.

The third kind of evidence sought should reveal their basic

philosophy of life. The essays described in Chapters XI and XII from the Junior High young people are examples. Projective techniques are usually designed to get such information. These can include such simple devices as stating their three strongest wishes, describing the kind of person they would like to be, the things they would like to see done to make their communities better, and similar topics.

This information should be organized in two ways. In the first place, summaries of it—both part by part, and general summaries —should be prepared and put on cards and coded in such a way as to make direct identification impossible. The treatment of the Junior High essays described in Chapter XI illustrates the method.

In the second place, each part of the information needs to be quantified in some manner. I have indicated a number of ways of doing so in Chapter XII. These results can be put on punch cards for correlation analyses and the search for interaction dynamics.

Having collected all this information and put it into manageable form, the analysis of the qualitative data is based primarily on the methods of control ranks and characteristic differences. All sorts of studies are possible. Children can be compared in many different ways. For example, select comparable groups made up of those who participate in the activities of some agency and of those who do not participate in any agency. These can be ranked in terms of any of the factors concerning which information has been obtained. The average ranks of the agency and non-agency groups will indicate the effectiveness of the agency's program. The top and bottom halves of the groups in whatever way they have been ranked can be studied for characteristic differences. This should indicate what factors are accounting for this result.

The same method can be used to evaluate the effects of the other influences in the community to which children are exposed. TV programs can be analyzed for their probable influences, groups chosen who have and have not seen them, and the same methods of control ranks and characteristic differences used to formulate and test hypotheses and to discover influences not suspected.

As this evidence piles up, it will make it possible for interagency committees to construct a role theory for the various agencies, prepare interrelating programs based on these findings, which will reduce to a minimum the conflicts and overlapping among the agencies, and bring about the greatest possible influence in producing moral and spiritual education of value for the children and youth in the community. I would guess that the agencies in any city in this country could increase their effectiveness in the community by tenfold in ten years on the basis of such a program of research. Each of them ought to invest at least a third of its budget on research.

RELIGIOUS AND CHARACTER EDUCATORS MUST GET OUT OF THEIR BLIND ALLEYS IF THEY ARE TO LEAD ANYONE EXCEPT THEMSELVES

I could list ten names here—five of them professional athletic heroes and five of them stars in the entertainment world—who exert many times as much influence on our youth as all our religious and character-education leaders put together. We can change all that if we really set out to determine the nature and functions of the great social and moral forces which we call the will of God, and if we pray to learn that will with every tool placed at our disposal. The scientific method is one of the most powerful of these.

There are two annual conferences which I regularly attend each year. They are the meetings of the American Psychological Association, and of the Division of Christian Education of the National Council of Churches. I have been attending both for a considerable period of years. When I read the program of the former today, I find very little in common with the program of a decade ago. New hypotheses, new frames of reference, new evidence, new and more powerful tools are the order of the day. In the case of the latter, however, I find many fewer evidences of such change. And those changes which have occurred have been brought about very often by changes in the former group. I have just examined two programs for each organization several years apart. I think I could take twenty topics, ten each chosen at random from the National Council programs, mix them up, and you could not sort them into their respective years at all. If, however, I do the same for the American Psychological Association, you could sort most of them back into their respective groups with ease.

The papers read today at this annual religious-education conference differ very little from those of a decade ago. This does not mean that we in religious education do not wish to make progress.

It would be foolish to invest so much time and money if we did not. Why this contrast? The answer is that we have not introduced into our religious-education procedures the methods which bring about rapid progress.

I have no desire to offend and certainly not to antagonize my colleagues in religious education. I imagine a great many more of them will read this book than will my psychological colleagues. In fact, it is because I do have so much faith in them that I want to set forth these facts and their implications as well as I can see them. In the Section at National Council to which I belong, we have spent during the last decade cumulatively more than ten thousand hours in session. This would be equivalent to some fifty years in the working life of an individual. I wonder whether in these sessions we have achieved even a small fraction of what one able scientist could do in fifty years of research. As for the whole of this religious-education body, you would need to multiply this number by at least thirty. These meetings over that period of time have probably cost those attending at least $1,500,000. Give thirty scientists a research fund of that size, and what would have been the outcome? I am not proposing that that be done. I am simply trying to show what our potential is.

What I am trying to say is that, given the power and tools of the scientific method, those of us who have faith in the ultimate value of religion could have achieved many times as much as we have in our search for the truth which comes closer and closer to the will of God, in challenging our children to a stature far beyond that which most of us have been able to achieve.

The scientific method, of course, is not the whole story of our future. I would not for a moment have us lose the great spiritual values which have been gained over the centuries. The scientific method is one form of prayer, however, which we have sadly neglected.

If we do learn to use it, our program topics at National Council will change. This is not important in itself; but if God is infinite, and if we do use these powerful tools for testing our concepts about him and his will for us, it is inevitable that they will change. Not only that, if God is good, we need have no fear that they will change for the worse. Our research results may scare us from time to time, as we see our long-cherished concepts failing to meet the test of evidence. Nevertheless, they will inevitably be replaced with finer and nobler ones.

I STILL BELIEVE IN AN INFINITE GOD WHO WILL ALWAYS REVEAL NEW VISIONS OF HIS WILL TO THOSE WHO SEEK TO LEARN IT

When you read this heading you may be inclined to say, "This is where I came in." And so it is, in a way. The point is, however, the cycle is a spiral, not a circle. Each year, in the history of the Character Research Project, our new insights are so thrilling that we are sure there can never be another year to match it. The next one is regularly more productive. In other words, the spiral goes up at an increasing rate of acceleration.

As you will recall, this is another of our CRP concepts. We call it the *positively accelerating curve*. Look at the two curves drawn below:

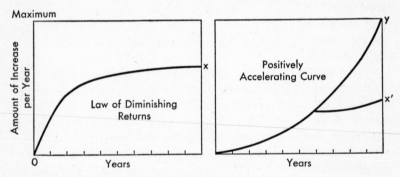

In the left-hand graph the curve goes up rapidly at first, and then less and less rapidly as time passes. Curves that look like this represent, graphically, the law of diminishing returns. The right-hand curve—the one that ends at "y"—is of a different sort. Here progress gets more and more rapid with the passing of time. It is a positively accelerating curve, because the acceleration is constantly increasing positively. The x′ is, of course, the terminus of the curve representing no progress.

Now what sort of curve can we expect in the field of religious and character-education research? I feel completely certain that it can be the one ending in y. In fact, has that not always been the case with scientific research?

One recurring tragedy in the development of our social order is that from time to time we have made some good progress, only to assume in our enthusiasm that this is all there could be, a final answer.

At the time of this writing, the world is being torn asunder between two ideologies, Democracy and Communism. As I am writing this, a speaker on the radio has just made an often repeated assertion, "Communism and Democracy cannot continue to exist in the same world." By this, the speaker seems to imply the hopeless conclusion that a third world war is inevitable. Almost everyone is agreed that such a war spells the end of our civilization. Must we see that as inevitable?

Perhaps what follows is only wishful thinking. But suppose that in our international conferences we tried such a method as that suggested in Chapter I in our concept of group design. We are proud of our Democracy, but does any one of us imagine that it could not be infinitely greater? Suppose that, together with those who hold another political philosophy, we used the full power of our conflict, not in war but by each being stimulated by the other, to seek a new and greater level of his own political philosophy.

All this emphasis on the infinity principle may seem discouraging to those who like to finish things. A very good friend writes, after reading an early draft of this volume: "One thing that has raised a question in our minds has been your constant reference to revision of methods and materials and projection of techniques unaccomplished. This leads us to wonder whether CRP will ever be wrapped up in a package and the experiment considered accomplished."

Of course, in one way the answer is "No." If our concepts of an infinite God and the positively accelerating curve are correct, then not only will further research always be possible, but ever more significant findings will be the results of such efforts.

Finally, let's combine this natural desire for finishing things with the infinity principle in the frame of reference of such a comprehensive research design as this one. It is true that in the past when "answers" have been found which seemed to constitute significant advances over previous answers, we have often become ego-involved with them, and found it emotionally difficult to be objective toward seeing their weaknesses. I think you will agree that such emotional conflicts have too often been a very prominent characteristic of religion. We need a research design which constitutes a frame of reference which makes it possible for us to study any problem with complete intensity and yet without losing sight of the forest for the trees. It needs to be motivated by the infinity principle which makes us able to feel a justifiable sense of achievement at the completion of each stage of the research, and at the same time see one of its main values as being a steppingstone to a better answer. Is it possible that something of this dream is behind the statement of the one who once said, "I came not to destroy but to fulfill"?

SOME IMPORTANT CONCEPTS DESCRIBED IN THIS CHAPTER

The few millions being spent on religious and character education have greater potential for man's good than the billions spent on war have for his destruction. However, good intentions have never been the best road to the achievement of any potential. Religious and character education, today, is using only a small fraction of its maximum potential.

Effective religious and character education must be based on the realization that the child's growth takes place in a highly complex universe of interacting forces. Religious and character educators must come to realize that the curriculum can play an important role in this process only when it is an integrated and challenging part of these interacting forces. Shotgun approaches to religious education, consisting of the addition of many "good materials," are uneconomical and of minimum effectiveness.

The church-school teacher is the forgotten man of religious education. More emphasis is put on new buildings than on the teacher. Parents are given little beyond "oughts" for their work. Homes are assumed to be alike. Effective religious and character education will need to find methods that challenge and can be done by these people. We have not even begun to tap the sources of power which parents and teachers can and will invest in this process. Even today professional scientists are regarded by most lay people as supermen who deal only with higher mathematics and highly technical instruments. The truth is that lay people, too, can master and use many of the methods of science. When they do, we shall make far greater changes in our social order than have the automobile, the airplane, the movies, television, radio, and the comics combined.

Youth does more to his environment than the environment does to him. Newspapers, movies, TV, and radio have erred on the side of assuming that he does it all. They have in general tried only to discover what he wants. Education and particularly religious education have erred in the other direction of thinking of him as plastic clay, and of creating curricula with only passing nods at what he wants. A far more powerful approach would emphasize both factors.

There are now being developed many calibrating guides for the curricular writer, which will increasingly free him from the fatal errors of personal opinion, and make it possible to double the effectiveness of our curricula at least once a decade. These include the skills of pragmatic eclecticism, various types of age-level calibrations, future age-level predictors, home types, and sources of teacher effectiveness, to mention only a few.

There are methods now available for community surveys which make possible the increasingly effective use of the potential which the various character-building agencies have at their disposal. At present they probably do not achieve one-tenth of their maximum potential. These new methods are not critical evaluators so much as they are methods for assessing present achievement and further possibilities.

BIBLIOGRAPHY

Four annotated bibliographies are included in the following general bibliography. They are recommended for those who wish to read more widely in these areas. They are designated as follows:

    c Child psychology and development
    r Religious and character education
    p Personality and trait theory
    x Experimental design and statistics

Each of them could have been extended to many times its present length. These are not presented as necessarily the best. The purpose is to include an adequate representation in the fields covered.

1. *Adventures in Character Education.* Published 36 times each year by the Union College Character Research Project, Union College, Schenectady.

p 2. Allport, Gordon W., *Personality.* Henry Holt and Company, New York, 1937. Parts III and IV. This is one of the classic volumes in the history of psychology. No one who works in this field of personality should fail to read it. It was perhaps the strongest argument against the extreme doctrine of specificity.

c 3. Almy, Millie, *Child Development.* Henry Holt and Company, New York, 1955. For anyone, whether parent or psychologist, who wants a highly readable and interesting account of child psychology, this is an ideal book. I consider it the most interesting textbook I have ever read.

p 4. Anastasi, Anne, *Psychological Testing.* The Macmillan Company, New York, 1954. For those who are interested in the meaning of psychological testing. Principles of testing are described at a semi-technical level. Covers almost all parts of the Profile.

p 5. ———, and John P. Foley, Jr., *Differential Psychology.* The Macmillan Company, New York, 1949. A comprehensive survey of the problem of individual differences in personality research.

6. Anderson, Harold H., and Gladys L. Anderson, editors, *An Introduction to Projective Techniques*. Prentice-Hall, Inc., New York, 1951.

7. Anderson, John E., "Personality Organization in Children," *American Psychologist*, 1948, Vol. 3, No. 9.

p 8. ————, *The Psychology of Development and Personal Adjustment*. Henry Holt and Company, New York, 1949. This college text develops in great detail especially parts I, II, and IV of the Personality Profile. Emphasis is on interpretation of the characteristics rather than on the process of testing and measurement.

x 9. Andrews, Thomas G., editor, *Methods of Psychology*. John Wiley and Sons, Inc., New York, 1948. Here is an excellent summary of psychological methods. Students primarily interested in social psychology and personality, however, will find that too much of it is oriented to laboratory experimental psychology to suit them.

10. Baker, Winifred A., "Longitudinal Study of the Effect of Experience in the Character Research Project on the Learning of Concepts," *Union College Studies in Character Research*, 1954, Vol. 1, No. 4.

c 11. Barker, Roger G., Jacob S. Kounin, and Herbert F. Wright, *Child Behavior and Development*. McGraw-Hill Book Company, Inc., New York, 1943. A series of reports of thirty-five outstanding pieces of research in the area of child development. The reader will find in these a description of methods of research as well as findings.

x 12. ————, and Herbert F. Wright, *Midwest and Its Children*. Row, Peterson and Company, Evanston, Ill., 1955. This study will revolutionize community research. The many new procedures described in it will interest everyone concerned with such research.

x 13. Bingham, Walter Van Dyke, and Bruce Vernon Moore, *How to Interview*. Harper and Brothers, New York, 1941. This is the basic text in the field for those who want to grasp the principles of scientific interviewing.

14. Brand, Howard, editor, *The Study of Personality*. John Wiley and Sons, Inc., New York, 1954.

15. Bunting, James F., *More Effective Character Development*. Union College Character Research Project, Union College, Schenectady, 1950.

16. Buros, Oscar Krisen, editor, *The Fourth Mental Measurements Yearbook*. The Gryphon Press, Highland Park, N.J., 1953.

17. Cantril, Hadley, *The "Why" of Man's Experience*. The Macmillan Company, New York, 1950.

x 18. Carmichael, Leonard, editor, *Manual of Child Psychology*. John Wiley and Sons, Inc., New York, 1954. Second Edition. This is another of the basic handbooks now available in the field of psychology. This one is a must for those who need comprehensive grounding in child development.

x 19. Cartwright, Dorwin, and Alvin Zander, *Group Dynamics, Research and Theory*. Row, Peterson and Company, Evanston, Ill., 1953.

x 20. Cattell, Raymond B., *Description and Measurement of Personality*. World Book Company, Yonkers-on-Hudson, 1946.

p,x 21. ———, *Personality*. McGraw-Hill Book Company, Inc., New York, 1950. This is probably the most ambitious effort that has thus far been made to carry the philosophy of factor analysis to its ultimate point in the description of trait theory. This is highly technical reading, but worth while if you have the statistical background to understand it.

x 22. ———, *Factor Analysis*. Harper and Brothers, New York, 1952. While this is one of the most elementary texts on factor analysis, it is still far beyond the elementary statistics student. For those who have gone far enough in theoretical statistics, however, it is one of the best texts by which to gain a basic understanding of factor analysis.

p 23. Character Education Inquiry, *Studies in the Nature of Character*:
   I, *Studies in Deceit*, by Hugh Hartshorne and Mark A. May. The Macmillan Company, New York, 1928.
   II, *Studies in Service and Self-Control*, by Hugh Hartshorne, Mark A. May, and Julius B. Maller. The Macmillan Company, New York, 1929.
   III, *Studies in the Organization of Character*, by Hugh Hartshorne, Mark A. May, and Frank K. Shuttleworth. The Macmillan Company, New York, 1930.

24. Cox, Catharine Marie, *The Early Mental Traits of Three Hundred Geniuses*, Vol. II of *Genetic Studies of Genius*, edited by Lewis M. Terman. Stanford University Press, Stanford University, Calif., 1926.

p 25. Dennis, Wayne, *Readings in Child Psychology*. Prentice-Hall, Inc., New York, 1951. This collection of readings will be particularly useful to those who are interested in the experimental evidence that underlies assumptions in psychological testing. Profile items under the headings "Use of Language," "Intelligence," "Emotional Maturity," and "Social Adjustment" are covered better than other sections.

p 26. Department of Superintendence, *Tenth Yearbook: Character Edu-*

cation. National Education Association, Washington, D.C., 1932.

27. Diederich, Paul B., "Methods of Studying Ethical Development," *Religious Education*, 1955, Vol. L, No. 3.

28. Dollard, J., L. W. Doob, N. E. Miller, *et al, Frustration and Aggression*. Yale University Press, New Haven, 1939.

29. Doty, Richard S., "Help Your Campers Develop Desirable Character Traits," *Camping*, 1951, Vol. 23, No. 7.

30. ———, "Character Education in Gra-Y Work," *Y Work with Youth*, 1951, Vol. 7, No. 5.

31. ———, "A Study of the Relationship of Boys' Wishes to Their Sociometric Status," *Union College Studies in Character Research*, 1955, Vol. 1, No. 12.

32. ———, The Third Dimension of Camping. To be published.

33. ———, and John Stettner, assisted by the Camp Chingachgook Staff, "Growth Toward Attitude Objectives in a Summer Camp as Indicated by Two Sociometric Devices," *Union College Studies in Character Research*, 1954, Vol. 1, No. 8.

34. Eakin, Mildred Moody, "Newer Techniques in Teaching," in *Orientation in Religious Education*, edited by P. Henry Lotz. Abingdon-Cokesbury Press, Nashville, 1950.

x 35. Edwards, Allen L., *Statistical Methods for the Behavioral Sciences*. Rinehart and Company, Inc., New York, 1954. This is one of the best among the many medium-difficult introductions to statistical analysis of the kind of data we use in psychology and education.

36. Eysenck, H. S., *Dimensions of Personality*. Routledge and Kegan Paul, Ltd., London, 1947.

37. Fallaw, Wesner, *The Modern Parent and the Teaching Church*. The Macmillan Company, New York, 1946.

38. ———, "The Home and Parent Education," in *Orientation in Religious Education*, edited by P. Henry Lotz. Abingdon-Cokesbury Press, Nashville, 1950.

39. Fisher, R. A., *The Design of Experiments*. Oliver and Boyd, Ltd., London, 1951. Sixth Revision.

x 40. Garrett, Henry E., *Great Experiments in Psychology*. Appleton-Century-Crofts, Inc., New York, 1951. Third Edition.

x 41. ———, *Statistics in Psychology and Education*. Longmans, Green and Company, New York, 1954. This is the fourth edition of a longtime popular text for beginning statistics. It will be preferred by many statisticians.

42. Godcharles, Charles, "Problems of Character Training in a Summer Camp," *Y Work with Youth*, 1948, Vol. 4, No. 5.

x 43. Goodenough, Florence L., and John E. Anderson, *Experimental Child Study*. The Century Company, New York, 1931.

*44. Greene, Edward B., *Measurements of Human Behavior*. Odyssey Press, New York, 1941. Although it is somewhat outdated, this is probably one of the more comprehensive texts in psychological measurement. Besides the process of measurement, most popular tests are discussed at an understandable level. Tests include most of those on the Profile.

45. *The Growth and Development of Christian Personality*. A chart published by the Union College Character Research Project, Union College, Schenectady.

46. Guilford, J. P., "Creativity," *American Psychologist*, 1950, Vol. 5, No. 9.

*47. ————, *Fundamental Statistics in Psychology and Education*. McGraw-Hill Book Company, Inc., New York, 1950. Second Edition. This is my own favorite elementary statistics text. It is readable, thorough, and usable.

*48. ————, *Psychometric Methods*. McGraw-Hill Book Company, Inc., New York, 1954. As a text describing the various ways there are to measure psychological data, this book has no superior. It is fairly technical reading, but probably the best in the field.

49. Havighurst, Robert J., *Human Development and Education*. Longmans, Green and Company, New York, 1953.

c50. ————, and Hilda Taba, *Adolescent Character and Personality*. John Wiley and Sons, Inc., New York, 1949.

51. Hilgard, Ernest R., *Theories of Learning*. Appleton-Century-Crofts, Inc., New York, 1948.

p52. Horrocks, John E., *The Psychology of Adolescence*. Houghton Mifflin and Company, New York, 1951. For those who are most concerned with the adolescent. Many of the characteristics on the Profile are interpreted at this age.

53. Hovey, Elizabeth H., *et al.* To be published in *Union College Studies in Character Research*.

54. Hunt, J. McV., editor, *Personality and the Behavior Disorders*. The Ronald Press, New York, 1944, 2 vols.

55. *The Interpreter's Bible*. Abingdon-Cokesbury Press, Nashville, 1951. Vol. VII.

*56. Jahoda, Marie, Morton Deutsch, and Stuart W. Cook, *Research Methods in Social Relations:* Part One: *Basic Processes;* Part Two: *Selected Techniques*. The Dryden Press, New York, 1951. This text is oriented especially with research in the area of prejudice, but for that very reason has a realism which many texts do not have. They show the difficulties of the experimental-control group method, assuming that for the most part it is applicable only *ex post facto,* and not as a planned research in the first place.

r 57. Johnson, Paul E., *Christian Love*. Abingdon-Cokesbury Press, Nashville, 1951.

r 58. Jones, Vernon, *Character and Citizenship Training in the Public School*. The University of Chicago Press, Chicago, 1936.

x 59. Kendall, Maurice G., *Rank Correlation Methods*. Charles Griffin and Company, Ltd., London, 1948. This is a specialized book which relatively few people not doing a great deal of statistical work will want.

60. Kluckhohn, Clyde, and Henry A. Murray, editors, *Personality in Nature, Society, and Culture*. Alfred A. Knopf, New York, 1948.

61. Koppe, William A., Studies in Psychological Ecology: A Behavior-Setting Survey of the Town of Midwest. Unpublished thesis, University of Kansas, 1954.

62. ———, "Attitude Measurement by Use of Worksheets" (Attitude Measurement Studies), *Union College Studies in Character Research*, 1954, Vol. 1, No. 11.

63. ———, "A Report to Co-Scientists," *Adventures in Character Education*, 1955, Vol. 8, No. 7. Union College Character Research Project, Union College, Schenectady.

x 64. Lacey, Oliver L., *Statistical Methods in Experimentation*. The Macmillan Company, New York, 1953. Although this book is oriented toward biology, it is an excellent simple text in experimental design.

65. Lewin, Kurt, *Field Theory in Social Science* (Dorwin Cartwright, editor). Harper and Brothers, New York, 1954.

66. ———, Ronald Lippitt, and Ralph K. White, "Patterns of Aggressive Behavior in Experimentally Created 'Social Climates,'" *Journal of Social Psychology*, 1939, Vol. 10, No. 2.

r 67. Ligon, Ernest M., *The Psychology of Christian Personality*. The Macmillan Company, New York, 1935.

68. ———, "A Plea for the Child," *Presbyterian Tribune*, January 23, 1936.

69. ———, "The Church in the Scientific Study of Character," *Sigma Xi Quarterly*, 1936, Vol. 24, No. 1.

70. ———, "Character, Science, and Religion," *Religion in Life*, 1937, Vol. 5, Spring Number.

71. ———, "Measuring the Total Personality," *Proceedings* of the Eleventh International Congress of Psychology, 1937.

72. ———, "Positive Mental Hygiene in Personality Development." Comptes redus du IIe Congres International d'Hygiene Mentale, Paris, July, 1937.

p 73. ———, *Their Future Is Now*. The Macmillan Company, New York, 1939.

74. ———, A Study of the Influence of Philosophical Attitudes on Personality Adjustment. Unpublished paper read at September 1941 meeting of American Psychological Association at Evanston, Ill.

75. ———, "The Administration of Group Tests," *Educational and Psychological Measurement*, 1942, Vol. II, No. 4.

76. ———, "Minimum Essentials of Character Education," *Religious Education*, 1944, Vol. XXXIX, No. 6. ([Part] I of a Symposium on Character Education in the Church School.)

77. ———, "A Commentary on the Commentaries," *Religious Education*, 1944, Vol. XXXIX, No. 6. ([Part] II of a Symposium on Character Education in the Church School.)

78. ———, "Individual Character Education," *Religious Education*, 1944, Vol. XXXIX, No. 6. ([Part] VI of a Symposium on Character Education in the Church School.)

79. ———, "An Outline of Trait-Habit Attitude Goals for Character Education," *Religious Education*, 1944, Vol. XXXIX, No. 6. ([Part] VIII of a Symposium on Character Education in the Church School.)

80. ———, "Contributions of Psychology to Religious Education," *Religious Education*, 1946, Vol. XLI, No. 5.

81. ———, "Partiality Is the Best Policy," *Camping Magazine*, 1947, Vol. 19, No. 9.

r 82. ———, *A Greater Generation*. The Macmillan Company, New York, 1948.

83. ———, "Experimental Design for Character Research," *American Psychologist*, 1949, Vol. 4, No. 7. (Abstract of paper read at September 1949 meeting of American Psychological Association at Denver, Colo.)

84. ———, "Possible Contributions of Recent Researches in Psychology to Religious Education," *Religious Education*, 1949, Vol. XLIV, No. 4.

85. ———, "Basic Psychological Concepts," in *Orientation in Religious Education*, edited by P. Henry Lotz. Abingdon-Cokesbury Press, Nashville, 1950.

86. ———, "An Outline of the Conceptual History of the Union College Character Research Project, 1935–1953. Historical Introduction," *Union College Studies in Character Research*, 1953.

87. ———, "The Y Goes Home," *Y Work with Youth*, 1955, Vol. XI, No. 6.

88. ———, and Mary O'Brien, "The Method of Characteristic Differences," *Religious Education*, 1954, Vol. XLIX, No. 4.

x 89. Lindquist, E. F., *Statistical Analysis in Educational Research*.

Houghton Mifflin Company, New York, 1940. This text is one of the best from the point of view of small-sample theory. It starts with the basic principles of small-sample research and continues until the reader has a grasp of the tools necessary for most experimental designs using small samples.

x 90. ———, *Design and Analysis of Experiments in Psychology and Education.* Houghton Mifflin Company, New York, 1953. This is a fairly advanced text, describing the many kinds of designs which are possible for the most economic solution to complex problems. Only those with a fairly solid foundation in statistics will find this text of value to them.

x 91. Lindzey, Gardner, editor, *Handbook of Social Psychology.* Addison-Wesley Publishing Company, Inc., Cambridge, 1954. Volume I, *Theory and Method.* Volume II, *Special Fields and Applications,* is an excellent summary of the research done in the field of social psychology up to now.

r 92. Lotz, P. Henry, editor, *Orientation in Religious Education.* Abingdon-Cokesbury Press, Nashville, 1950. A series of papers by leaders in the field. It represents the most comprehensive description of modern religious education available.

93. Marquis, Donald G., "Research Planning at the Frontiers of Science," *American Psychologist,* 1948, Vol. 3, No. 10.

94. Maslow, Abraham H., and Béla Mittelmann, *Principles of Abnormal Psychology.* Harper and Brothers, New York, 1941.

95. Maynard, Donald M., "The Total Church as an Agency in Religious Education," in *Orientation in Religious Education,* edited by P. Henry Lotz. Abingdon-Cokesbury Press, Nashville, 1950.

96. McDougall, William, *An Introduction to Social Psychology.* John W. Luce and Company, Boston, 1921.

97. McGraw, Myrtle, "Later Development of Children Specially Trained During Infancy," in *Readings in Child Psychology,* edited by Wayne Dennis. Prentice-Hall, Inc., New York, 1951.

r 98. McKibben, Frank M., *Christian Education Through the Church.* Abingdon-Cokesbury Press, Nashville, 1947.

99. ———, "Trends in Educational Philosophy," in *Orientation in Religious Education,* edited by P. Henry Lotz. Abingdon-Cokesbury Press, Nashville, 1950.

100. McLane, Edwin D., Mary A. O'Brien, Sallie Ann Wemple, "A Comparison of the Effectiveness of the Teaching-Learning Process in Groups Participating and Not Participating in the Character Research Project," *Union College Studies in Character Research,* 1954, Vol. 7, No. 7.

ˣ 101. McNemar, Quinn, *Psychological Statistics*. John Wiley and Sons, New York, 1955. Second Edition. This is one of the more popular elementary texts. It is not easy reading, but quite within the range of people interested in learning the fundamentals of statistics.

ʳ 102. Miller, Randolph Crump, *The Clue to Christian Education*. Charles Scribner's Sons, New York, 1950. This little volume shows how the doctrinal concepts of theology can be included in a religious-education program.

ˣ 103. Monroe, Walter S., *Encyclopedia of Educational Research*. The Macmillan Company, New York, 1950. Revised Edition. (1520 large pages) Here is a source volume, encyclopedic in scope, but valuable for those who want to know what has been done in educational research.

104. Morse, Mervyn M., "The Effectiveness of Individual Classroom Adaptation in Bringing About Attitude Growth in Class Groups," *Union College Studies in Character Research*, 1953, Vol. 1, No. 1.

105. ———, "Some Factors Which Relate to the Three Categories of Attitude Growth: Significant Growth, Ordinary Growth, and No Growth," *Union College Studies in Character Research*, 1953, Vol. 1, No. 2.

106. Mould, Ralph D., "Principles and Procedures of Curriculum Building," *Religious Education*, 1952, Vol. XLVII, No. 5.

107. Munro, Harry C., "The Christian Education of Adults," in *Orientation in Religious Education*, edited by P. Henry Lotz. Abingdon-Cokesbury Press, Nashville, 1950.

ᵖ 108. Murphy, Gardner, *Personality*. Harper and Brothers, New York, 1947. Parts IV and V. This book is especially noteworthy because of its treatment of the difficult concept of the self. Murphy's trait concepts are closely related to self psychology.

109. ———, *An Introduction to Psychology*. Harper and Brothers, New York, 1951. This is a good source for most readers.

ˣ 110. ———, Lois B. Murphy, and Theodore M. Newcomb, *Experimental Social Psychology*. Harper and Brothers, New York, 1937. Revised Edition.

111. Newcomb, Theodore M., *Social Psychology*. The Dryden Press, New York, 1950.

112. O'Brien, Mary A., Leonard A. Sibley, Jr., Ernest M. Ligon, assisted by the Curricular Staff of the Character Research Project, "Developing Creativity in Children's Use of Imagination: Theoretical Statement," *Union College Studies in Character Research*, 1953, Vol. 1, No. 3.

113. ———, Rachel A. Elder, Polly Putnam, Miriam R. Sewell, "De-

veloping Creativity in Children's Use of Imagination: Nursery, Ages Two and Three," *Union College Studies in Character Research,* 1954, Vol. 1, No. 5.

c 114. Olson, Willard C., *Child Development.* D. C. Heath and Company, Boston, 1949. A standard text in child psychology, with special emphasis on the implications for education. The characteristics on the Profile are integrated into a pattern of total growth as it applies to curriculum. Should be valuable to religious educators in conjunction with the Personality Profile.

115. *Parents' Manual.* Union College Character Research Project, Union College, Schenectady.

116. Parsons, Talcott, and Edward A. Shils, *Toward a General Theory of Action.* Harvard University Press, Cambridge, 1951.

x 117. Peatman, J. G., *Descriptive and Sampling Statistics.* Harper and Brothers, New York, 1947.

118. *The Personal Equation.* Union College Character Research Project, Union College, Schenectady.

119. Poincaré, Henri, *The Foundations of Science,* p. 544, quoted from *Handbook of Experimental Psychology,* edited by S. Smith Stevens. John Wiley and Sons, Inc., New York, 1951.

120. Rennick, Verle G., Jane E. Grupe, Emmy Lu Reich, and Miriam R. Sewell, "Exploratory Study of Rating Procedures Used to Analyze Material Received on Parents' Reports," *Union College Studies in Character Research,* 1954, Vol. 1, No. 9.

121. Rogers, William L., and Paul H. Vieth, *Visual Aids in the Church.* Christian Education Press, Philadelphia, 1946.

122. Rosenzweig, Saul, "An Outline of Frustration Theory," in *Personality and the Behavior Disorders,* edited by J. McV. Hunt. The Ronald Press, New York, 1944.

123. Schwilck, Gene. An evaluation of the Park School Counseling Program. In a study still in process and later to be published.

124. Setchko, Penelope Sayre, "Readability of Character Research Project Lessons," *Union College Studies in Character Research,* 1954, Vol. 1, No. 10.

r 125. Sherrill, Lewis J., *The Rise of Christian Education.* The Macmillan Company, New York, 1944.

126. Smith, Leona J., Ernest M. Ligon, Joan Lohmann, Mary A. O'Brien, and Richard B. Seymour, "A Search for Dimensions of the Family Climate Based on Dynamic Interrelationships Among Factors Influencing Parental Attitudes: Orientation to the Problem," *Union College Studies in Character Research,* 1954, Vol. 1, No. 6.

127. Snyder, Ross, "Experimentation and Research," in *Orientation in*

Religious Education, edited by P. Henry Lotz. Abingdon-Cokesbury Press, Nashville, 1950.

128. Snygg, Donald, and Arthur W. Combs, *Individual Behavior.* Harper and Brothers, New York, 1949.

129. *Sociometry in Group Relations,* edited by H. H. Jennings. The American Council on Education, Washington, D.C., 1948.

130. Spaulding, Helen, and Olga Haley, *A Study of Youth Work in Protestant Churches.* National Council of Churches of Christ in the U.S.A., Chicago, 1955.

p 131. Stagner, Ross, *Psychology of Personality.* McGraw-Hill Book Company, New York, 1948. Second Edition, Section II. This is probably as general a treatment of the position held by most psychologists as you could find. This is a good solid book in which to study the present thinking in the psychology of personality. It is a conservative, middle-of-the-road presentation.

x 132. Stevens, S. Smith, editor, *Handbook of Experimental Psychology.* John Wiley and Sons, Inc., New York, 1951. This is one of an increasing group of source volumes, which attempt to cover the whole field of research involved. This is most certainly not vacation reading, but it is a source for those who are willing and prepared to plow through its encyclopedic chapters, to know what experimental psychologists have been and are doing.

r 133. Stidley, Leonard A., "A Selected Bibliography of Religious Education," in *Orientation in Religious Education,* edited by P. Henry Lotz. Abingdon-Cokesbury Press, Nashville, 1950. This chapter from the *Orientation* volume is listed separately because it constitutes such a complete bibliography in the field of religious education.

x 134. Symonds, P. M., *Diagnosing Personality and Conduct.* The Century Company, New York, 1931. Although an old text, it still has invaluable sections, especially in the construction of rating scales and questionnaires.

x 135. ————, *The Dynamics of Human Adjustment.* Appleton-Century, New York, 1946.

x 136. Terman, Lewis M., editor, *Genetic Studies of Genius.* Stanford University Press, Stanford University, 1925 ff. Several volumes.

c 137. Thompson, George G., *Child Psychology.* Houghton Mifflin Company, Boston, 1952.

138. Thurstone, L. L., and E. J. Chave, *The Measurement of Attitude.* University of Chicago Press, Chicago, 1929.

139. Trumbull, Richard S., "A Psychogenic Study of Dark Adaptation," *Journal of General Psychology,* 1941, Vol. 24, Second Half.

140. *Union College Studies in Character Research.* A series of technical

papers describing the researches of the Union College Character Research Project.

141. Vieth, Paul H., "The Content of the Curriculum," *Religious Education*, 1952, Vol. XLVII, No. 5.

x 142. Walker, Helen M., *Mathematics Essential for Elementary Statistics*. Henry Holt and Company, New York, 1951. Revised Edition. For those who are a little rusty on their high-school mathematics, this is an excellent book to read along with an elementary statistics course. It is interesting to note that with the exception of a small section on trigonometry and another on logarithms, no mathematics is involved beyond algebra.

143. Weigle, Luther A., "The Aim and Scope of Religious Education," in *Orientation in Religious Education*, edited by P. Henry Lotz. Abingdon-Cokesbury Press, Nashville, 1950.

144. *The Why and How of Adaptation*. Union College Character Research Project, Schenectady. In three parts: Nursery-Primary Departments (Age 2 through Grade 2); Secondary-Junior High Departments (Grades 3 through 8); Senior I and II Departments (Grades 9 through 12).

r 145. Williams, J. Paul, *The New Education and Religion*. Association Press, New York, 1945.

p 146. Witmer, Helen L., and Ruth Kotinsky, *Personality in the Making: The Fact-Finding Report of the Midcentury White House Conference on Children and Youth*. Harper and Brothers, New York, 1952. This book has interested us in CRP especially, because the eight "components of the healthy personality," set forth in it, are in such close relationship with our eight general objectives of the Christian personality that we were able to match them almost perfectly.

147. Woodworth, Robert S., *Contemporary Schools of Psychology*. The Ronald Press Company, New York, 1948.

INDEX

Psychological theories, 33, 438

Psychological validity, 139-144

Psychology of Christian Personality, The, 40, 210

Psychophysical methods, 340

Putnam, Polly, 479

Questionnaire, most difficult of all measuring instruments, 335, 368

Randomization: *the choice of a representative sample, so chosen that every individual in the population being sampled has an equal chance of being selected*, 301, 305, 325

Rank-difference method, 330, 341, 342

Reich, Emmy Lu, 353, 384, 480

Reliability, 331, 362

Religion: defined, 176; and psychologists, 209

Religious education: in our culture, 82, 387; new formats in, 387; experiments in, 289 ff.; greatest opportunity, 31; taught by home and the culture, 354

Religious philosophy, essential to achieving man's maximum potential, 123

Religious self attitudes, 176

Rennick, Verle G., 353, 384, 480

Research: basic nature of, 1, 2, 7-15, 56; budgets, 29, 82; creative, 30, 343 f., exploratory, 48; infinity principle in, 423; planning, 21; and progress, 39; and service, 29 f.; teams, 17-22; tools, 16, 288-344; vision for, 25

Research curriculum: *a curriculum so constructed that it contains within itself the techniques for its own evaluation and scientific revision*, 30, 348, 355, 356, 378, 445 f.

Research design, 8, 48-53, 60, 427, 443, 444

Research Design Chart, 348-351; (cut of), 350-351; 362, 363 f., 364, 374, 382-387

Responsibilities, chores and, 110

Restructuring the field, 12

Retroactive inhibition, xii, 430

Rogers, Will, 400

Rogers, William L., 480

Roles: application in, 95; contemporary, 408; developmental, 408; determinants, 395, 408

Rosenzweig, Saul, 203, 480

Sample: *the group of individuals actually studied, in an experiment designed to study a larger population of which they are a sample*, 397; choosing best possible, 303, 402, 404 f.; from selected samples, 405; stratified random, 306; voluntary, 306, 403

Sampling distributions, 304 f., 307-316

Sampling problem, 375, 405

Satisfaction of needs, 117

Schenectady Public Schools, 120

Schenectady YMCA, 114-118, 360

Schmidt, Louis G., xiii

Schwilck, Gene, 120, 395, 480

Science: concept of, 38; creative tools of, 332 ff.; gateway to, 7; in the home, 111

Scientific method: 2, 7, 31-35, 37, 54, 68, 79, 443 ff.; attitude, 38; co-scientist role in, 358; evidence, 118, 379; generalization in, 413; interpreting the evidence, 380-414; in the home, 106 f.; humility, 19; laws, 4; levels of, 3; moral and spiritual growth, ix; people who use it, 142; forms of prayer, 465; tools of, 2, 48, 129, 452; total personality, 319; youth problem and, 101, 104

Secular schools, character education in, 120

Selected samples, 401 f.

Self: attitudes, 172, 173; concept of, 13, 77, 173 f.; development of, 77; goals, 135, 175; image, 174; other, 135

Sensitiveness to criticism, 110

Sensitivity to the needs of others, 241-246

Setchko, Penelope Sayre, 387, 480

Sewell, Miriam R., 353, 384, 479, 480

Seymour, Richard B., 480

Sherrill, Lewis J., 104, 480

Shils, Edward A., 480

CONCEPTS, PRINCIPLES AND METHODS
A STUDY OUTLINE

In order to make this book of the greatest possible value to you, you will need to master thoroughly its major concepts, principles and methods. The following outline has been prepared to help you do that. Referring to index entries, you can use this outline as a study guide for achieving this purpose.

I. BASIC CONCEPTS. There are some basic concepts which underlie the whole book. They are set forth here in three major groups.

A. *Personality.* To gain a grasp of the concept of personality on which this book is based, examine the index entry topics listed below:

Personality	Personality Profile
Total personality	Emotions
Traits	Needs
Attitudes	Potential

B. *Basic Assumptions.* Every book starts with certain basic assumptions. The topics listed below will identify most of those included in this volume:

Science	Character Research Project
Insight-hypothesis	Basic decisions
The infinity principle	Types
Co-scientist concept	Positive goodness
Creative research	Creative conflict
	Maximum potential

C. *Frames of Reference.* Although frames of reference are simply convenient ways for organizing one's ideas, it is much easier to use any book, if you are familiar with its major frames of reference.

Attitudes	Christian Hypothesis
Character	White House Conference stages
Hypotheses	of development
Dimensions	Dynamics, interaction
Dimensional-traits	Dynamics Diagram
Value dimensions	Personal equation
	Personality Profile

II. THE SCIENTIFIC METHOD. Few lay people have a grasp of what is meant by the scientific method. To make this possible is the major purpose of this book. The following topics may help you gain a picture of the scope of the scientific attitude.

A. *Methods and Procedures.* If one is to use the scientific method he must have learned some of its techniques. Below are listed the ones described in this book.

Co-scientist procedures	*More technical procedures*
Scientific method	Evidence
Co-scientist skills	Insight-hypothesis
Evaluation	Questionnaires
Unbiased evidence	Psychometrics
Pro-con method	Pragmatic eclecticism
Observation	Projective techniques
Open-end data	Developmental calibration
Characteristic differences	Generalization
Roles	

B. *Experimental Design.* Most common sense experiments are useless because they are so badly designed that their results are uninterpretable. Under the index entries listed below are some principles of experimental design you ought to know.

Research design	Statistical tools
Research Design Chart	Measurement
Reliability	Correlation
Validity	Statistics
Research	Units
Experiment	Variables
Experimental design	Sampling
Program design	Population
Group design	Stratification
Factorial design	Randomization
Guinea-pigism	Parameters
Research curriculum	Cluster analysis

III. LEARNING AND THE CURRICULUM. The curriculum is the embodiment of our hypotheses of what learning is hoped for and how it is to be brought about. On the principles underlying the construction of the curriculum lie our success and failure.

Curriculum	Lesson plans
Education	Objectives
Educational goals	Adaptation procedure
Learning	Projects
Transfer	Teachers
Curriculum kit	Motivated capacity
Psychological order	Workshops

Religious education   Typical class
Research curriculum   Teacher Opinion Study

IV. A GREATER GENERATION. If we are to produce a greater generation, it must begin with the growing child in the home and the community. Note the topics listed below.

A. *Developmental Psychology.* The principles of development are, of course, basic to any kind of education.

Child   Developmental calibration
Youth   Vocational guidance
Individual differences   Vision
Child of God concept   Character

B. *Home and Community.* Almost all available evidence shows that home participation is the basic prerequisite to any effective religious or character education, with community agencies acting as augmenting forces.

Family   Camping
Home   Character-building agencies
Parental behavior   Culture
Discipline   Projects, church-school
Parents' Reports

DUE DATE

	201-6503		Printed in USA